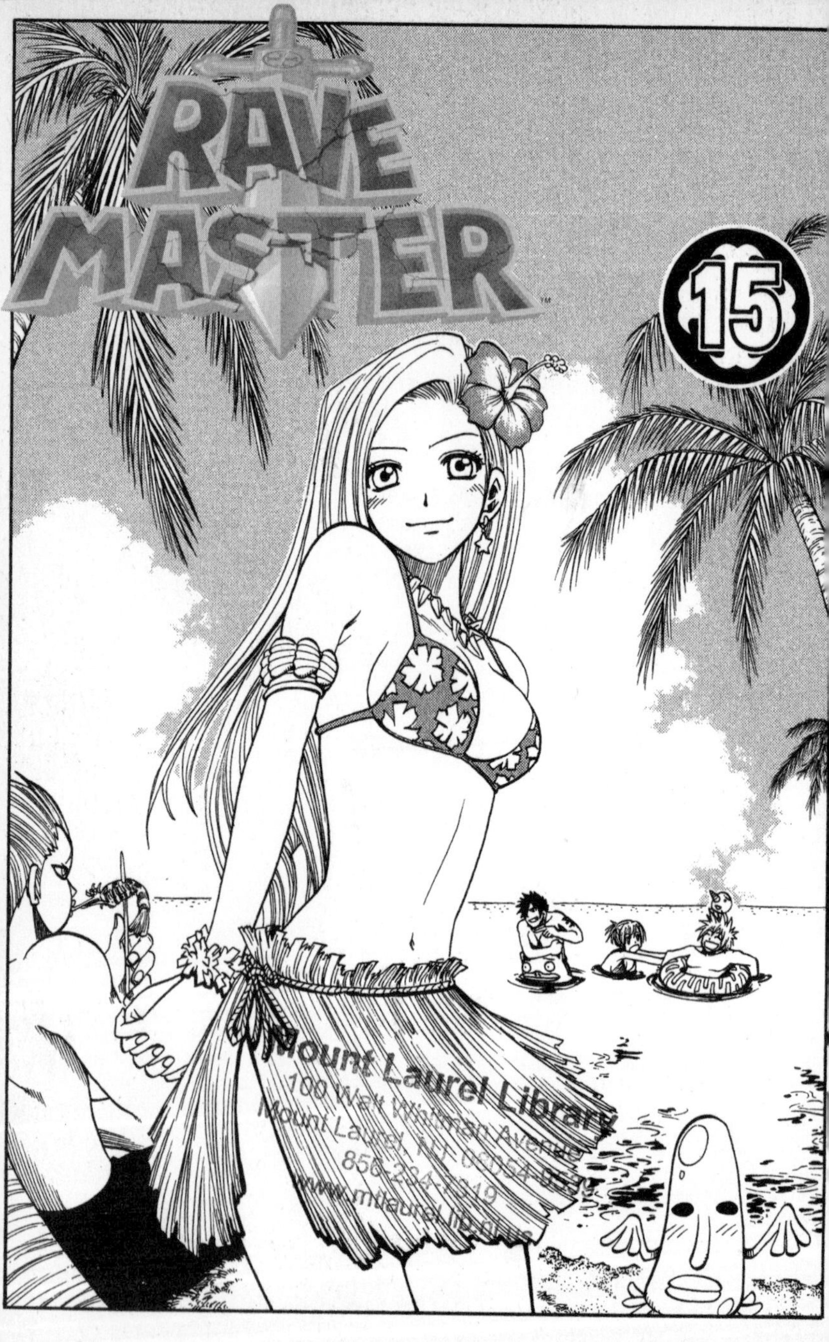
RAVE MASTER
15

Rave Master Vol. 15
Created by Hiro Mashima

Translation - Jeremiah Bourque
English Adaptation - Jake Forbes
Retouch and Lettering - Abelardo Bigting
Production Artist - Jason Milligan
Cover Design - Al-Insan Lashley

Editor - Tim Beedle
Digital Imaging Manager - Chris Buford
Pre-Press Manager - Antonio DePietro
Production Managers - Jennifer Miller and Mutsumi Miyazaki
Art Director - Matt Alford
Managing Editor - Jill Freshney
VP of Production - Ron Klamert
Editor-in-Chief - Mike Kiley
President and C.O.O. - John Parker
Publisher and C.E.O. - Stuart Levy

A 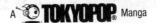 Manga

TOKYOPOP Inc.
5900 Wilshire Blvd. Suite 2000
Los Angeles, CA 90036

E-mail: info@TOKYOPOP.com
Come visit us online at www.TOKYOPOP.com

ISBN: 1-59532-020-2

First TOKYOPOP printing: June 2005
10 9 8 7 6 5 4 3 2 1
Printed in the USA

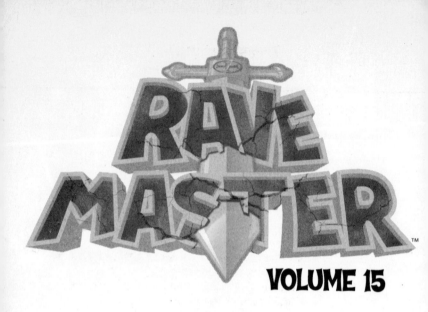

VOLUME 15

Story and Art by

HIRO MASHIMA

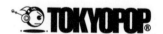

HAMBURG // LONDON // LOS ANGELES // TOKYO

THE STORY SO FAR...

Haru and friends have journeyed south in search of the fourth **Rave Stone**, but so far, they've found nothing but trouble. Having put a stop to the water-dwelling **Onigami's** genocide of the **mermaid** race, the group has now incurred the wrath of their allies, the **Ghost Attack Squad**. But it is not mere vengeance the Squad desires. They seek **Elie**, who possesses the destructive power of **Etherion**. With Haru busy fending off the Onigami, the Ghost Attack Squad saw the perfect opportunity to seize the feisty gambler. Elie is now the captive of **Pumpkin Doryu**, the gang's leader. **Ruby** was taken captive as well, and even worse, **Musica** has fallen in battle—the victim of Pumpkin Doryu's hideous Sinclaire, **Mother**.

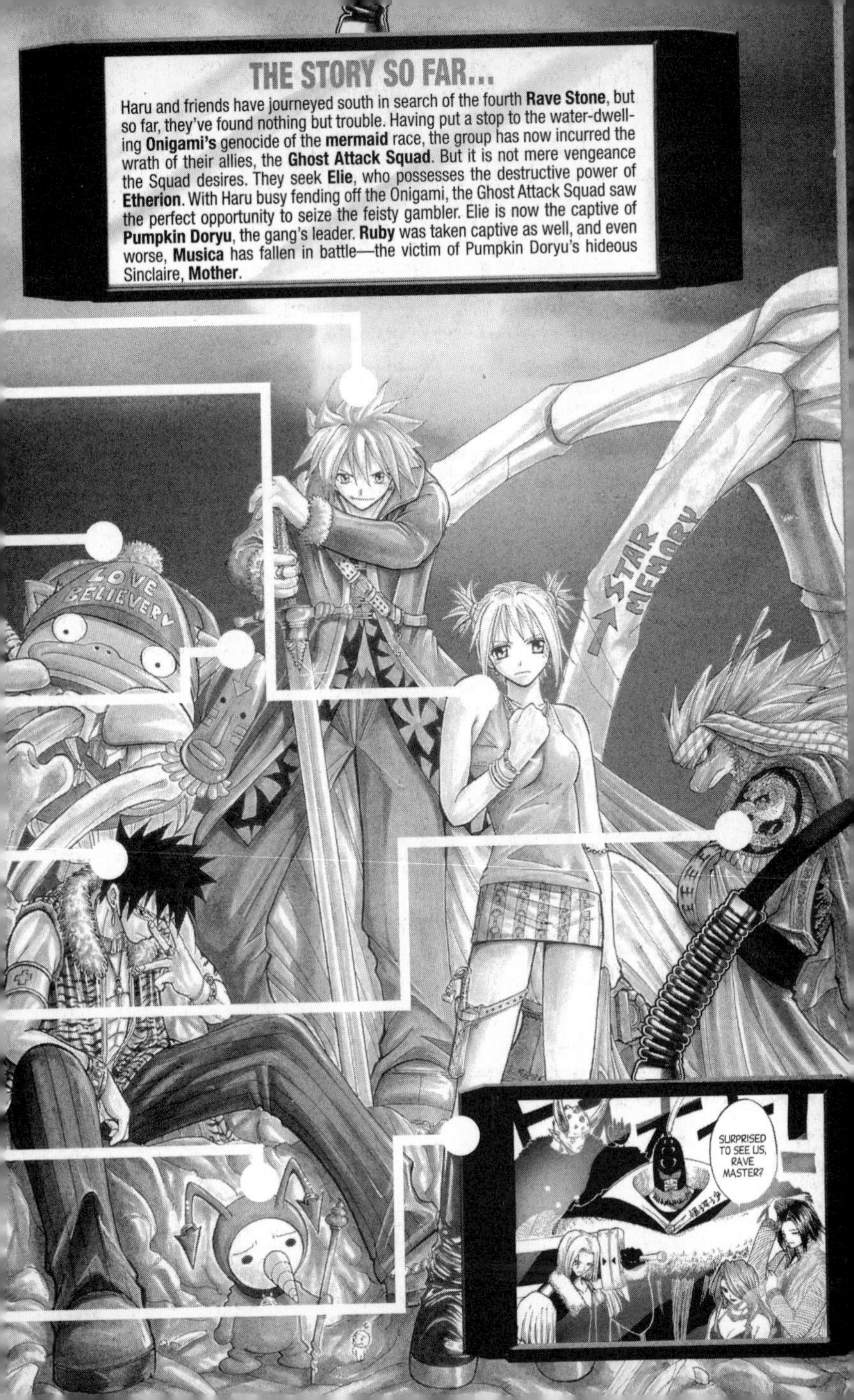
LOVE BELIEVER
STAR MEMORY
SURPRISED TO SEE US, RAVE MASTER?

THE RAVE MASTER CREW

HARU GLORY
A small-town boy turned savior of the world. As the **Rave Master** (the only one capable of using the holy weapon RAVE), Haru set forth to find the missing Rave Stones and defeat **Demon Card.** He fights with the **Ten Powers Sword,** a weapon that takes on different forms at his command. With Demon Card seemingly out of the way, Haru now seeks the remaining two Rave Stones in order to open the way to Star Memory.

ELIE
The girl without memories. Elie joined Haru on his quest when he promised to help her find out about her past. She's cute, spunky and loves gambling and shopping in equal measure. Locked inside of her is the power of **Etherion.**

RUBY
A "penguin-type" sentenoid, Ruby loves rare and unusual items. After Haru saved him from Pumpkin Doryu's gang, Ruby agreed to sponsor Haru's team in their search for the ultimate rare treasures: the Rave Stones!

GRIFFON KATO (GRIFF)
Griff is a loyal friend, even if he is a bit of a coward. His rubbery body can stretch and change shape as needed. Griff's two greatest pleasures in life are mapmaking and peeping on Elie.

MUSICA
A **"Silverclaimer"** (an alchemist who can shape silver at will) and a former street punk who made good. He joined Haru for the adventure, but now that Demon Card is defeated, does he have any reason to stick around?

LET
A member of the **Dragon Race,** he was formerly a member of the Demon Card's Five Palace Guardians. He was so impressed by Haru's fighting skills and pureness of heart that he made a truce with the Rave Master. After passing his Dragon Trial, he gained a human body, but his blood is still Dragon Race.

PLUE
The **Rave Bearer,** Plue is the faithful companion to the Rave Master. In addition to being Haru's guide, Plue also has powers of his own. When he's not getting Haru into or out of trouble, Plue can be found enjoying a sucker, his favorite treat.

THE ORACION SIX
Demon Card's six generals. Haru defeated **Shuda** after finding the Rave of Wisdom. The other five generals were presumed dead after King destroyed Demon Card Headquarters.

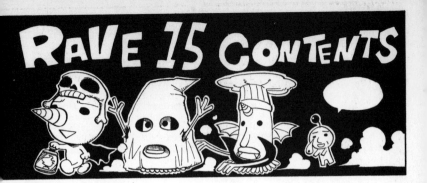

RAVE 15 CONTENTS

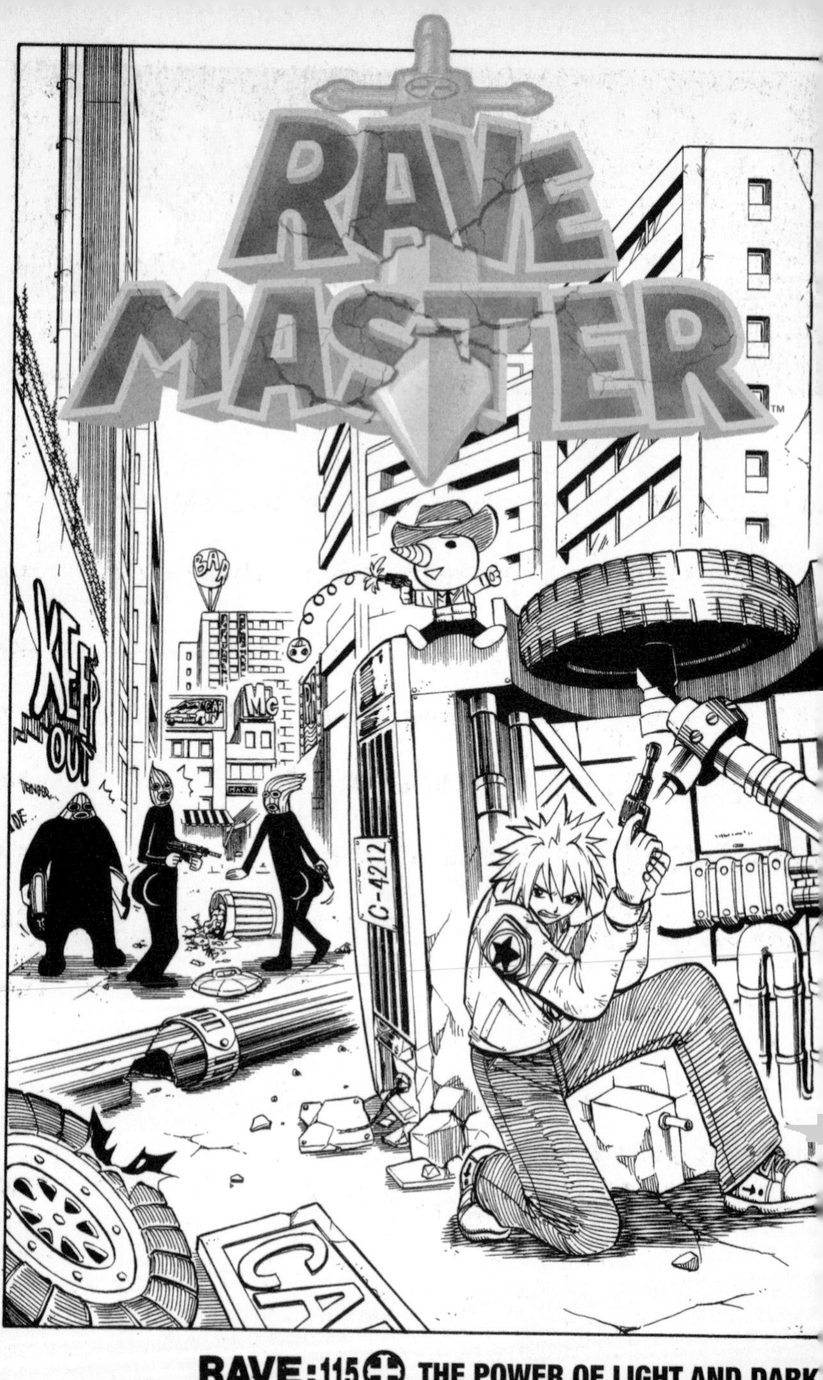
RAVE MASTER™
KEEP OUT
BAR
Mc
C-4212

RAVE:115 ✠ THE POWER OF LIGHT AND DARK

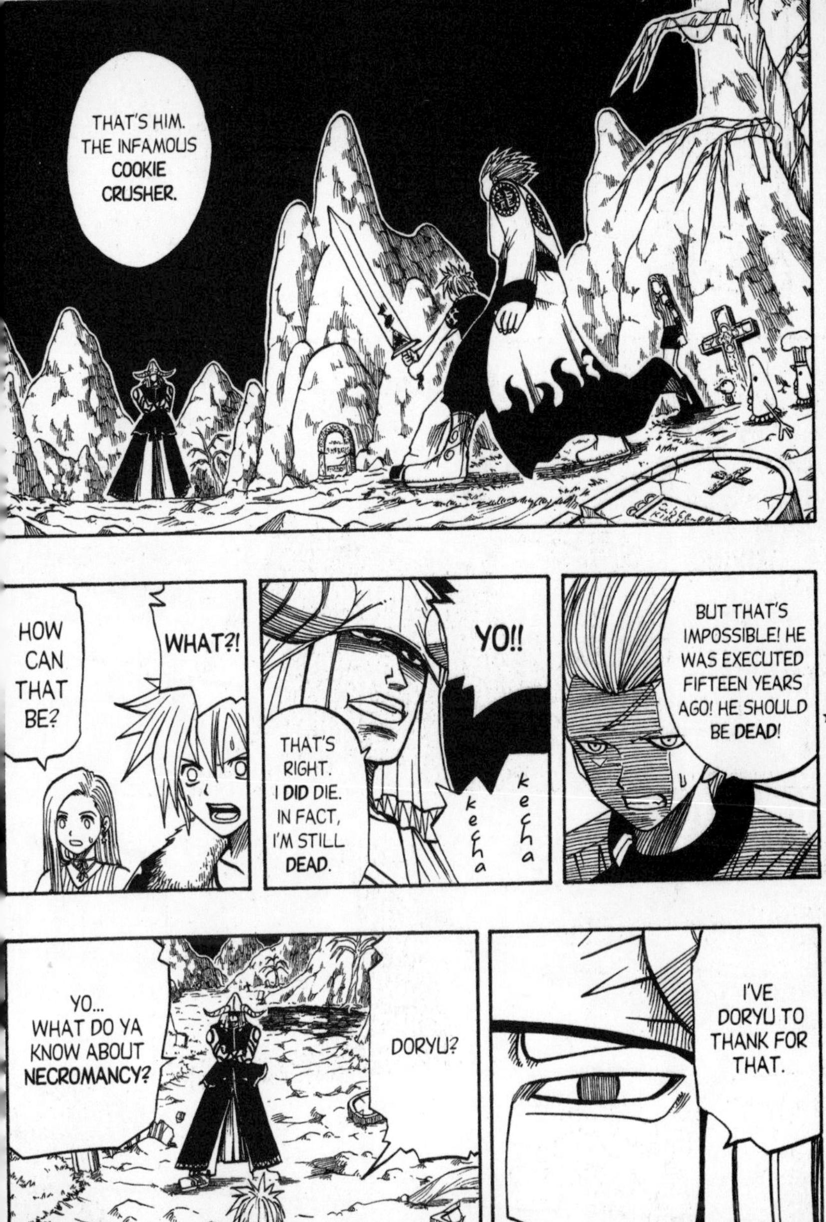
THAT'S HIM. THE INFAMOUS COOKIE CRUSHER.
BUT THAT'S IMPOSSIBLE! HE WAS EXECUTED FIFTEEN YEARS AGO! HE SHOULD BE DEAD!
YO!!
kecha kecha
THAT'S RIGHT. I DID DIE. IN FACT, I'M STILL DEAD.
WHAT?!
HOW CAN THAT BE?
I'VE DORYU TO THANK FOR THAT.
DORYU?
YO... WHAT DO YA KNOW ABOUT NECROMANCY?

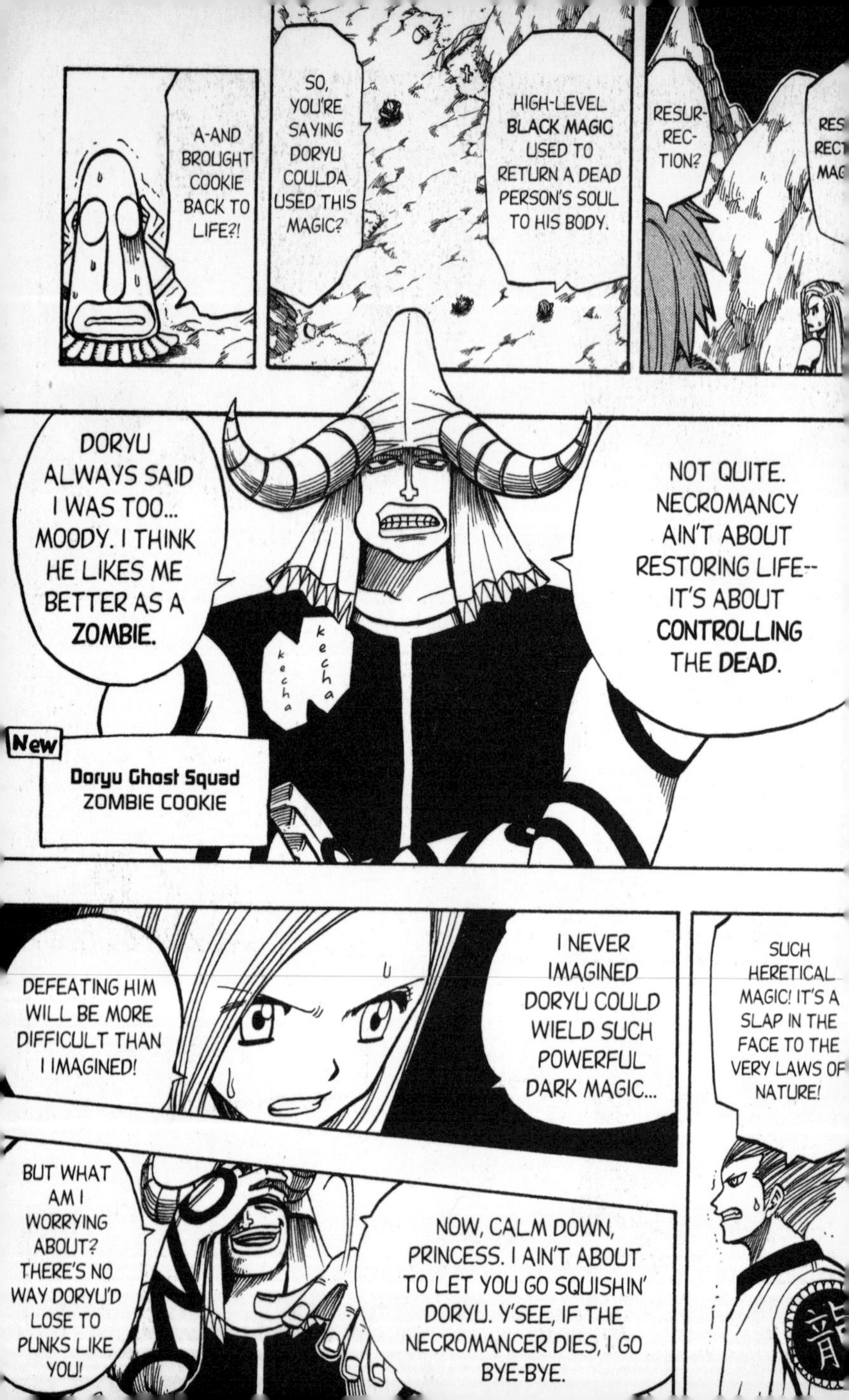
RESUR-REC-TION?
HIGH-LEVEL BLACK MAGIC USED TO RETURN A DEAD PERSON'S SOUL TO HIS BODY.
SO, YOU'RE SAYING DORYU COULDA USED THIS MAGIC?
A-AND BROUGHT COOKIE BACK TO LIFE?!
NOT QUITE. NECROMANCY AIN'T ABOUT RESTORING LIFE-- IT'S ABOUT CONTROLLING THE DEAD.
DORYU ALWAYS SAID I WAS TOO... MOODY. I THINK HE LIKES ME BETTER AS A ZOMBIE.
kecha kecha
New
Doryu Ghost Squad
ZOMBIE COOKIE
SUCH HERETICAL MAGIC! IT'S A SLAP IN THE FACE TO THE VERY LAWS OF NATURE!
I NEVER IMAGINED DORYU COULD WIELD SUCH POWERFUL DARK MAGIC...
DEFEATING HIM WILL BE MORE DIFFICULT THAN I IMAGINED!
NOW, CALM DOWN, PRINCESS. I AIN'T ABOUT TO LET YOU GO SQUISHIN' DORYU. Y'SEE, IF THE NECROMANCER DIES, I GO BYE-BYE.
BUT WHAT AM I WORRYING ABOUT? THERE'S NO WAY DORYU'D LOSE TO PUNKS LIKE YOU!

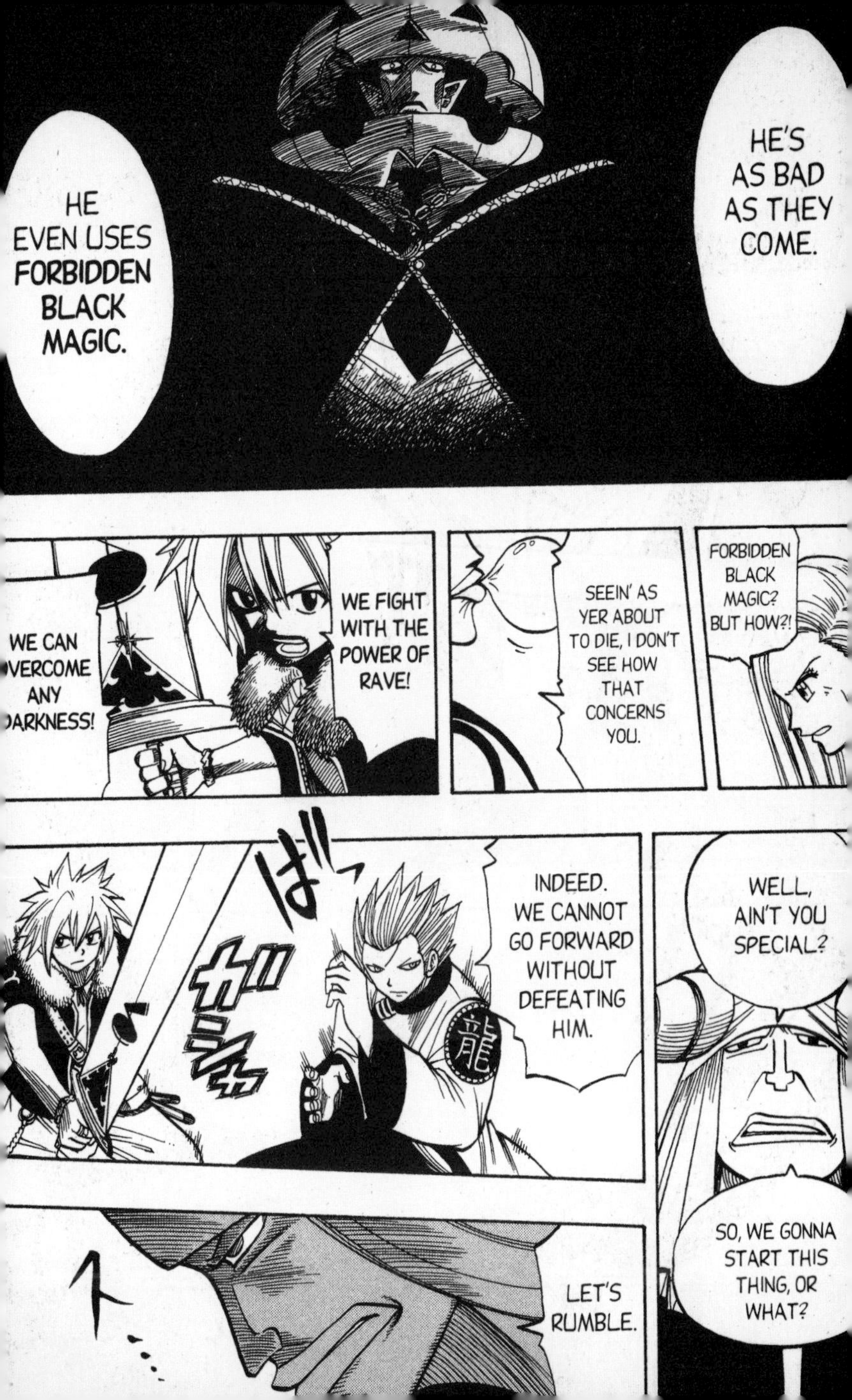
HE'S AS BAD AS THEY COME.
HE EVEN USES FORBIDDEN BLACK MAGIC.
FORBIDDEN BLACK MAGIC? BUT HOW?!
SEEIN' AS YER ABOUT TO DIE, I DON'T SEE HOW THAT CONCERNS YOU.
WE FIGHT WITH THE POWER OF RAVE!
WE CAN VERCOME ANY ARKNESS!
WELL, AIN'T YOU SPECIAL?
SO, WE GONNA START THIS THING, OR WHAT?
ばっ
ガシャ
INDEED. WE CANNOT GO FORWARD WITHOUT DEFEATING HIM.
LET'S RUMBLE.

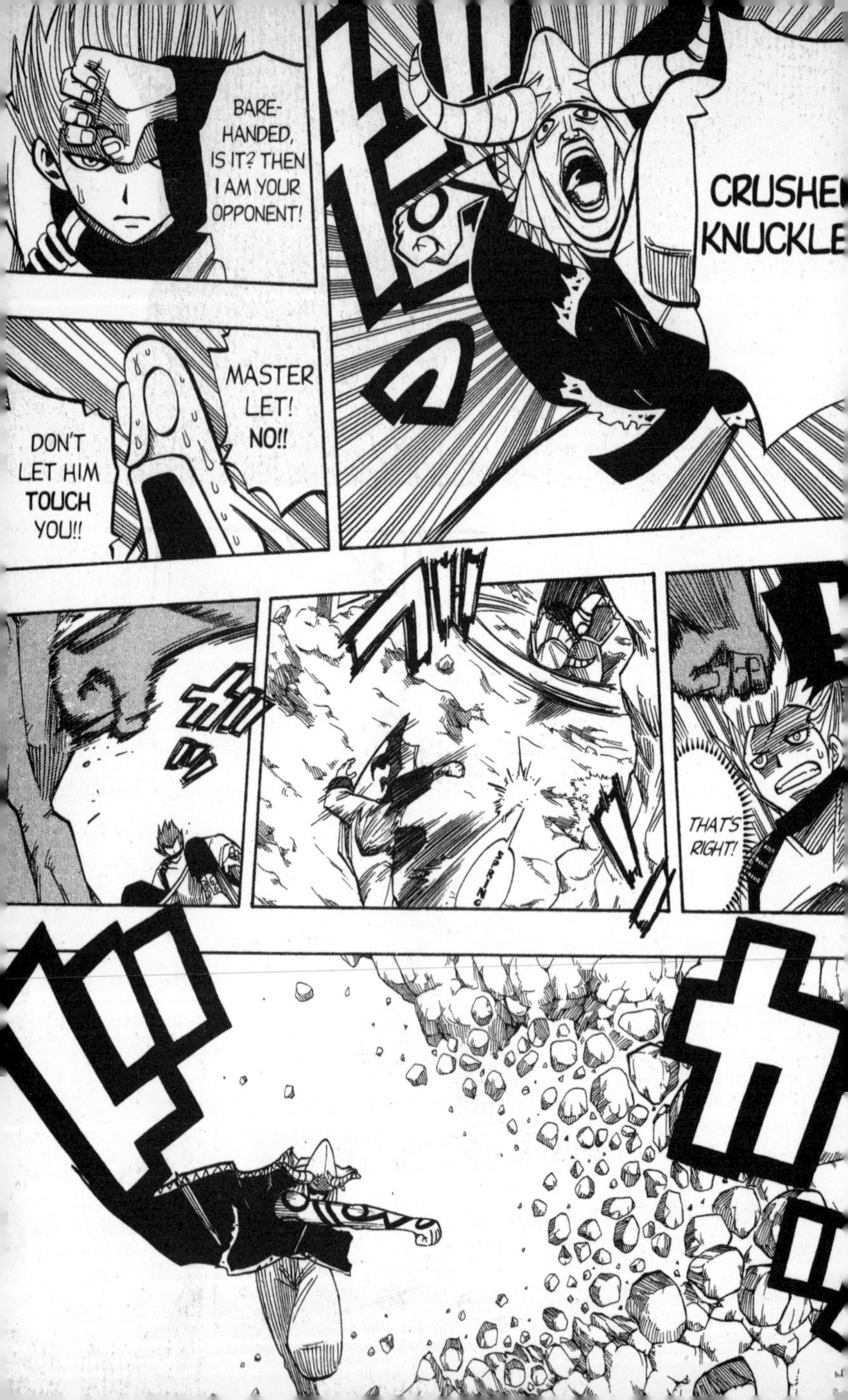
CRUSHE
KNUCKLE
BARE-HANDED, IS IT? THEN I AM YOUR OPPONENT!
MASTER LET! NO!!
DON'T LET HIM TOUCH YOU!!
THAT'S RIGHT!
SPRING

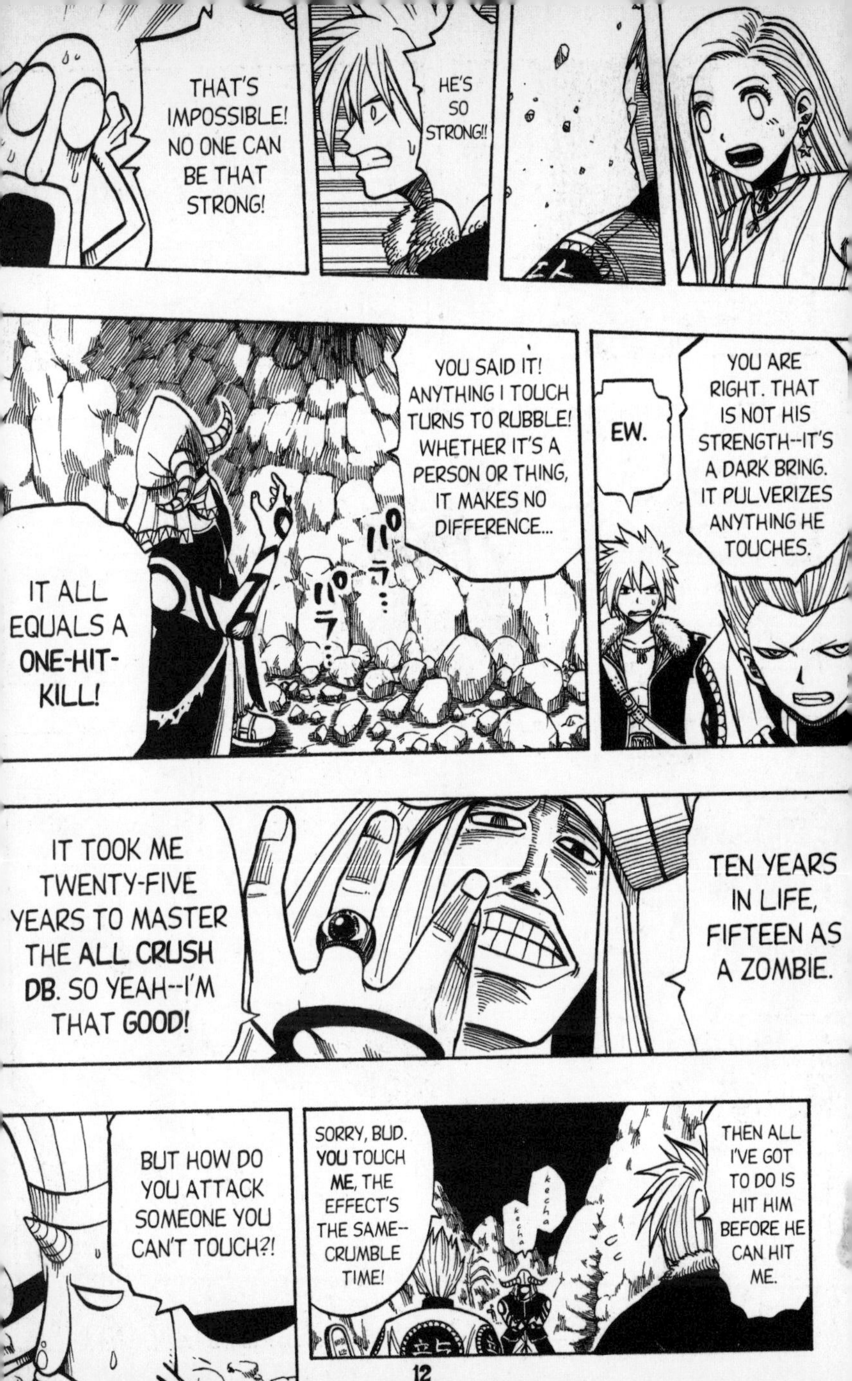
HE'S SO STRONG!!
THAT'S IMPOSSIBLE! NO ONE CAN BE THAT STRONG!
YOU ARE RIGHT. THAT IS NOT HIS STRENGTH--IT'S A DARK BRING. IT PULVERIZES ANYTHING HE TOUCHES.
EW.
YOU SAID IT! ANYTHING I TOUCH TURNS TO RUBBLE! WHETHER IT'S A PERSON OR THING, IT MAKES NO DIFFERENCE...
IT ALL EQUALS A **ONE-HIT-KILL!**
IT TOOK ME TWENTY-FIVE YEARS TO MASTER THE **ALL CRUSH DB**. SO YEAH--I'M THAT **GOOD!**
TEN YEARS IN LIFE, FIFTEEN AS A ZOMBIE.
THEN ALL I'VE GOT TO DO IS HIT HIM BEFORE HE CAN HIT ME.
kecha
kecha
SORRY, BUD. **YOU** TOUCH **ME**, THE EFFECT'S THE SAME--CRUMBLE TIME!
BUT HOW DO YOU ATTACK SOMEONE YOU CAN'T TOUCH?!

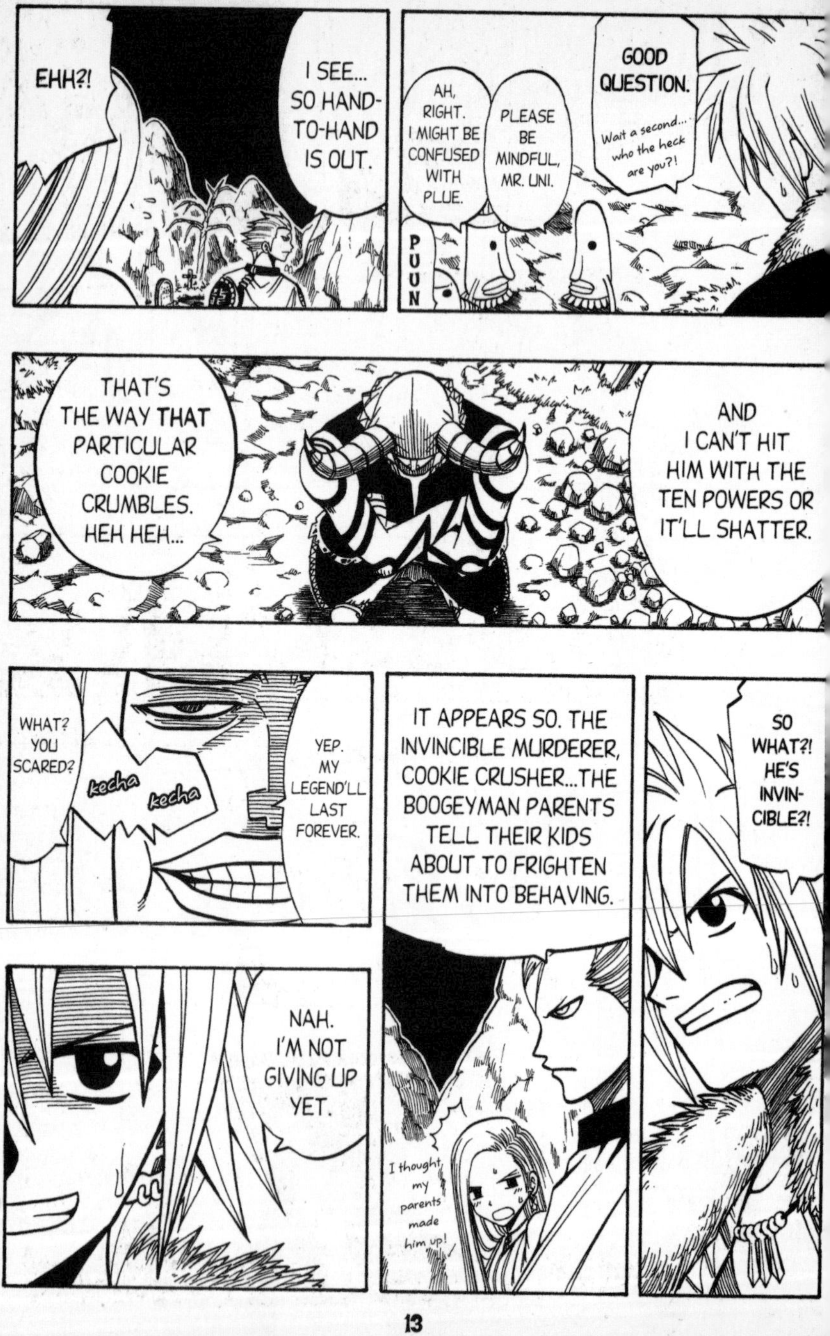
GOOD QUESTION.
Wait a second... who the heck are you?!
PLEASE BE MINDFUL, MR. UNI.
AH, RIGHT. I MIGHT BE CONFUSED WITH PLUE.
PUUN
I SEE... SO HAND-TO-HAND IS OUT.
EHH?!
AND I CAN'T HIT HIM WITH THE TEN POWERS OR IT'LL SHATTER.
THAT'S THE WAY THAT PARTICULAR COOKIE CRUMBLES. HEH HEH...
SO WHAT?! HE'S INVINCIBLE?!
IT APPEARS SO. THE INVINCIBLE MURDERER, COOKIE CRUSHER...THE BOOGEYMAN PARENTS TELL THEIR KIDS ABOUT TO FRIGHTEN THEM INTO BEHAVING.
I thought my parents made him up!
YEP. MY LEGEND'LL LAST FOREVER.
kecha kecha
WHAT? YOU SCARED?
NAH. I'M NOT GIVING UP YET.

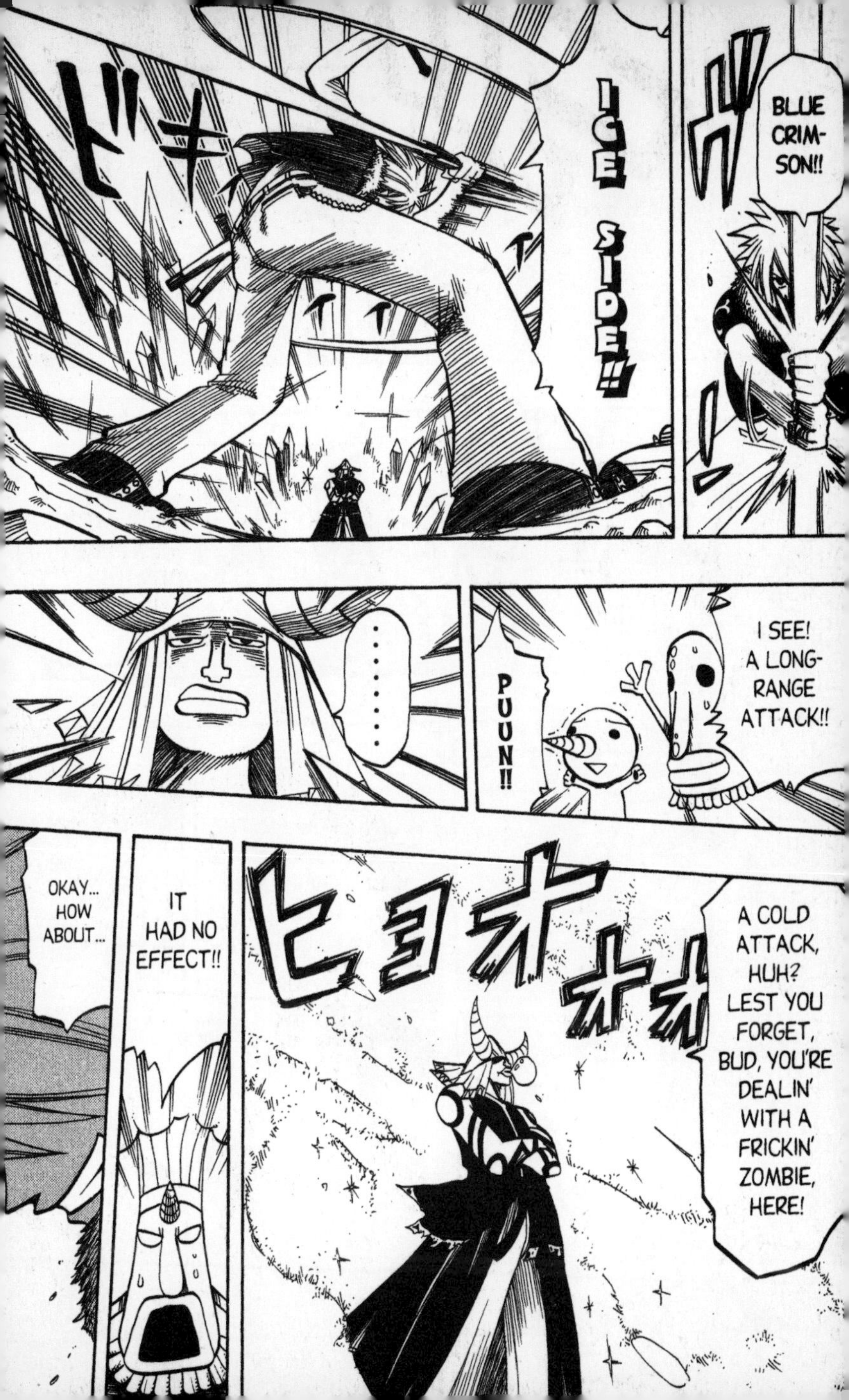
BLUE CRIMSON!!
ICE SIDE!!
I SEE! A LONG-RANGE ATTACK!!
PUUN!!
......
A COLD ATTACK, HUH? LEST YOU FORGET, BUD, YOU'RE DEALIN' WITH A FRICKIN' ZOMBIE, HERE!
ヒョオ
IT HAD NO EFFECT!!
OKAY... HOW ABOUT...

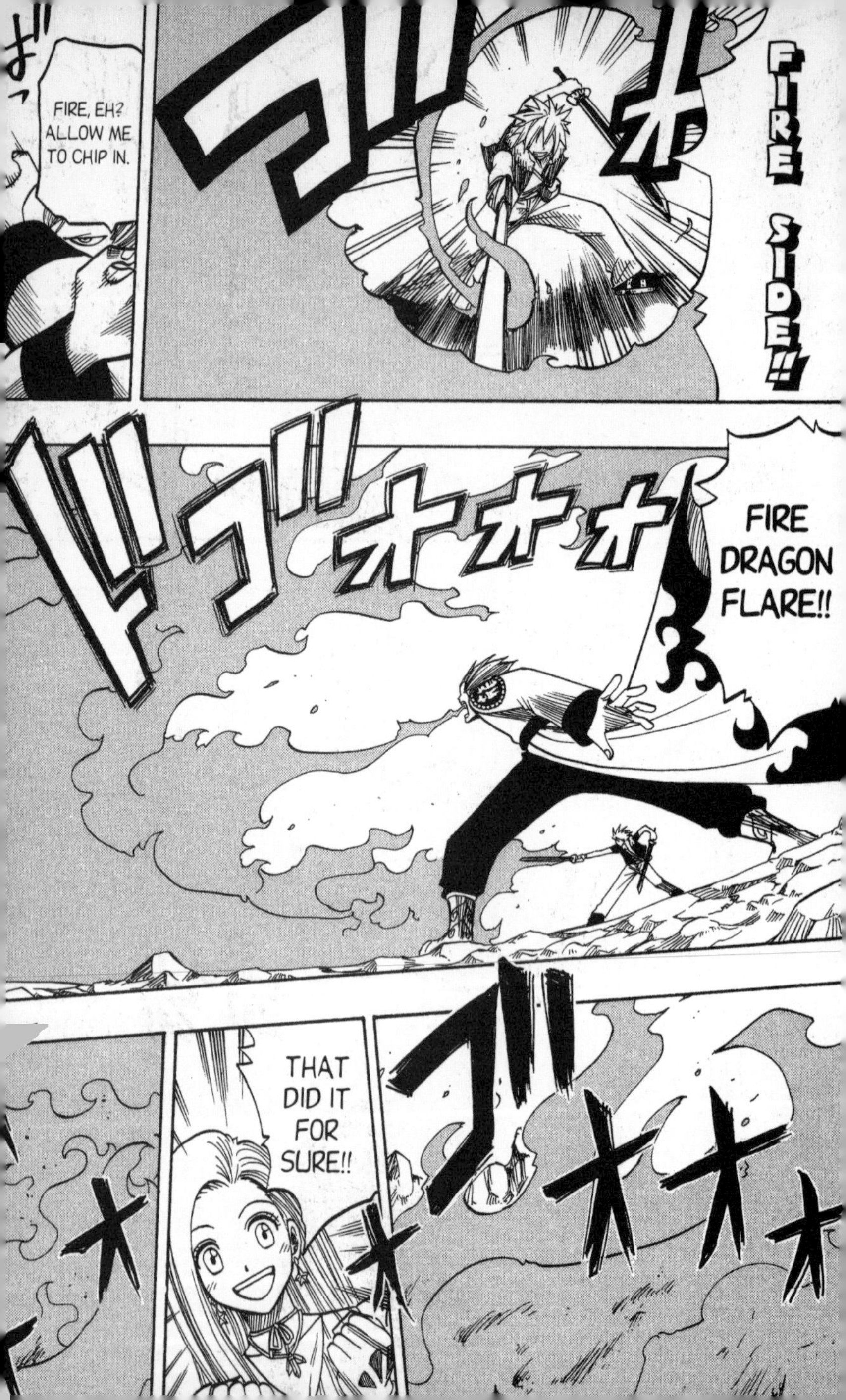
FIRE SIDE!!
FIRE, EH? ALLOW ME TO CHIP IN.
FIRE DRAGON FLARE!!
THAT DID IT FOR SURE!!

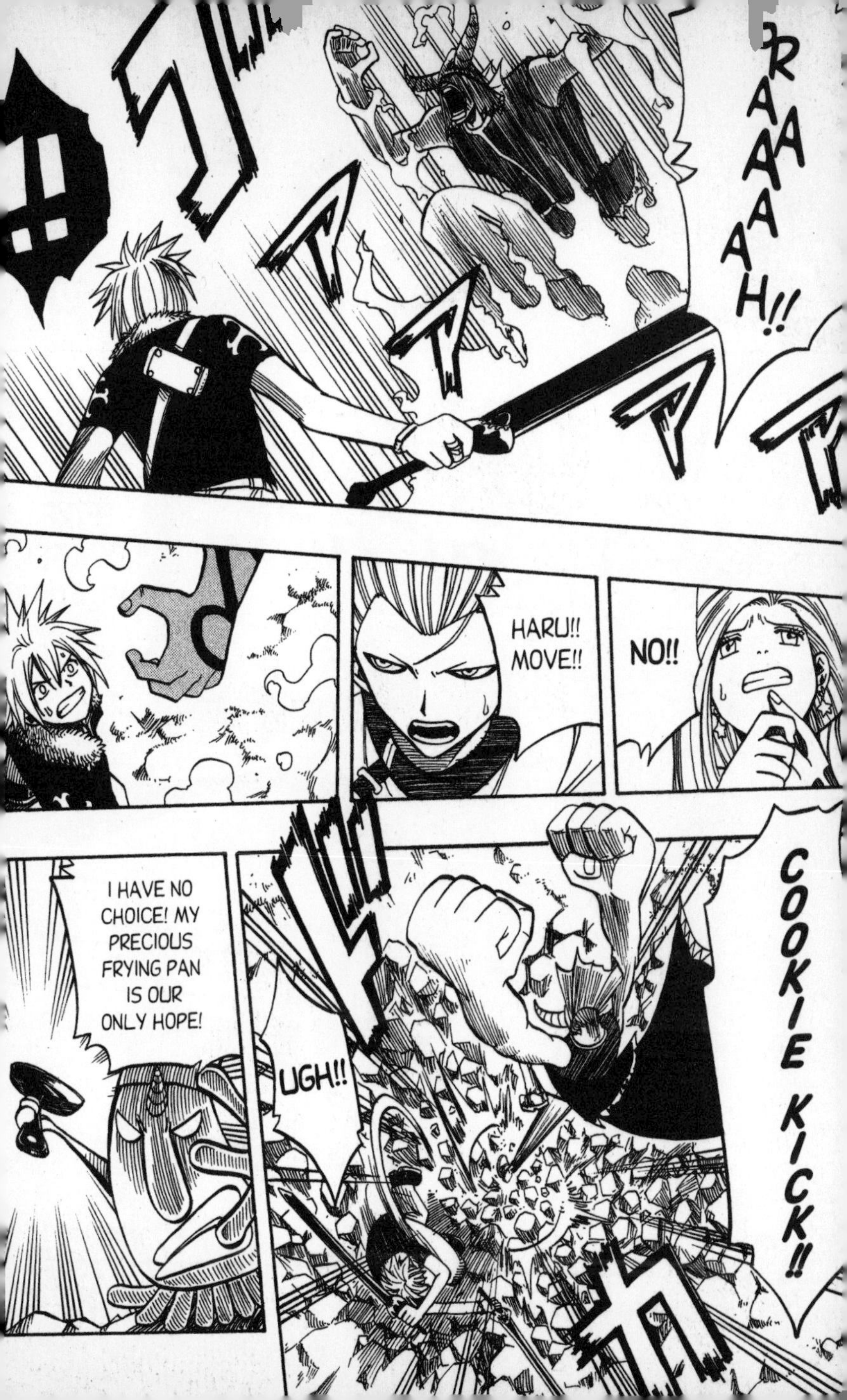
RAAAAAH!!
HARU!! MOVE!!
NO!!
COOOKIE KICK!!
UGH!!
I HAVE NO CHOICE! MY PRECIOUS FRYING PAN IS OUR ONLY HOPE!

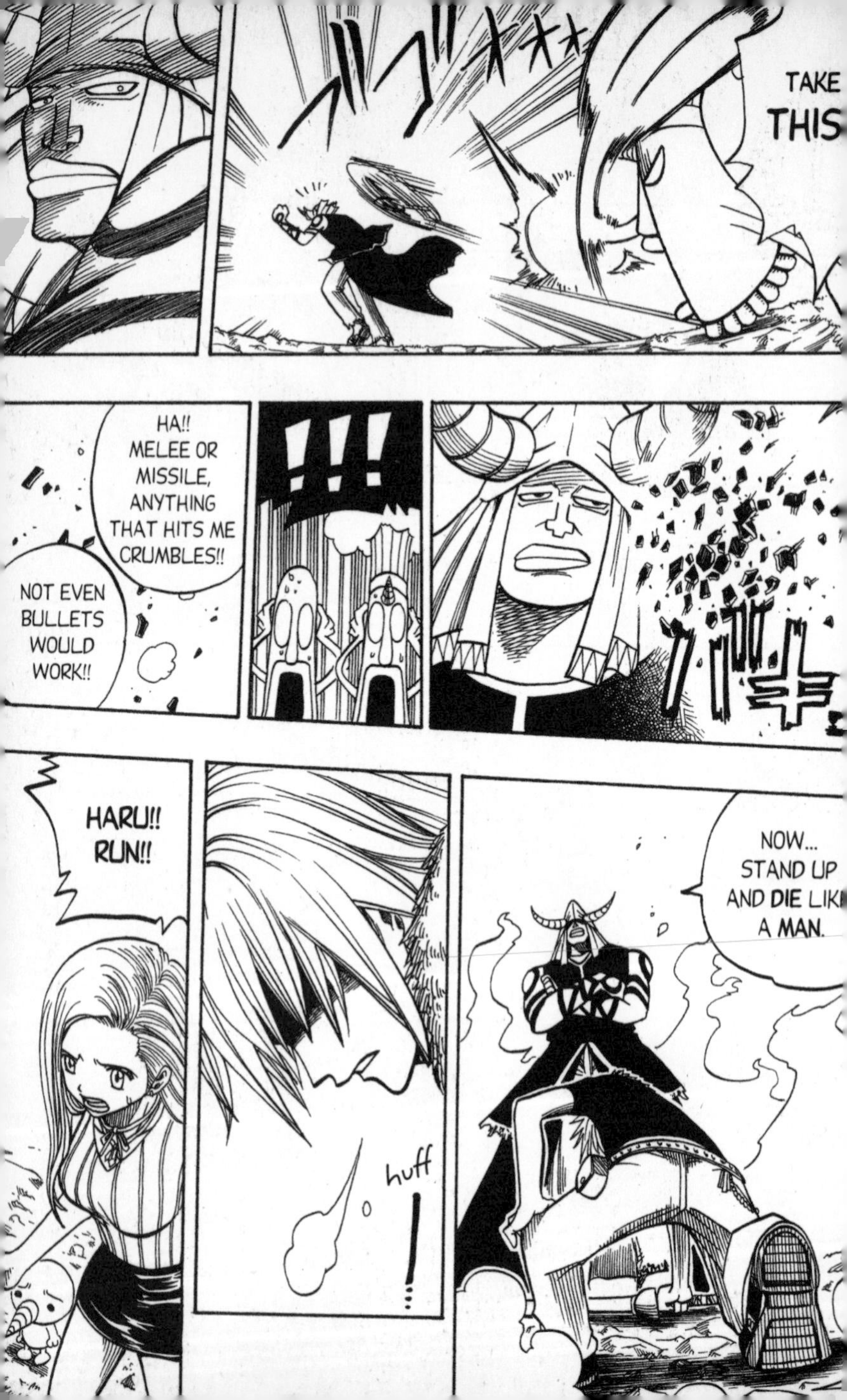

TAKE THIS
!!!
HA!! MELEE OR MISSILE, ANYTHING THAT HITS ME CRUMBLES!!
NOT EVEN BULLETS WOULD WORK!!
NOW... STAND UP AND DIE LIK
A MAN.
huff
HARU!! RUN!!

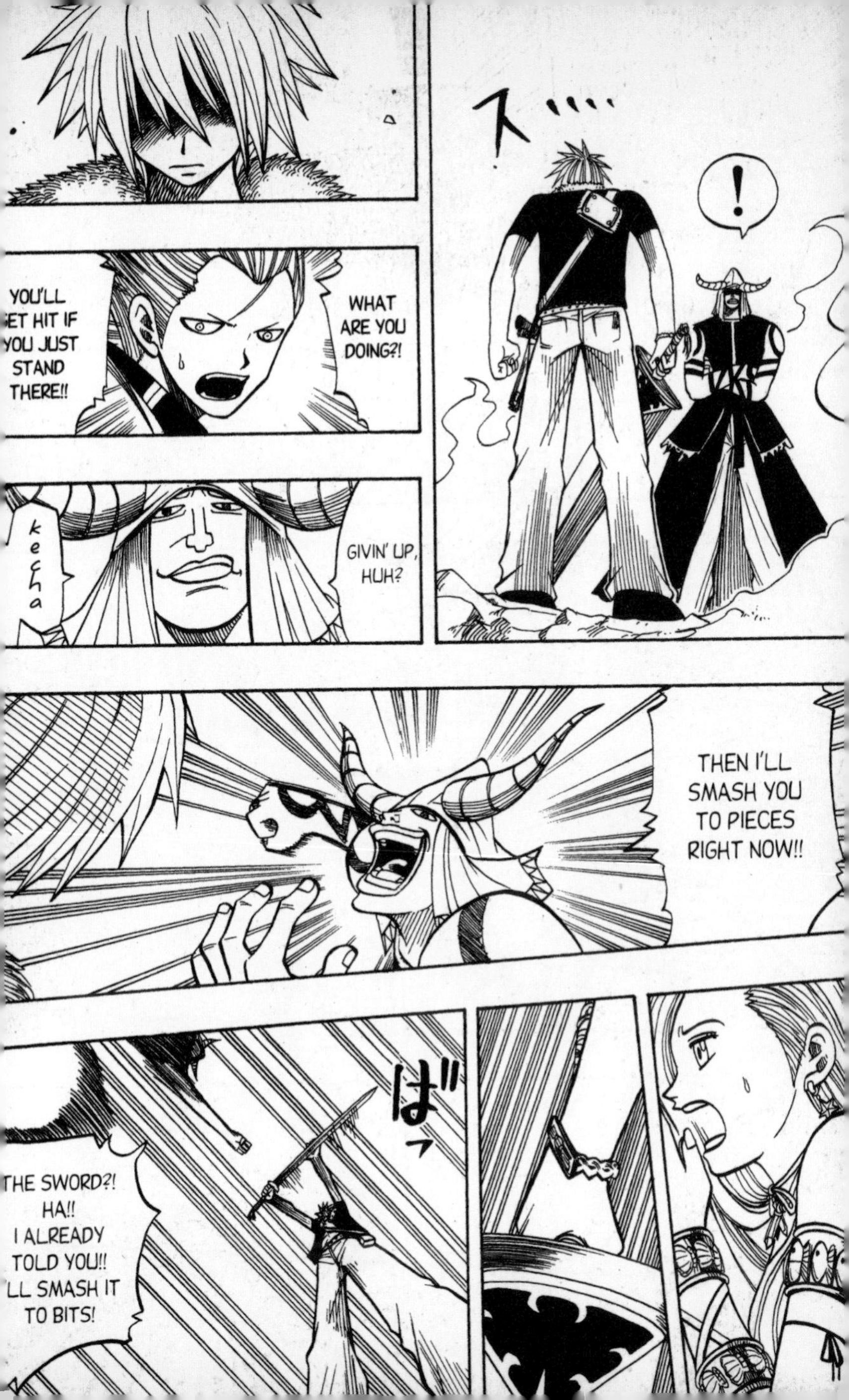
ス…
!
WHAT ARE YOU DOING?!
YOU'LL ET HIT IF YOU JUST STAND THERE!!
GIVIN' UP, HUH?
kecha
THEN I'LL SMASH YOU TO PIECES RIGHT NOW!!
ばっ
THE SWORD?! HA!! I ALREADY TOLD YOU!! LL SMASH IT TO BITS!

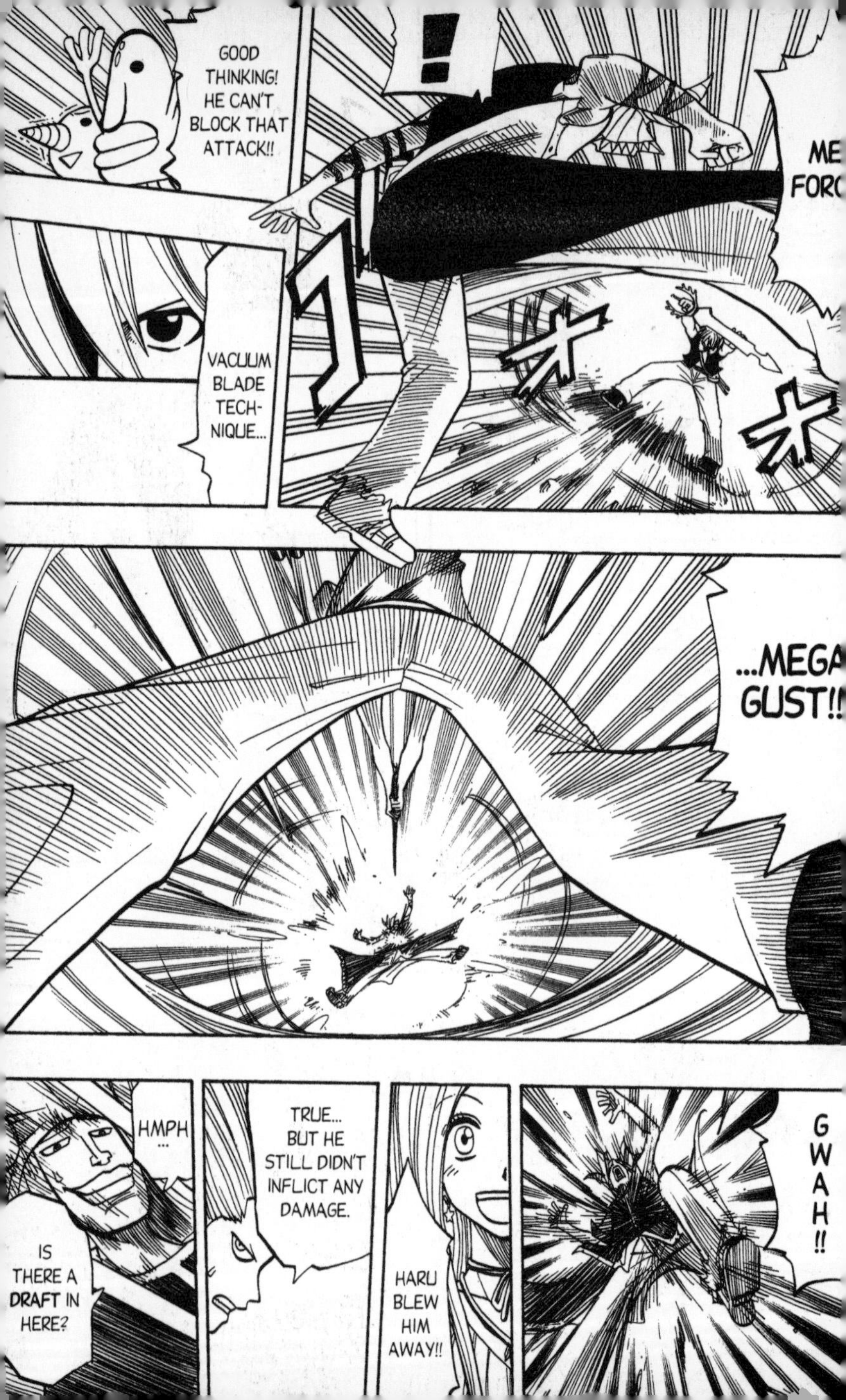
!
ME
FORC
GOOD THINKING! HE CAN'T BLOCK THAT ATTACK!!
VACUUM BLADE TECH-NIQUE...
...MEGA GUST!!
GWAH!!
HARU BLEW HIM AWAY!!
TRUE... BUT HE STILL DIDN'T INFLICT ANY DAMAGE.
HMPH ...
IS THERE A **DRAFT** IN HERE?

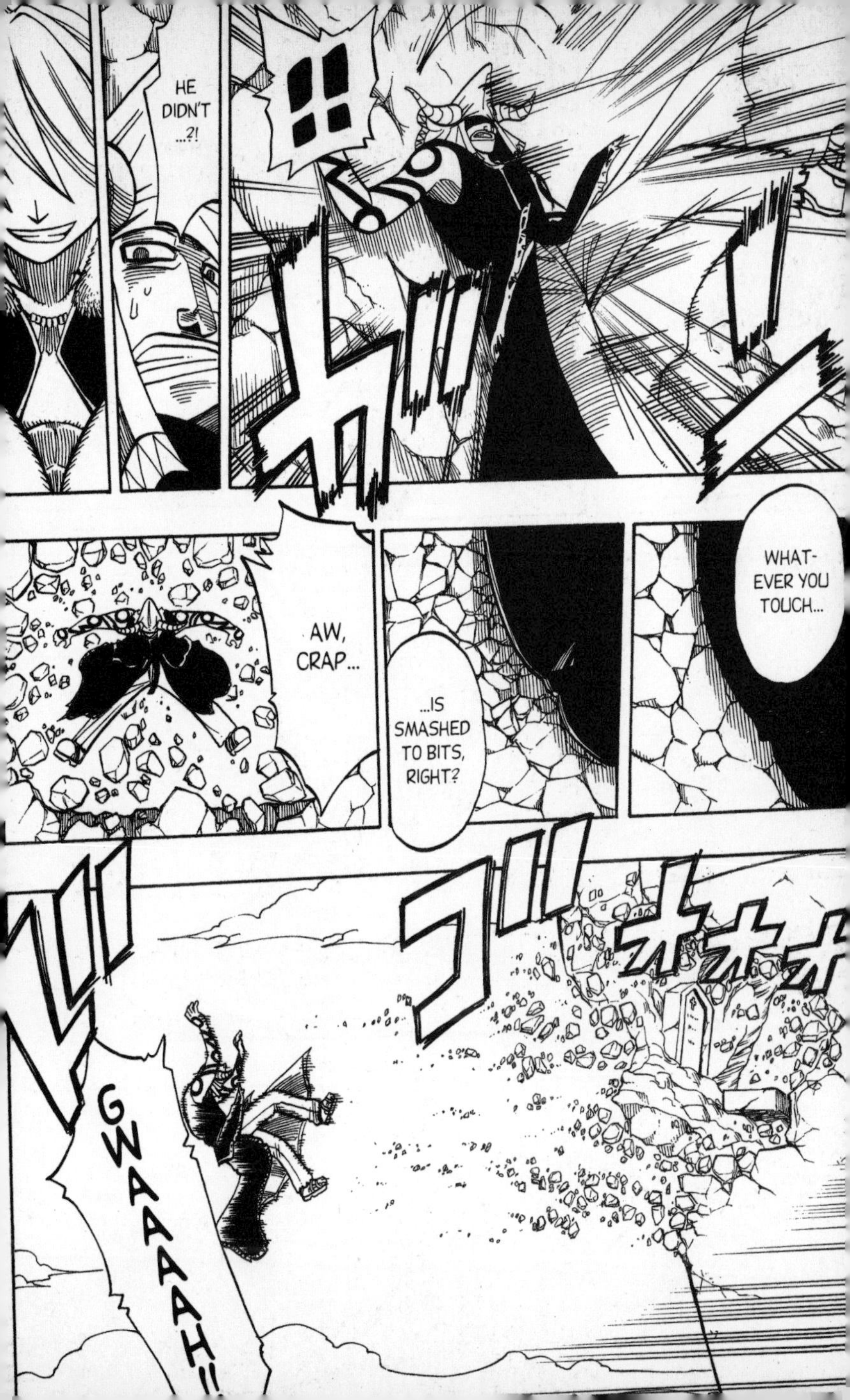
HE DIDN'T ...?!
WHAT-EVER YOU TOUCH...
...IS SMASHED TO BITS, RIGHT?
AW, CRAP...
GWAAAAAH!!

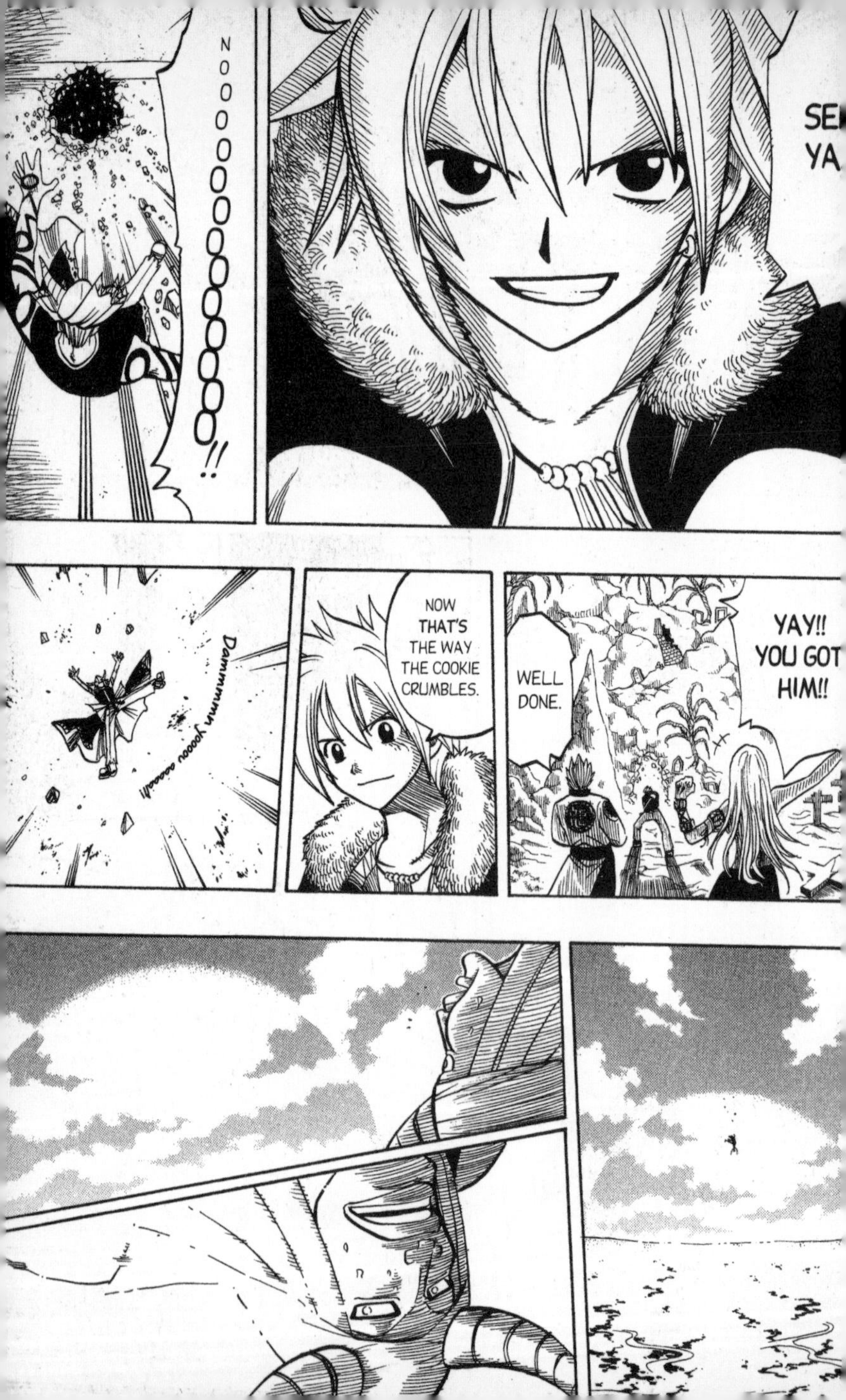
SE
YA
NOOOOOOOOOOOOOOO!!
YAY!! YOU GOT HIM!!
WELL DONE.
NOW THAT'S THE WAY THE COOKIE CRUMBLES.
Dammmmn yoooou oooooo!!

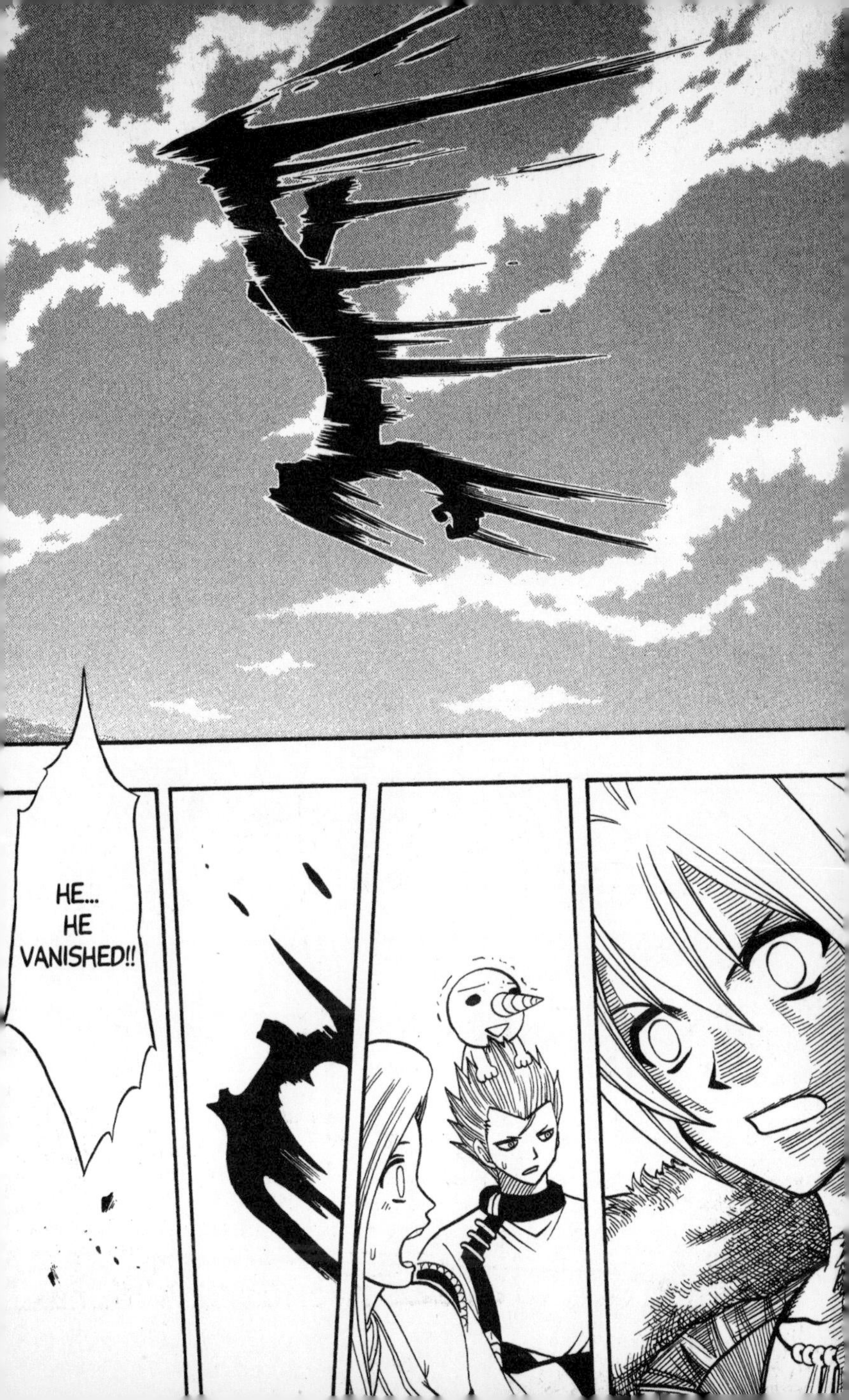
HE... HE VANISHED!!

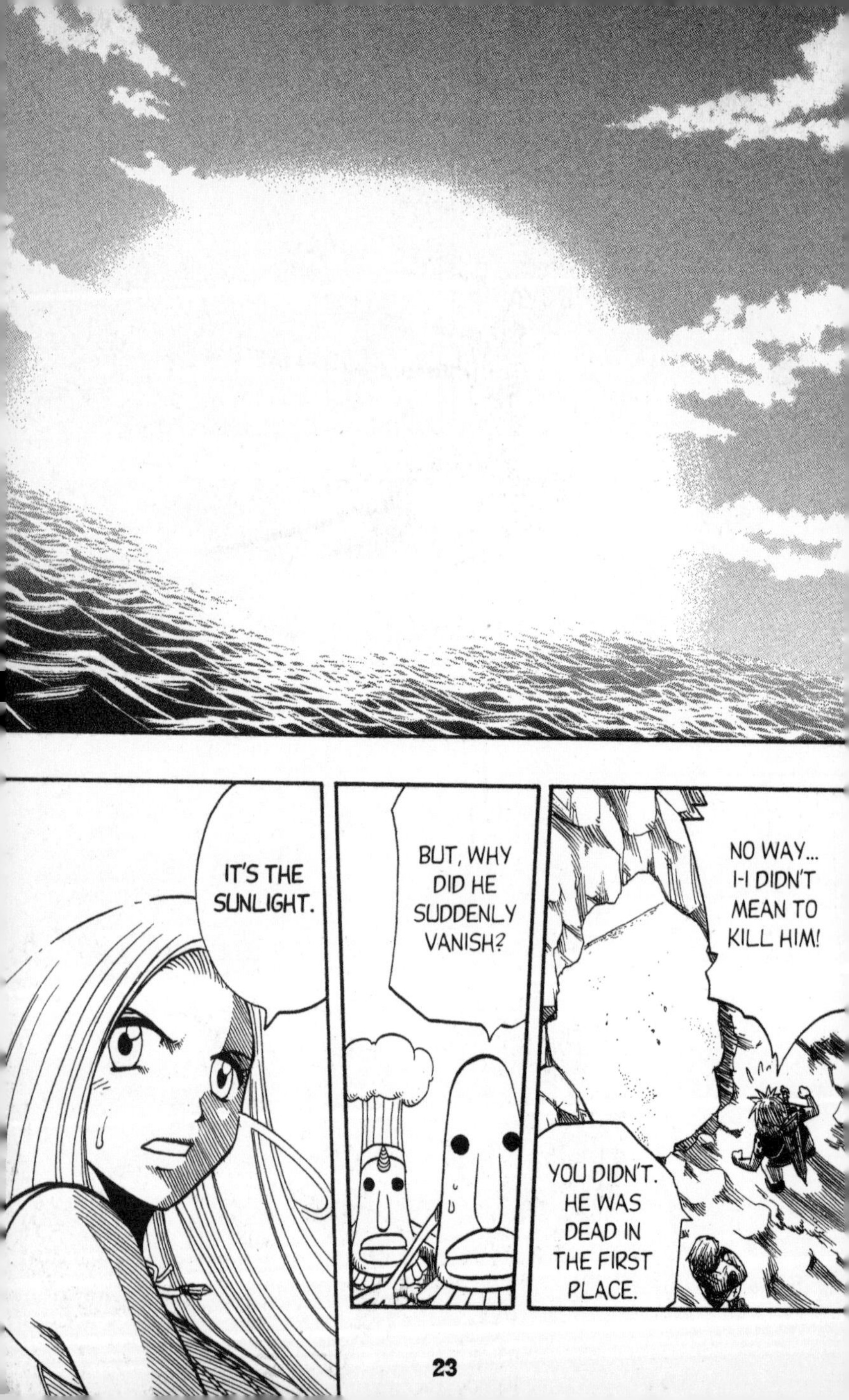
NO WAY... I-I DIDN'T MEAN TO KILL HIM!
YOU DIDN'T. HE WAS DEAD IN THE FIRST PLACE.
BUT, WHY DID HE SUDDENLY VANISH?
IT'S THE SUNLIGHT.

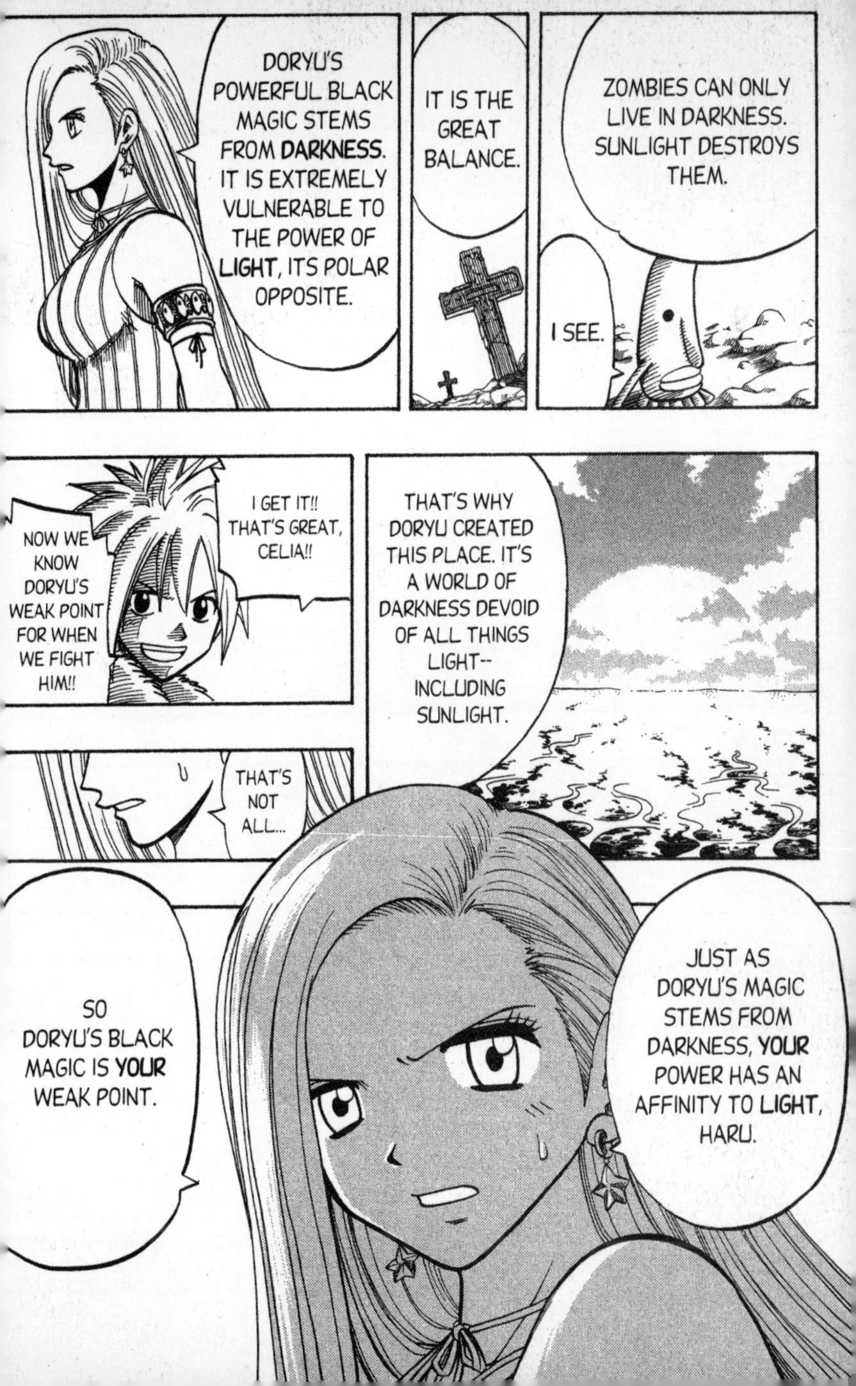
ZOMBIES CAN ONLY LIVE IN DARKNESS. SUNLIGHT DESTROYS THEM.
I SEE.
IT IS THE GREAT BALANCE.
DORYU'S POWERFUL BLACK MAGIC STEMS FROM DARKNESS. IT IS EXTREMELY VULNERABLE TO THE POWER OF LIGHT, ITS POLAR OPPOSITE.
THAT'S WHY DORYU CREATED THIS PLACE. IT'S A WORLD OF DARKNESS DEVOID OF ALL THINGS LIGHT-- INCLUDING SUNLIGHT.
I GET IT!! THAT'S GREAT, CELIA!!
NOW WE KNOW DORYU'S WEAK POINT FOR WHEN WE FIGHT HIM!!
THAT'S NOT ALL...
JUST AS DORYU'S MAGIC STEMS FROM DARKNESS, YOUR POWER HAS AN AFFINITY TO LIGHT, HARU.
SO DORYU'S BLACK MAGIC IS YOUR WEAK POINT.

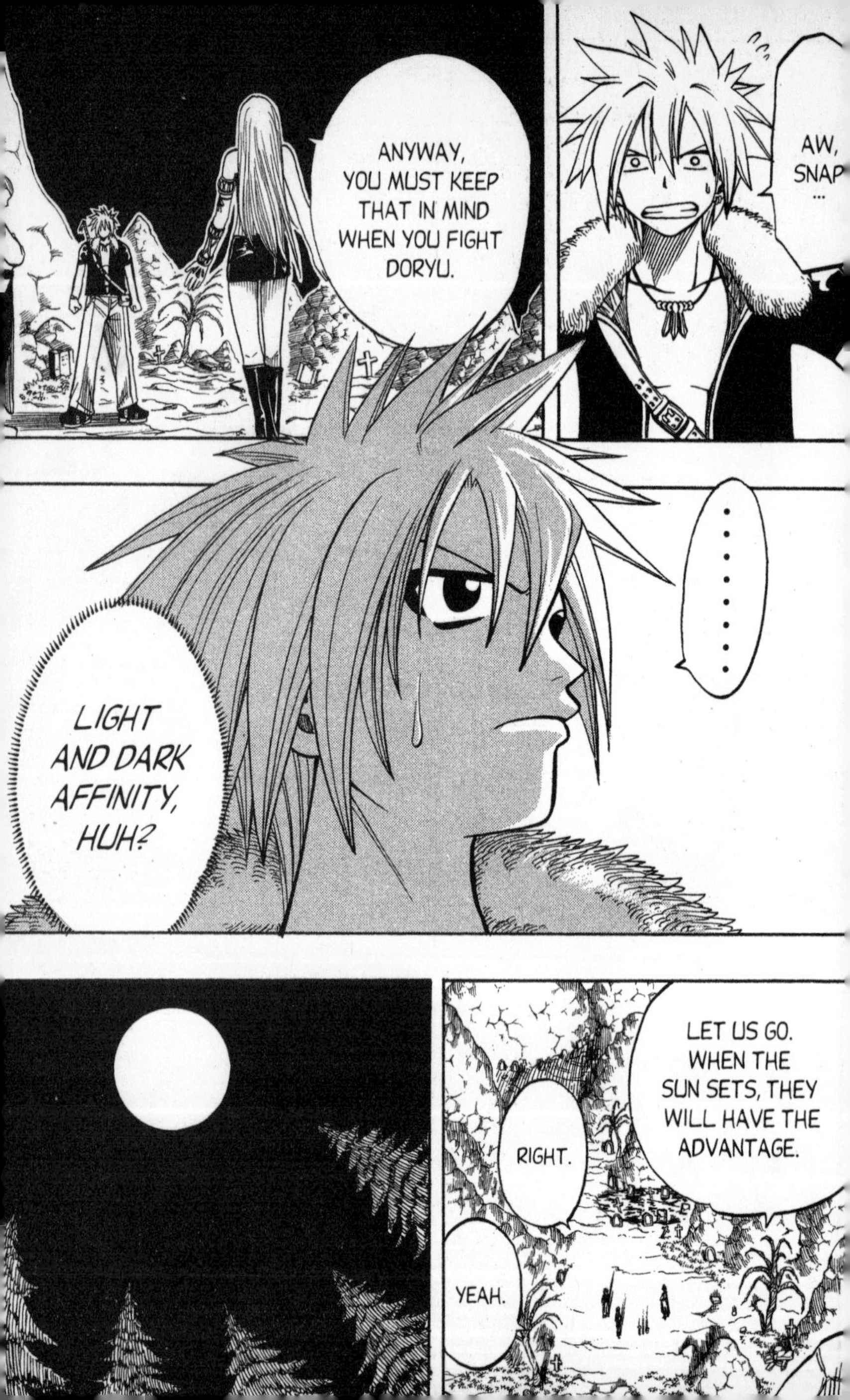
AW, SNAP ...
ANYWAY, YOU MUST KEEP THAT IN MIND WHEN YOU FIGHT DORYU.
......
LIGHT AND DARK AFFINITY, HUH?
LET US GO. WHEN THE SUN SETS, THEY WILL HAVE THE ADVANTAGE.
RIGHT.
YEAH.

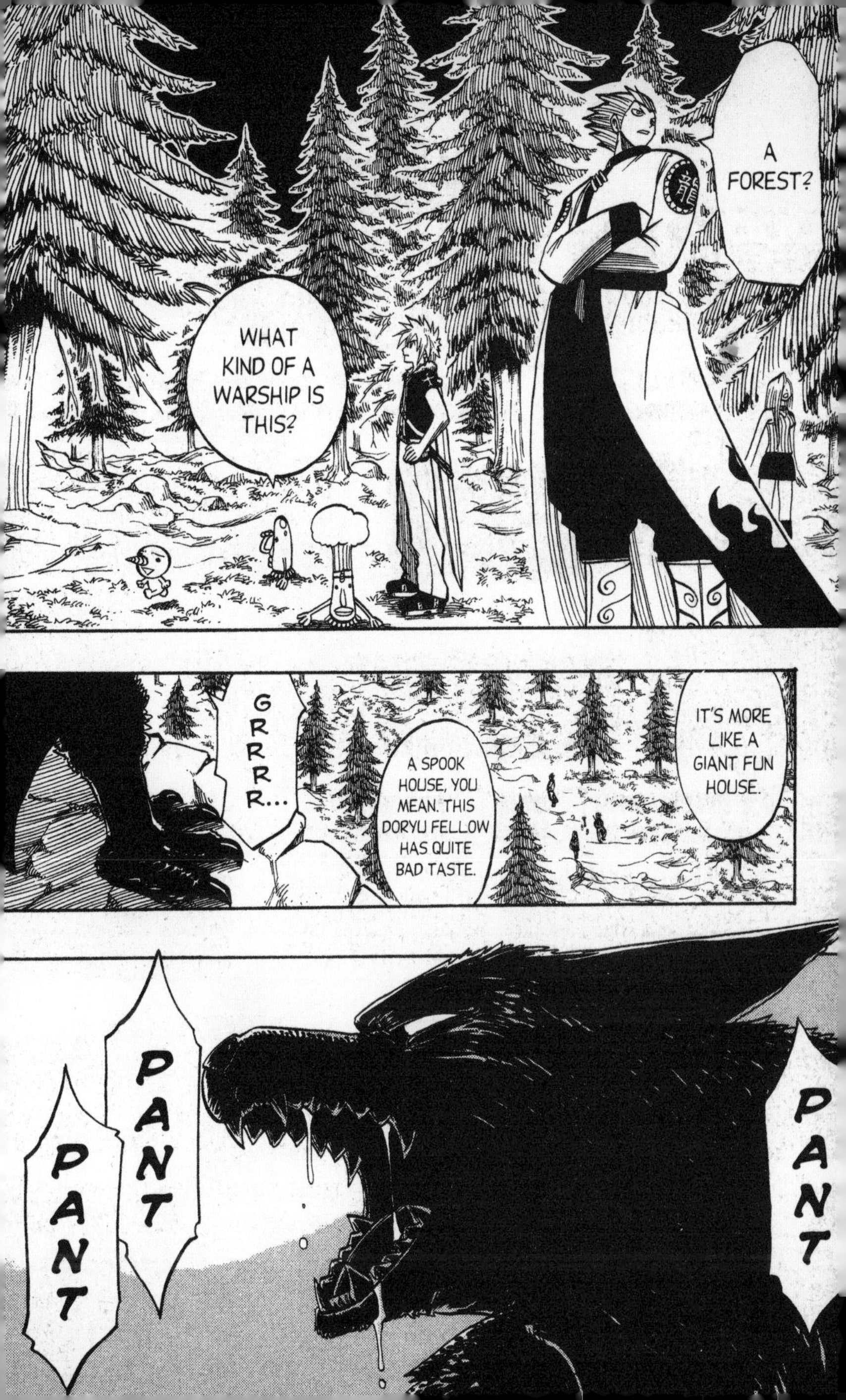
A FOREST?
WHAT KIND OF A WARSHIP IS THIS?
IT'S MORE LIKE A GIANT FUN HOUSE.
A SPOOK HOUSE, YOU MEAN. THIS DORYU FELLOW HAS QUITE BAD TASTE.
GRRRR....
PANT
PANT
PANT

HISTORY OF RAVE

Latest Version

0000
- Jan 1, New Calendar begins
- Resha born

0015
- Rave & DB are created, Kingdom Wars begin
- Shiba appointed Rave Master
- Sept 9, Resha's death

0016
- Overdrive occurs, 1 / 10th of the world destroyed
- Rave scattered
- Plue vanishes

0021
- Sept 9, Gale Glory and Gale Raregroove (King) born

0041
- Sept 9, Gale & King form Demon Card
- Before the end of 0041, Gale Glory secedes from DC and goes to Garage

0050
- August 7, Haru born on Garage Island
- Also August 7, Lucia born

0051
- Gale leaves Garage

0056
- Demon Card wiped out by the Empire
- Sakura, Haru's mother, dies
- King rebuilds Demon Card
- Gale spends 10 years in the desert

0060
- Nakajima arrives at Haru's house

0065
- Plue and Griff battle the Pudding Army

0066
- Haru hooks Plue at Garage Island
- Haru declared second Rave Master

0066.9.9
- Demon Card HQ destroyed
- Gale Glory and King die

0067
- Haru, now 17, arrives at Southernberg in search of the fourth Rave stone

0067.6
- DC restored, Lucia named 2nd King

0077
- Nakajima arrives at Levin's house

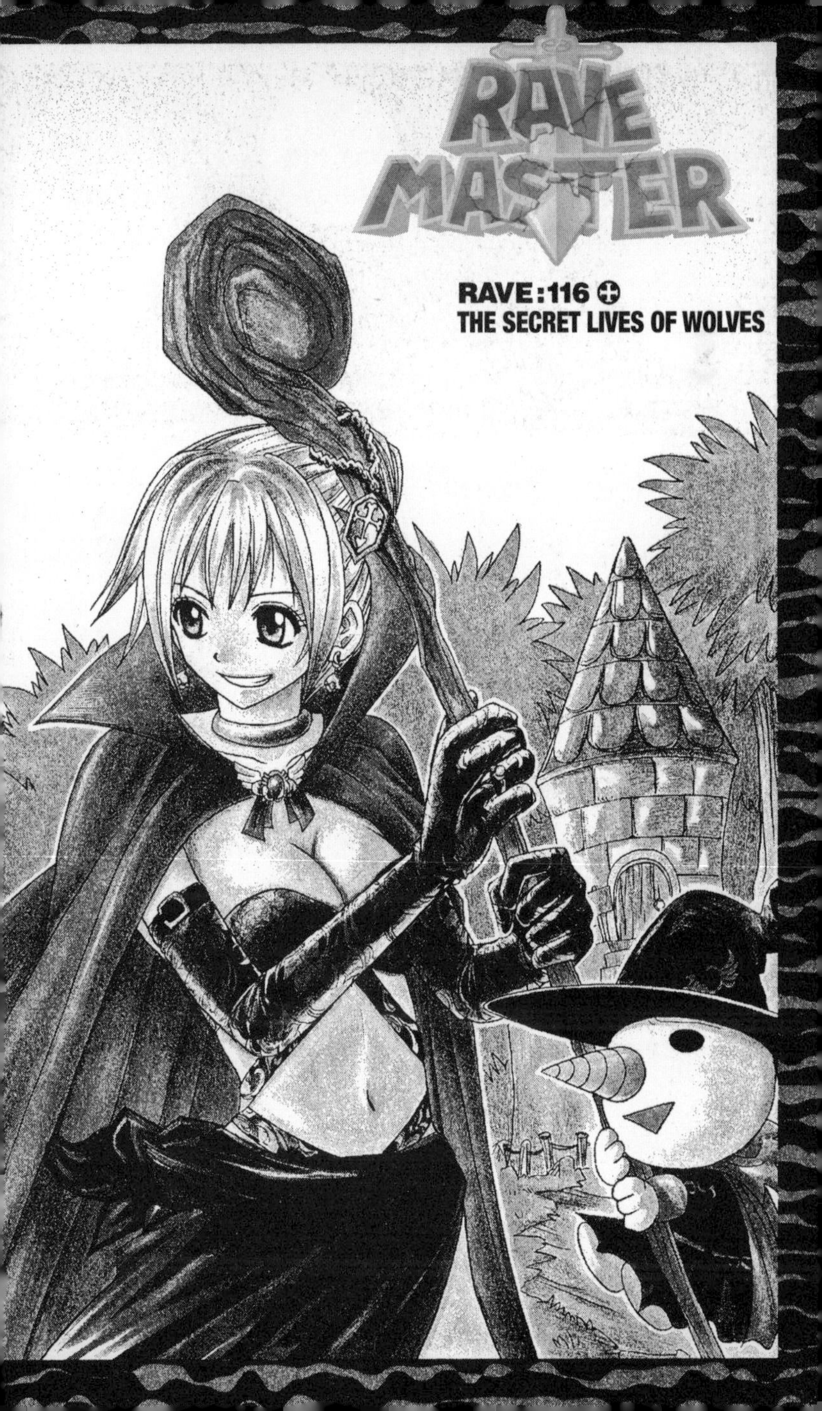
RAVE MASTER
RAVE:116
THE SECRET LIVES OF WOLVES

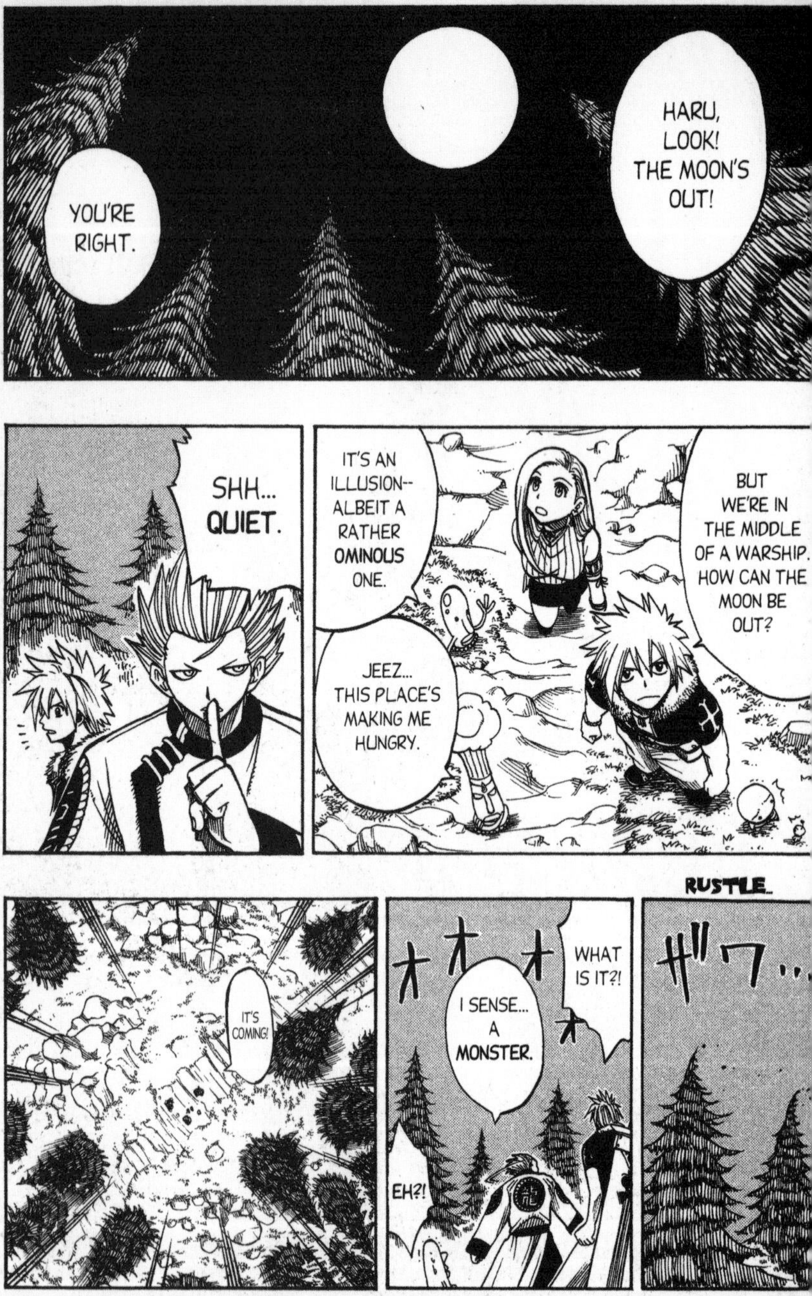
HARU, LOOK! THE MOON'S OUT!
YOU'RE RIGHT.
BUT WE'RE IN THE MIDDLE OF A WARSHIP. HOW CAN THE MOON BE OUT?
IT'S AN ILLUSION-- ALBEIT A RATHER OMINOUS ONE.
JEEZ... THIS PLACE'S MAKING ME HUNGRY.
SHH... QUIET.
RUSTLE...
ザワ...
WHAT IS IT?!
オオオオ
I SENSE... A MONSTER.
EH?!
IT'S COMING!

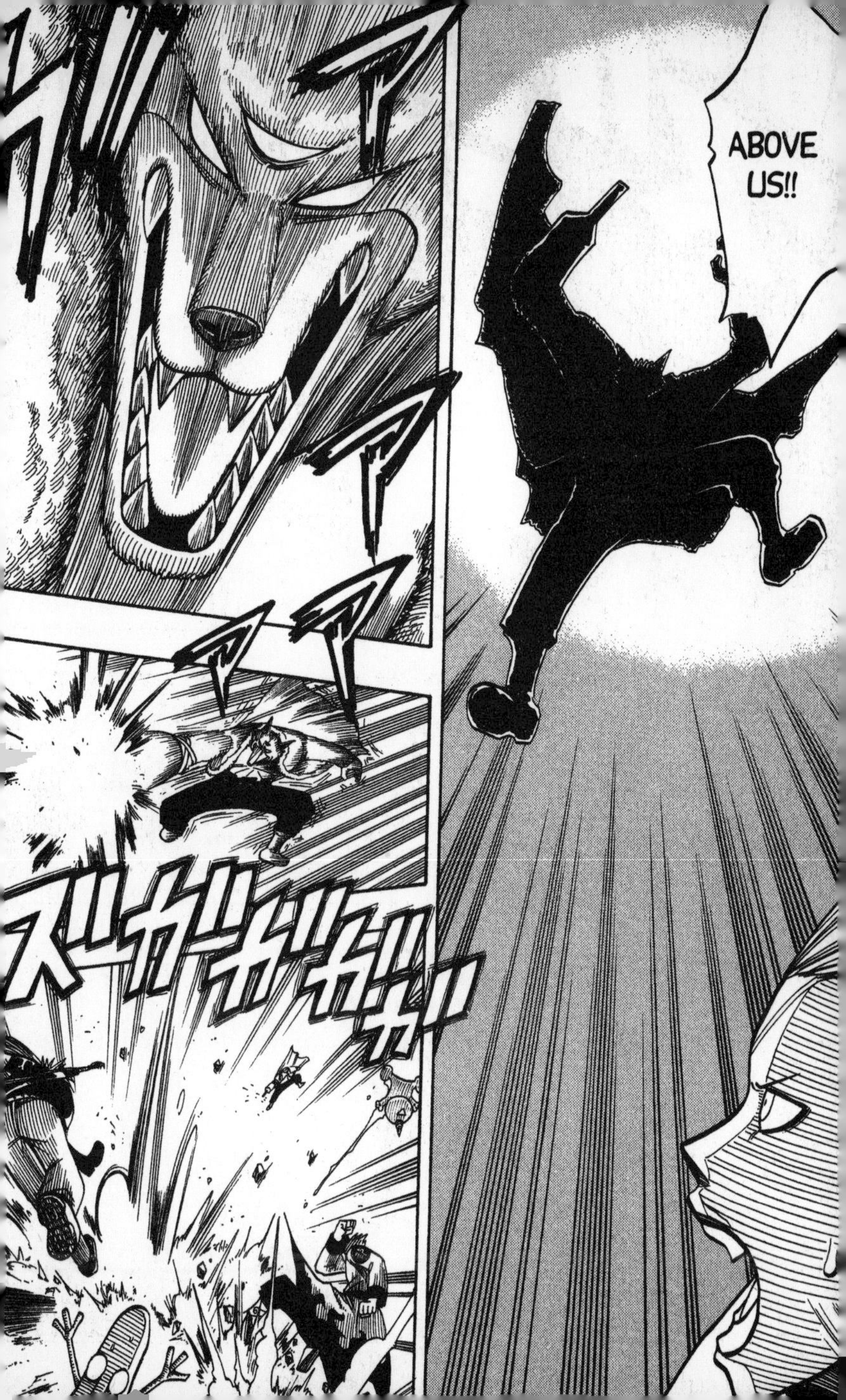
ABOVE US!!

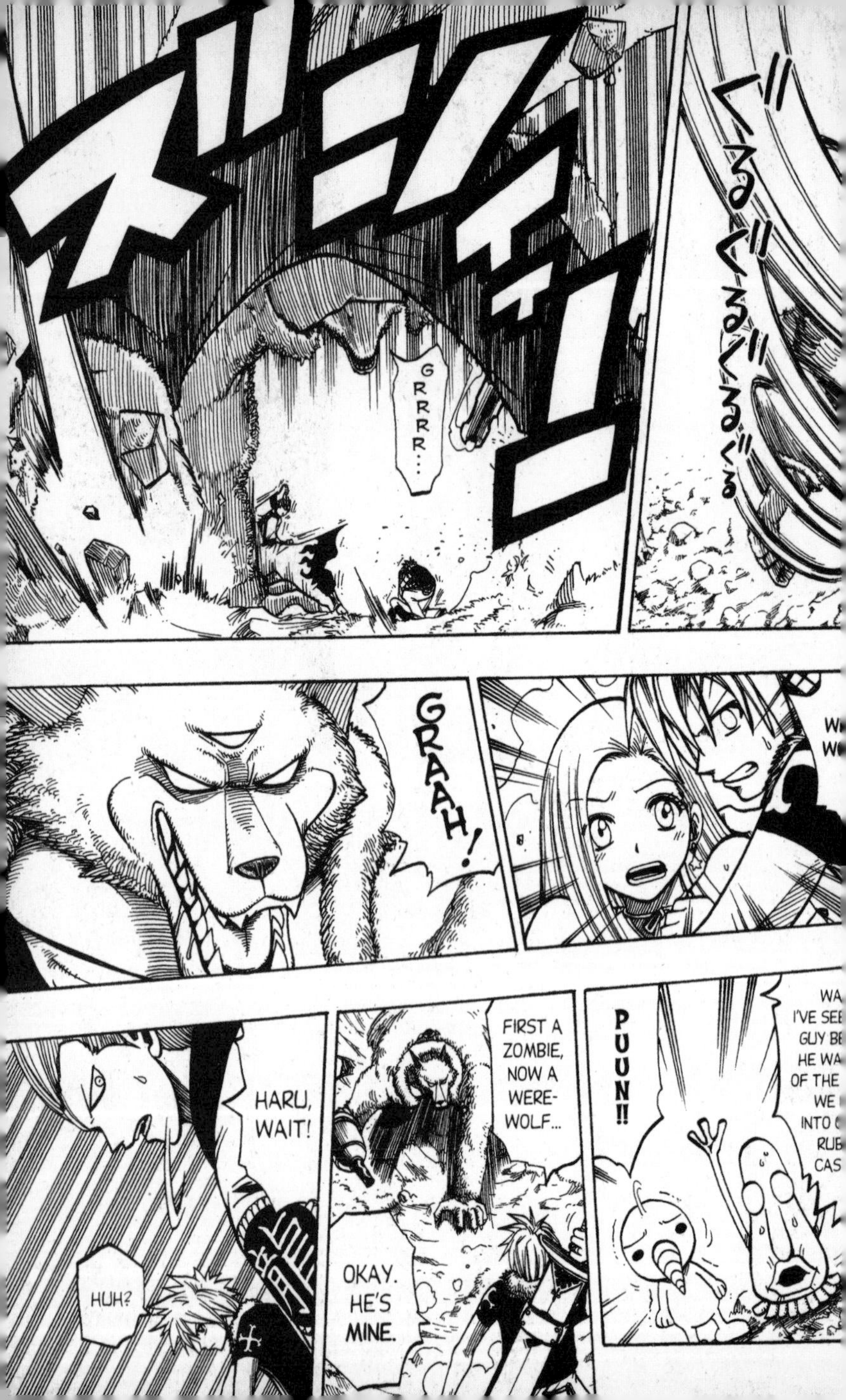

ぐるぐるぐるぐる
GRRRR...
GRAAH!
PUUN!!
FIRST A ZOMBIE, NOW A WERE-WOLF...
OKAY. HE'S MINE.
HARU, WAIT!
HUH?

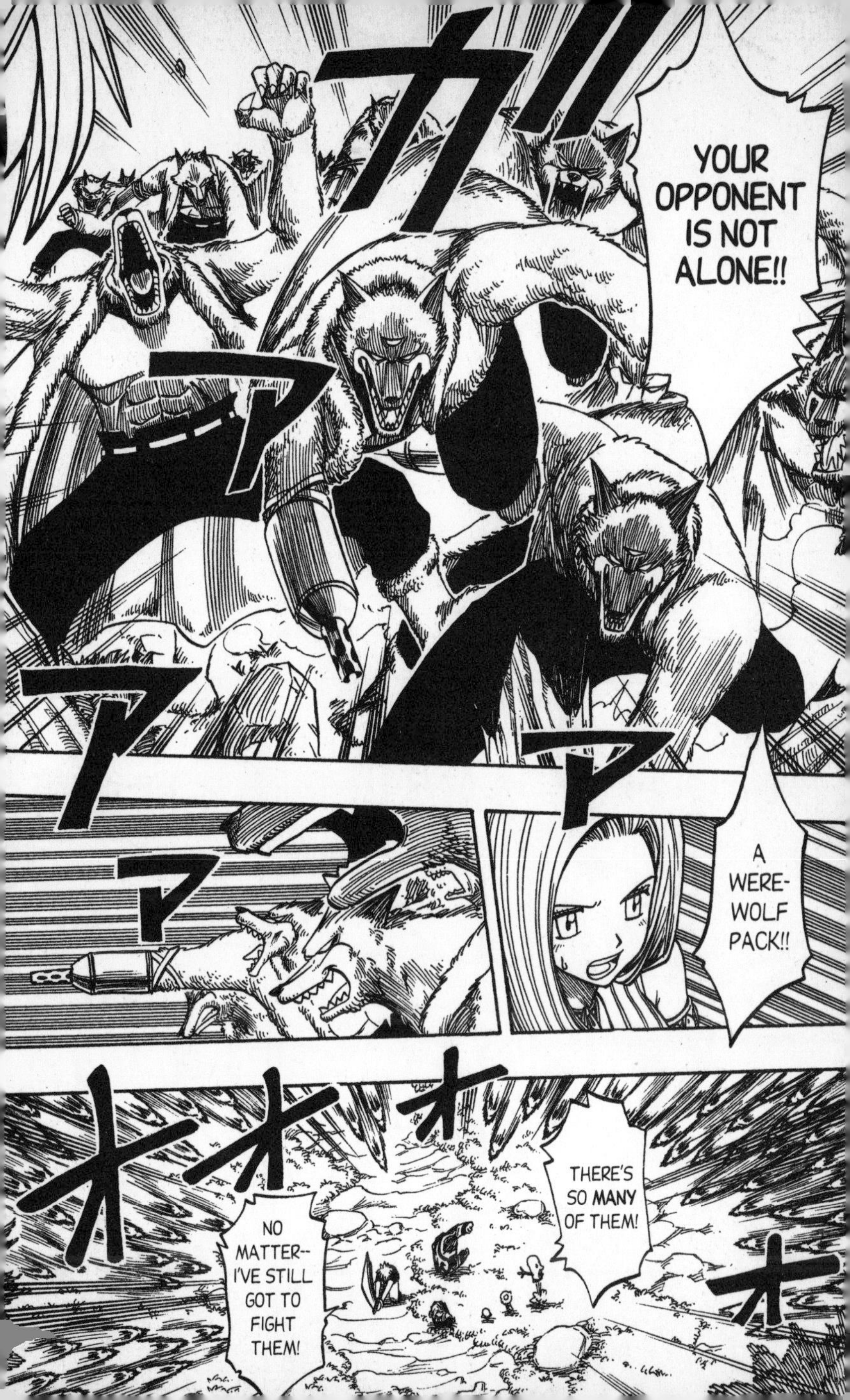
YOUR OPPONENT IS NOT ALONE!!
A WERE-WOLF PACK!!
THERE'S SO MANY OF THEM!
NO MATTER-- I'VE STILL GOT TO FIGHT THEM!

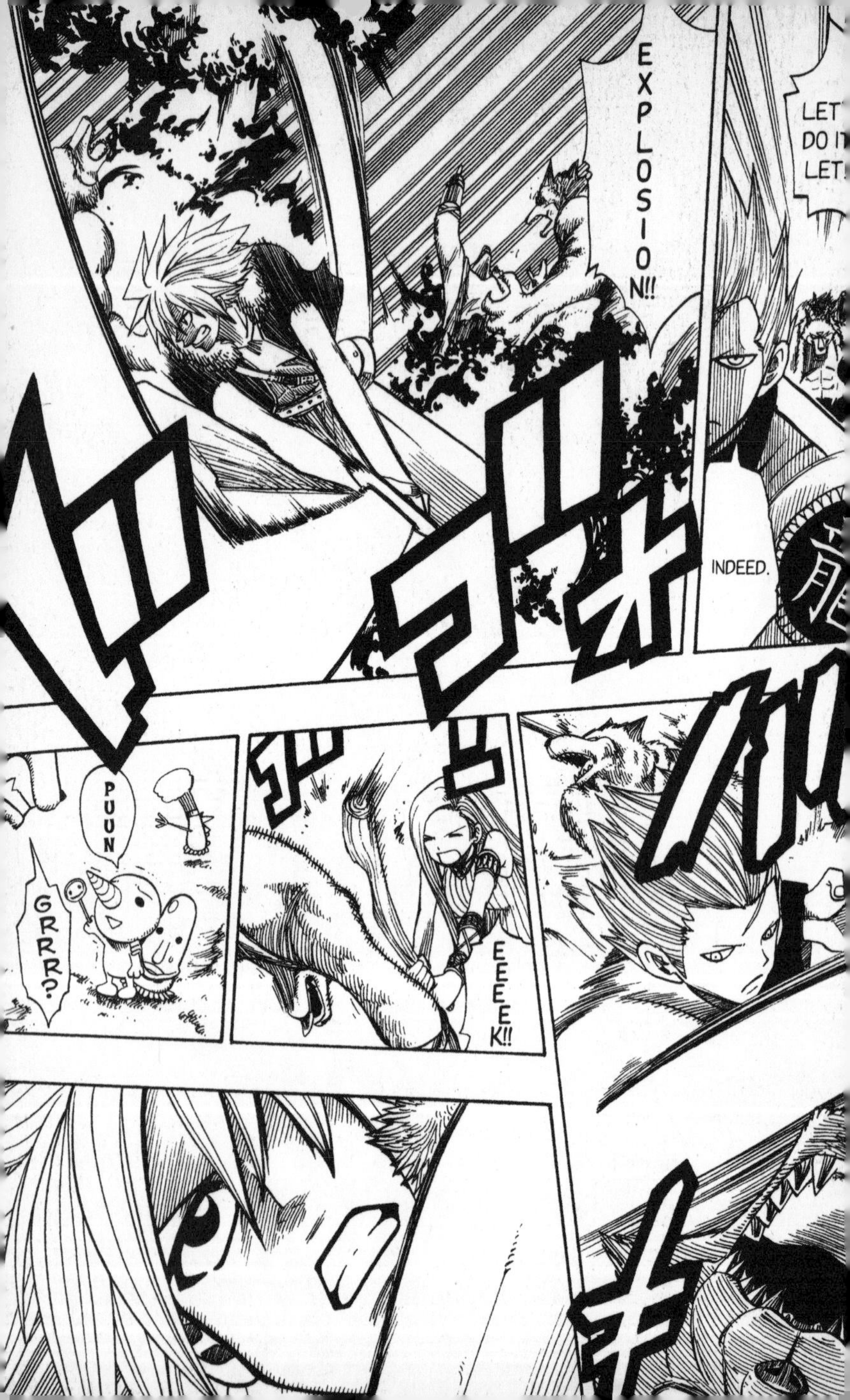
LET
DO IT
LET
INDEED.
EXPLOSION!!
EEEEK!!
PUUN
GRRR?

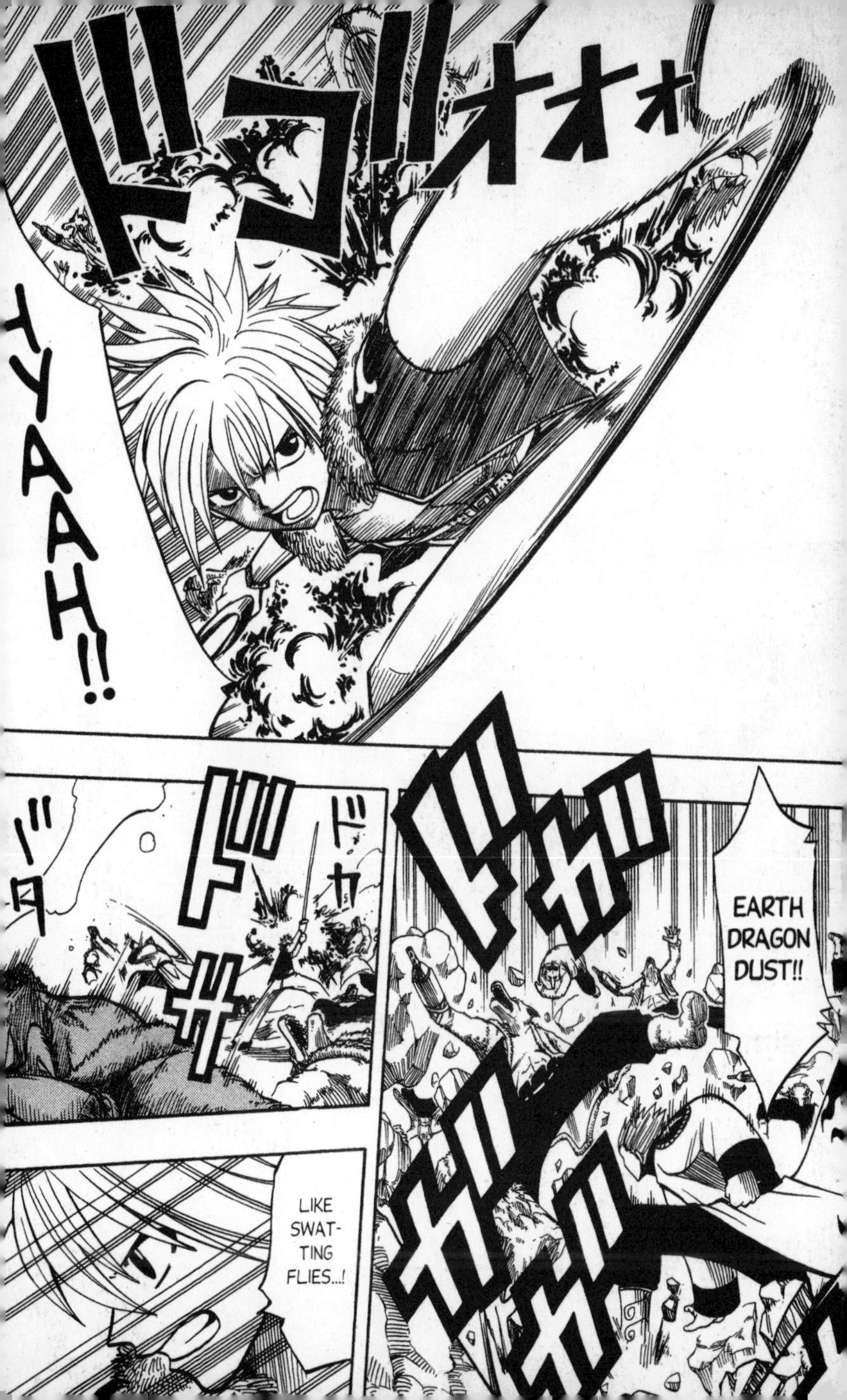

ドゴオオォ
TYAAAH!!
EARTH DRAGON DUST!!
LIKE SWAT-TING FLIES...!

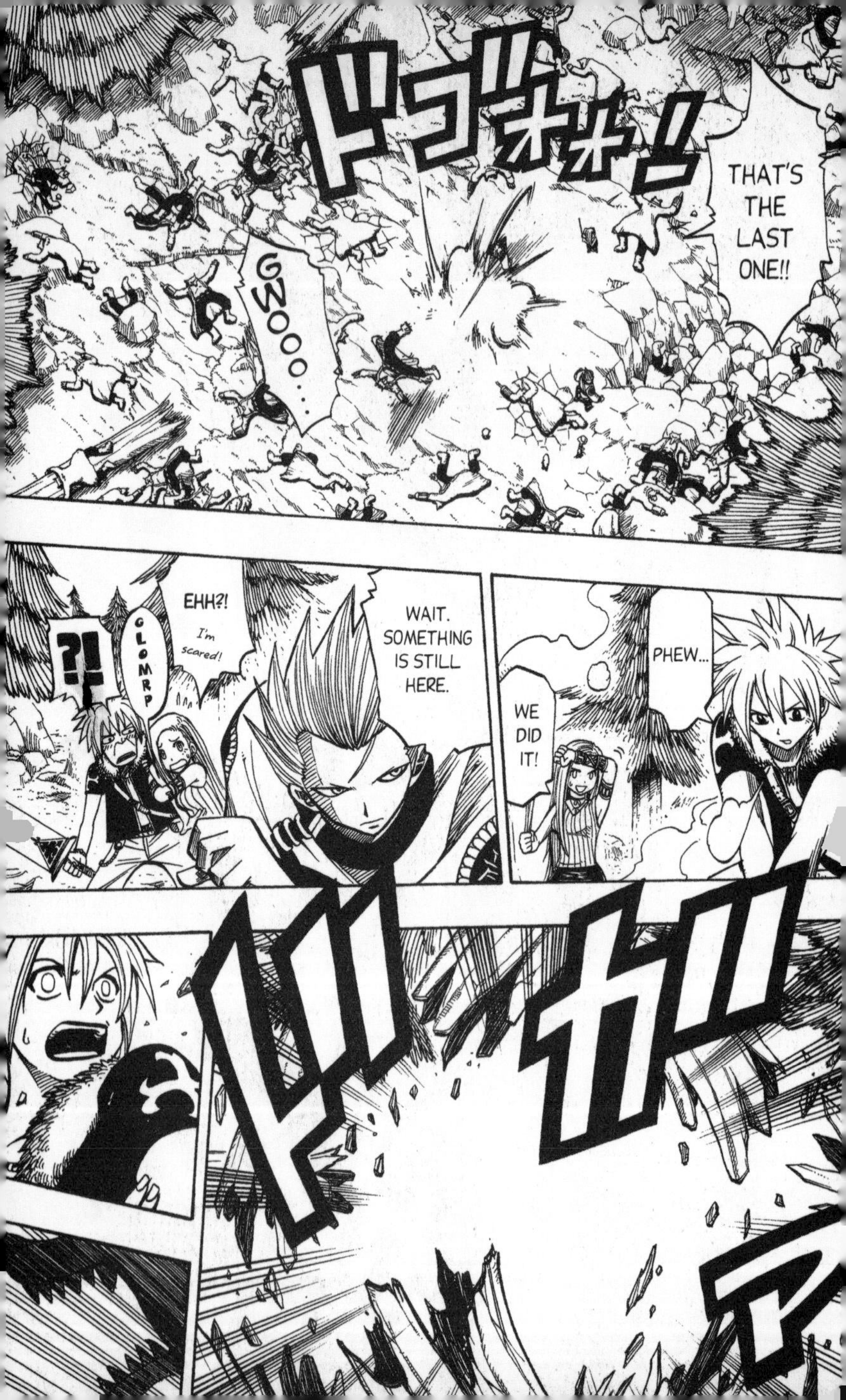

ドゴォォ!
THAT'S THE LAST ONE!!
GWOOOO...
PHEW...
WE DID IT!
WAIT. SOMETHING IS STILL HERE.
EHH?!
GLOMRP
I'm scared!
?!

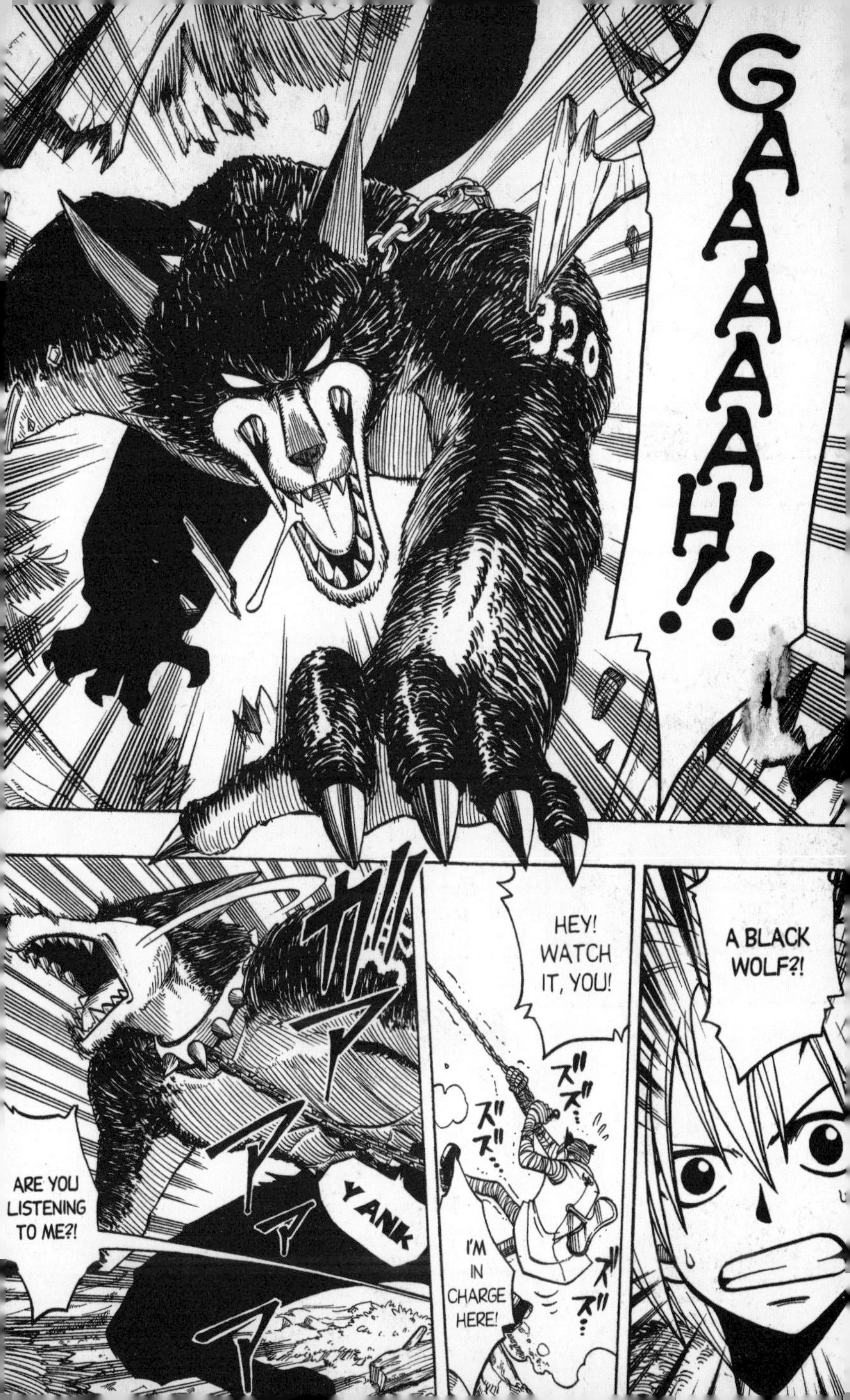
GAAAAAH!!
320
A BLACK WOLF?!
HEY! WATCH IT, YOU!
ズズ...
ズズ...
I'M IN CHARGE HERE!
ズズ...
YANK
ARE YOU LISTENING TO ME?!

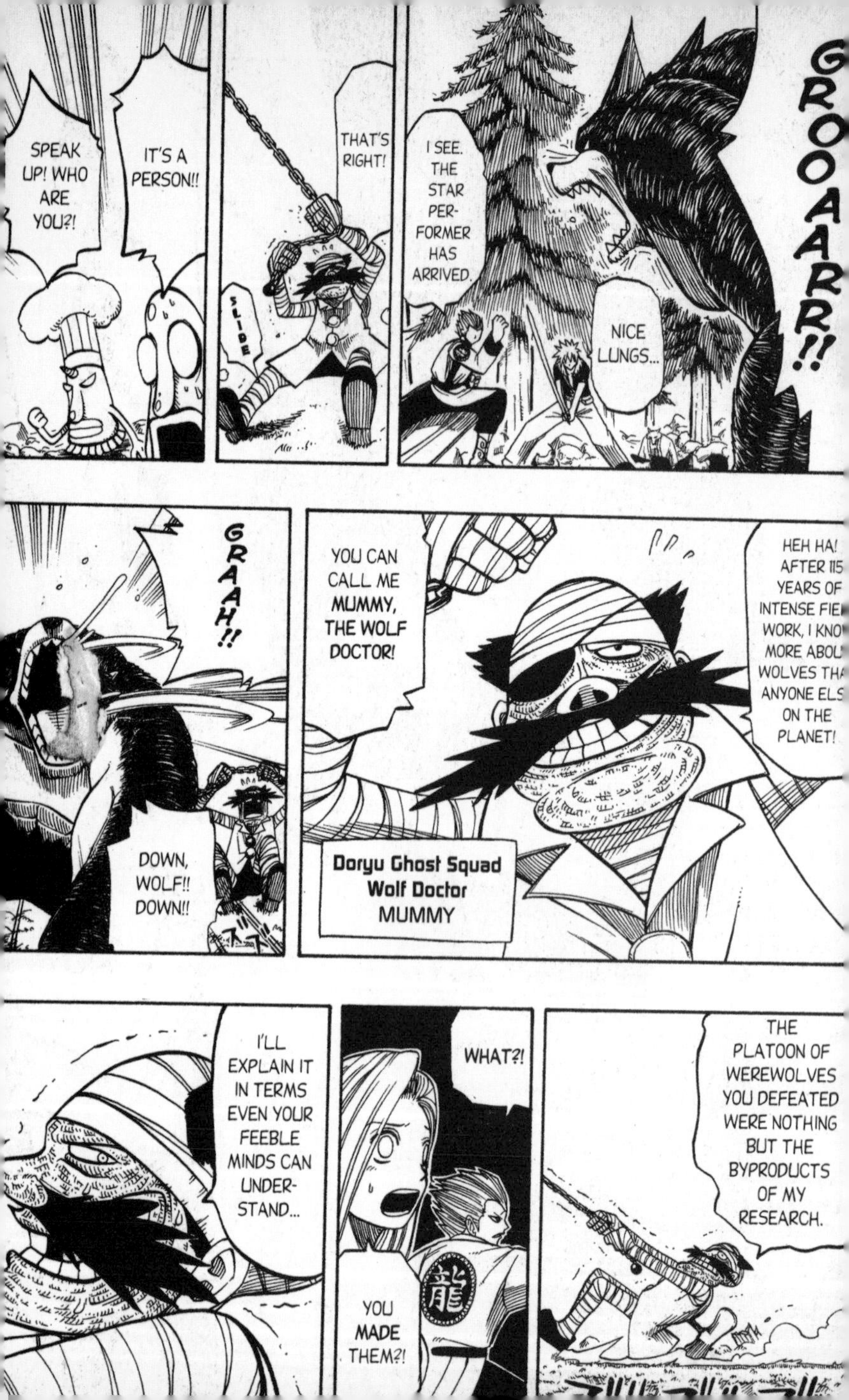
GROOOAARR!!
I SEE. THE STAR PERFORMER HAS ARRIVED.
NICE LUNGS...
THAT'S RIGHT!
SLIDE
IT'S A PERSON!!
SPEAK UP! WHO ARE YOU?!
HEH HA! AFTER 115 YEARS OF INTENSE FIE WORK, I KNO MORE ABOU WOLVES THA ANYONE ELS ON THE PLANET!
YOU CAN CALL ME MUMMY, THE WOLF DOCTOR!
Doryu Ghost Squad Wolf Doctor MUMMY
GRAAH!!
DOWN, WOLF!! DOWN!!
THE PLATOON OF WEREWOLVES YOU DEFEATED WERE NOTHING BUT THE BYPRODUCTS OF MY RESEARCH.
WHAT?!
YOU MADE THEM?!
I'LL EXPLAIN IT IN TERMS EVEN YOUR FEEBLE MINDS CAN UNDERSTAND...

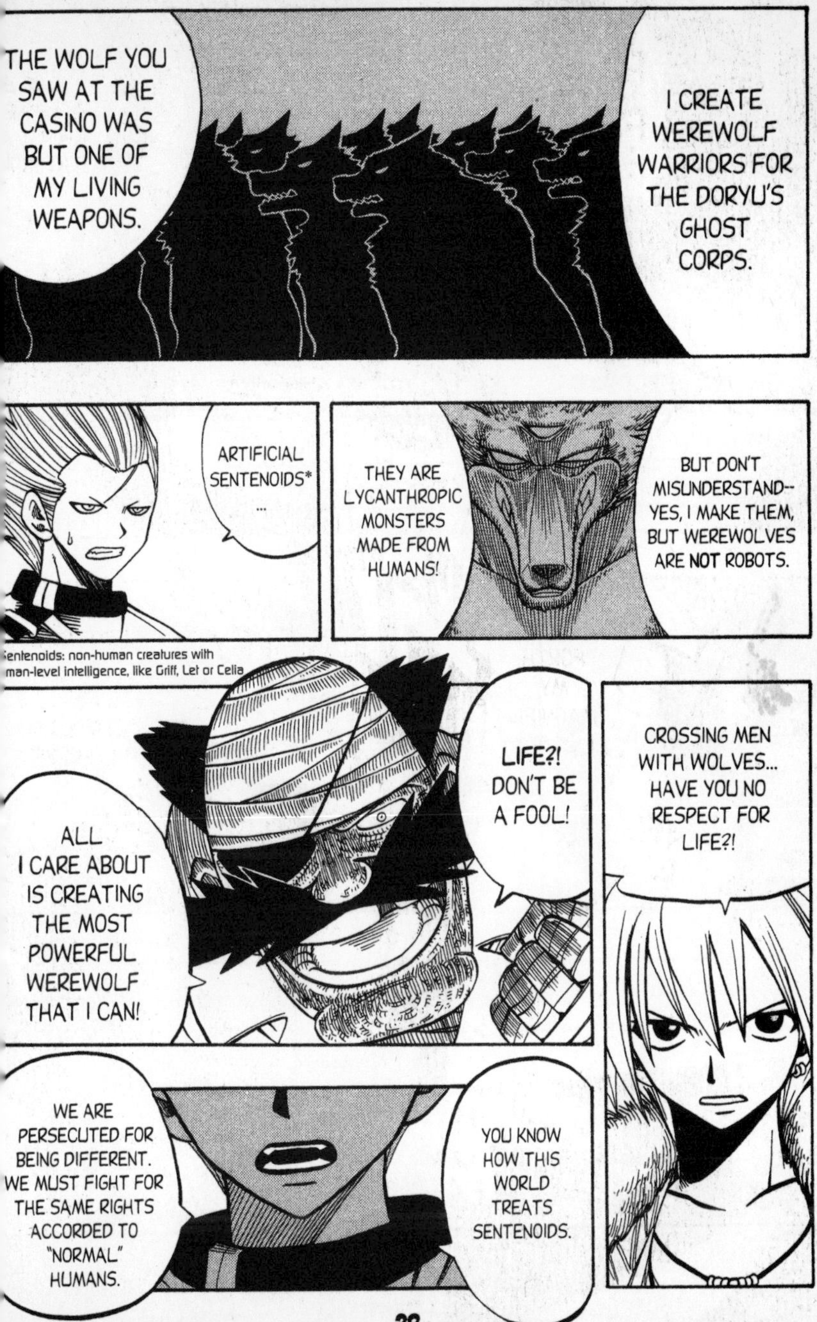
I CREATE WEREWOLF WARRIORS FOR THE DORYU'S GHOST CORPS.
THE WOLF YOU SAW AT THE CASINO WAS BUT ONE OF MY LIVING WEAPONS.
BUT DON'T MISUNDERSTAND-- YES, I MAKE THEM, BUT WEREWOLVES ARE **NOT** ROBOTS.
THEY ARE LYCANTHROPIC MONSTERS MADE FROM HUMANS!
ARTIFICIAL SENTENOIDS* ...
Sentenoids: non-human creatures with man-level intelligence, like Griff, Let or Celia
CROSSING MEN WITH WOLVES... HAVE YOU NO RESPECT FOR LIFE?!
LIFE?! DON'T BE A FOOL!
ALL I CARE ABOUT IS CREATING THE MOST POWERFUL WEREWOLF THAT I CAN!
YOU KNOW HOW THIS WORLD TREATS SENTENOIDS.
WE ARE PERSECUTED FOR BEING DIFFERENT. WE MUST FIGHT FOR THE SAME RIGHTS ACCORDED TO "NORMAL" HUMANS.

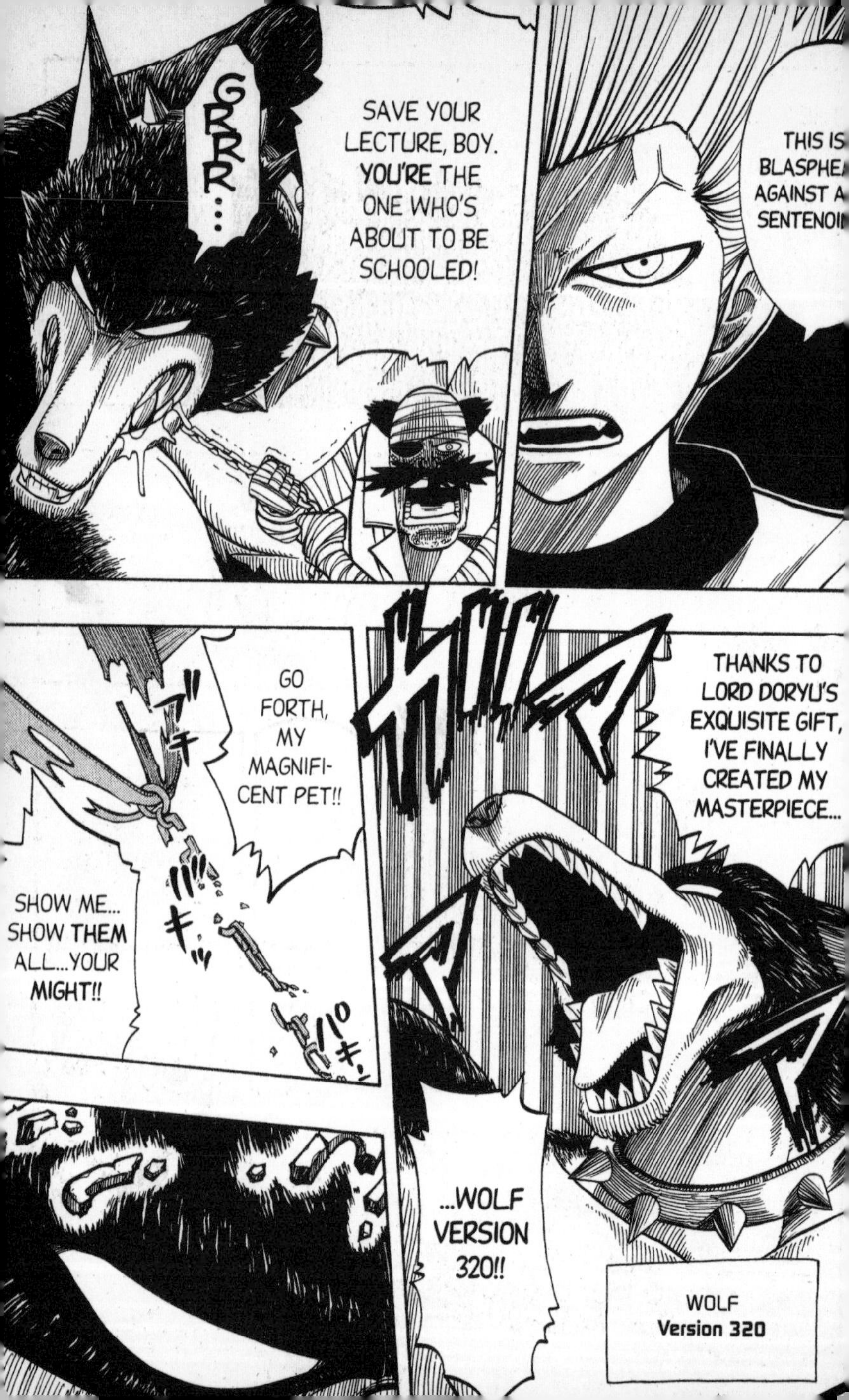
THIS IS BLASPHE AGAINST A SENTENOI
SAVE YOUR LECTURE, BOY. YOU'RE THE ONE WHO'S ABOUT TO BE SCHOOLED!
GRRR...
THANKS TO LORD DORYU'S EXQUISITE GIFT, I'VE FINALLY CREATED MY MASTERPIECE...
...WOLF VERSION 320!!
WOLF Version 320
GO FORTH, MY MAGNIFI-CENT PET!!
SHOW ME... SHOW THEM ALL...YOUR MIGHT!!

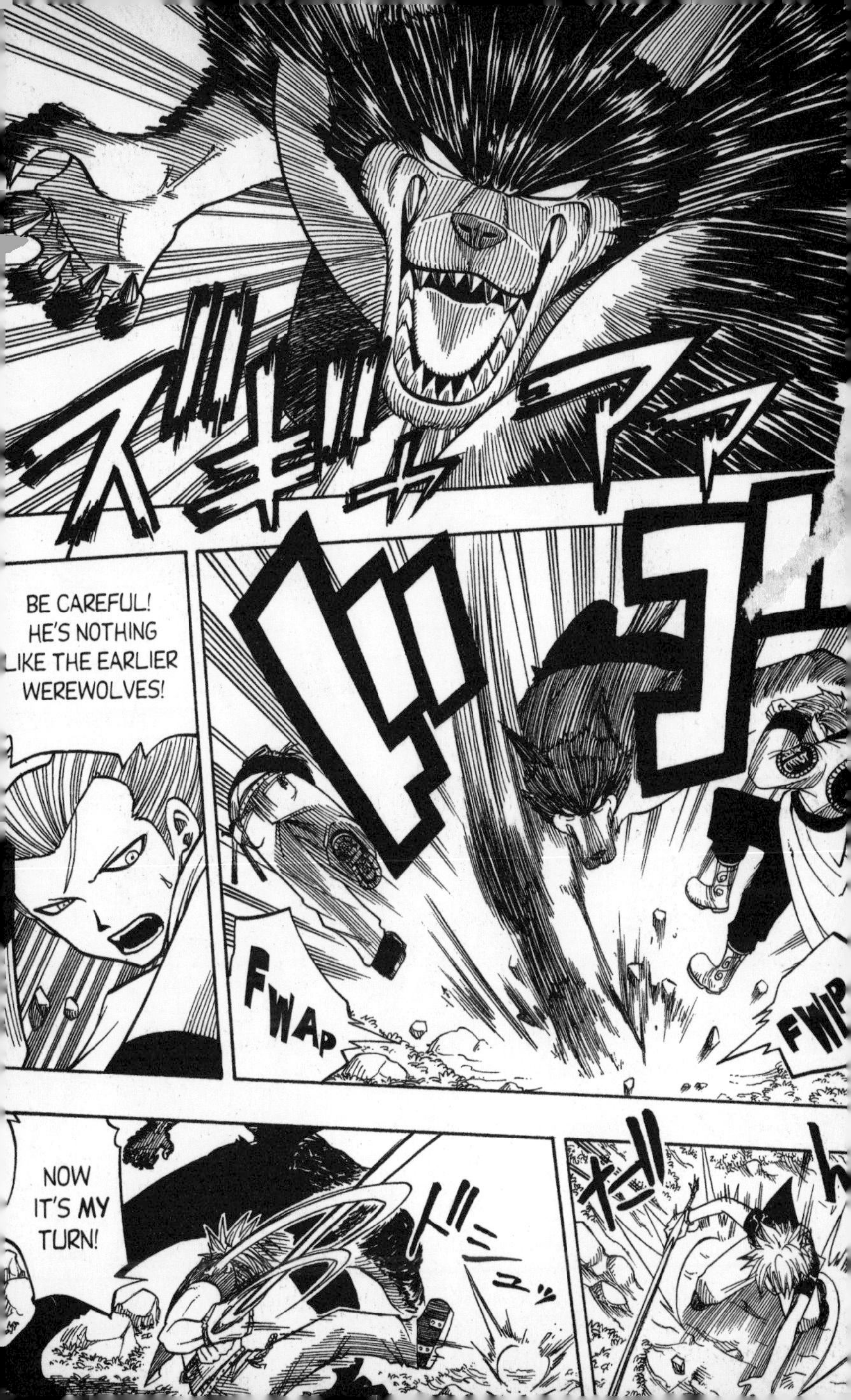
FWIP
FWAP
BE CAREFUL! HE'S NOTHING LIKE THE EARLIER WEREWOLVES!
NOW IT'S MY TURN!

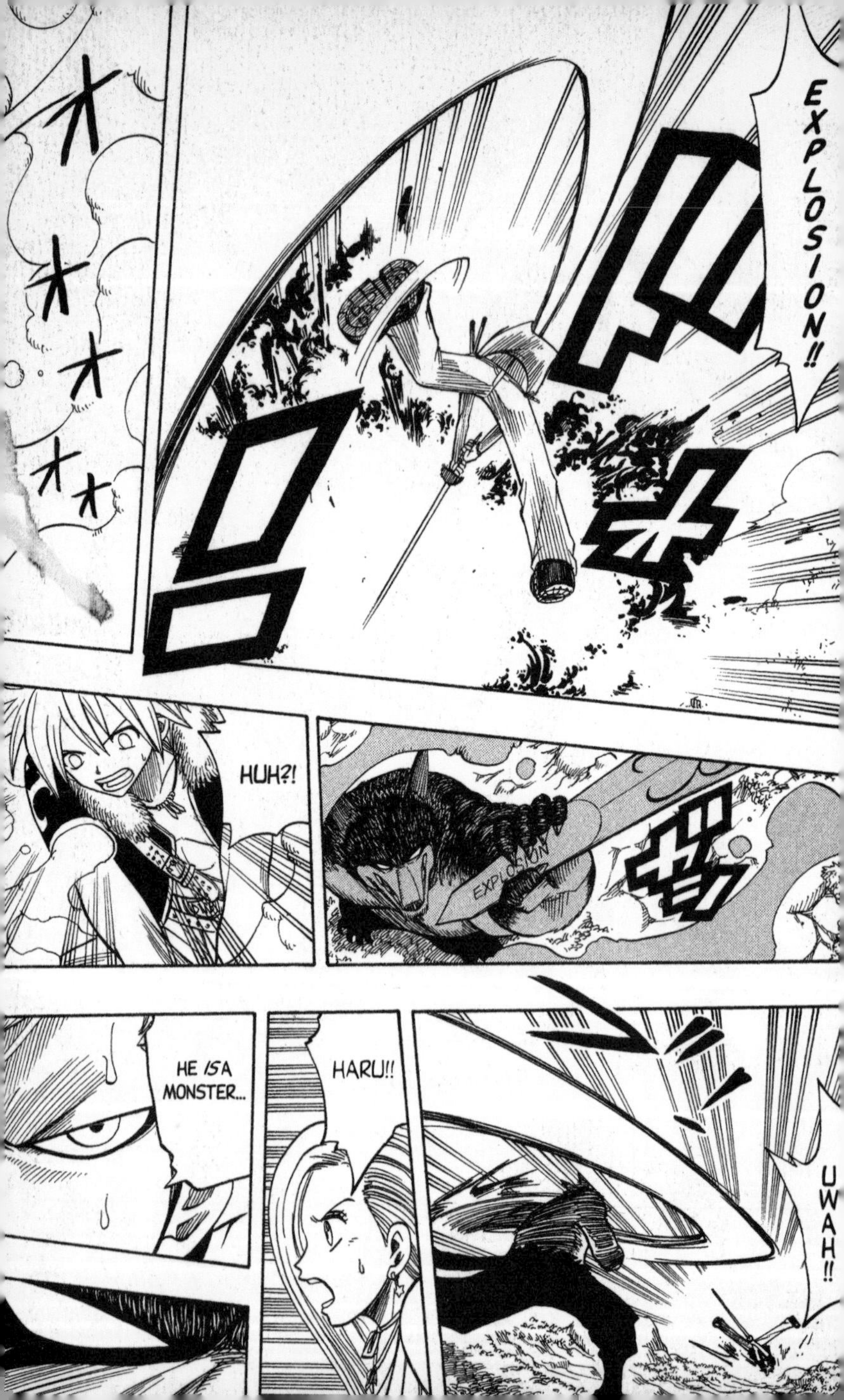
EXPLOSION!!
EXPLOSION
HUH?!
UWAH!!
HARU!!
HE IS A MONSTER...

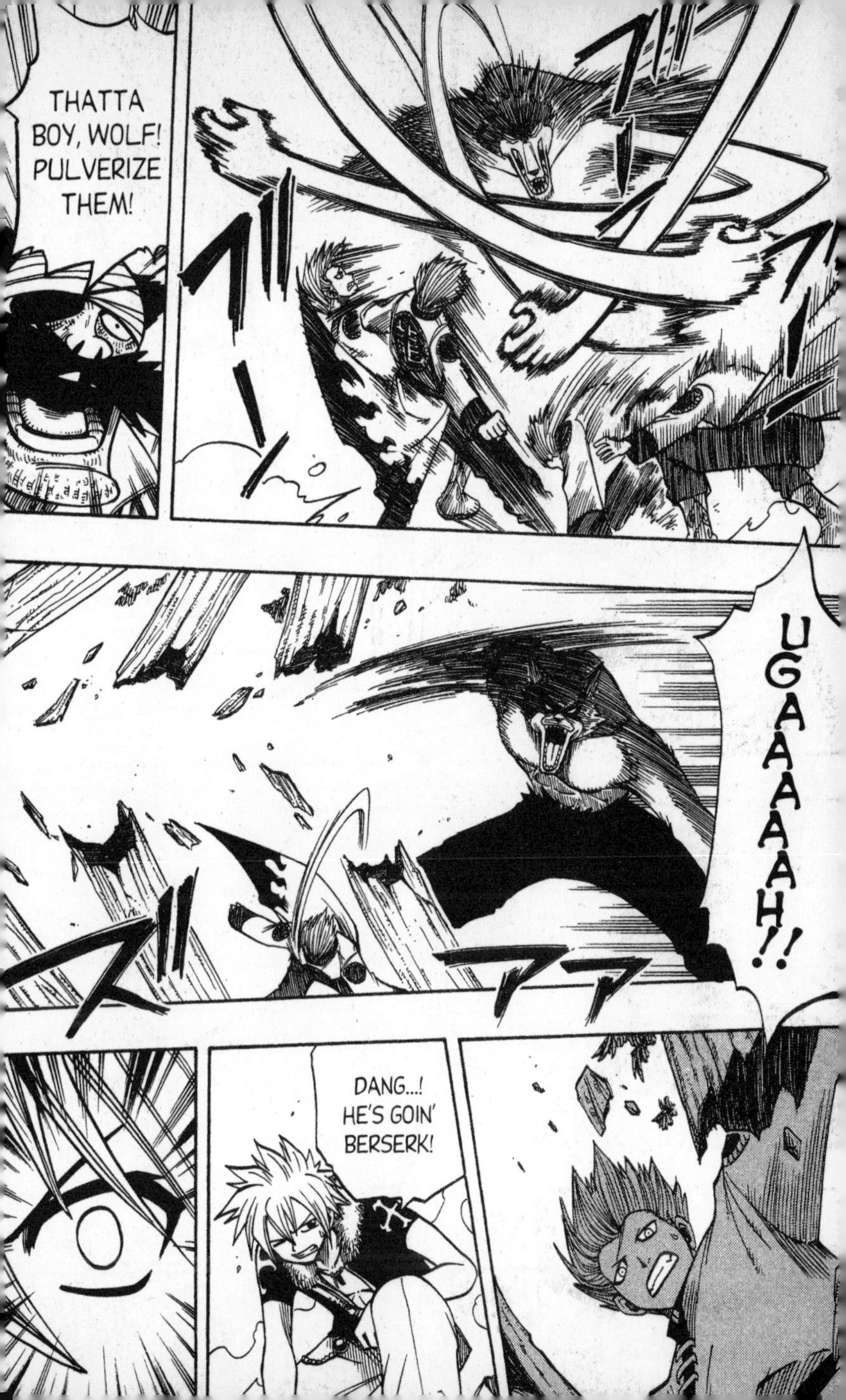
THATTA BOY, WOLF! PULVERIZE THEM!
UGAAAAAH!!
DANG...! HE'S GOIN' BERSERK!

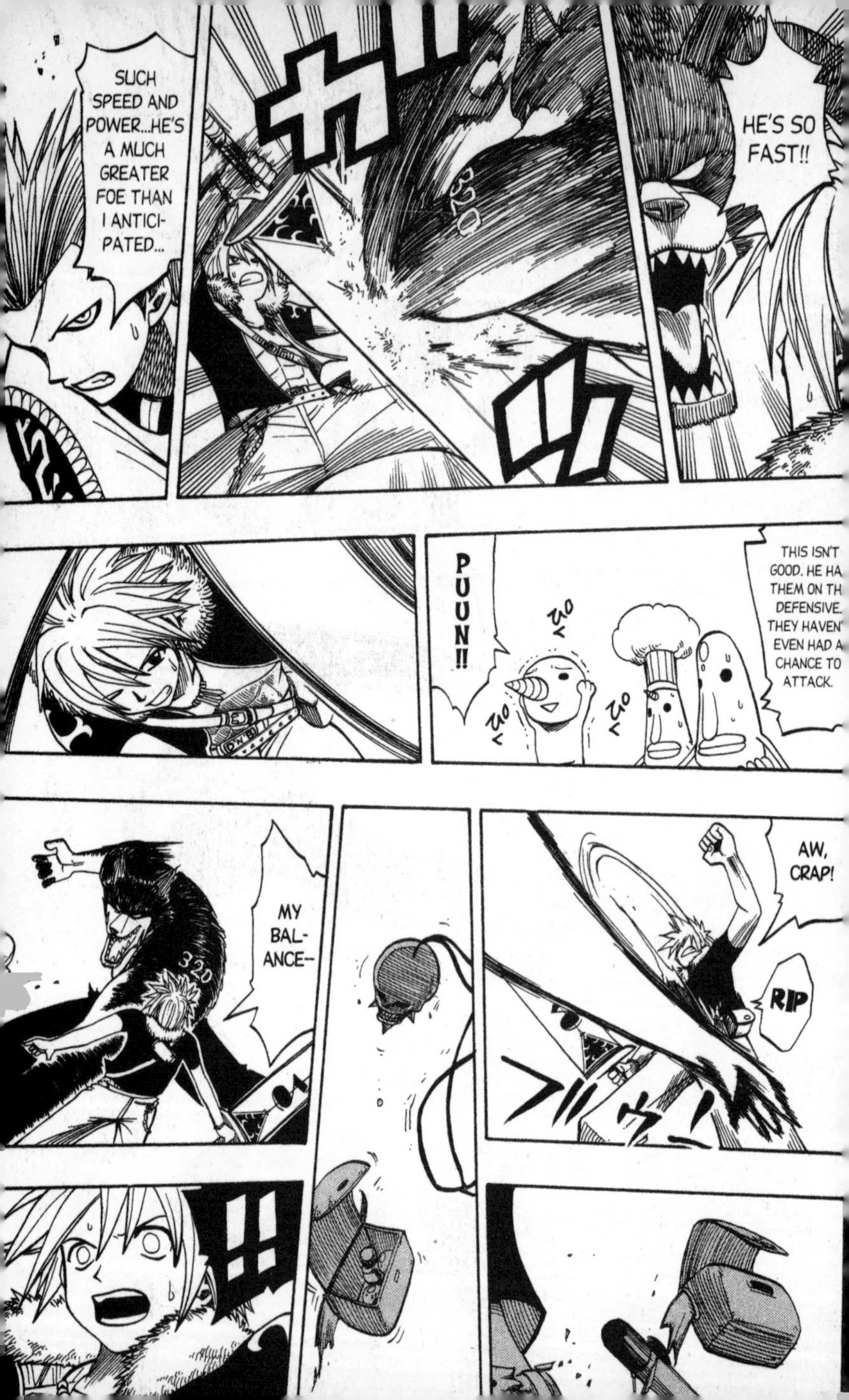
HE'S SO FAST!!
SUCH SPEED AND POWER...HE'S A MUCH GREATER FOE THAN I ANTICI-PATED...
THIS ISN'T GOOD. HE HA THEM ON TH DEFENSIVE. THEY HAVEN' EVEN HAD A CHANCE TO ATTACK.
PUUN!!
AW, CRAP!
RIP
MY BAL-ANCE--

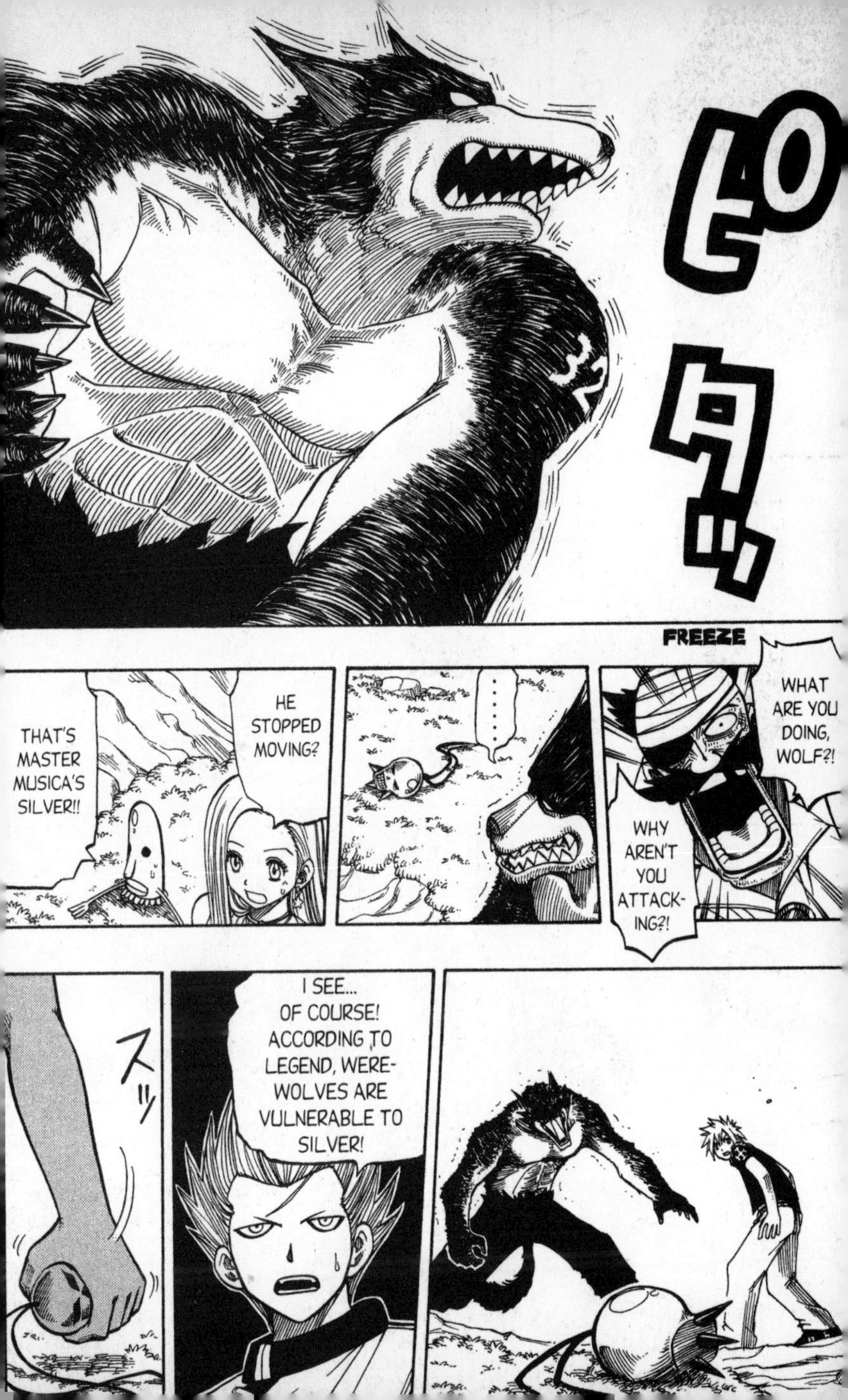
ピタッ
FREEZE
WHAT ARE YOU DOING, WOLF?!
WHY AREN'T YOU ATTACKING?!
......
HE STOPPED MOVING?
THAT'S MASTER MUSICA'S SILVER!!
I SEE... OF COURSE! ACCORDING TO LEGEND, WERE-WOLVES ARE VULNERABLE TO SILVER!
スッ

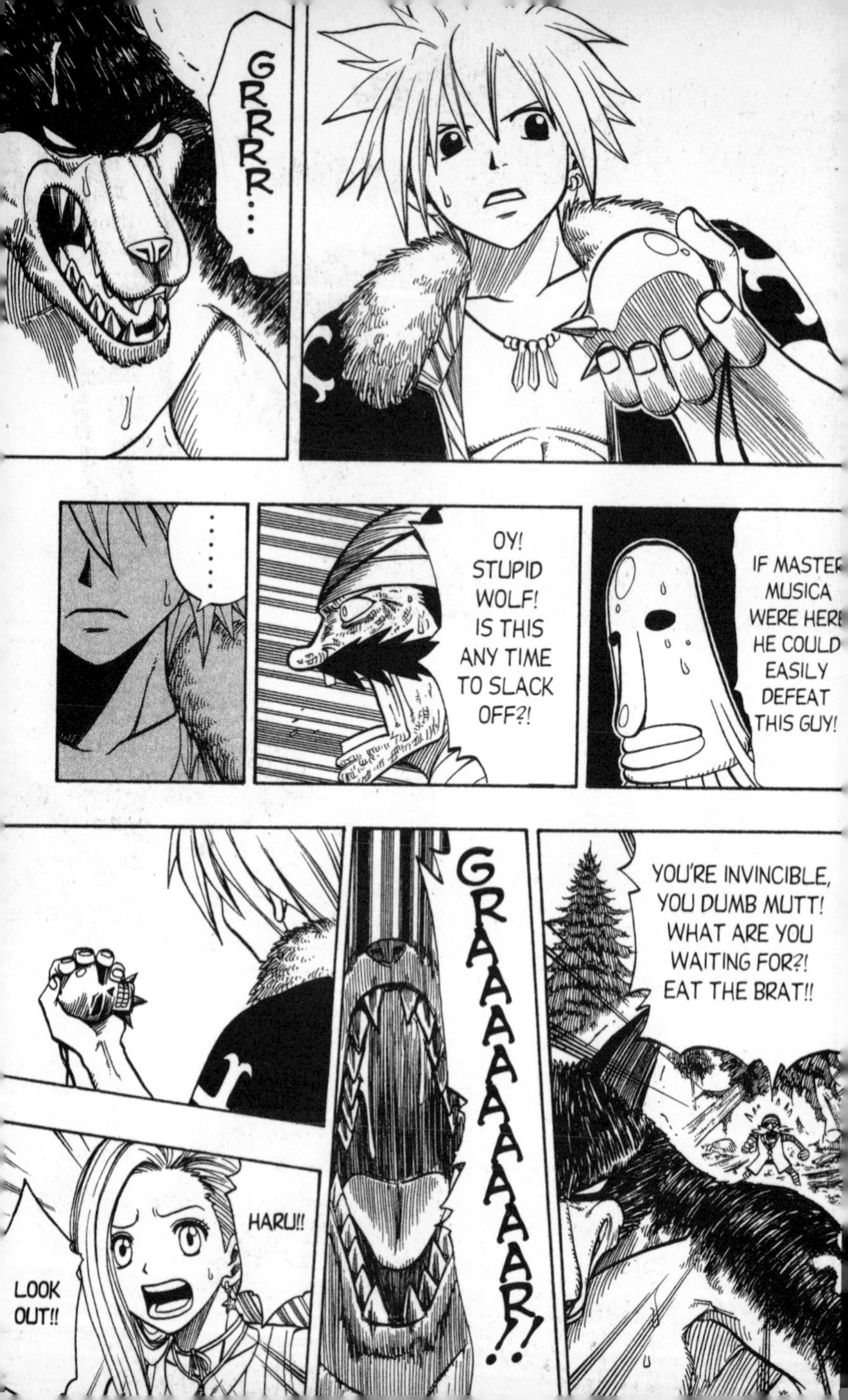
GRRRR...
IF MASTER MUSICA WERE HERE HE COULD EASILY DEFEAT THIS GUY!
OY! STUPID WOLF! IS THIS ANY TIME TO SLACK OFF?!
......
YOU'RE INVINCIBLE, YOU DUMB MUTT! WHAT ARE YOU WAITING FOR?! EAT THE BRAT!!
GRAAAAAAAR!!
HARU!!
LOOK OUT!!

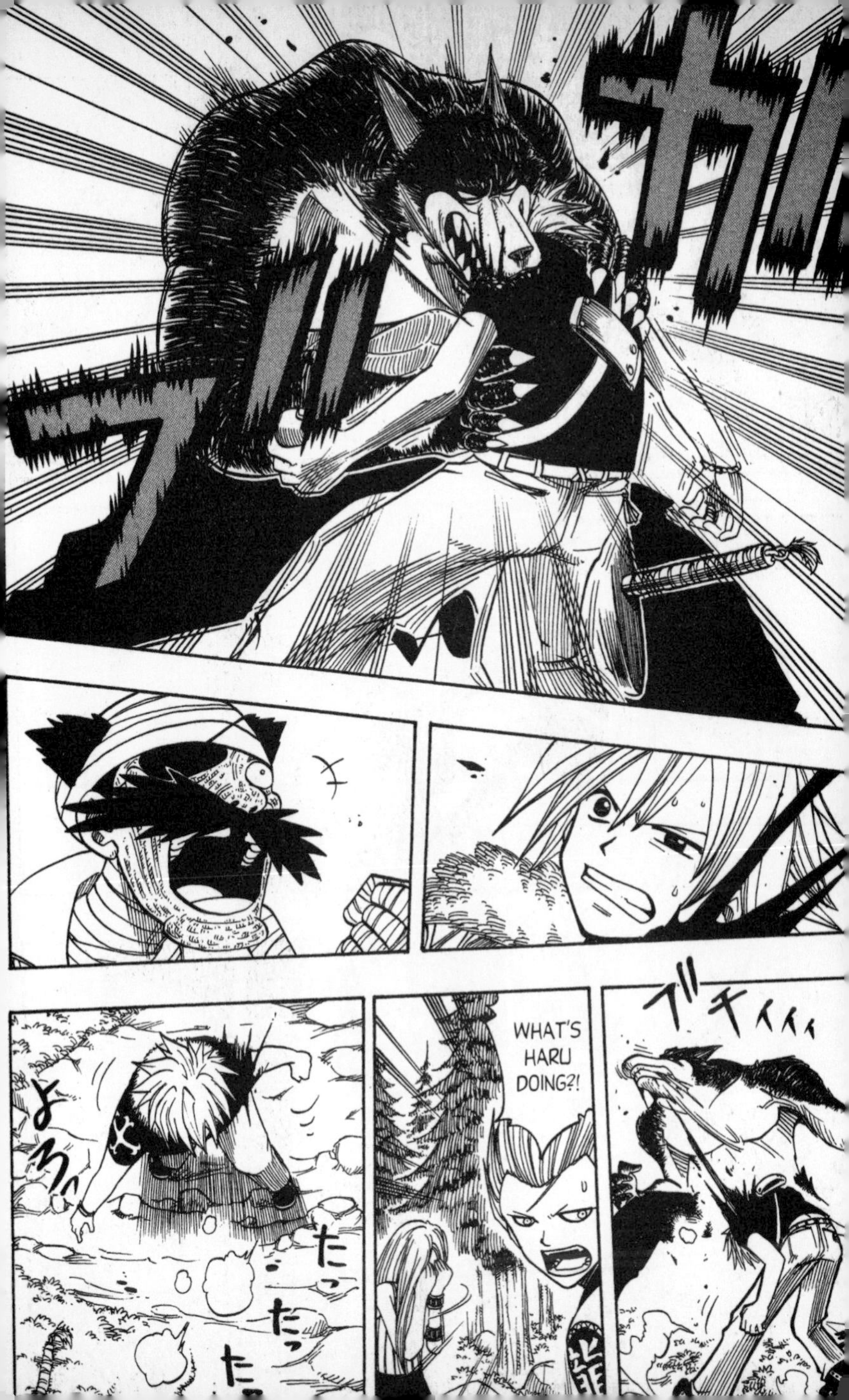
WHAT'S HARU DOING?!

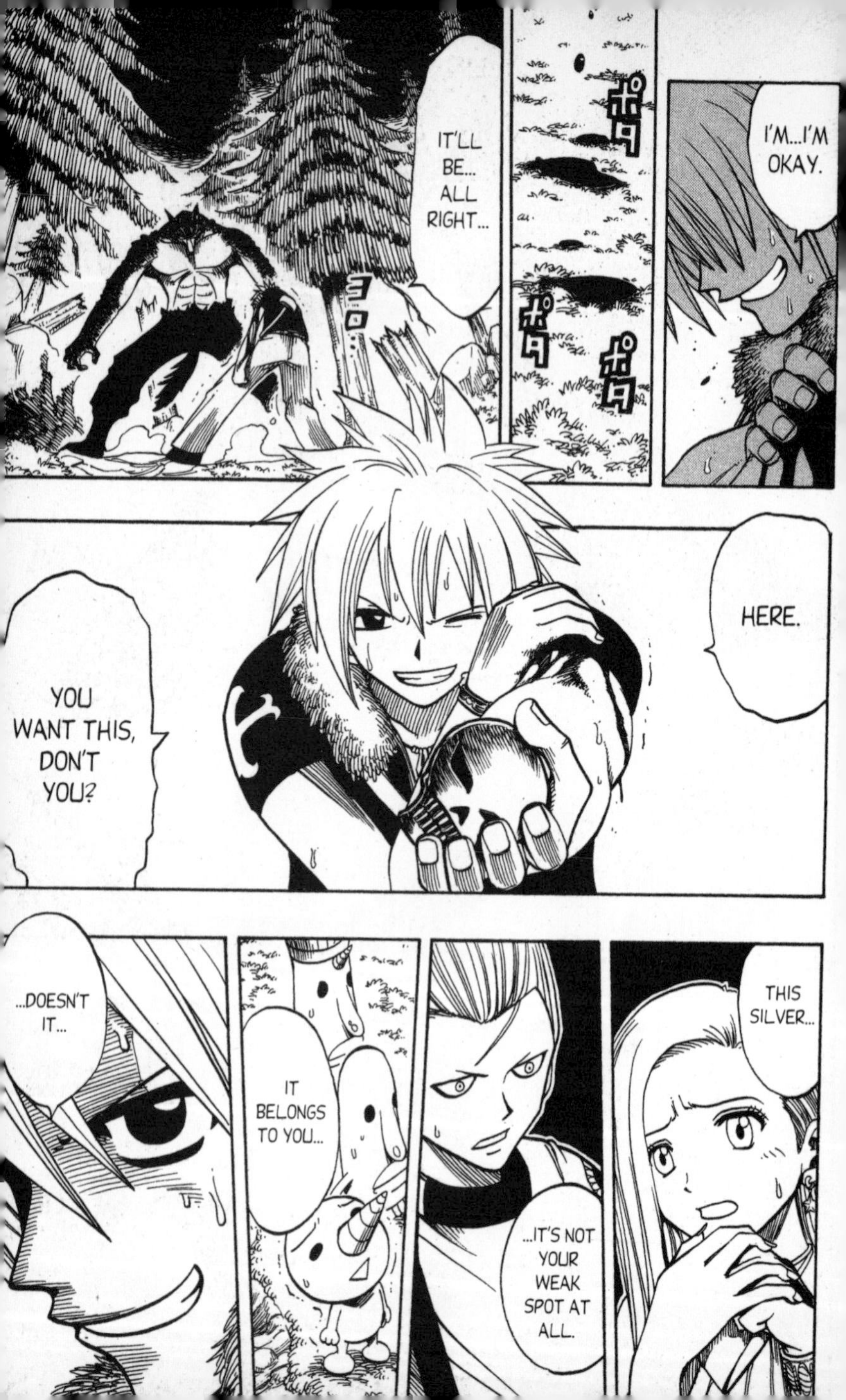
I'M...I'M OKAY.
ポタ
ポタ
ポタ
IT'LL BE... ALL RIGHT...
ヨロ...
HERE.
YOU WANT THIS, DON'T YOU?
THIS SILVER...
...IT'S NOT YOUR WEAK SPOT AT ALL.
IT BELONGS TO YOU...
...DOESN'T IT...

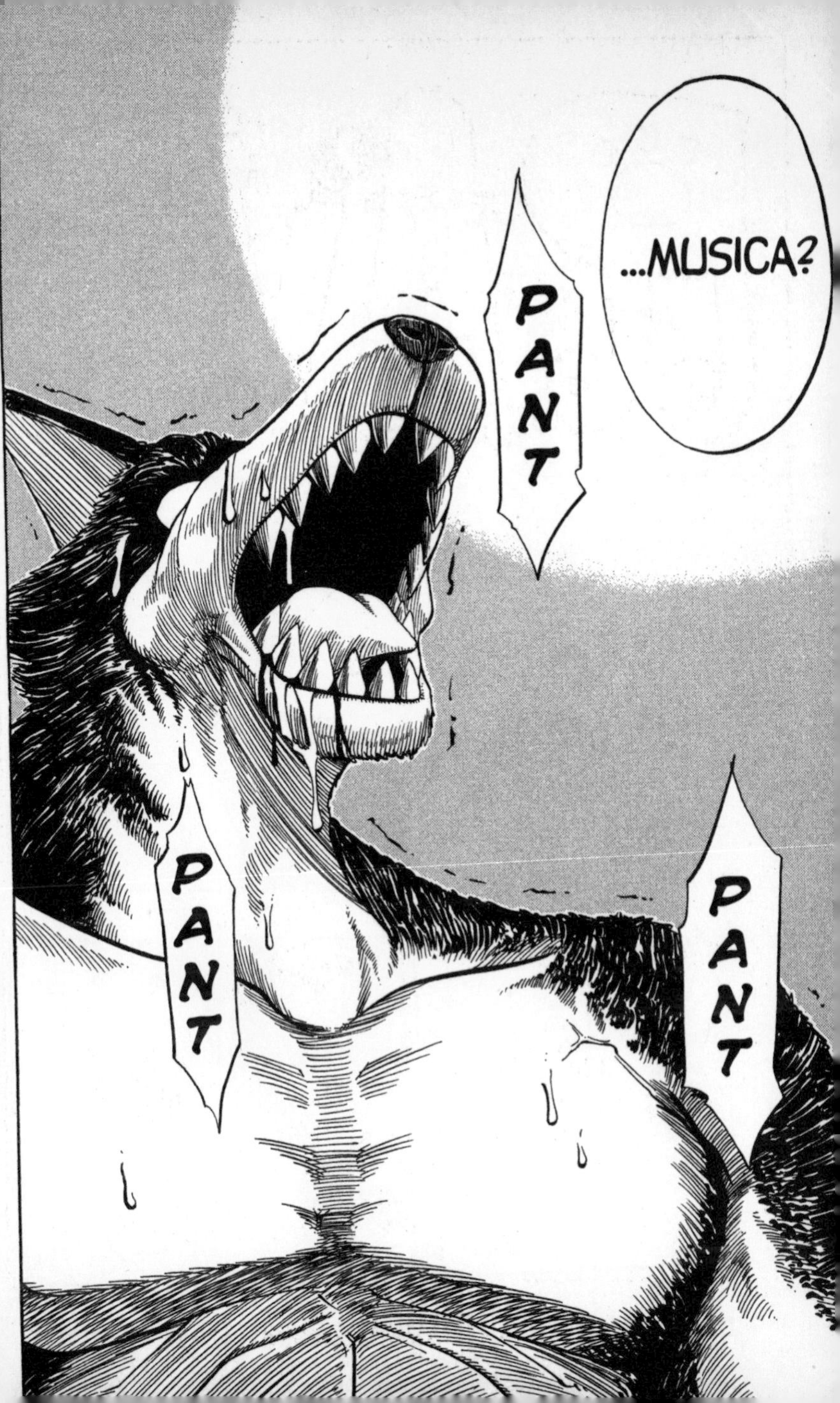
...MUSICA?
PANT
PANT
PANT

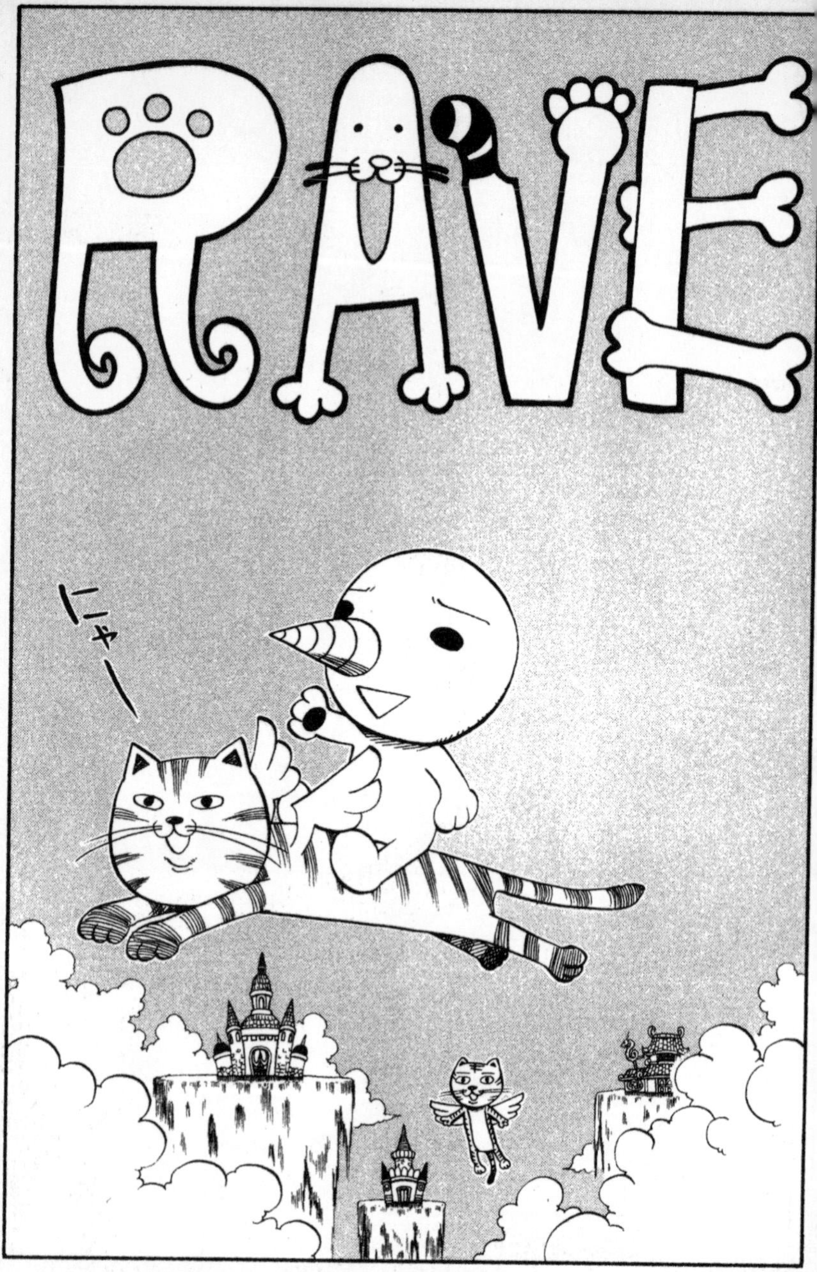
RAVE
にゃー

RAVE:117 BECAUSE WE'RE A TEAM!

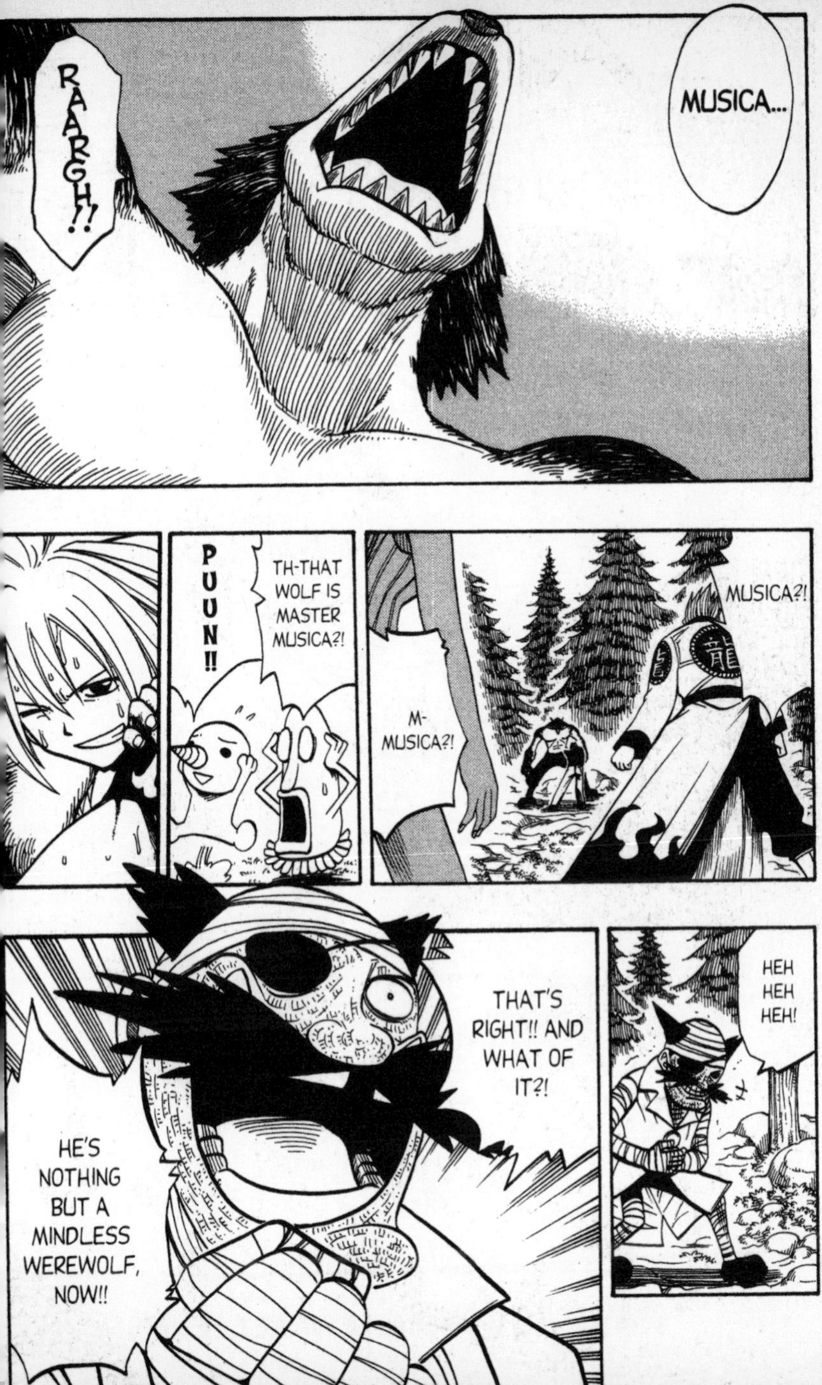
MUSICA...
RAARGH!!
MUSICA?!
M- MUSICA?!
TH-THAT WOLF IS MASTER MUSICA?!
PUUN!!
HEH HEH HEH!
THAT'S RIGHT!! AND WHAT OF IT?!
HE'S NOTHING BUT A MINDLESS WEREWOLF, NOW!!

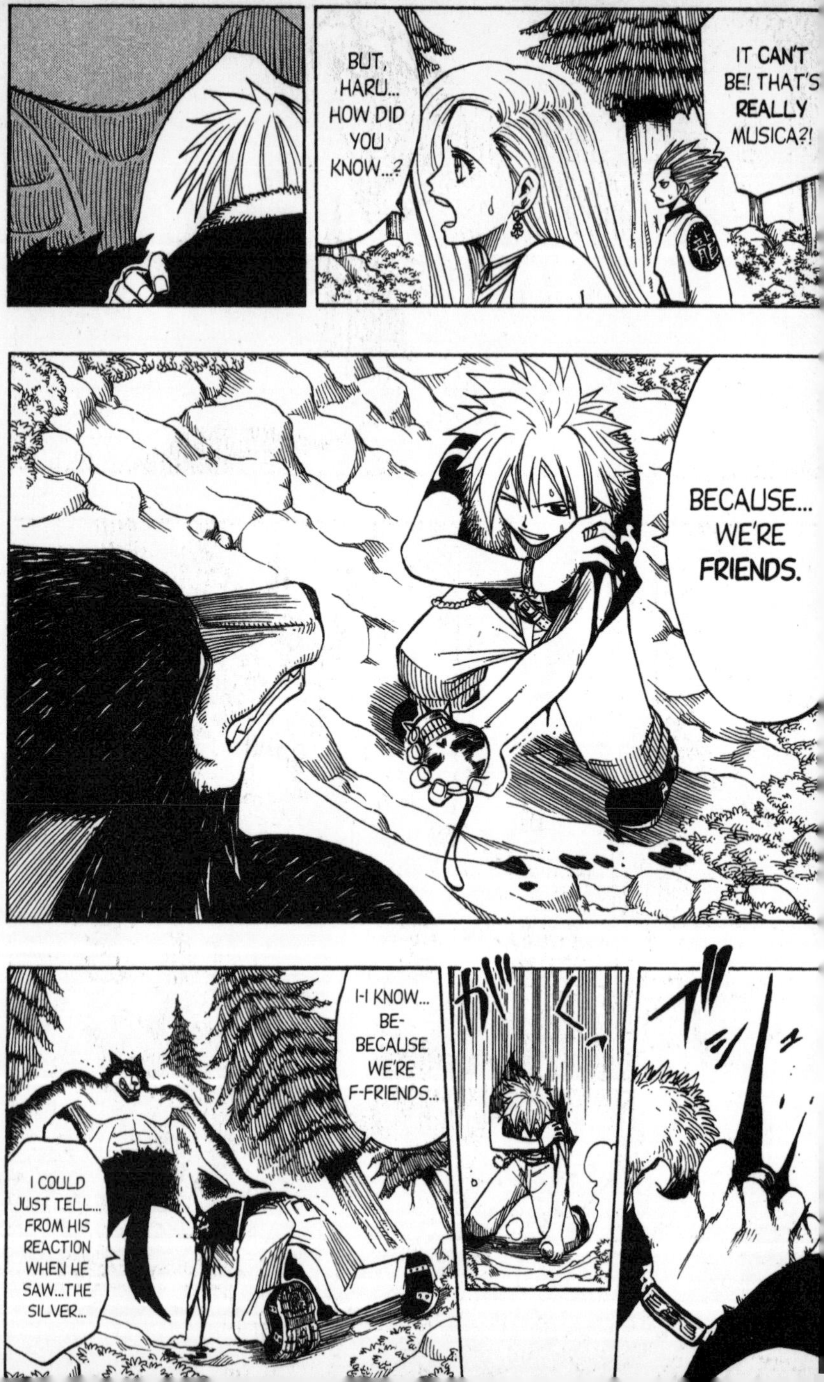
IT CAN'T BE! THAT'S REALLY MUSICA?!
BUT, HARU... HOW DID YOU KNOW...?
BECAUSE... WE'RE FRIENDS.
がくっ
I-I KNOW... BE-BECAUSE WE'RE F-FRIENDS...
I COULD JUST TELL... FROM HIS REACTION WHEN HE SAW...THE SILVER...

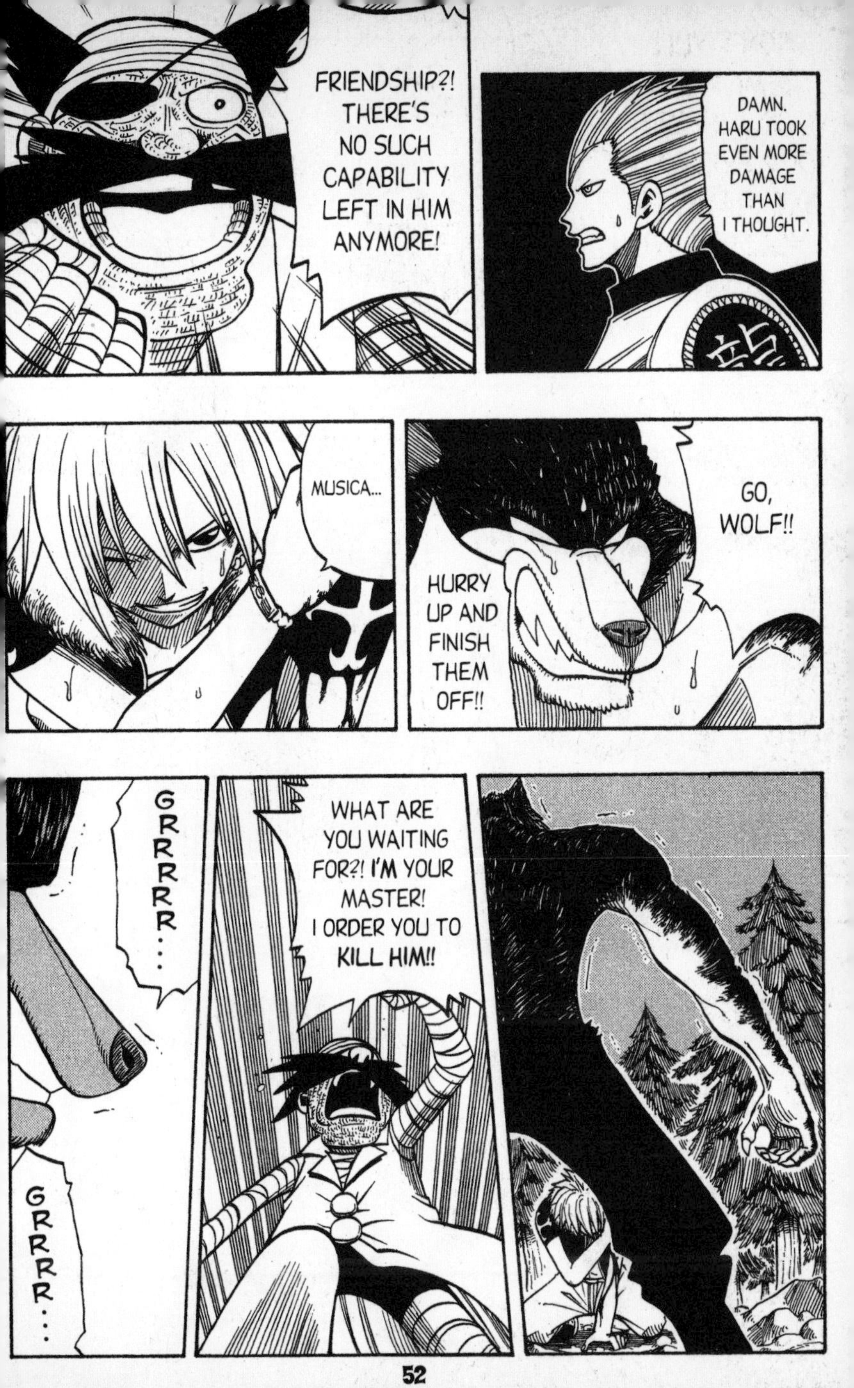
DAMN. HARU TOOK EVEN MORE DAMAGE THAN I THOUGHT.
FRIENDSHIP?! THERE'S NO SUCH CAPABILITY LEFT IN HIM ANYMORE!
GO, WOLF!!
HURRY UP AND FINISH THEM OFF!!
MUSICA...
WHAT ARE YOU WAITING FOR?! I'M YOUR MASTER! I ORDER YOU TO KILL HIM!!
GRRRRR...
GRRRR...

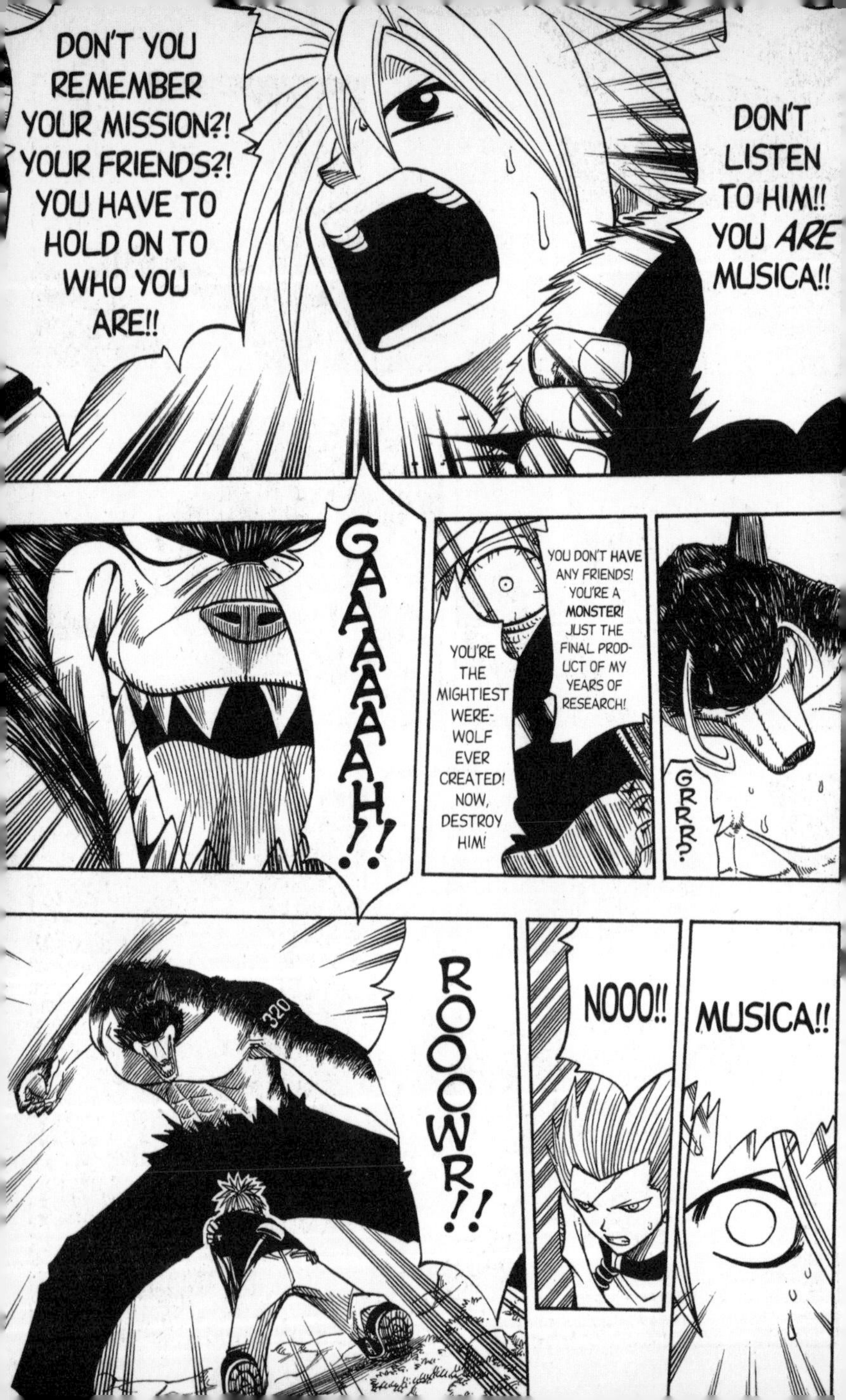
DON'T LISTEN TO HIM!! YOU ARE MUSICA!!
DON'T YOU REMEMBER YOUR MISSION?! YOUR FRIENDS?! YOU HAVE TO HOLD ON TO WHO YOU ARE!!
GRRR?
YOU DON'T HAVE ANY FRIENDS! YOU'RE A MONSTER! JUST THE FINAL PRODUCT OF MY YEARS OF RESEARCH!
YOU'RE THE MIGHTIEST WEREWOLF EVER CREATED! NOW, DESTROY HIM!
GAAAAAH!!
MUSICA!!
NOOO!!
ROOOOWR!!
320

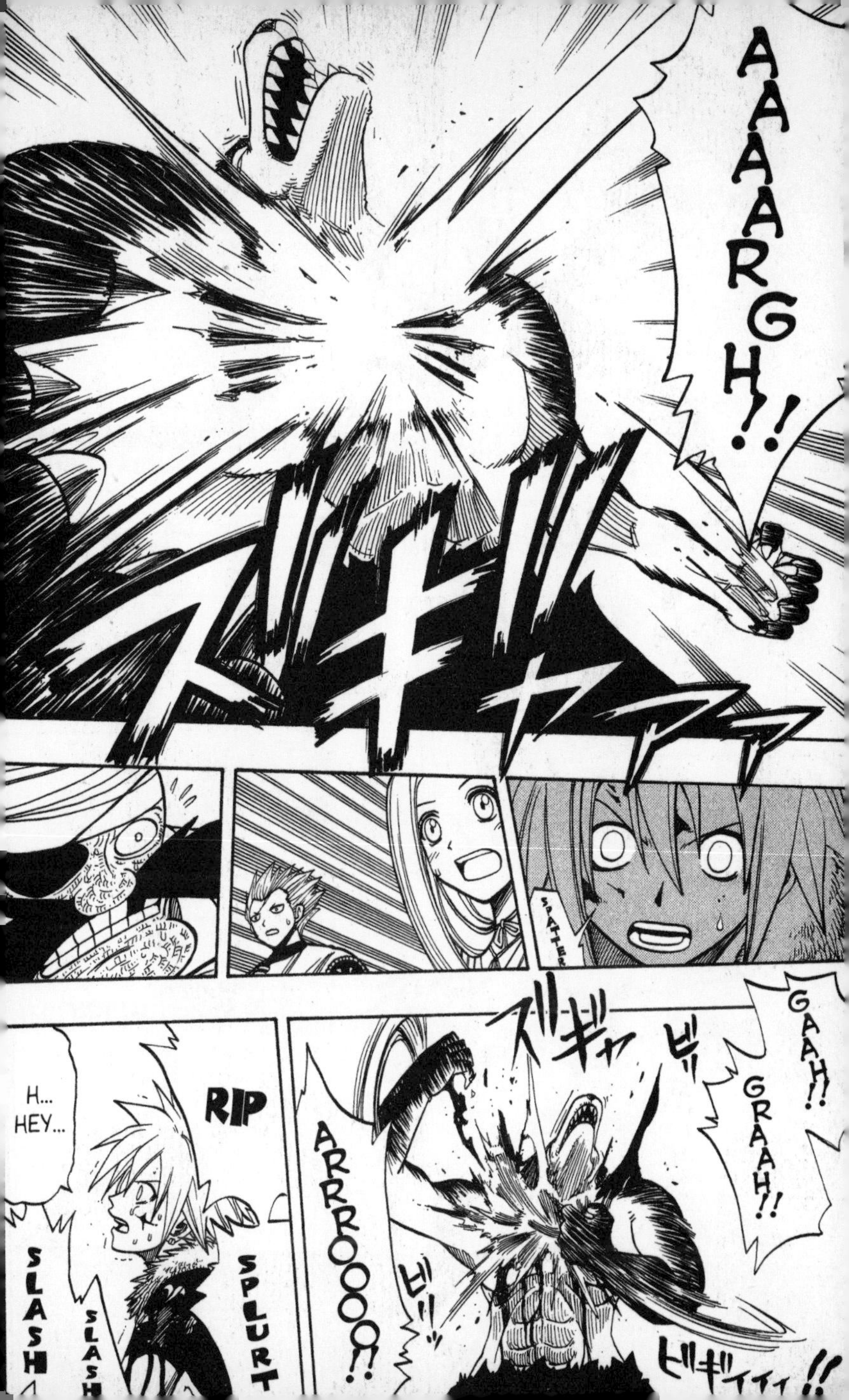

AAAARGH!!
SPATTER
GAAH!!
GRAAH!!
ARRROOOO!!
RIP
SPLURT
SLASH
SLASH
H... HEY...

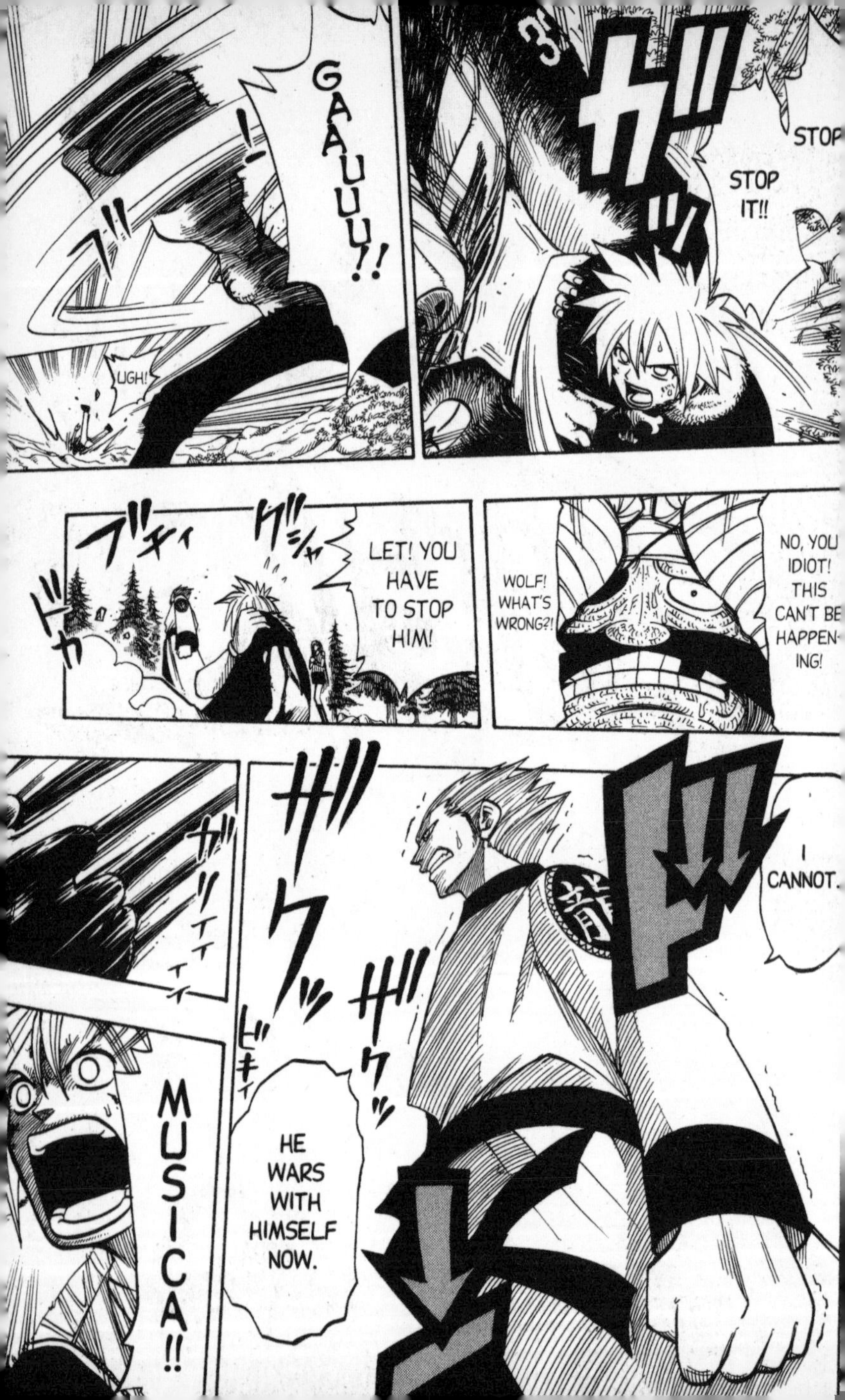
STOP
STOP IT!!
GAAUUU?!!
UGH!
NO, YOU IDIOT! THIS CAN'T BE HAPPENING!
WOLF! WHAT'S WRONG?!
LET! YOU HAVE TO STOP HIM!
I CANNOT.
HE WARS WITH HIMSELF NOW.
MUSICA!!

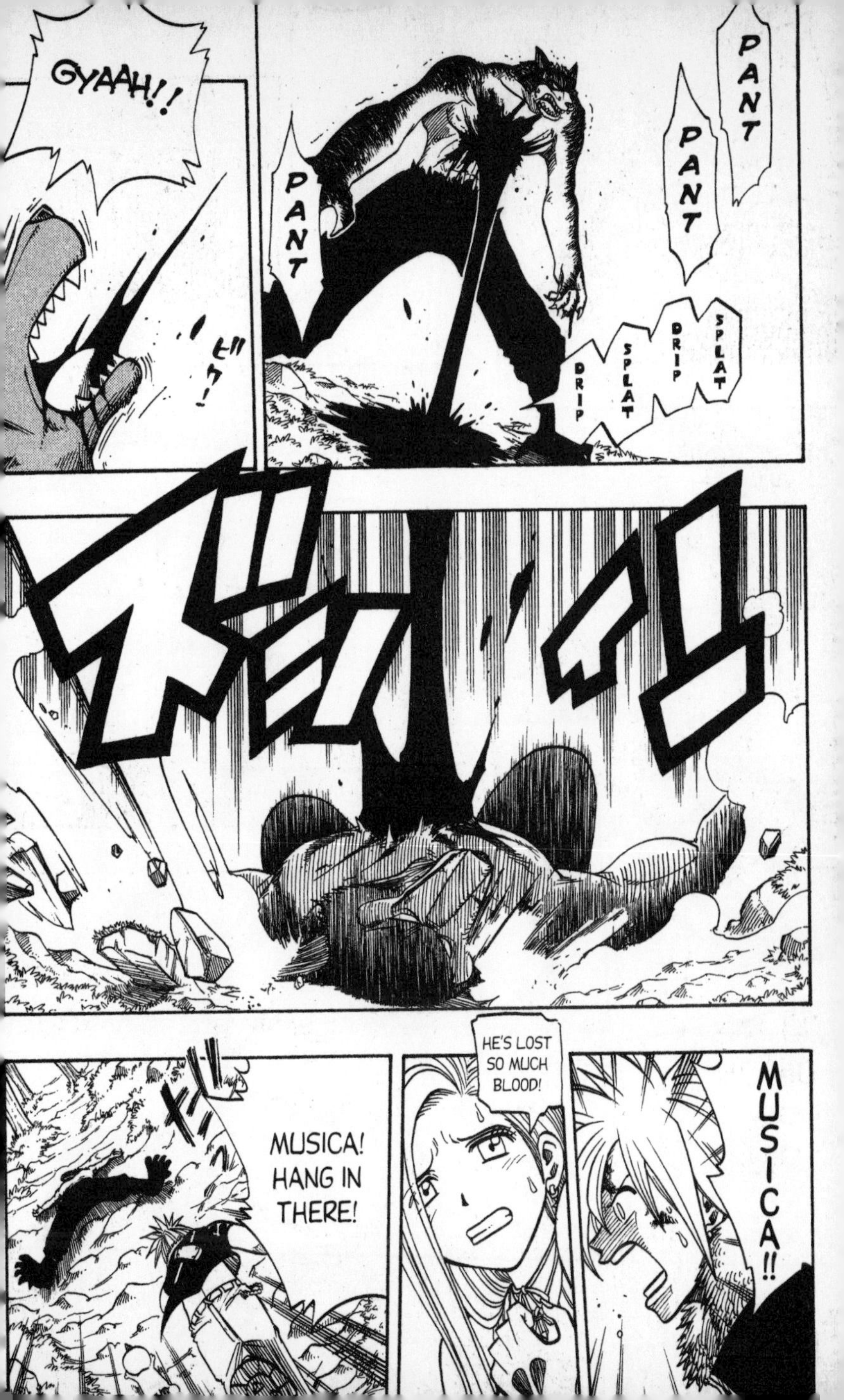
PANT
PANT
PANT PANT
DRIP SPLAT DRIP SPLAT
GYAAH!!
ビク!
MUSICA!!
HE'S LOST SO MUCH BLOOD!
MUSICA! HANG IN THERE!

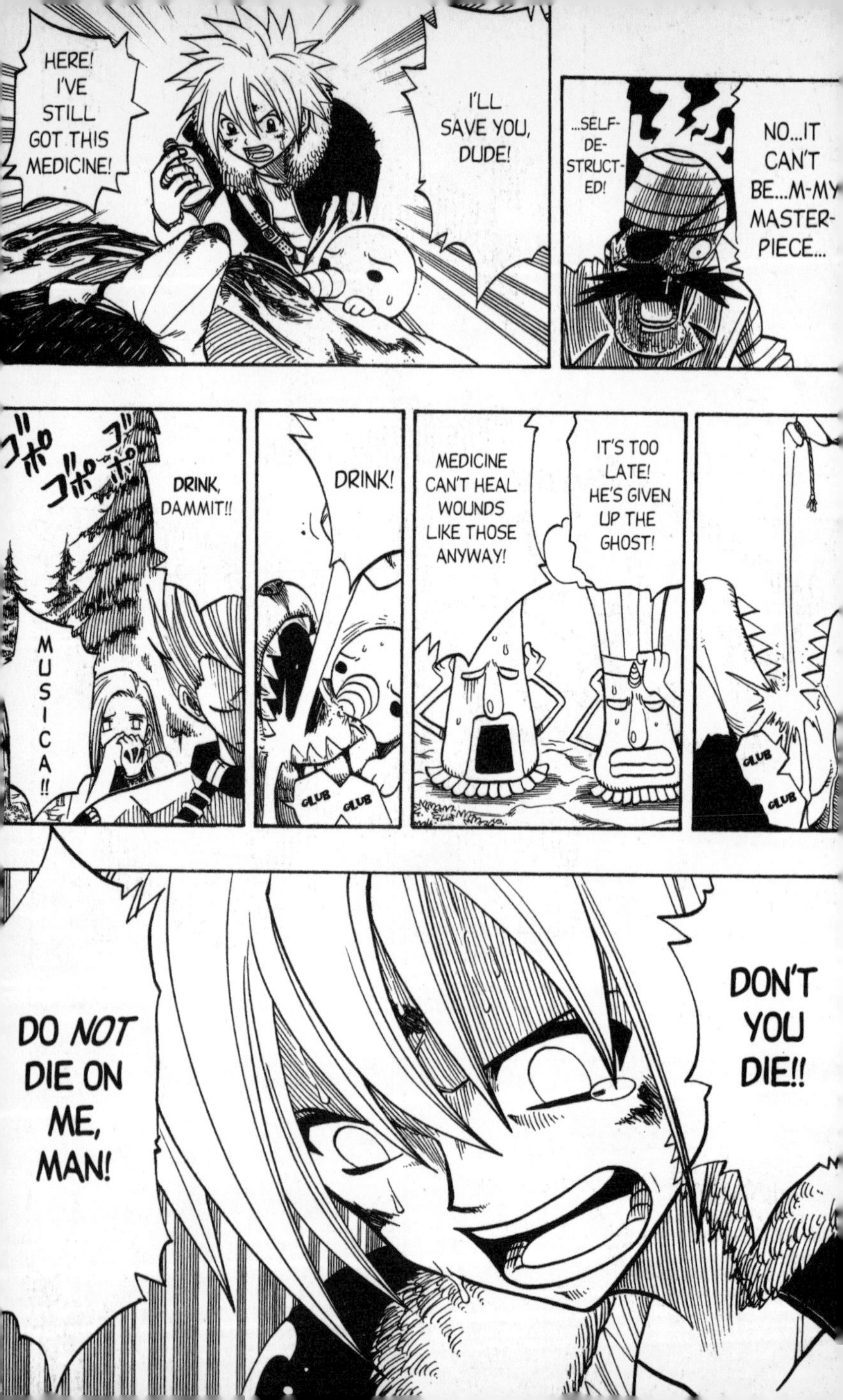
NO...IT CAN'T BE...M-MY MASTER-PIECE...
...SELF-DE-STRUCT-ED!
I'LL SAVE YOU, DUDE!
HERE! I'VE STILL GOT THIS MEDICINE!
GLUB
GLUB
IT'S TOO LATE! HE'S GIVEN UP THE GHOST!
MEDICINE CAN'T HEAL WOUNDS LIKE THOSE ANYWAY!
DRINK!
GLUB
GLUB
DRINK, DAMMIT!!
ゴポ ゴポ ゴポ
MUSICA!!
DON'T YOU DIE!!
DO *NOT* DIE ON ME, MAN!

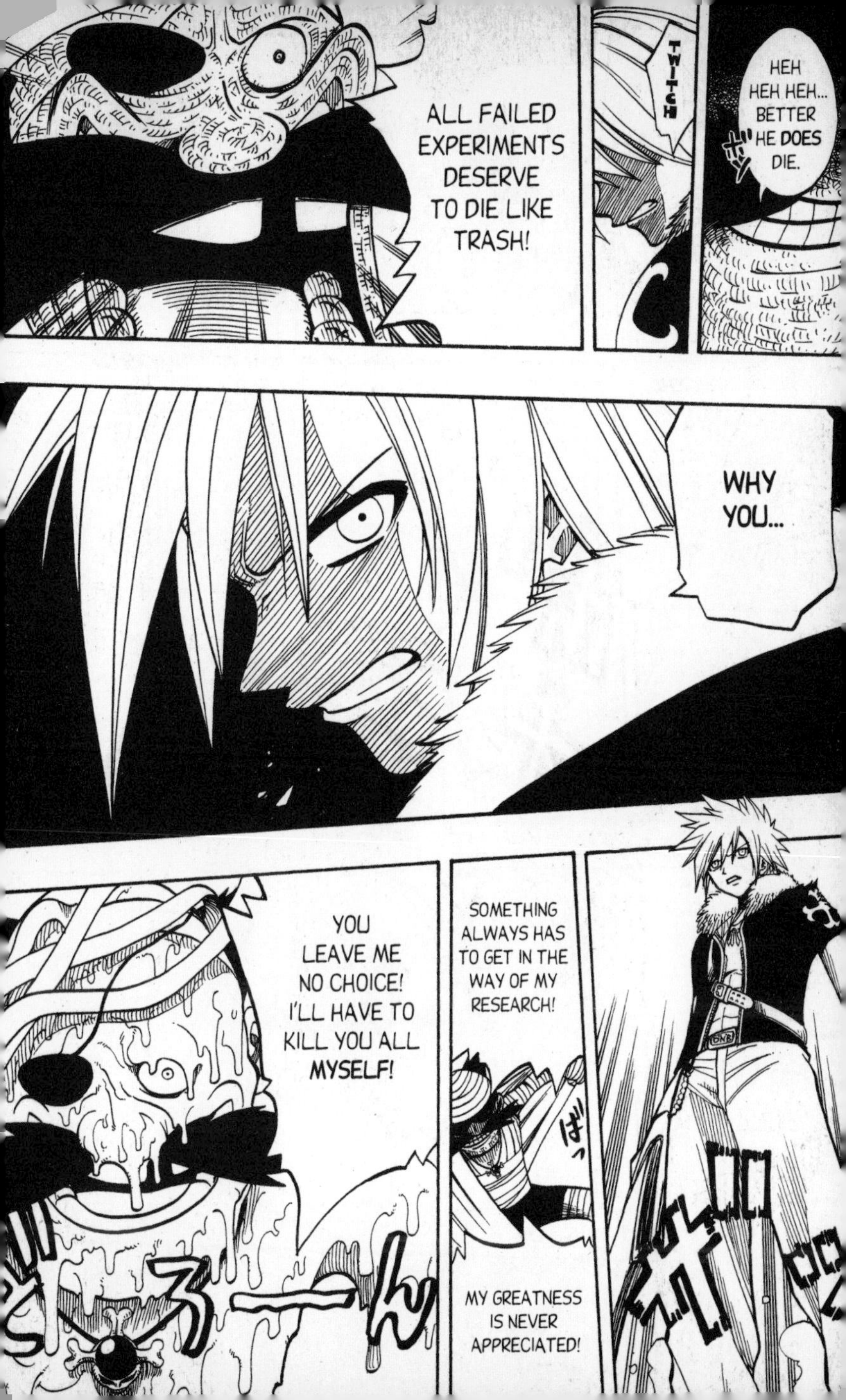
HEH HEH HEH... BETTER HE DOES DIE.
TWITCH
ALL FAILED EXPERIMENTS DESERVE TO DIE LIKE TRASH!
WHY YOU...
SOMETHING ALWAYS HAS TO GET IN THE WAY OF MY RESEARCH!
ばっ
MY GREATNESS IS NEVER APPRECIATED!
YOU LEAVE ME NO CHOICE! I'LL HAVE TO KILL YOU ALL MYSELF!

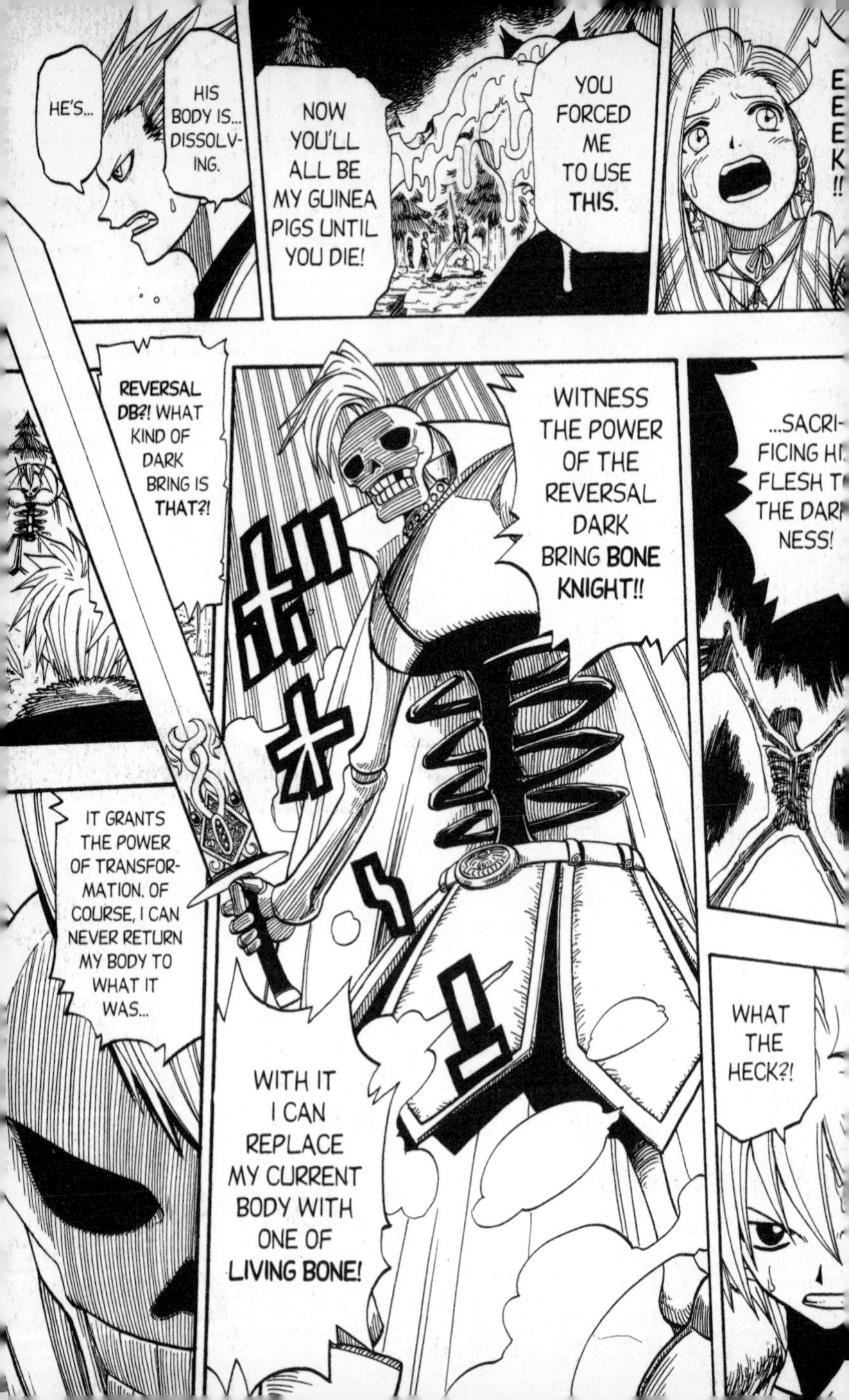
EEEEK!!
YOU FORCED ME TO USE THIS.
NOW YOU'LL ALL BE MY GUINEA PIGS UNTIL YOU DIE!
HIS BODY IS... DISSOLVING.
HE'S...
...SACRIFICING HI FLESH T THE DAR NESS!
WHAT THE HECK?!
WITNESS THE POWER OF THE REVERSAL DARK BRING BONE KNIGHT!!
WITH IT I CAN REPLACE MY CURRENT BODY WITH ONE OF LIVING BONE!
REVERSAL DB?! WHAT KIND OF DARK BRING IS THAT?!
IT GRANTS THE POWER OF TRANSFORMATION. OF COURSE, I CAN NEVER RETURN MY BODY TO WHAT IT WAS...

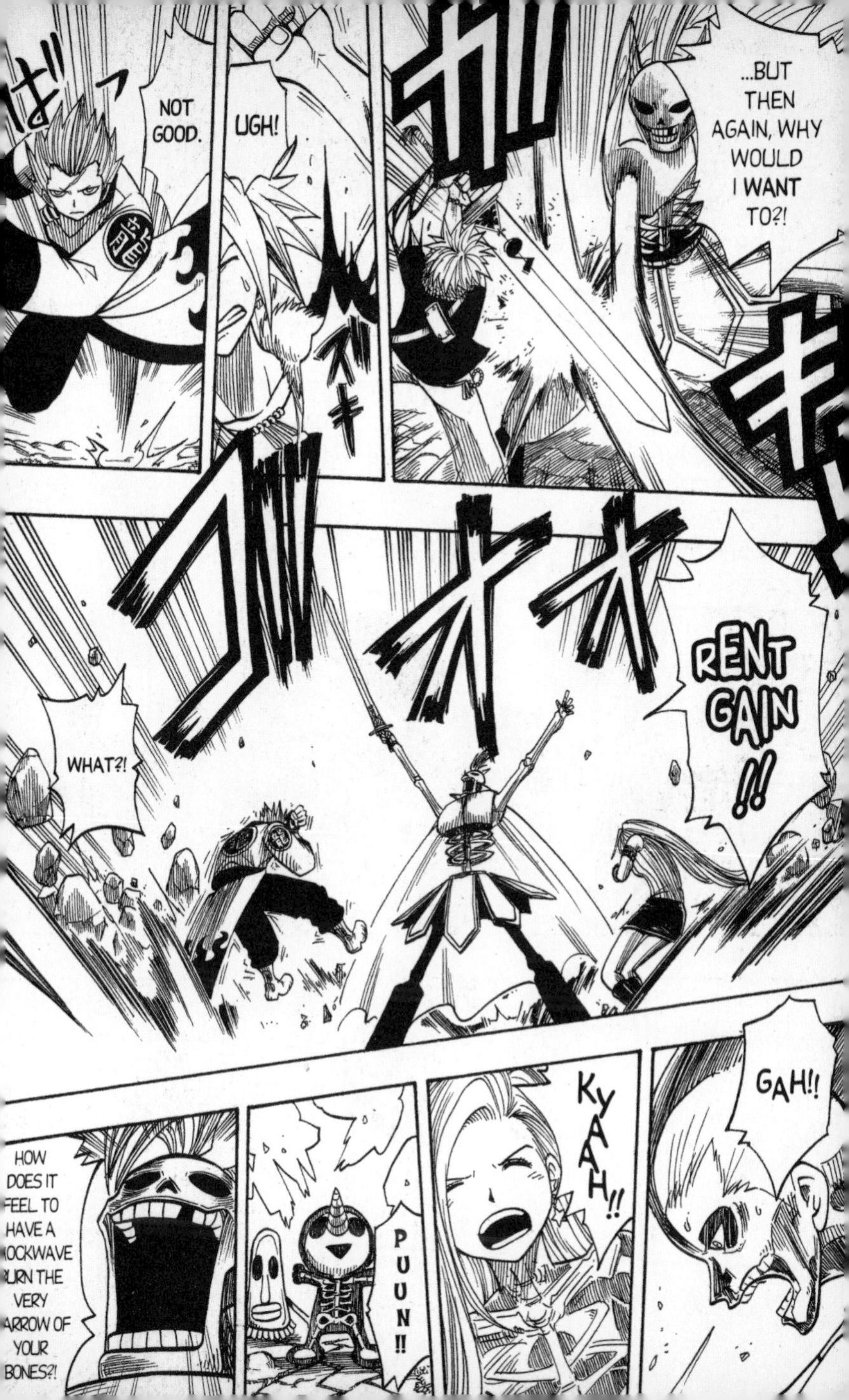
...BUT THEN AGAIN, WHY WOULD I WANT TO?!
UGH!
NOT GOOD.
RENT GAIN!!
WHAT?!
GAH!!
KYAAH!!
PUUN!!
HOW DOES IT FEEL TO HAVE A OCKWAVE URN THE VERY ARROW OF YOUR BONES?!

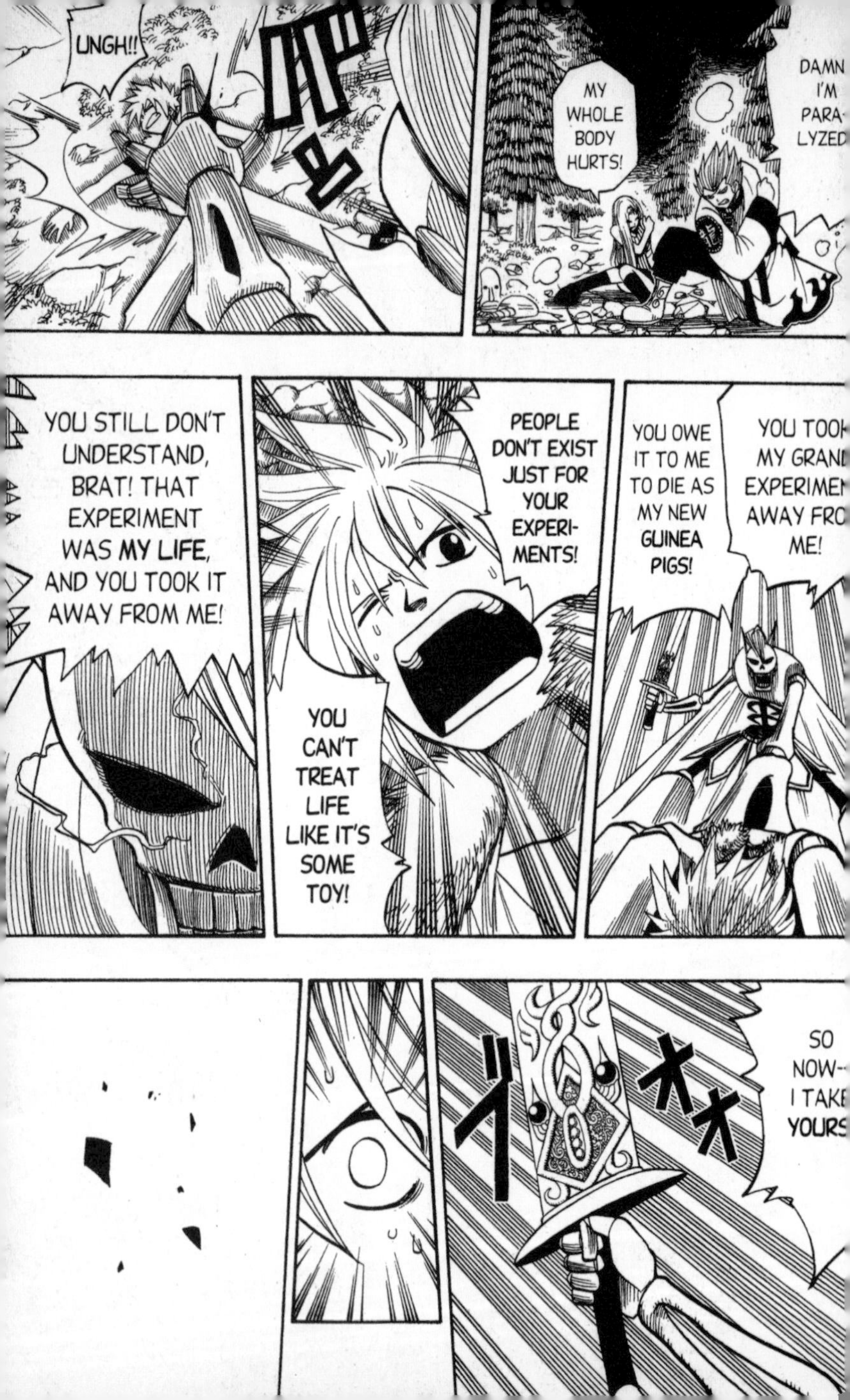
DAMN I'M PARA-LYZED
MY WHOLE BODY HURTS!
UNGH!!
YOU TOO MY GRAN EXPERIMEN AWAY FRO ME!
YOU OWE IT TO ME TO DIE AS MY NEW GUINEA PIGS!
PEOPLE DON'T EXIST JUST FOR YOUR EXPERI-MENTS!
YOU CAN'T TREAT LIFE LIKE IT'S SOME TOY!
YOU STILL DON'T UNDERSTAND, BRAT! THAT EXPERIMENT WAS MY LIFE, AND YOU TOOK IT AWAY FROM ME!
SO NOW- I TAK YOURS

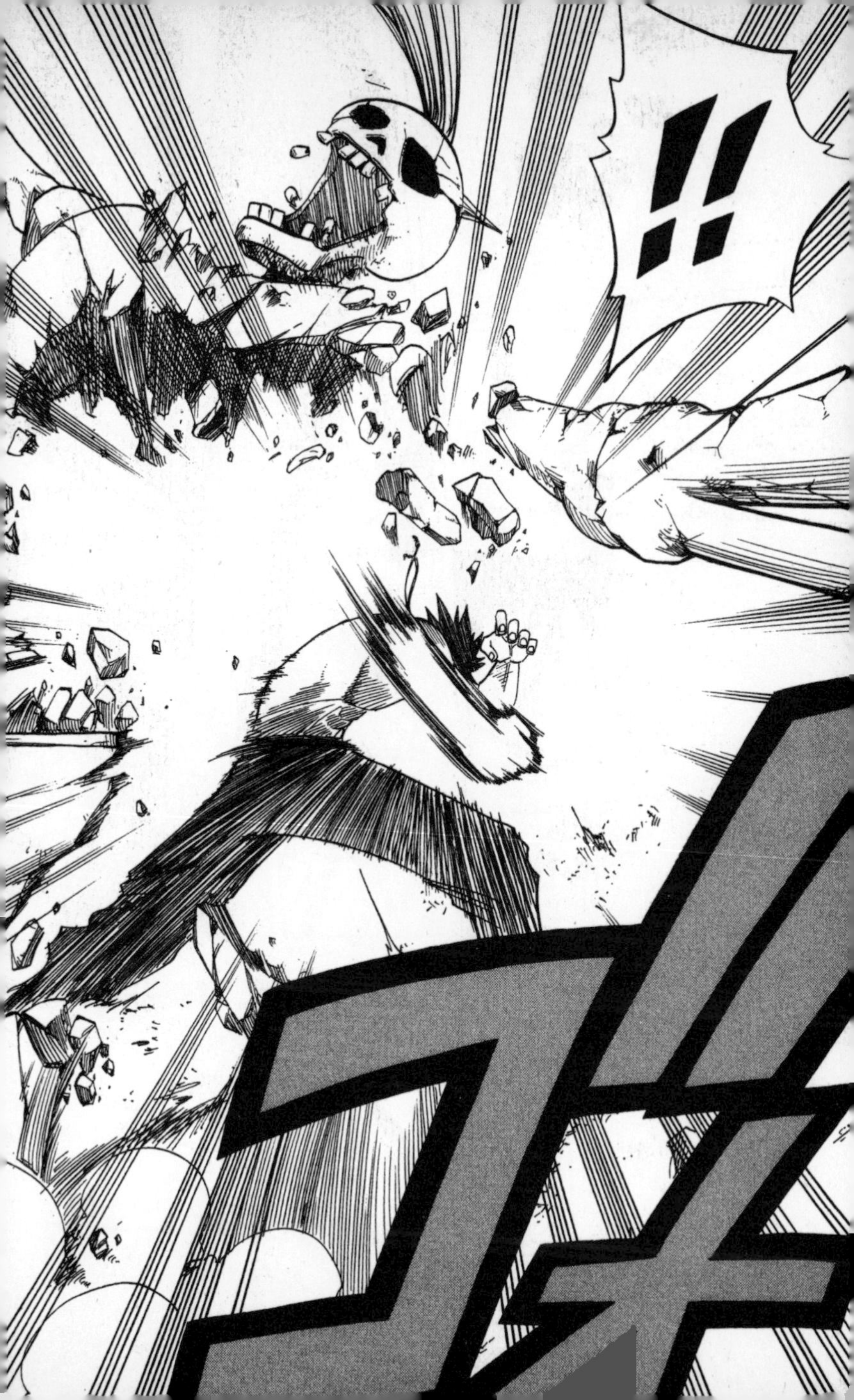
!!

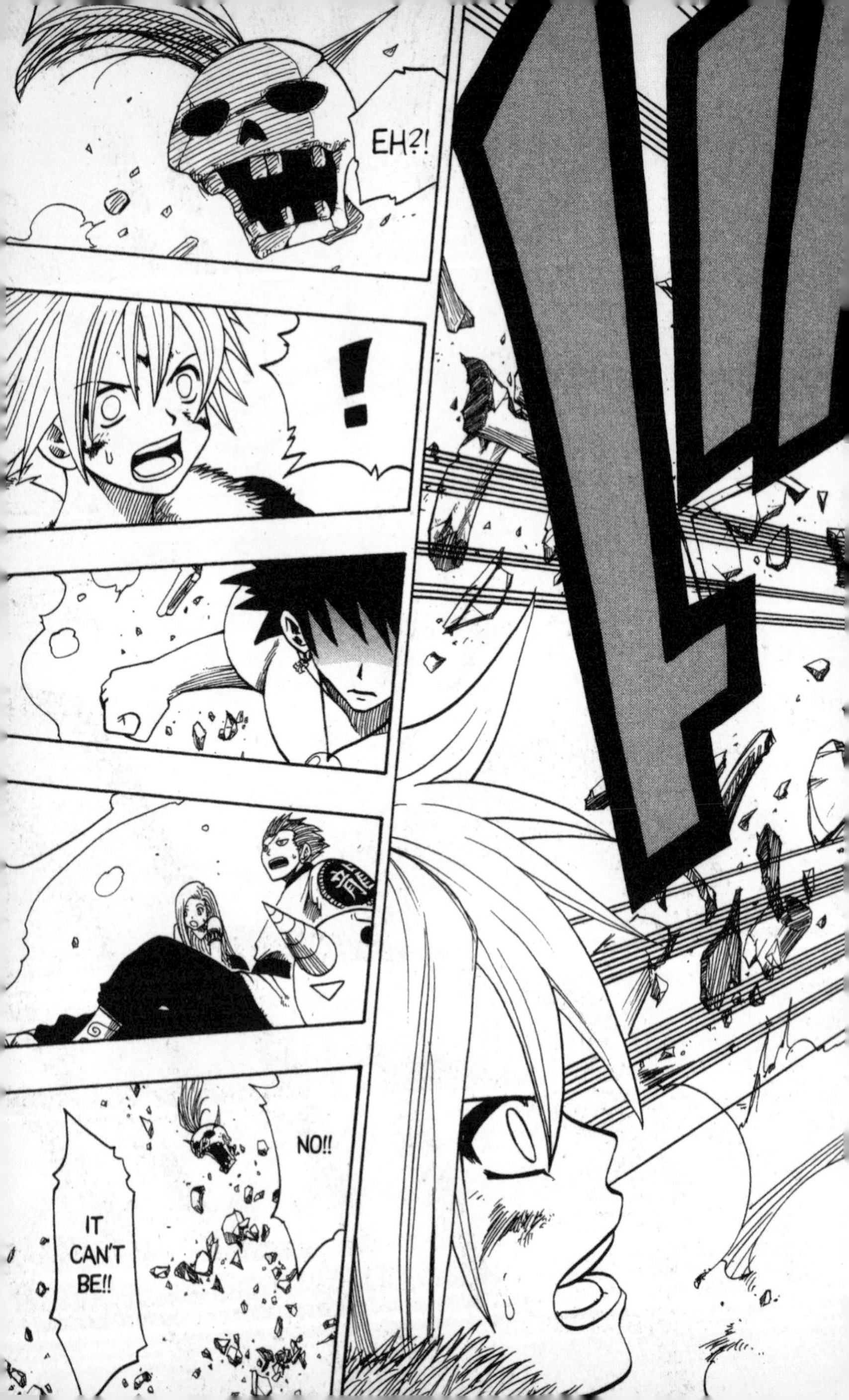
EH?!
!
NO!!
IT CAN'T BE!!

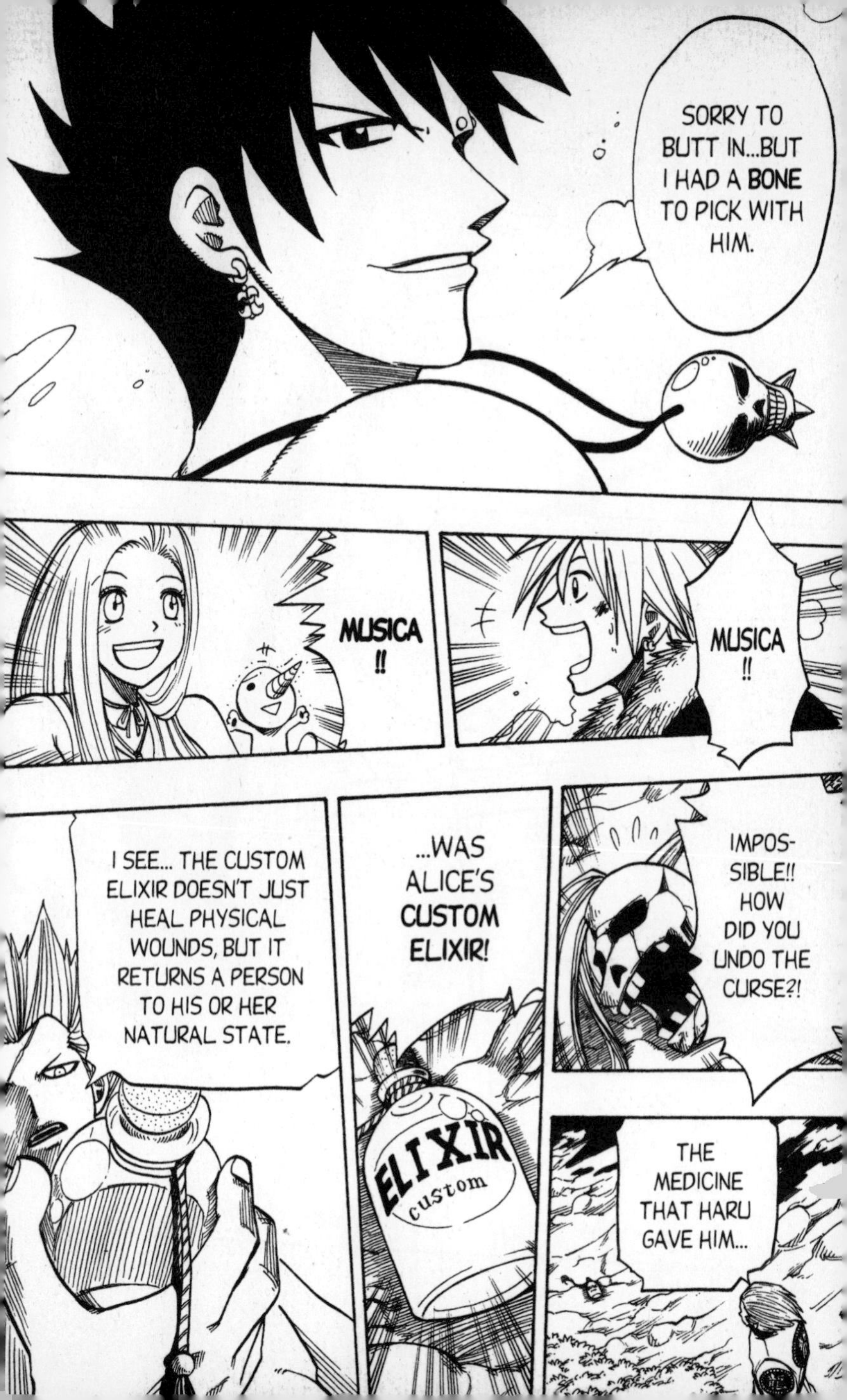
SORRY TO BUTT IN...BUT I HAD A BONE TO PICK WITH HIM.
MUSICA !!
MUSICA !!
IMPOS-SIBLE!! HOW DID YOU UNDO THE CURSE?!
THE MEDICINE THAT HARU GAVE HIM...
...WAS ALICE'S CUSTOM ELIXIR!
ELIXIR custom
I SEE... THE CUSTOM ELIXIR DOESN'T JUST HEAL PHYSICAL WOUNDS, BUT IT RETURNS A PERSON TO HIS OR HER NATURAL STATE.

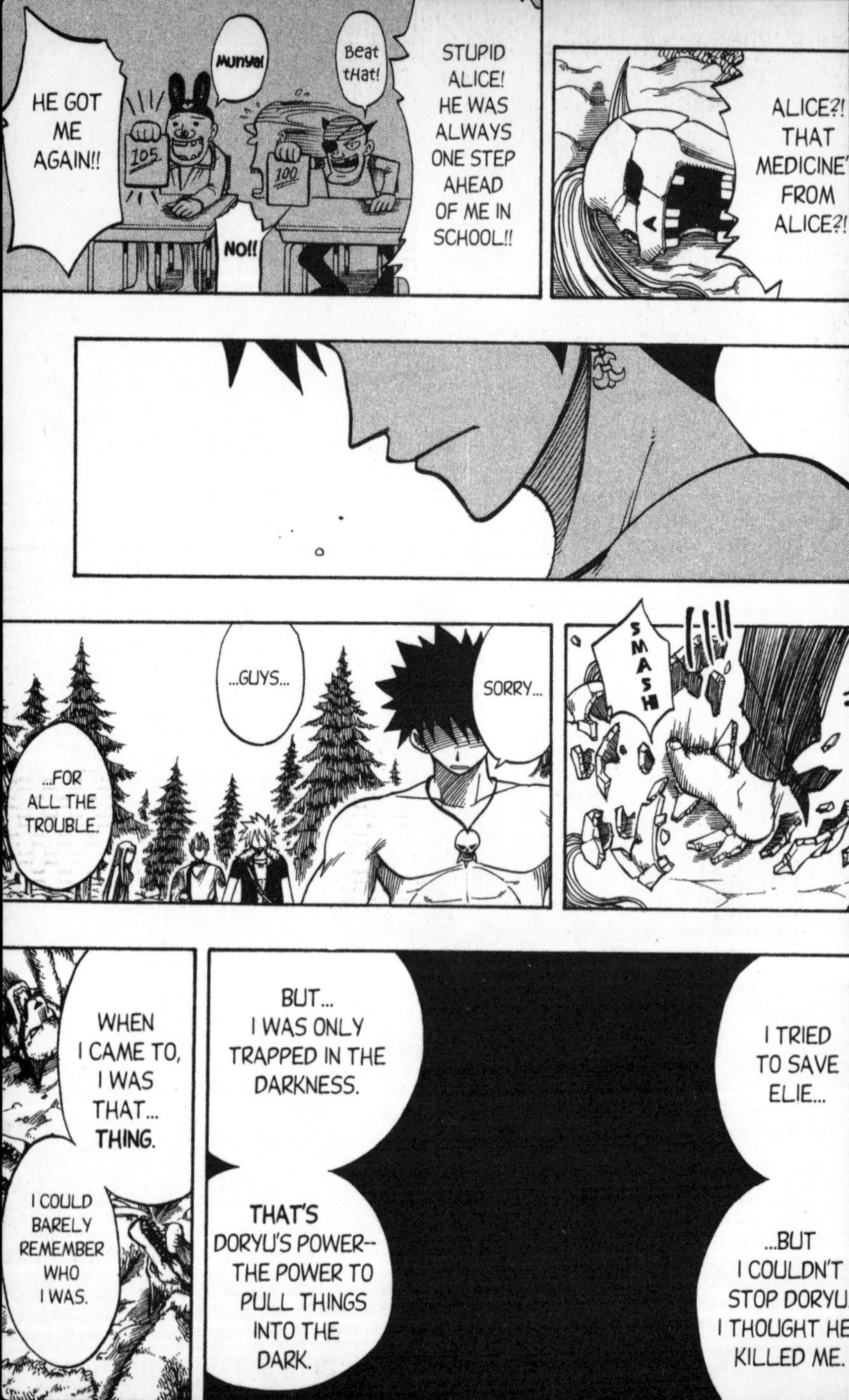
ALICE?! THAT MEDICINE FROM ALICE?!
STUPID ALICE! HE WAS ALWAYS ONE STEP AHEAD OF ME IN SCHOOL!!
Beat tHat!
Munya!
HE GOT ME AGAIN!!
NO!!
SMASH
SORRY...
...GUYS...
...FOR ALL THE TROUBLE.
I TRIED TO SAVE ELIE...
...BUT I COULDN'T STOP DORYU. I THOUGHT HE KILLED ME.
BUT... I WAS ONLY TRAPPED IN THE DARKNESS.
THAT'S DORYU'S POWER-- THE POWER TO PULL THINGS INTO THE DARK.
WHEN I CAME TO, I WAS THAT... THING.
I COULD BARELY REMEMBER WHO I WAS.

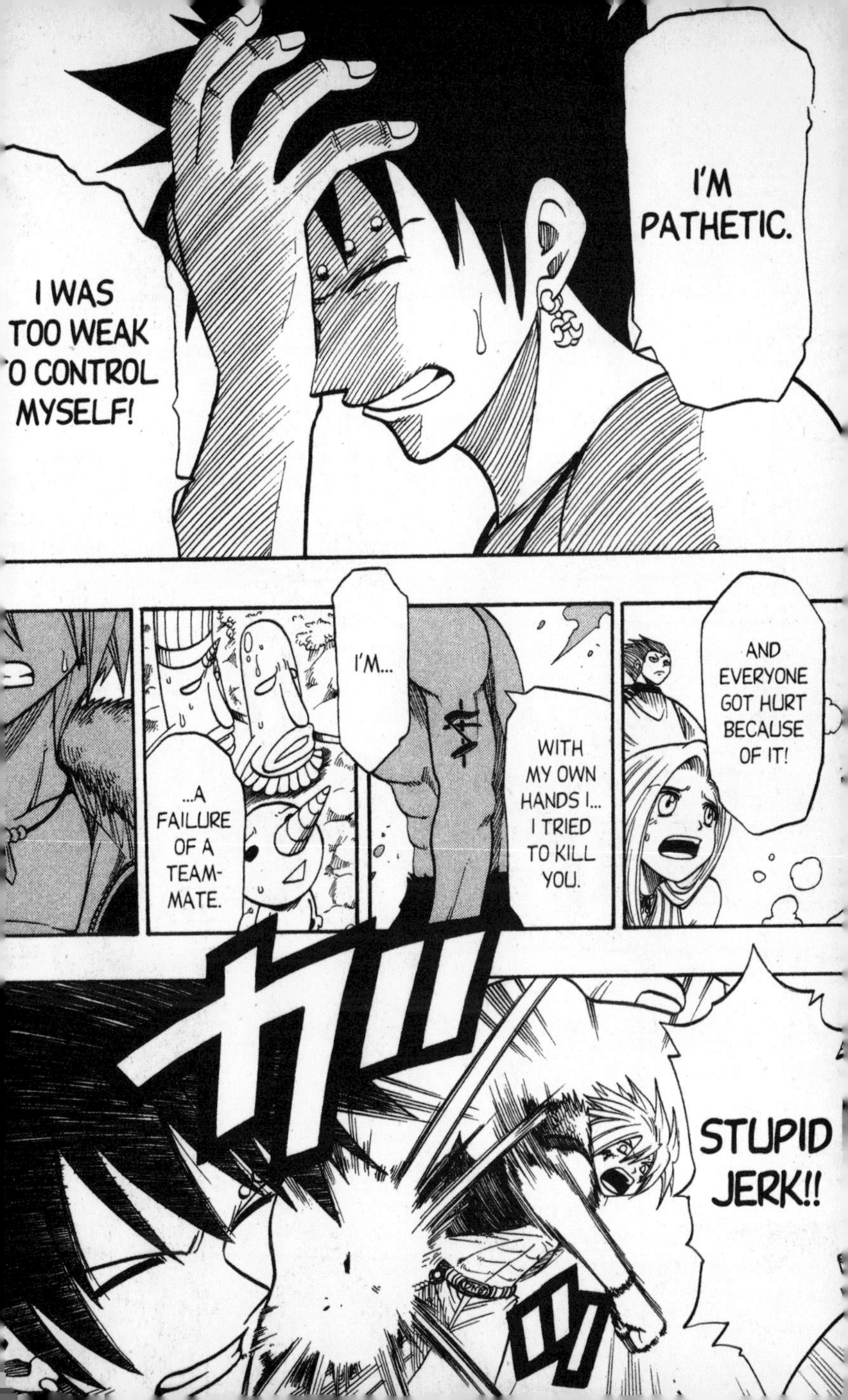
I'M PATHETIC.
I WAS TOO WEAK 'O CONTROL MYSELF!
AND EVERYONE GOT HURT BECAUSE OF IT!
WITH MY OWN HANDS I... I TRIED TO KILL YOU.
I'M...
...A FAILURE OF A TEAM-MATE.
カッ
STUPID JERK!!

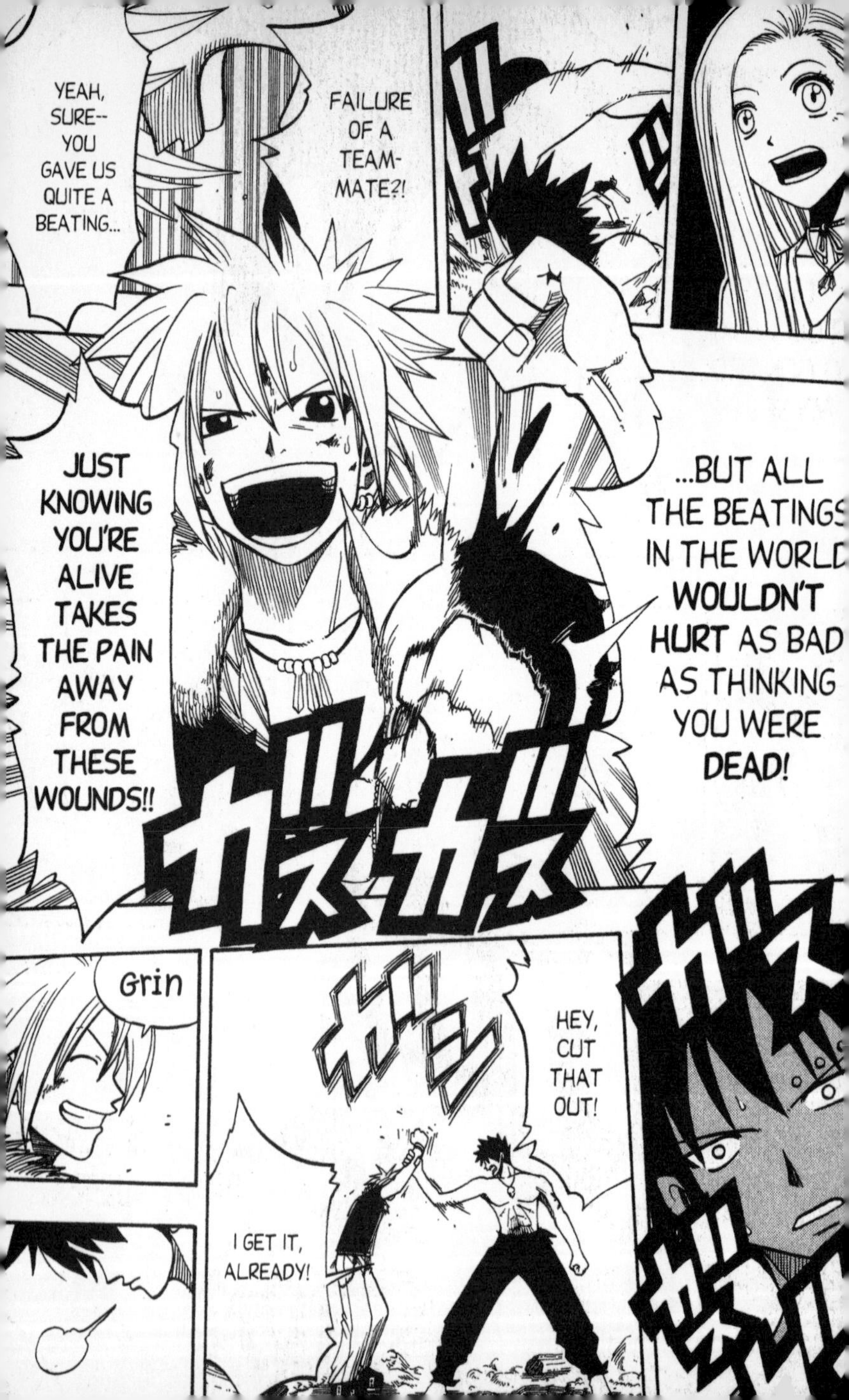
FAILURE OF A TEAM-MATE?!
YEAH, SURE-- YOU GAVE US QUITE A BEATING...
...BUT ALL THE BEATINGS IN THE WORLD WOULDN'T HURT AS BAD AS THINKING YOU WERE DEAD!
JUST KNOWING YOU'RE ALIVE TAKES THE PAIN AWAY FROM THESE WOUNDS!!
ガスガス
ガス
HEY, CUT THAT OUT!
ガシ
I GET IT, ALREADY!
Grin

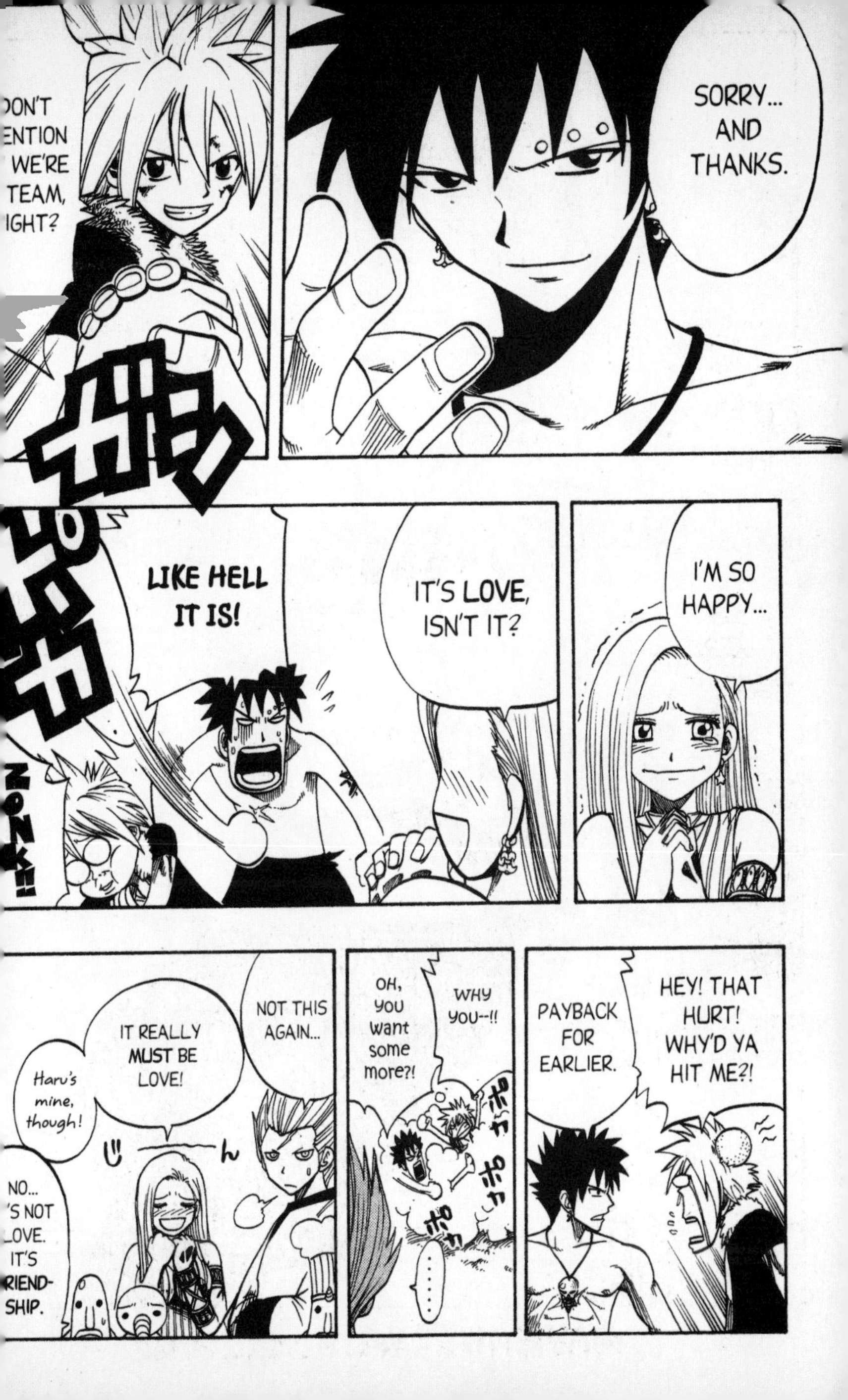
SORRY... AND THANKS.
DON'T ENTION WE'RE TEAM, IGHT?
I'M SO HAPPY...
IT'S LOVE, ISN'T IT?
LIKE HELL IT IS!
BONK!!
HEY! THAT HURT! WHY'D YA HIT ME?!
PAYBACK FOR EARLIER.
WHY YOU--!!
OH, you want some more?!
......
NOT THIS AGAIN...
IT REALLY MUST BE LOVE!
Haru's mine, though!
NO... 'S NOT LOVE. IT'S RIEND-SHIP.

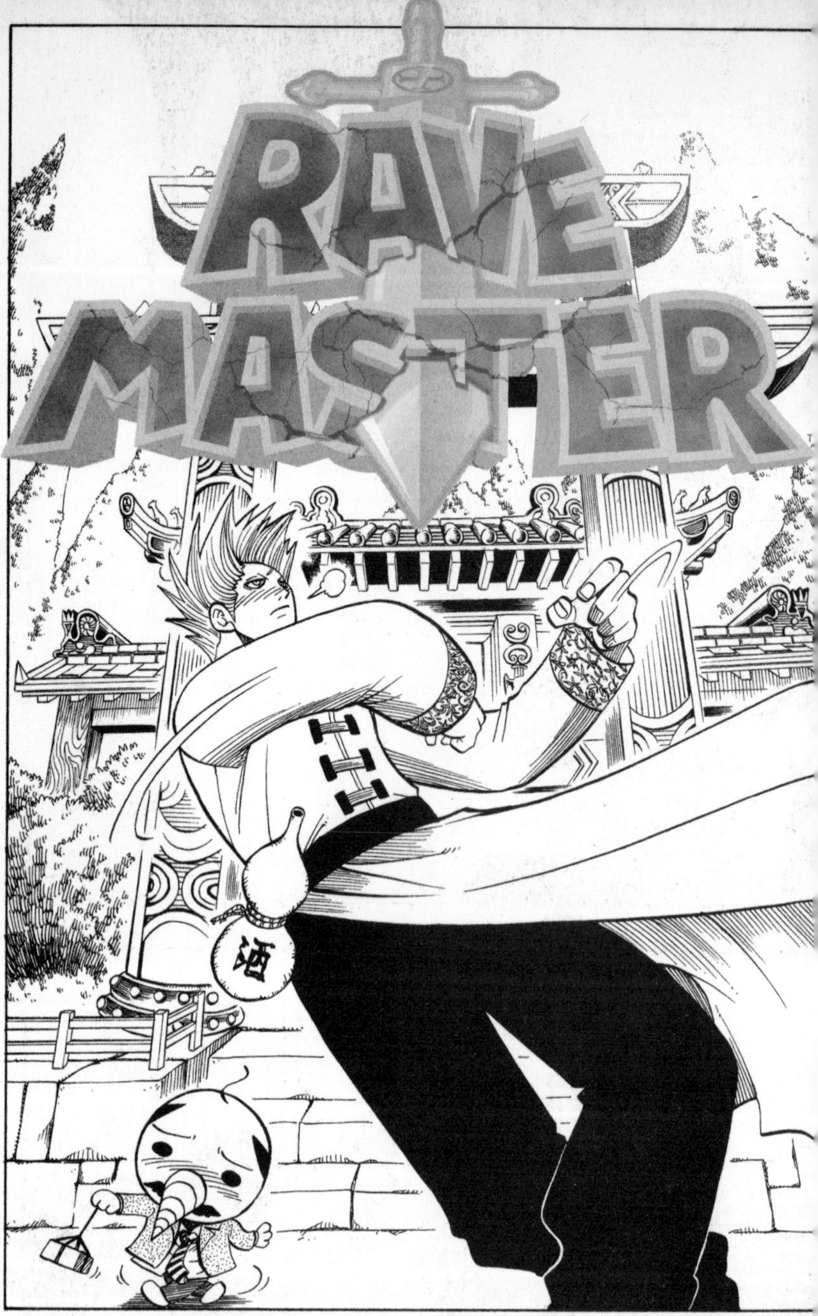
RAVE MASTER
酒

RAVE:118 ✠ THAT'S CRUEL, POYO!!

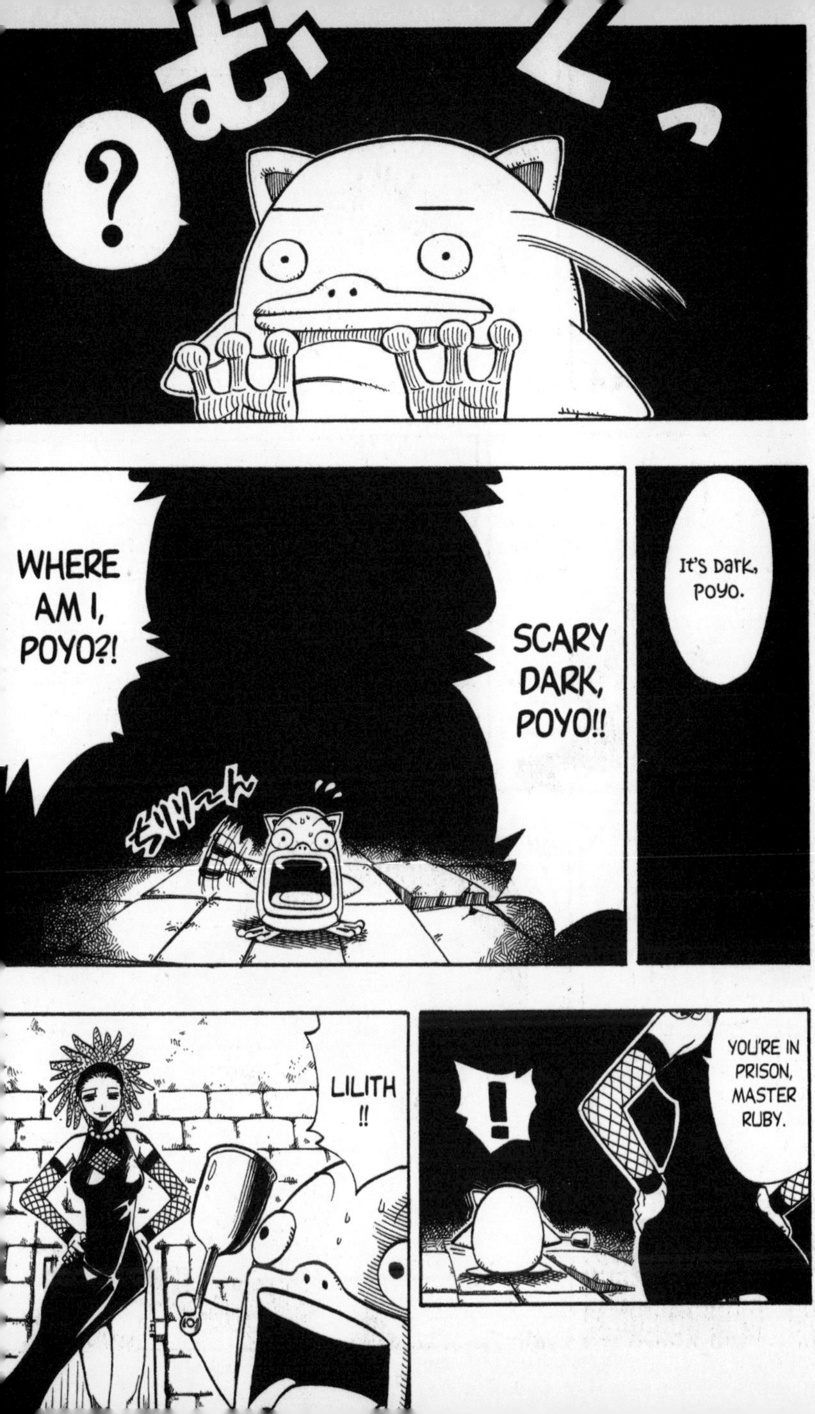
むくっ
?
It's Dark, Poyo.
SCARY DARK, POYO!!
WHERE AM I, POYO?!
!
YOU'RE IN PRISON, MASTER RUBY.
LILITH !!

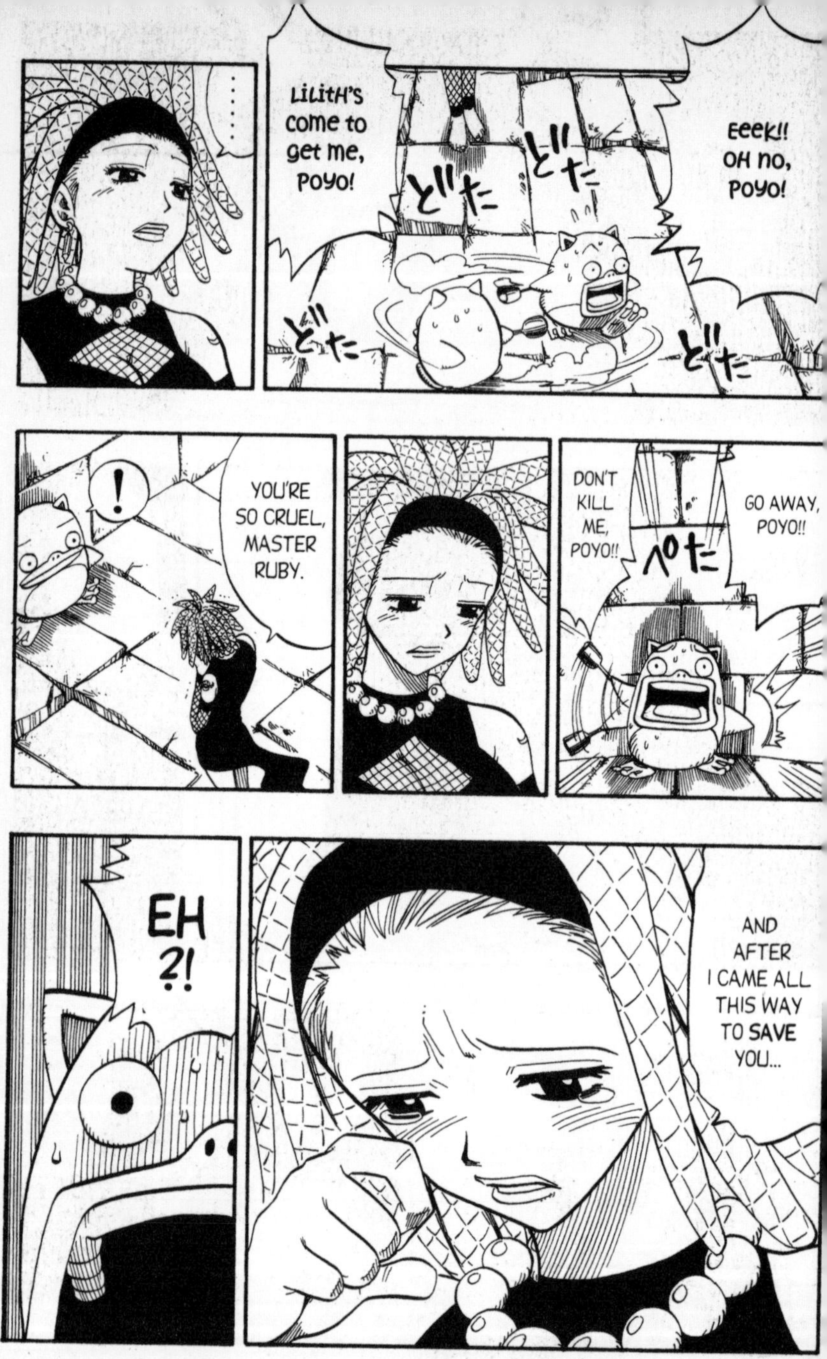
Eeek!! Oh no, Poyo!
どた
どた
Lilith's come to get me, Poyo!
どた
どた
......
GO AWAY, POYO!!
ぺた
DON'T KILL ME, POYO!!
YOU'RE SO CRUEL, MASTER RUBY.
!
AND AFTER I CAME ALL THIS WAY TO SAVE YOU...
EH ?!

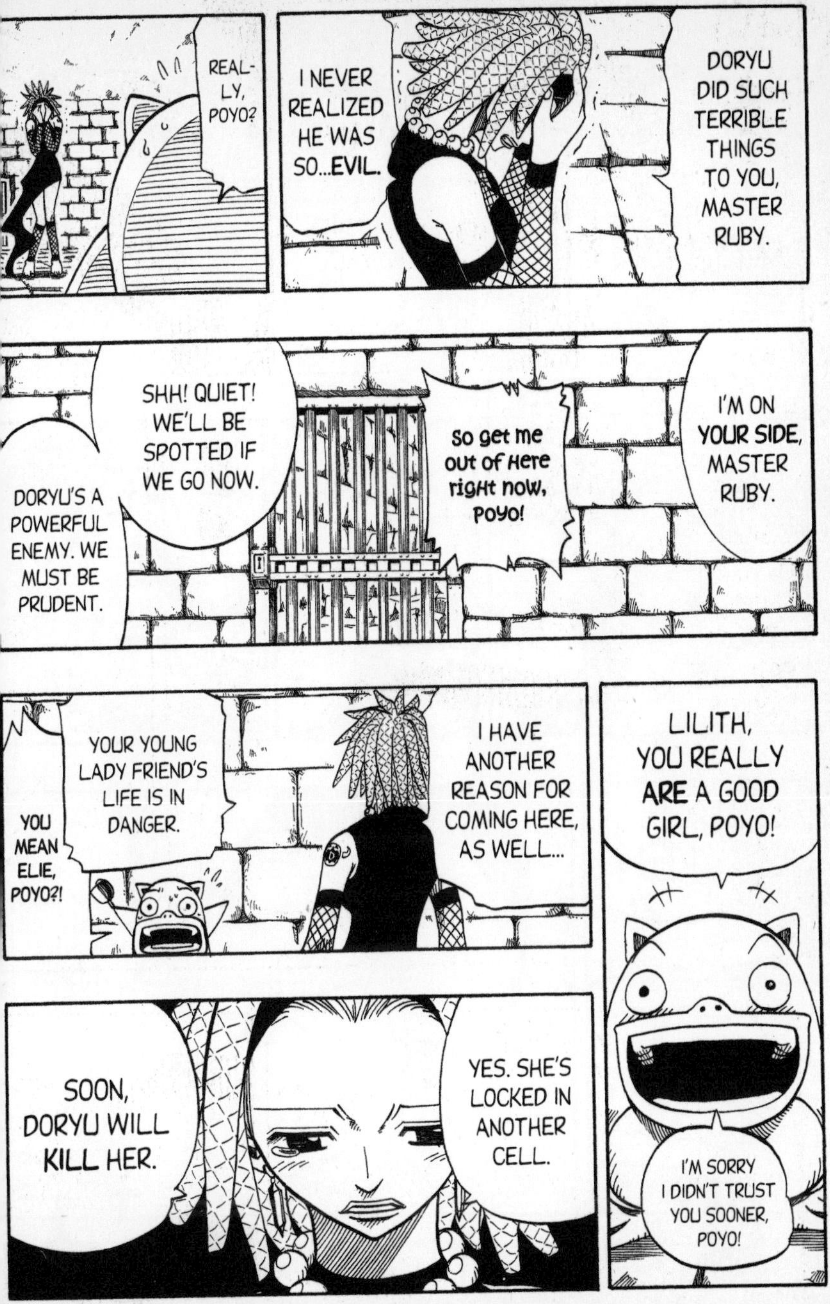
DORYU DID SUCH TERRIBLE THINGS TO YOU, MASTER RUBY.
I NEVER REALIZED HE WAS SO...**EVIL**.
REAL-LY, POYO?
I'M ON **YOUR SIDE**, MASTER RUBY.
So get me out of Here right now, POYO!
SHH! QUIET! WE'LL BE SPOTTED IF WE GO NOW.
DORYU'S A POWERFUL ENEMY. WE MUST BE PRUDENT.
LILITH, YOU REALLY **ARE** A GOOD GIRL, POYO!
I'M SORRY I DIDN'T TRUST YOU SOONER, POYO!
I HAVE ANOTHER REASON FOR COMING HERE, AS WELL...
YOUR YOUNG LADY FRIEND'S LIFE IS IN DANGER.
YOU MEAN ELIE, POYO?!
YES. SHE'S LOCKED IN ANOTHER CELL.
SOON, DORYU WILL **KILL** HER.

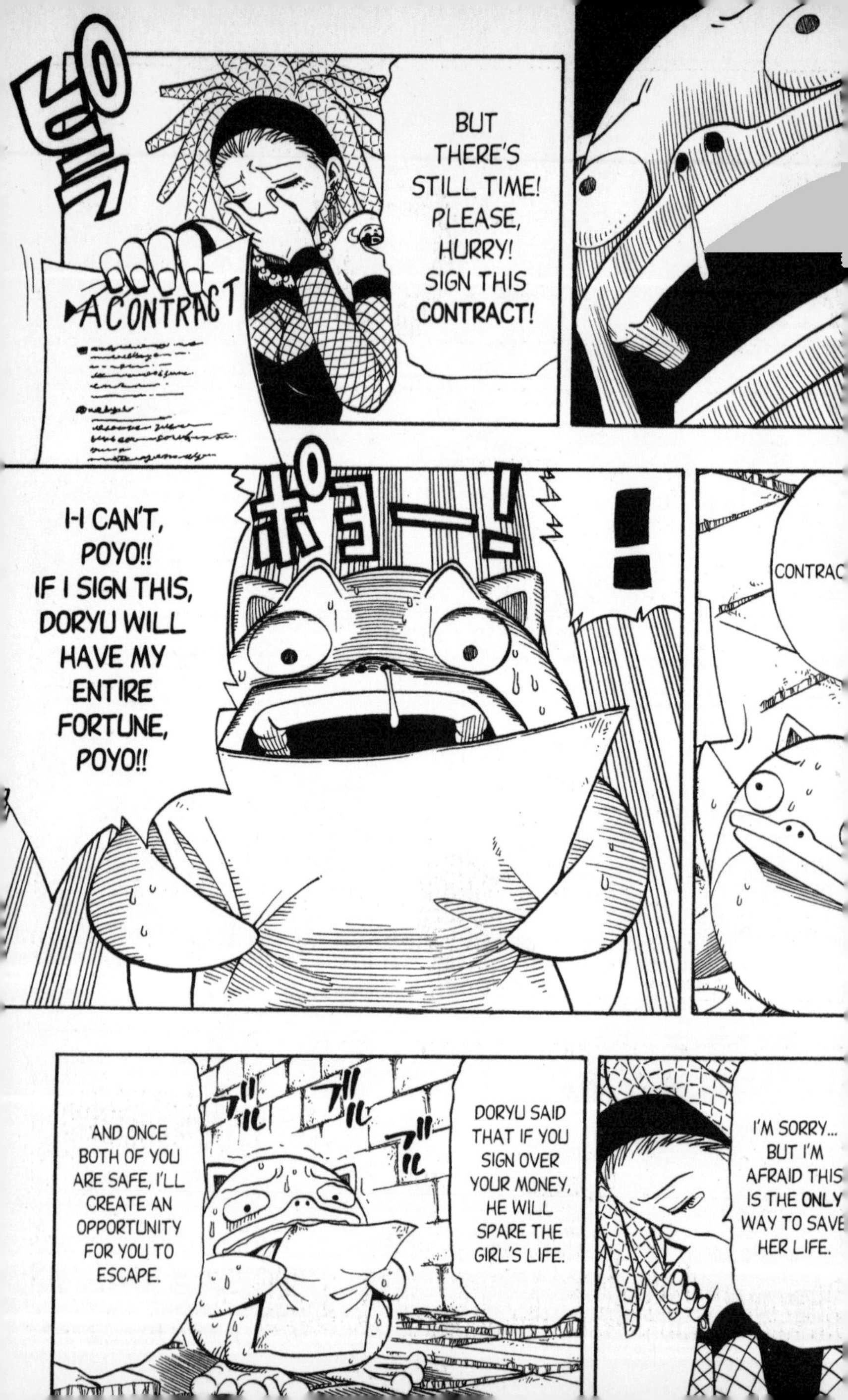
A CONTRACT
BUT THERE'S STILL TIME! PLEASE, HURRY! SIGN THIS CONTRACT!
CONTRAC
ポヨー!
!
I-I CAN'T, POYO!! IF I SIGN THIS, DORYU WILL HAVE MY ENTIRE FORTUNE, POYO!!
I'M SORRY... BUT I'M AFRAID THIS IS THE ONLY WAY TO SAVE HER LIFE.
ブル ブル ブル
DORYU SAID THAT IF YOU SIGN OVER YOUR MONEY, HE WILL SPARE THE GIRL'S LIFE.
AND ONCE BOTH OF YOU ARE SAFE, I'LL CREATE AN OPPORTUNITY FOR YOU TO ESCAPE.

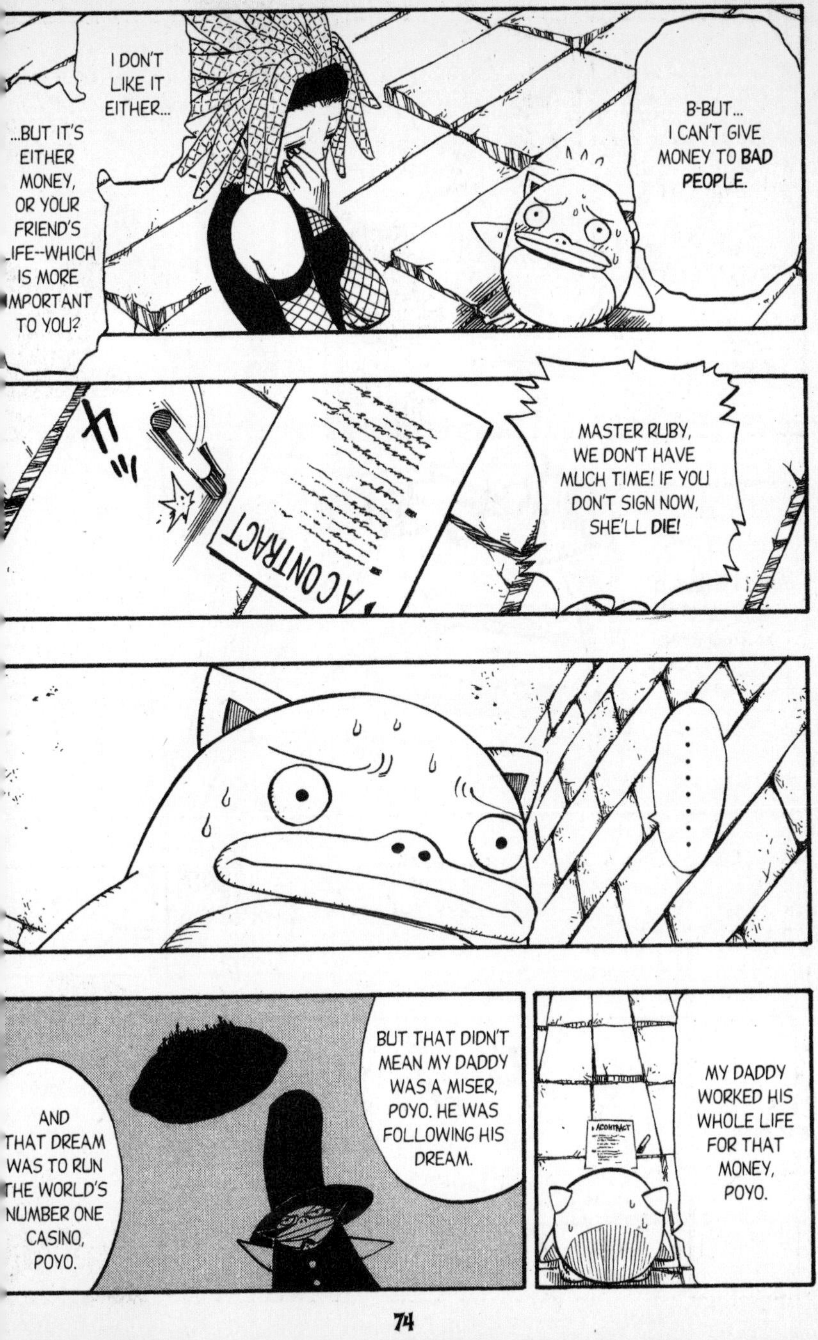
B-BUT... I CAN'T GIVE MONEY TO **BAD PEOPLE.**
I DON'T LIKE IT EITHER...
...BUT IT'S EITHER MONEY, OR YOUR FRIEND'S LIFE--WHICH IS MORE IMPORTANT TO YOU?
MASTER RUBY, WE DON'T HAVE MUCH TIME! IF YOU DON'T SIGN NOW, SHE'LL **DIE!**
A CONTRACT
......
MY DADDY WORKED HIS WHOLE LIFE FOR THAT MONEY, POYO.
BUT THAT DIDN'T MEAN MY DADDY WAS A MISER, POYO. HE WAS FOLLOWING HIS DREAM.
AND THAT DREAM WAS TO RUN THE WORLD'S NUMBER ONE CASINO, POYO.

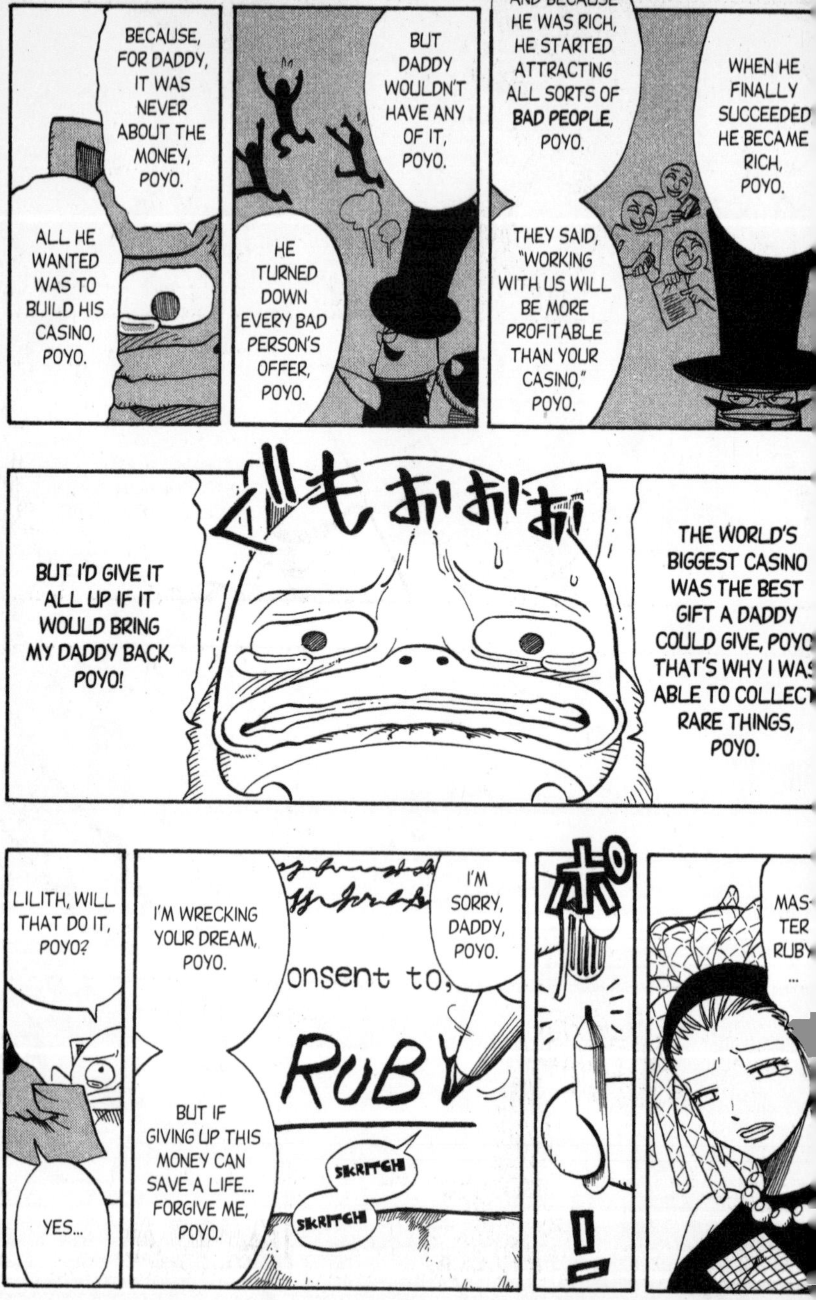
WHEN HE FINALLY SUCCEEDED HE BECAME RICH, POYO.
AND BECAUSE HE WAS RICH, HE STARTED ATTRACTING ALL SORTS OF BAD PEOPLE, POYO.
THEY SAID, "WORKING WITH US WILL BE MORE PROFITABLE THAN YOUR CASINO," POYO.
BUT DADDY WOULDN'T HAVE ANY OF IT, POYO.
HE TURNED DOWN EVERY BAD PERSON'S OFFER, POYO.
BECAUSE, FOR DADDY, IT WAS NEVER ABOUT THE MONEY, POYO.
ALL HE WANTED WAS TO BUILD HIS CASINO, POYO.
THE WORLD'S BIGGEST CASINO WAS THE BEST GIFT A DADDY COULD GIVE, POYO THAT'S WHY I WAS ABLE TO COLLECT RARE THINGS, POYO.
ぐもおおぉ
BUT I'D GIVE IT ALL UP IF IT WOULD BRING MY DADDY BACK, POYO!
MAS-TER RUBY...
ポ
!
I'M SORRY, DADDY, POYO.
onsent to,
RUBY
I'M WRECKING YOUR DREAM, POYO.
BUT IF GIVING UP THIS MONEY CAN SAVE A LIFE... FORGIVE ME, POYO.
SKRITCH
SKRITCH
LILITH, WILL THAT DO IT, POYO?
YES...

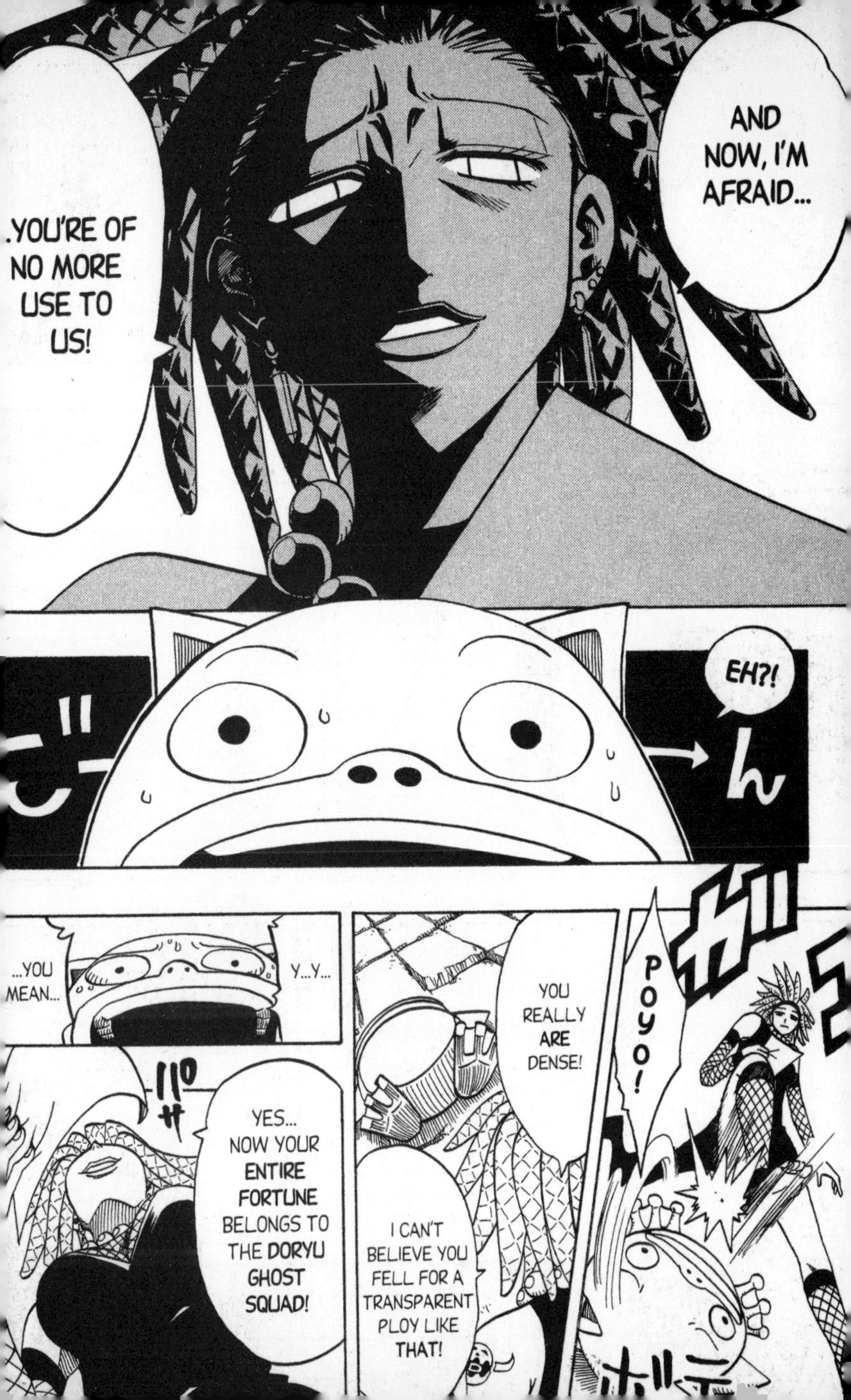
AND NOW, I'M AFRAID...
.YOU'RE OF NO MORE USE TO US!
EH?!
POYO!
YOU REALLY ARE DENSE!
I CAN'T BELIEVE YOU FELL FOR A TRANSPARENT PLOY LIKE THAT!
Y...Y...
...YOU MEAN...
YES... NOW YOUR ENTIRE FORTUNE BELONGS TO THE DORYU GHOST SQUAD!

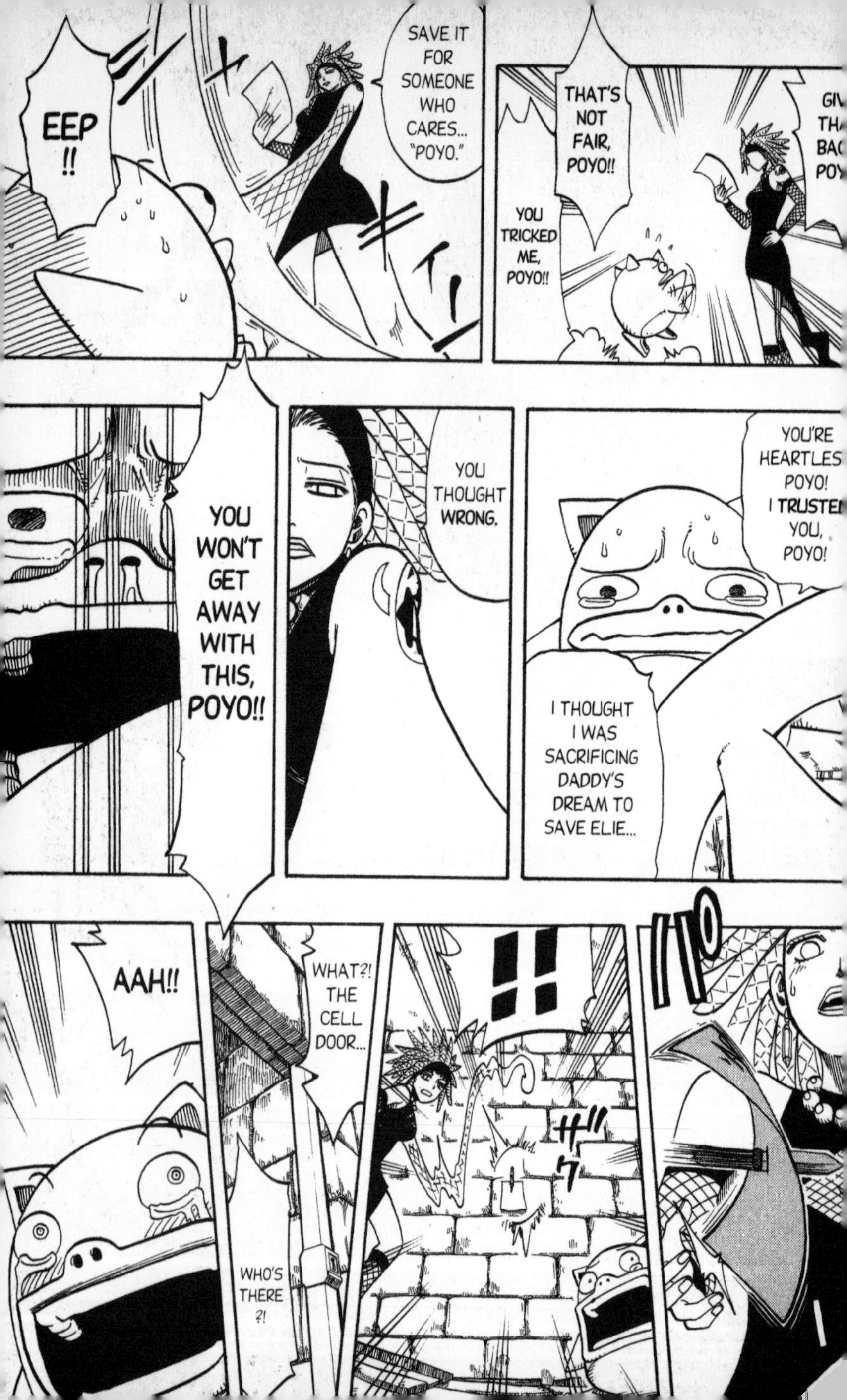
GIV
THA
BAC
POY
THAT'S NOT FAIR, POYO!!
YOU TRICKED ME, POYO!!
SAVE IT FOR SOMEONE WHO CARES... "POYO."
EEP !!
YOU'RE HEARTLES POYO! I TRUSTEI YOU, POYO!
I THOUGHT I WAS SACRIFICING DADDY'S DREAM TO SAVE ELIE...
YOU THOUGHT WRONG.
YOU WON'T GET AWAY WITH THIS, POYO!!
!!
WHAT?! THE CELL DOOR...
WHO'S THERE ?!
AAH!!

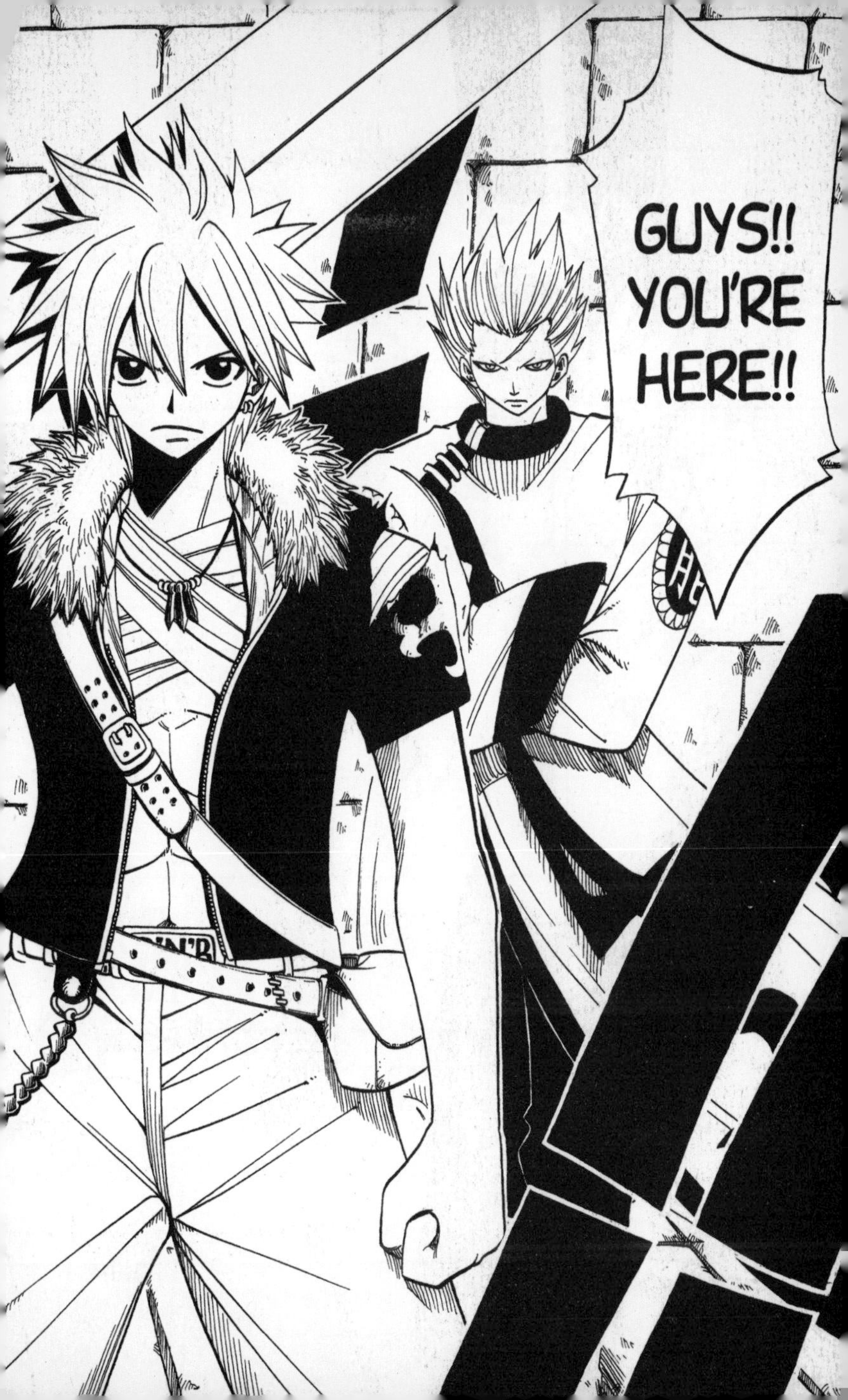
GUYS!! YOU'RE HERE!!

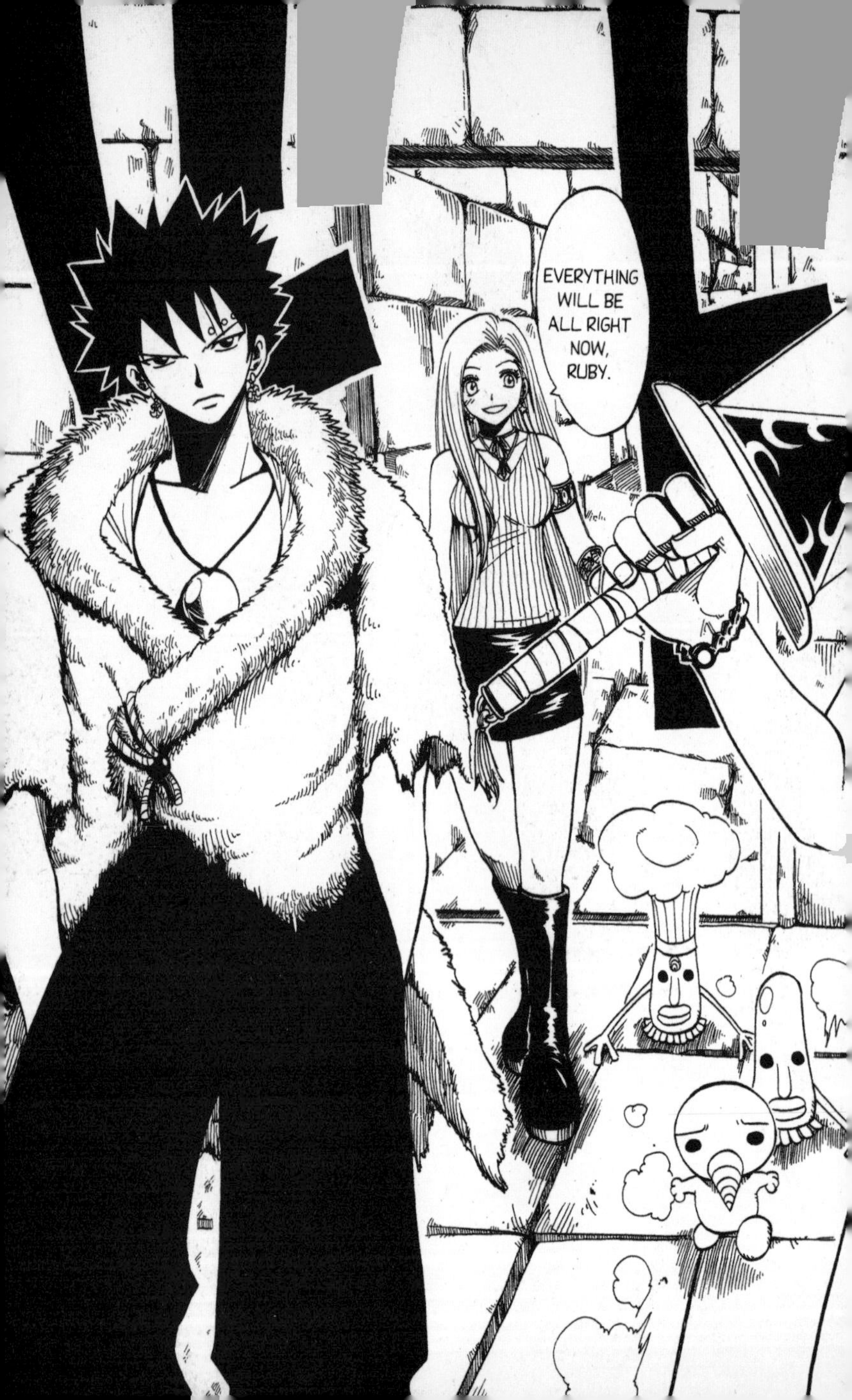
EVERYTHING WILL BE ALL RIGHT NOW, RUBY.

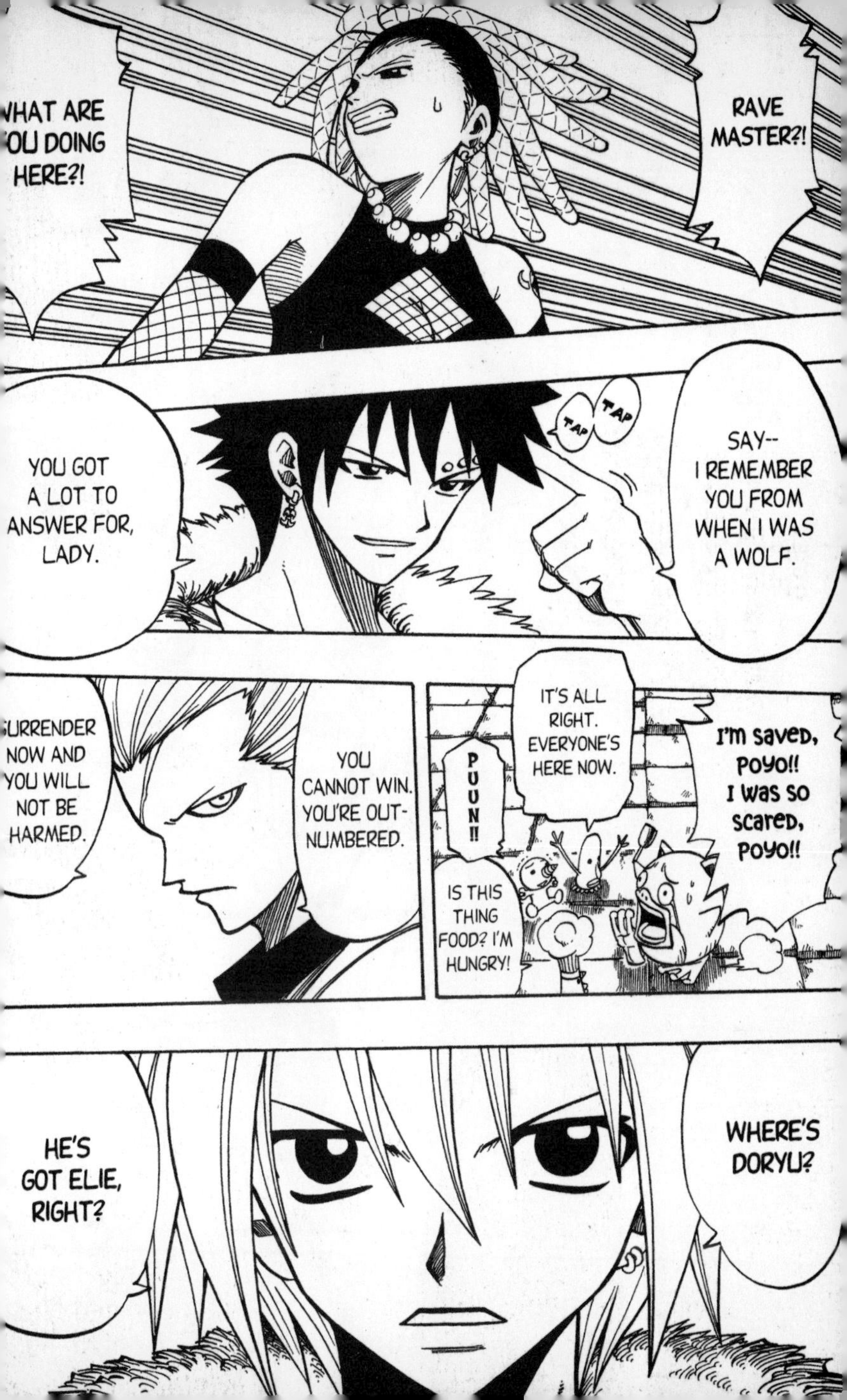
RAVE MASTER?!
WHAT ARE YOU DOING HERE?!
SAY-- I REMEMBER YOU FROM WHEN I WAS A WOLF.
TAP TAP
YOU GOT A LOT TO ANSWER FOR, LADY.
I'm saved, Poyo!! I was so scared, Poyo!!
IT'S ALL RIGHT. EVERYONE'S HERE NOW.
PUUN!!
IS THIS THING FOOD? I'M HUNGRY!
YOU CANNOT WIN. YOU'RE OUT-NUMBERED.
SURRENDER NOW AND YOU WILL NOT BE HARMED.
WHERE'S DORYU?
HE'S GOT ELIE, RIGHT?

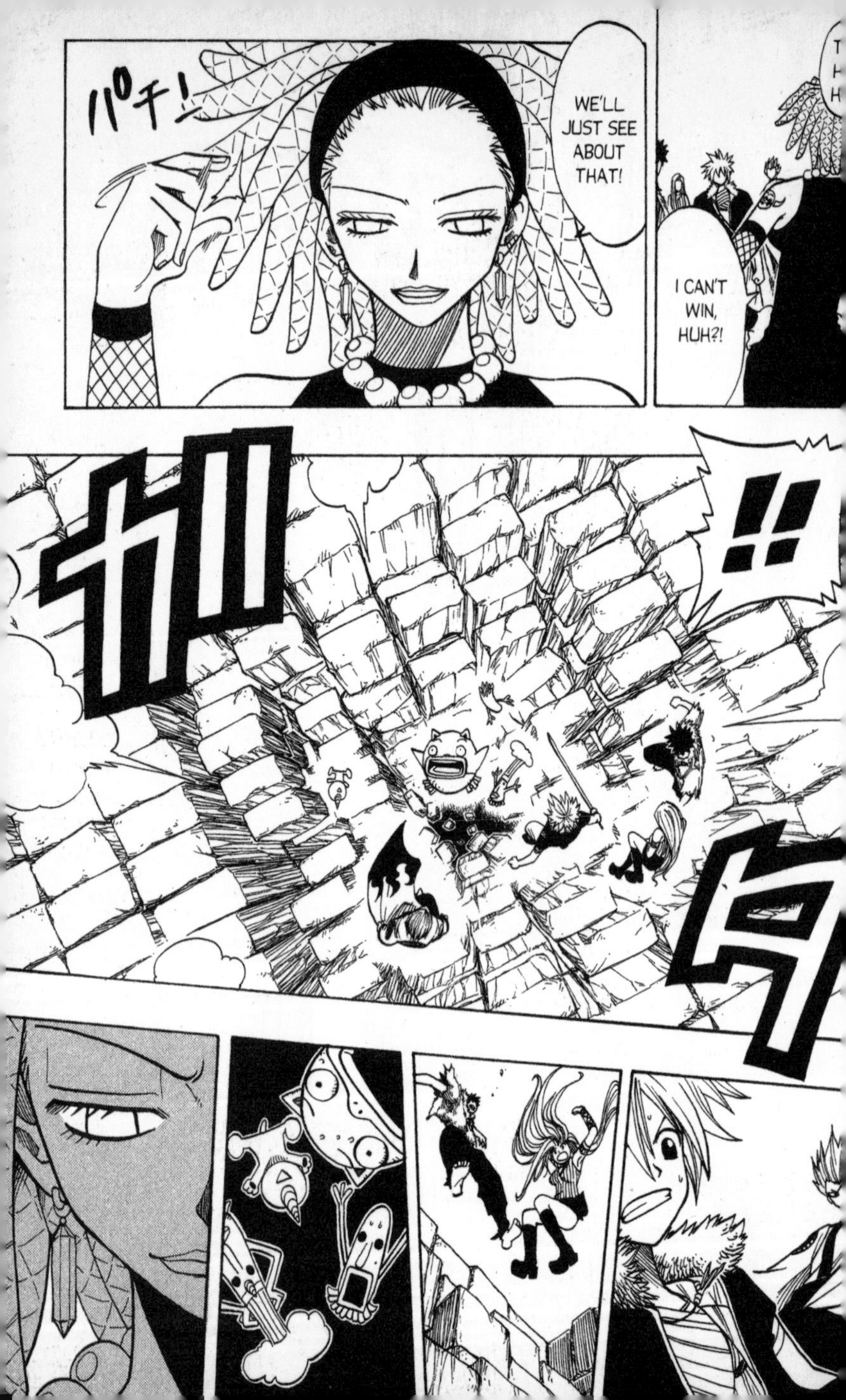
I CAN'T WIN, HUH?!
パチ！
WE'LL JUST SEE ABOUT THAT!
!!

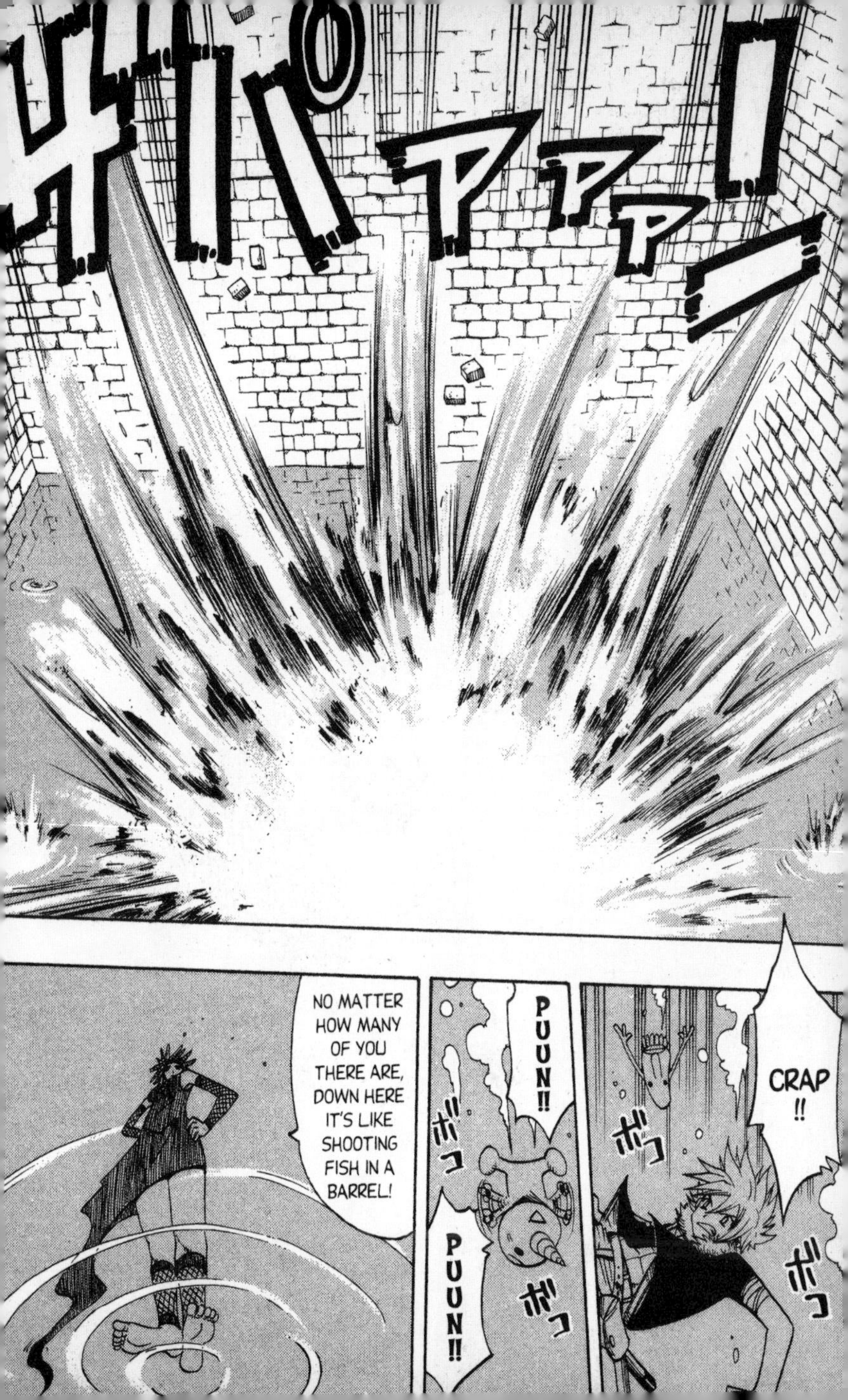
CRAP!!
ボコ
ボコ
PUUN!!
ボコ
PUUN!!
ボコ
NO MATTER HOW MANY OF YOU THERE ARE, DOWN HERE IT'S LIKE SHOOTING FISH IN A BARREL!

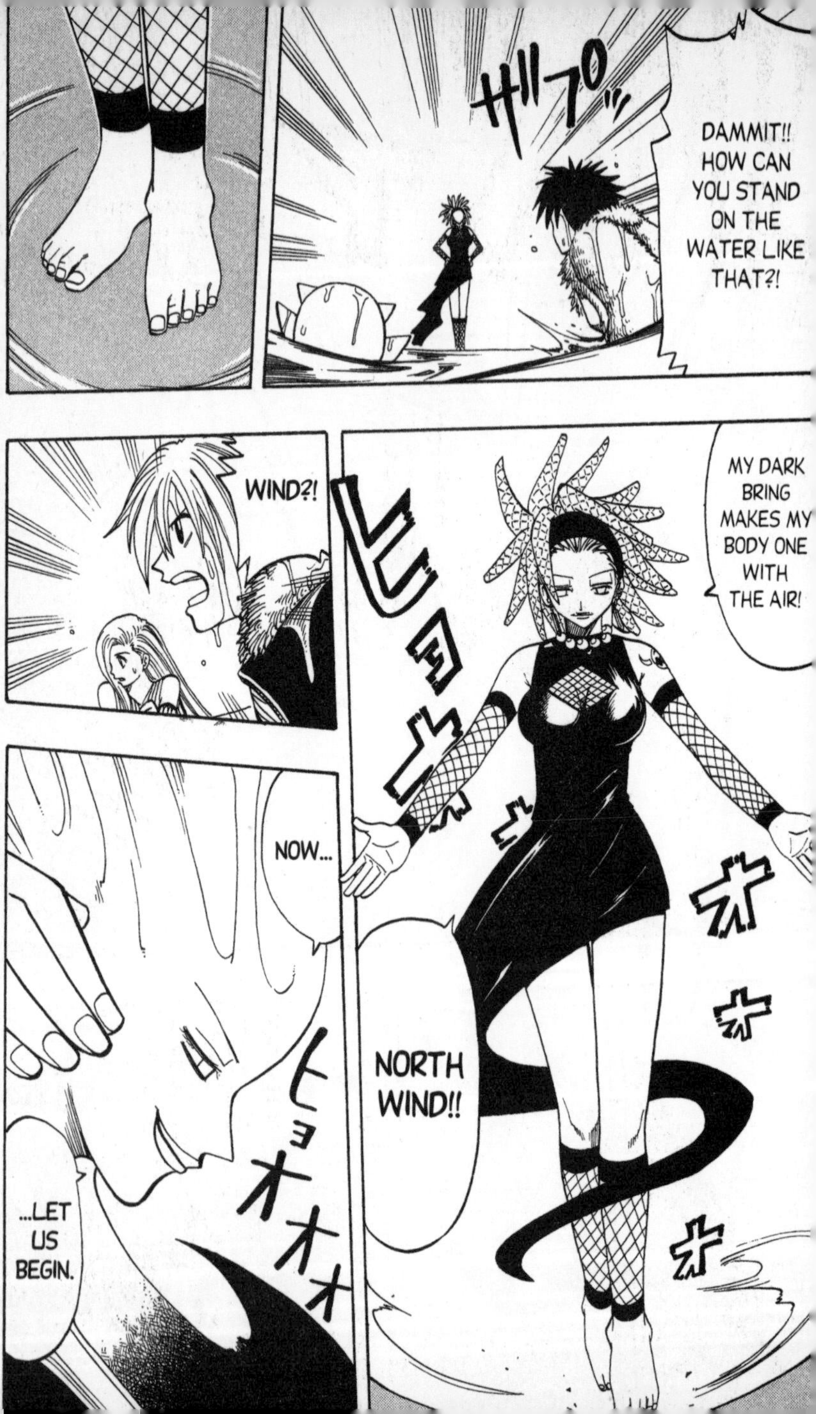
DAMMIT!! HOW CAN YOU STAND ON THE WATER LIKE THAT?!
MY DARK BRING MAKES MY BODY ONE WITH THE AIR!
NORTH WIND!!
WIND?!
NOW...
ヒョオオオ
...LET US BEGIN.

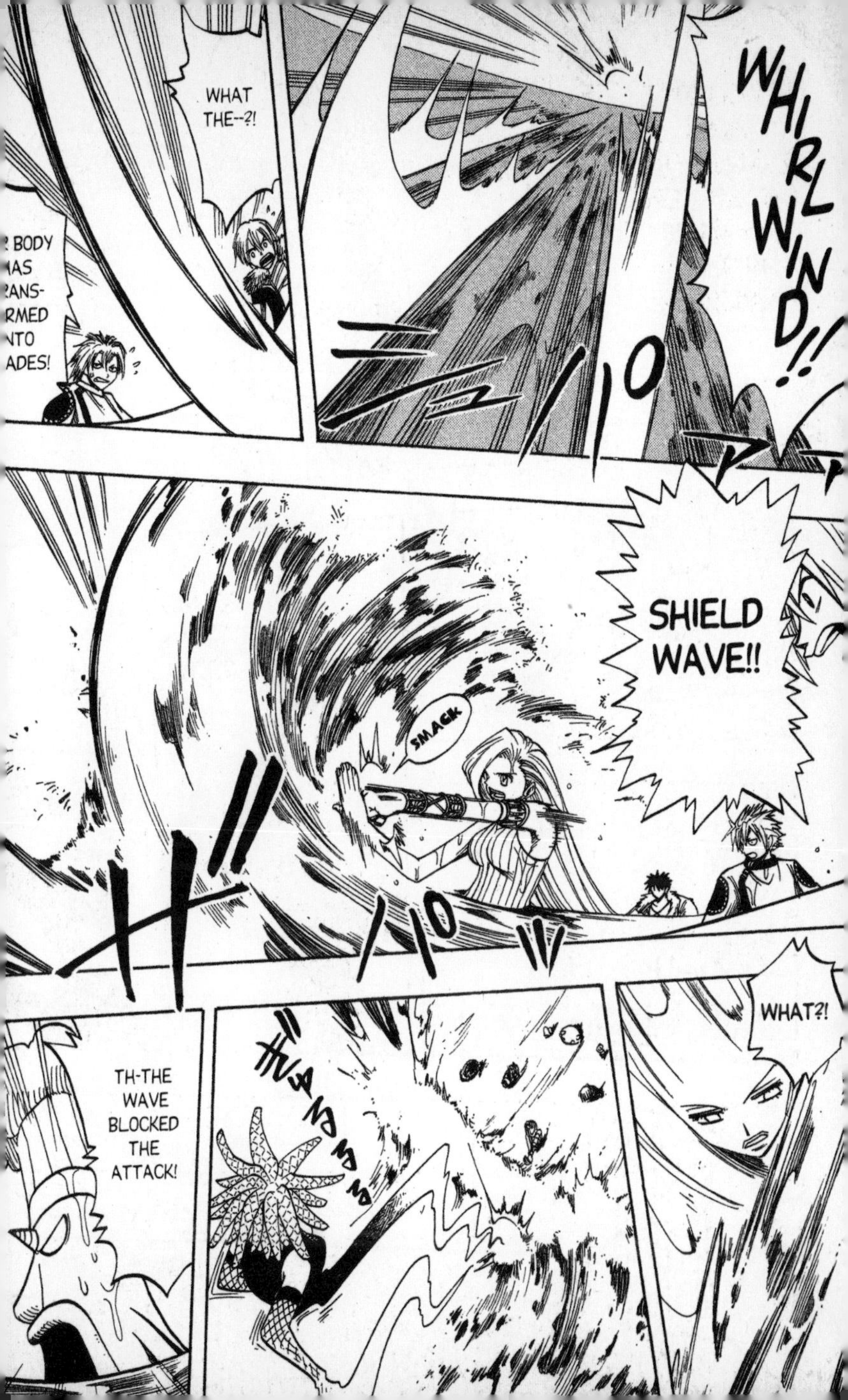
WHIRLWIND!!
WHAT THE--?!
BODY HAS ANS- RMED NTO ADES!
SHIELD WAVE!!
SMACK
WHAT?!
TH-THE WAVE BLOCKED THE ATTACK!

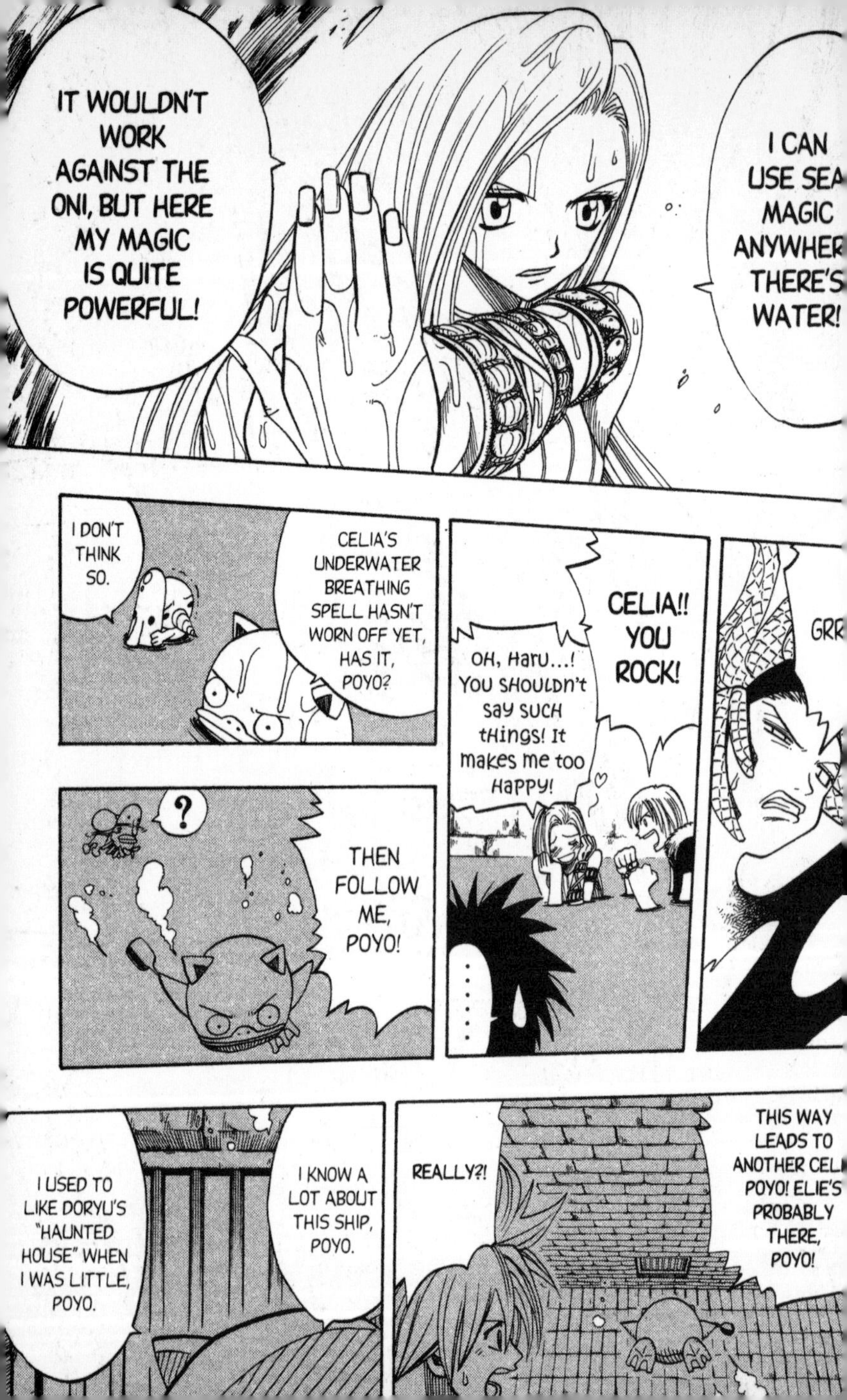
I CAN USE SEA MAGIC ANYWHER THERE'S WATER!
IT WOULDN'T WORK AGAINST THE ONI, BUT HERE MY MAGIC IS QUITE POWERFUL!
GRR
CELIA!! YOU ROCK!
OH, HARU...! YOU SHOULDN'T SAY SUCH THINGS! IT MAKES ME TOO HAPPY!
......
CELIA'S UNDERWATER BREATHING SPELL HASN'T WORN OFF YET, HAS IT, POYO?
I DON'T THINK SO.
?
THEN FOLLOW ME, POYO!
THIS WAY LEADS TO ANOTHER CEL POYO! ELIE'S PROBABLY THERE, POYO!
REALLY?!
I KNOW A LOT ABOUT THIS SHIP, POYO.
I USED TO LIKE DORYU'S "HAUNTED HOUSE" WHEN I WAS LITTLE, POYO.

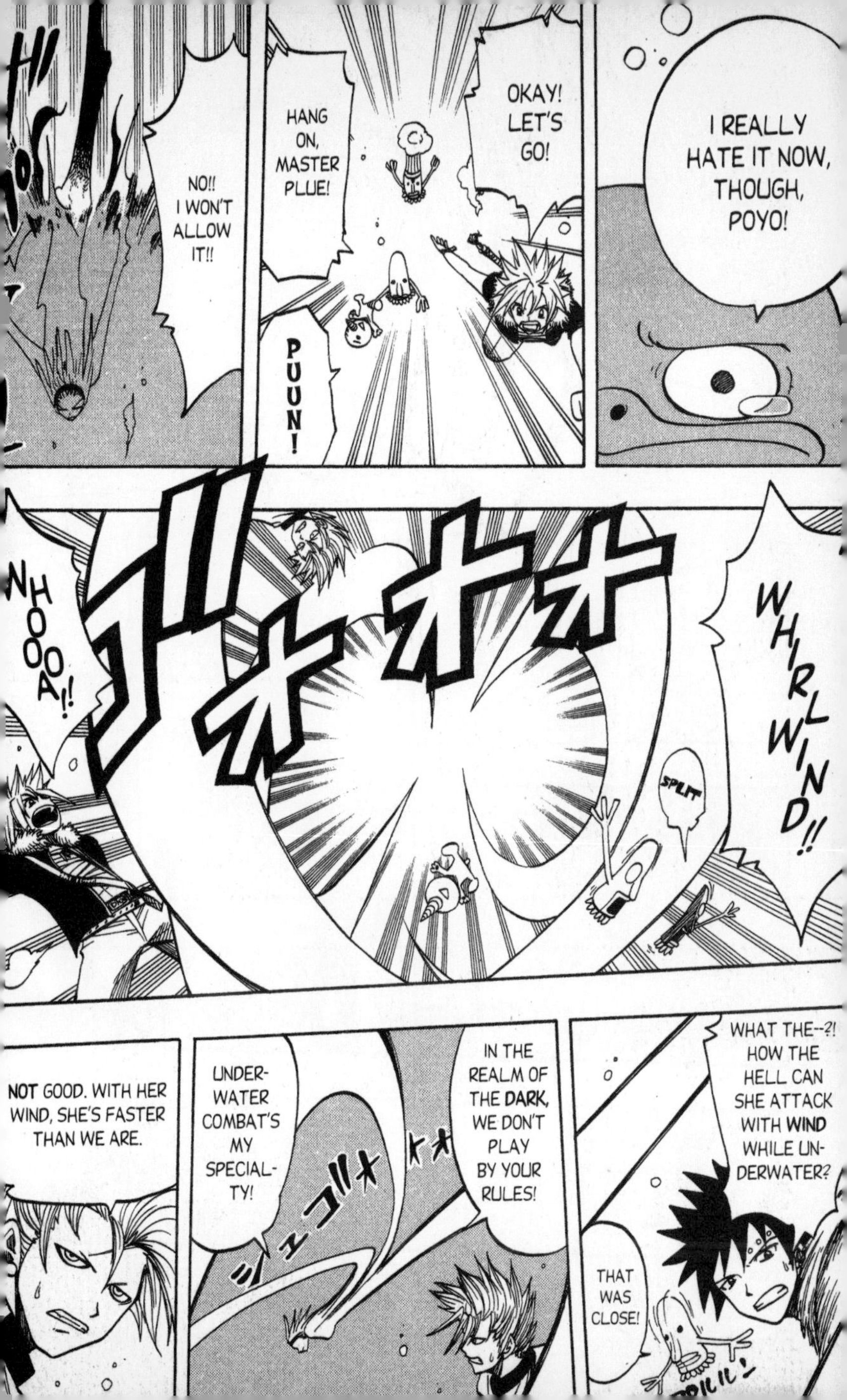
I REALLY HATE IT NOW, THOUGH, POYO!
OKAY! LET'S GO!
HANG ON, MASTER PLUE!
PUUN!
NO!! I WON'T ALLOW IT!!
WHIRLWIND!!
SPLIT
NHOOOA!!
WHAT THE--?! HOW THE HELL CAN SHE ATTACK WITH WIND WHILE UNDERWATER?
THAT WAS CLOSE!
IN THE REALM OF THE DARK, WE DON'T PLAY BY YOUR RULES!
UNDERWATER COMBAT'S MY SPECIALTY!
NOT GOOD. WITH HER WIND, SHE'S FASTER THAN WE ARE.

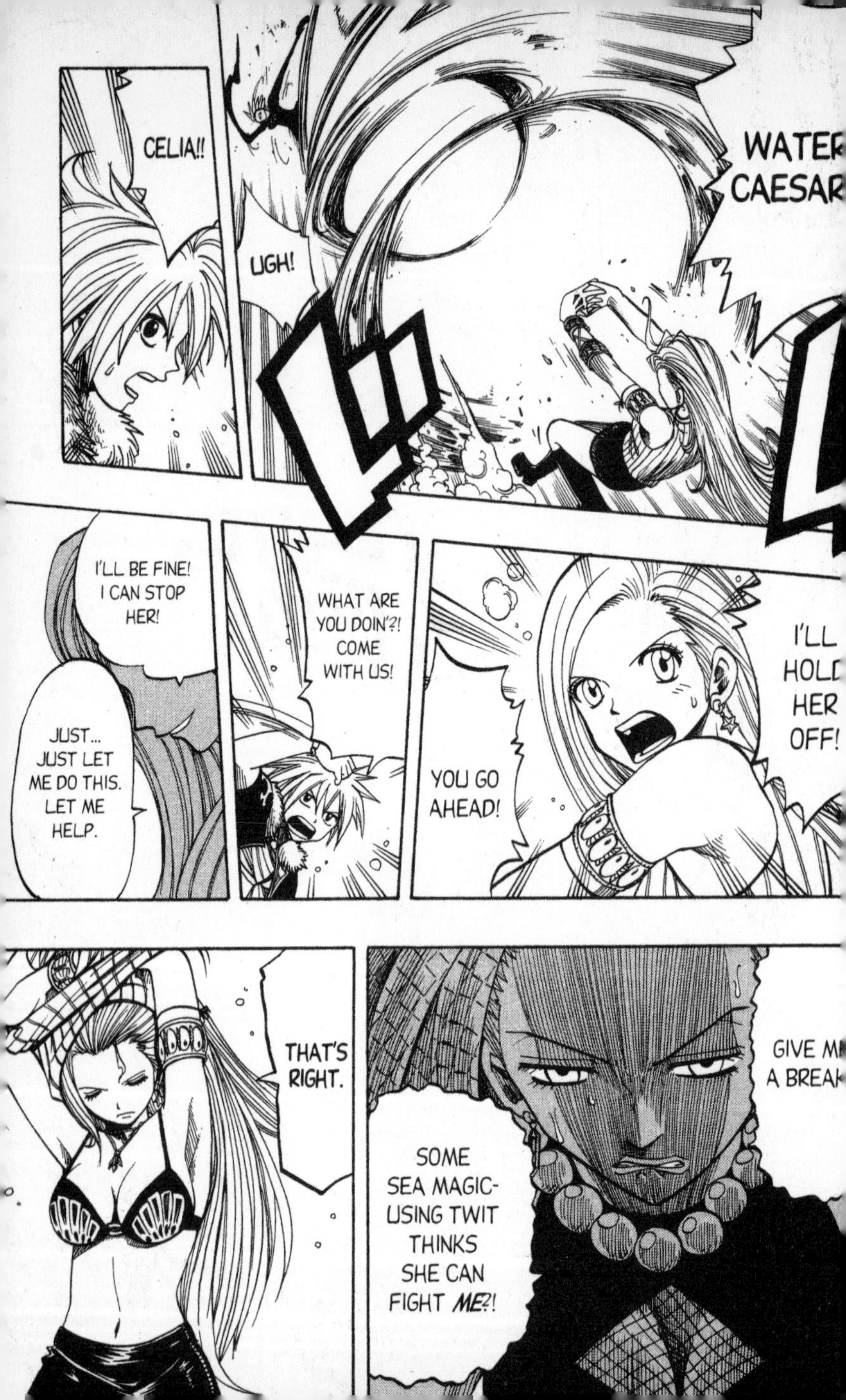
WATER CAESAR
UGH!
CELIA!!
I'LL HOLD HER OFF!
YOU GO AHEAD!
WHAT ARE YOU DOIN'?! COME WITH US!
I'LL BE FINE! I CAN STOP HER!
JUST... JUST LET ME DO THIS. LET ME HELP.
GIVE ME A BREAK
SOME SEA MAGIC-USING TWIT THINKS SHE CAN FIGHT *ME*?!
THAT'S RIGHT.

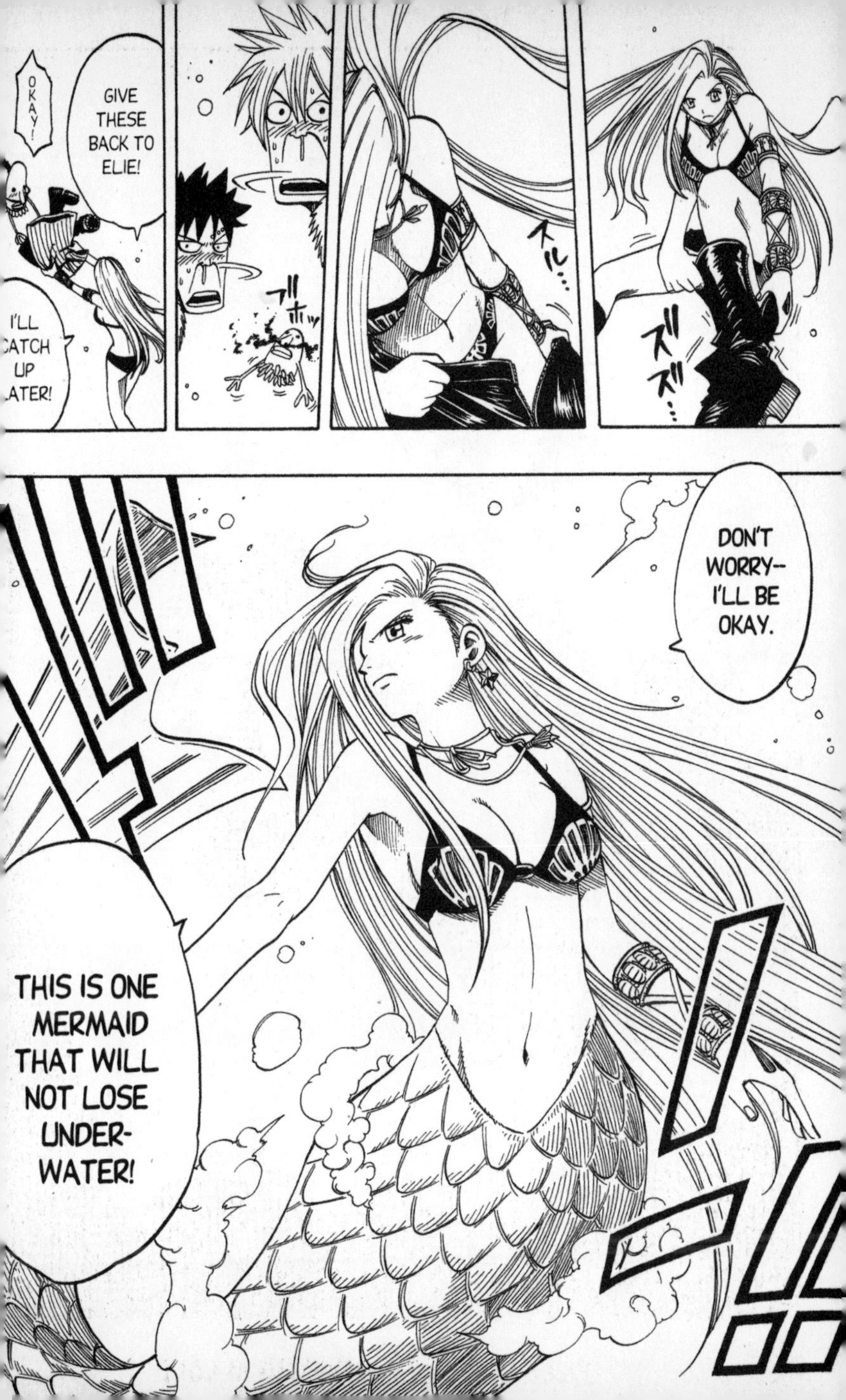
ズズ…
スル…
ブホッ
GIVE THESE BACK TO ELIE!
OKAY!
I'LL CATCH UP LATER!
DON'T WORRY-- I'LL BE OKAY.
THIS IS ONE MERMAID THAT WILL NOT LOSE UNDER-WATER!

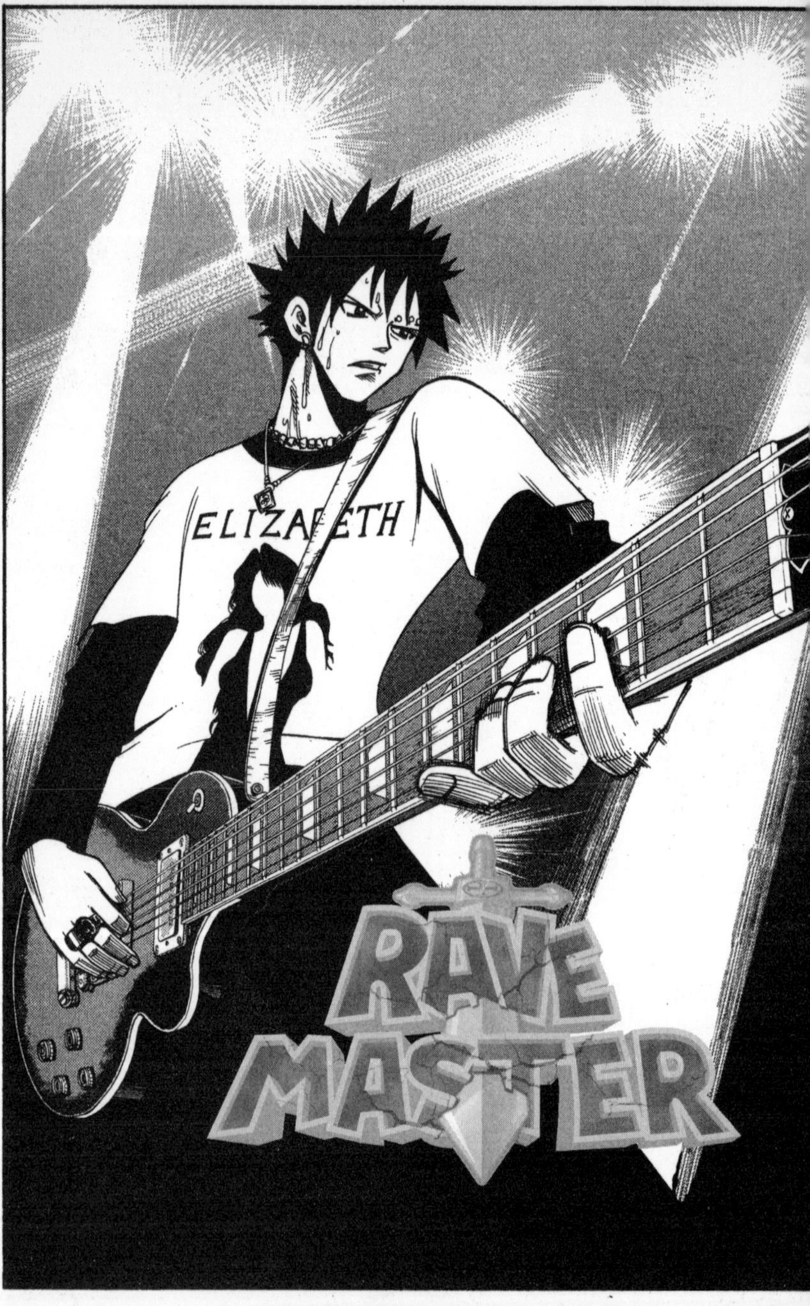
RAVE
MASTER

RAVE:119 MERMAID IN LOVE

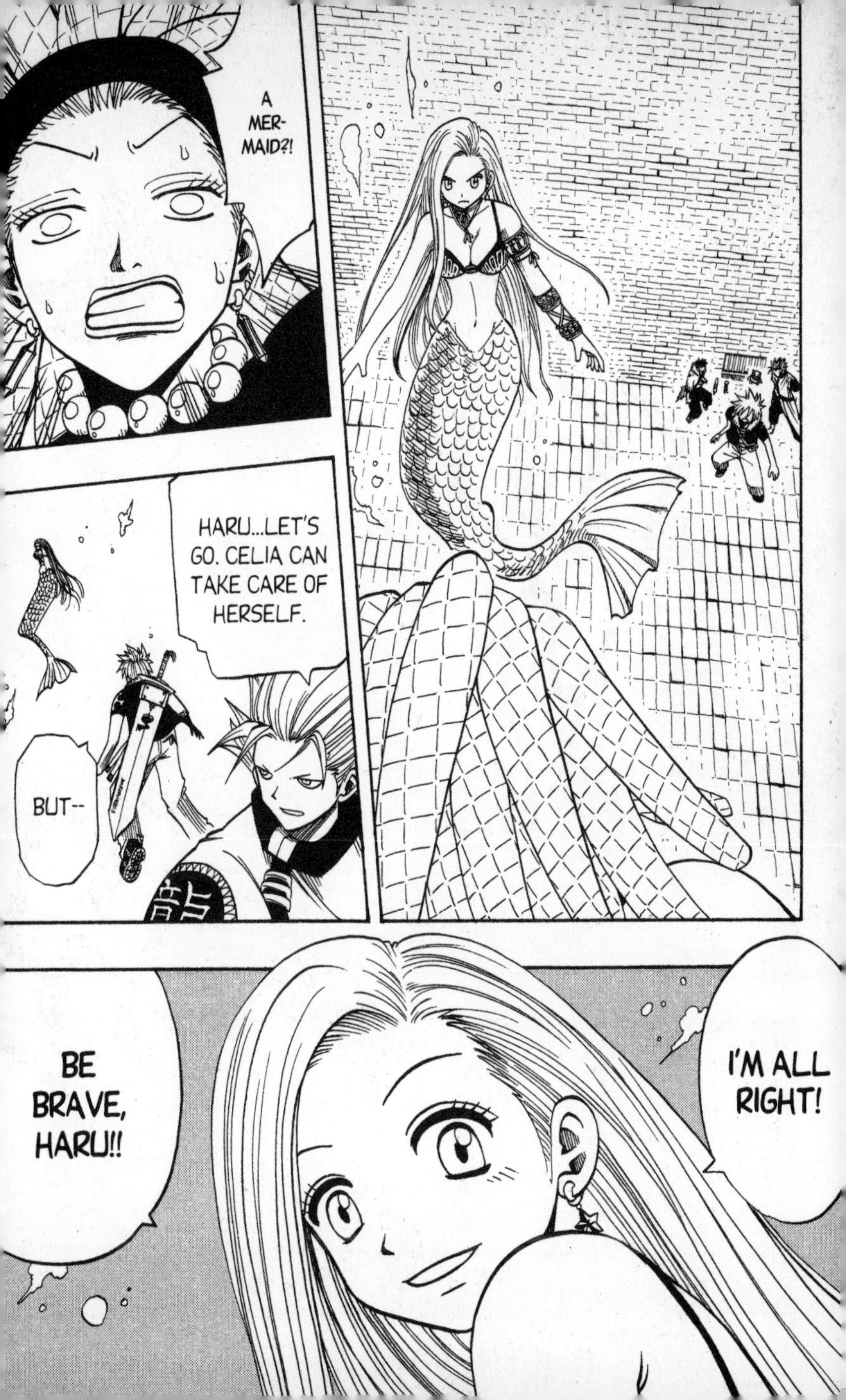
A MER-MAID?!
HARU...LET'S GO. CELIA CAN TAKE CARE OF HERSELF.
BUT--
I'M ALL RIGHT!
BE BRAVE, HARU!!

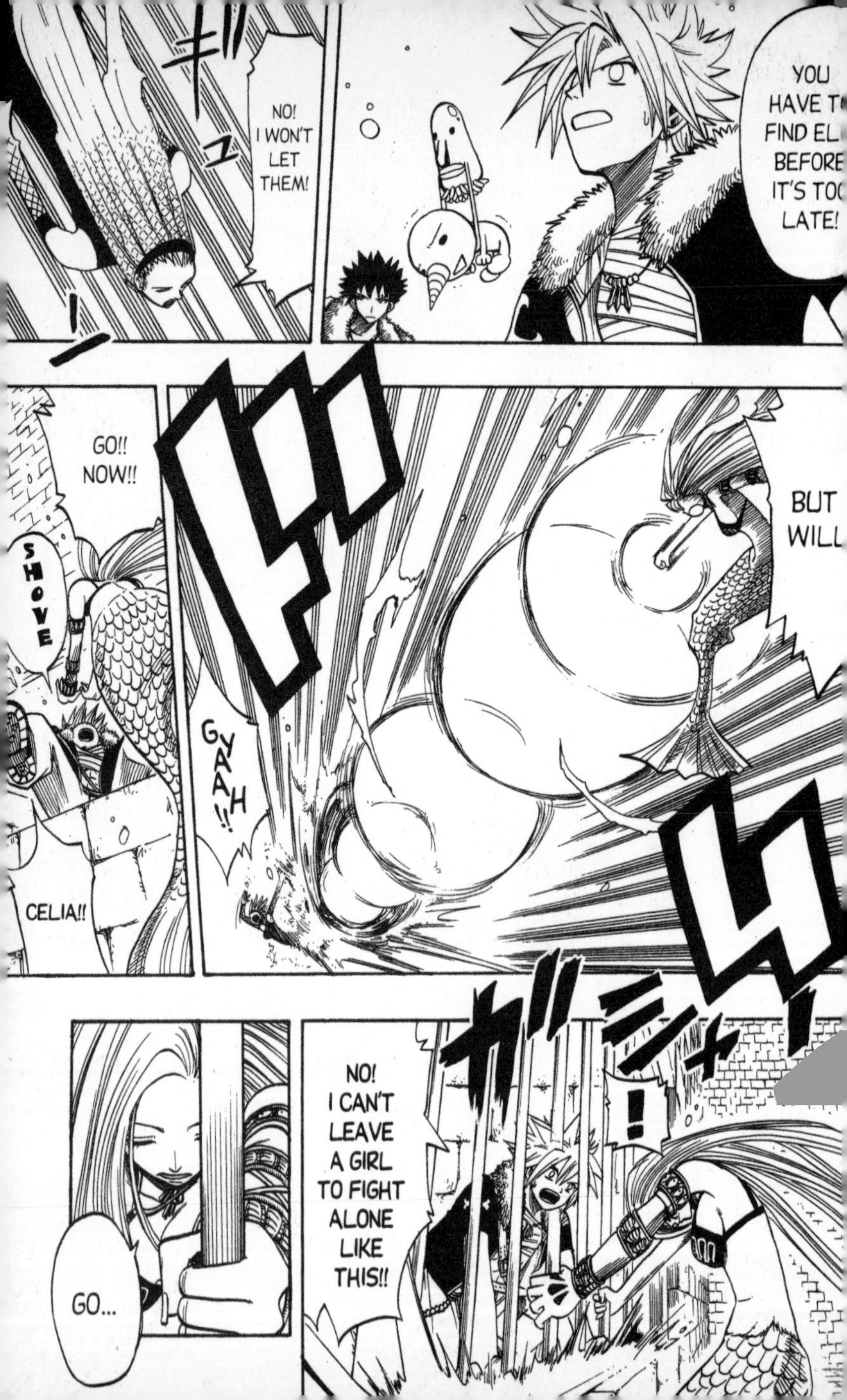
YOU HAVE T FIND EL BEFORE IT'S TO LATE!
NO! I WON'T LET THEM!
BUT WILL
GYAAH!!
GO!! NOW!!
SHOVE
CELIA!!
NO! I CAN'T LEAVE A GIRL TO FIGHT ALONE LIKE THIS!!
GO...

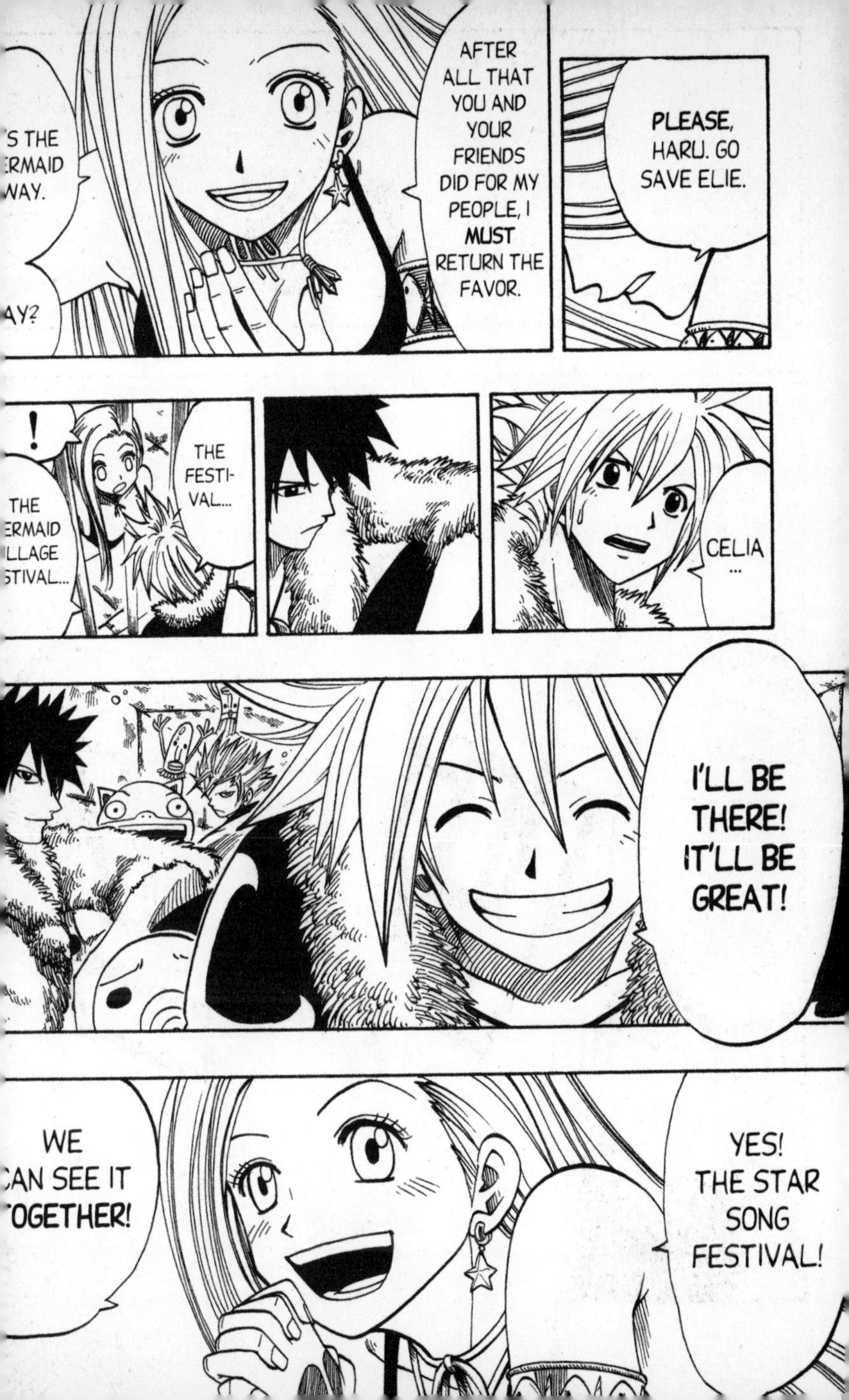
PLEASE, HARU. GO SAVE ELIE.
AFTER ALL THAT YOU AND YOUR FRIENDS DID FOR MY PEOPLE, I MUST RETURN THE FAVOR.
'S THE ERMAID WAY.
AY?
CELIA ...
THE FESTI-VAL...
!
THE ERMAID LLAGE STIVAL...
I'LL BE THERE! IT'LL BE GREAT!
YES! THE STAR SONG FESTIVAL!
WE CAN SEE IT TOGETHER!

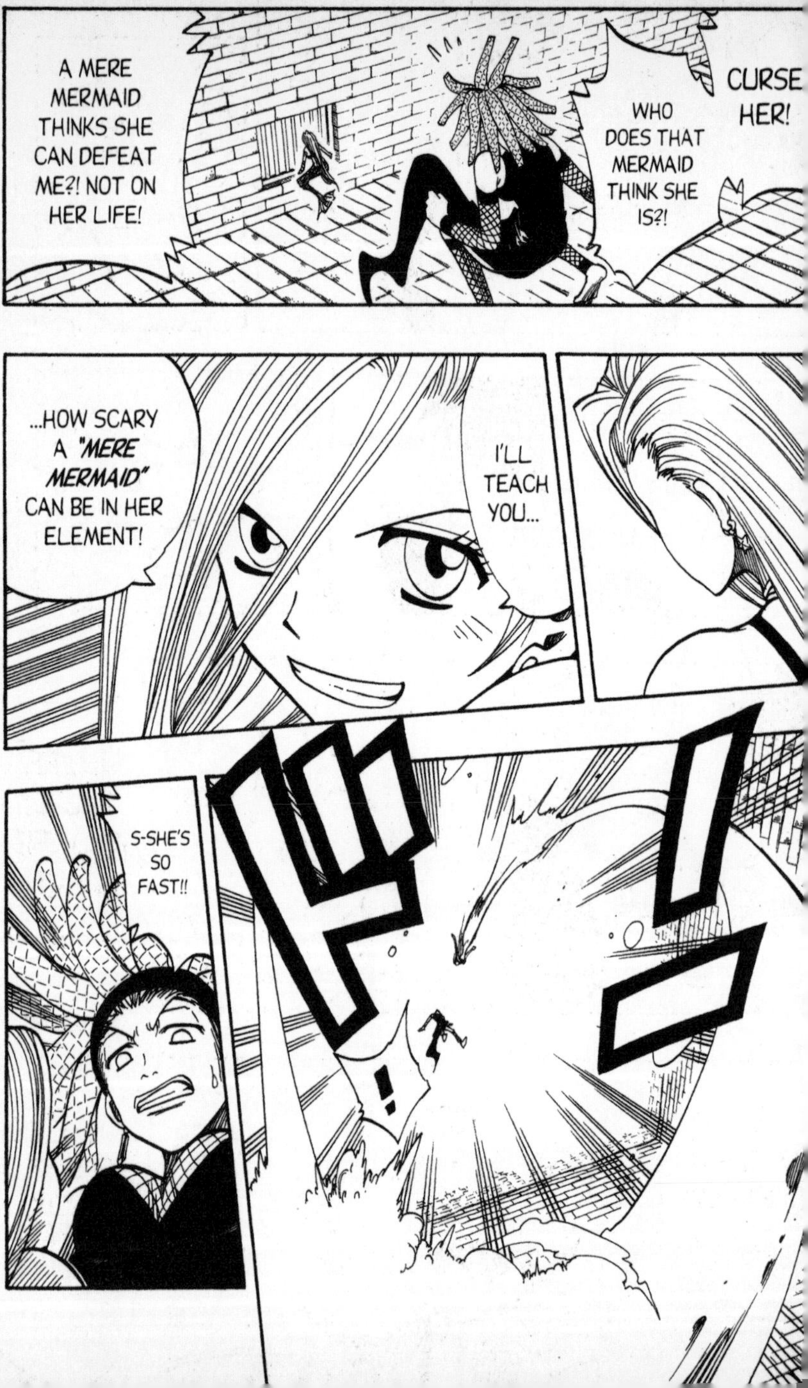
CURSE HER!
WHO DOES THAT MERMAID THINK SHE IS?!
A MERE MERMAID THINKS SHE CAN DEFEAT ME?! NOT ON HER LIFE!
I'LL TEACH YOU...
...HOW SCARY A "*MERE MERMAID*" CAN BE IN HER ELEMENT!
!
S-SHE'S SO FAST!!

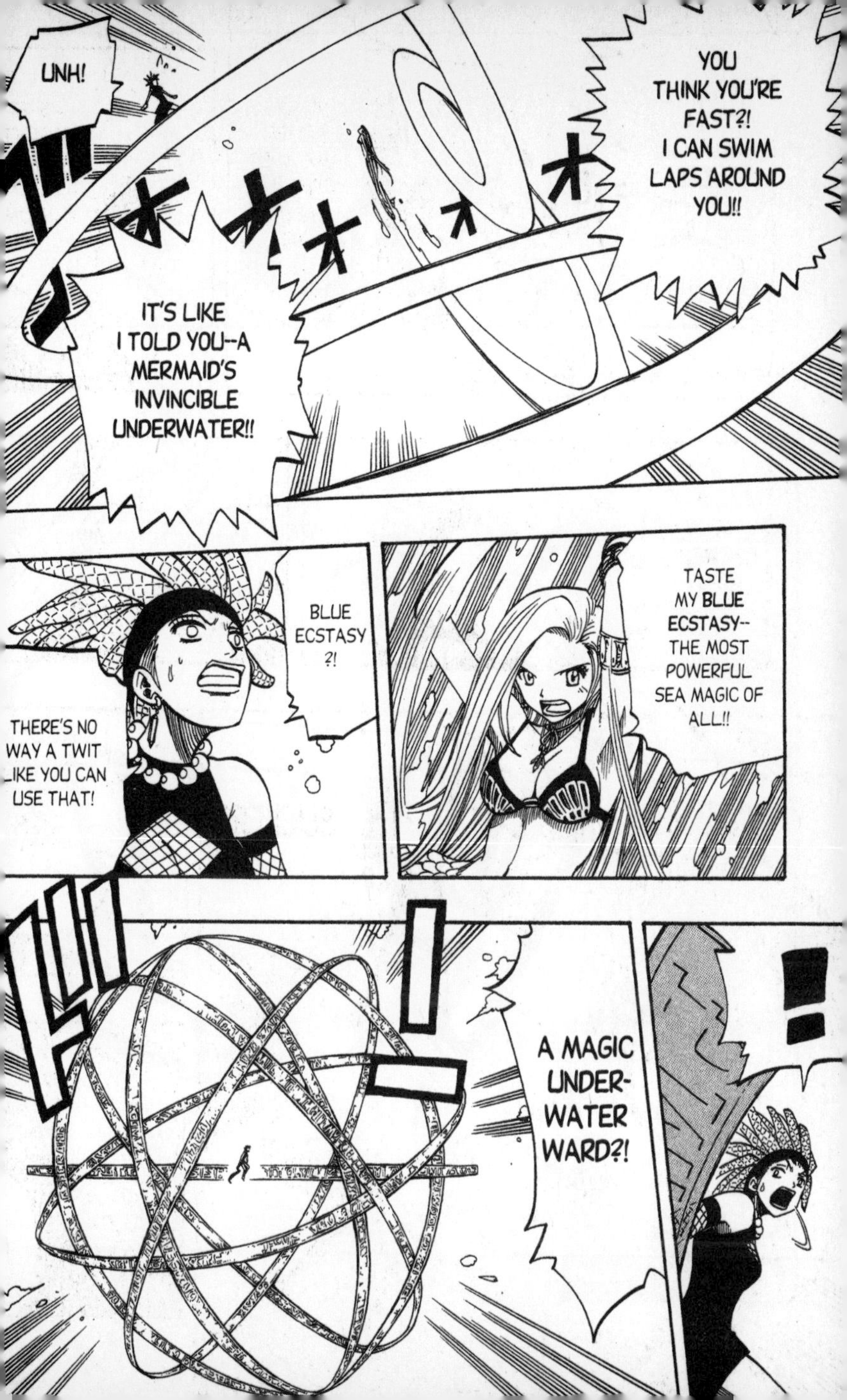
YOU THINK YOU'RE FAST?! I CAN SWIM LAPS AROUND YOU!!
UNH!
IT'S LIKE I TOLD YOU--A MERMAID'S INVINCIBLE UNDERWATER!!
TASTE MY BLUE ECSTASY-- THE MOST POWERFUL SEA MAGIC OF ALL!!
BLUE ECSTASY ?!
THERE'S NO WAY A TWIT LIKE YOU CAN USE THAT!
!!
A MAGIC UNDER-WATER WARD?!

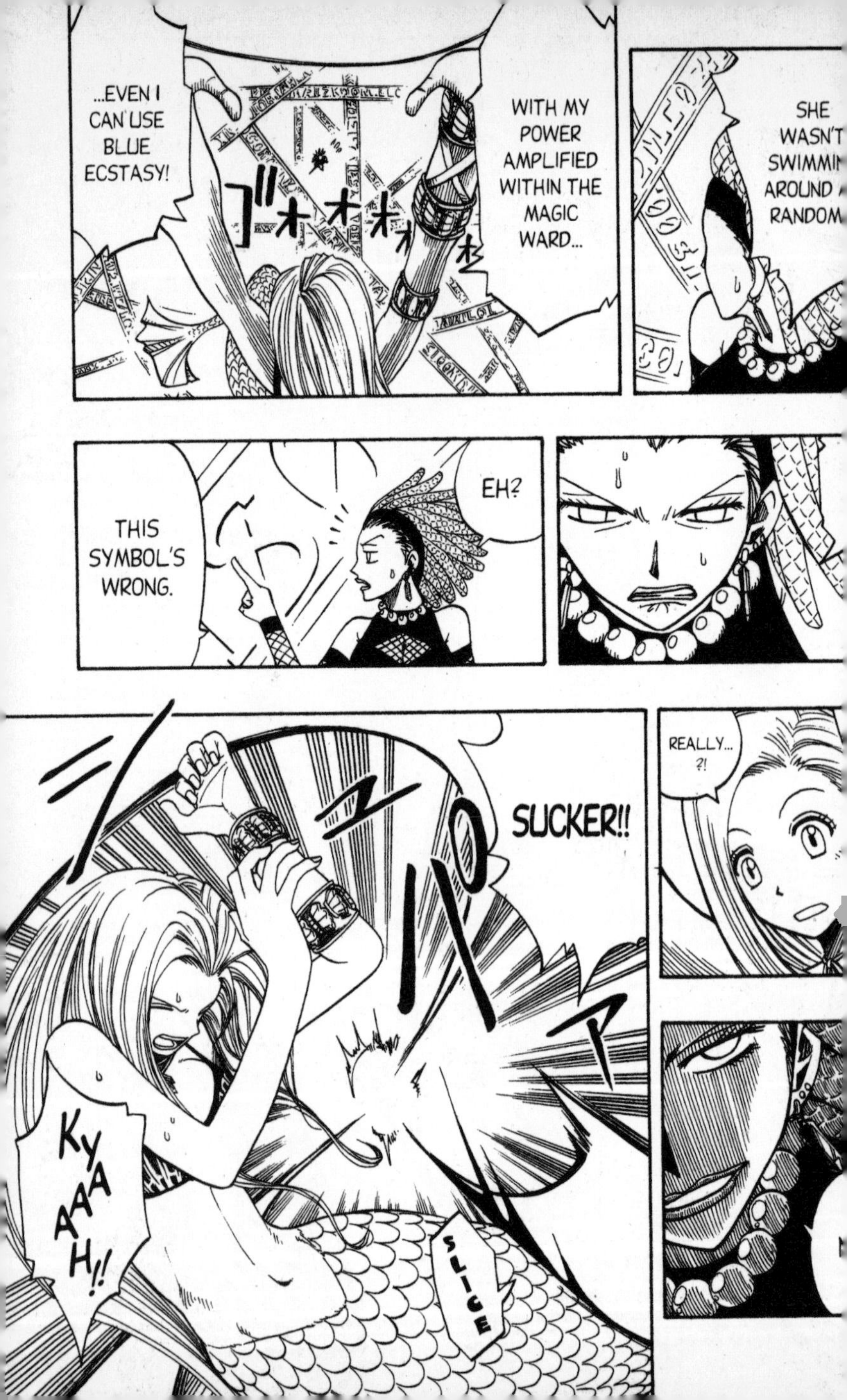
SHE WASN'T SWIMMIN AROUND A RANDOM
WITH MY POWER AMPLIFIED WITHIN THE MAGIC WARD...
...EVEN I CAN USE BLUE ECSTASY!
EH?
THIS SYMBOL'S WRONG.
REALLY... ?!
SUCKER!!
SLICE
KYAAAAH!!

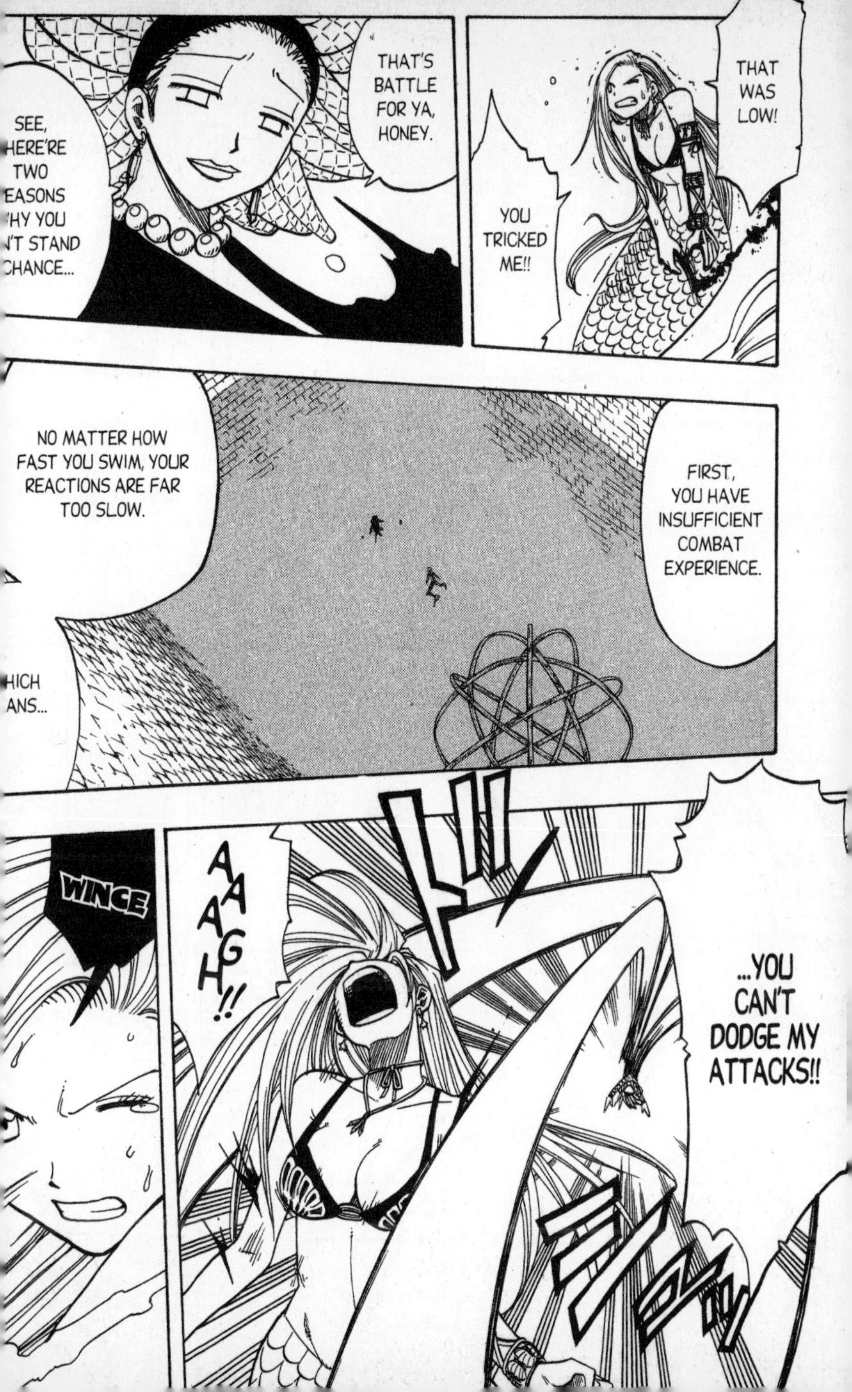
THAT WAS LOW!
YOU TRICKED ME!!
THAT'S BATTLE FOR YA, HONEY.
SEE, HERE'RE TWO EASONS HY YOU N'T STAND CHANCE...
FIRST, YOU HAVE INSUFFICIENT COMBAT EXPERIENCE.
NO MATTER HOW FAST YOU SWIM, YOUR REACTIONS ARE FAR TOO SLOW.
HICH ANS...
...YOU CAN'T DODGE MY ATTACKS!!
AAAGH!!
WINCE

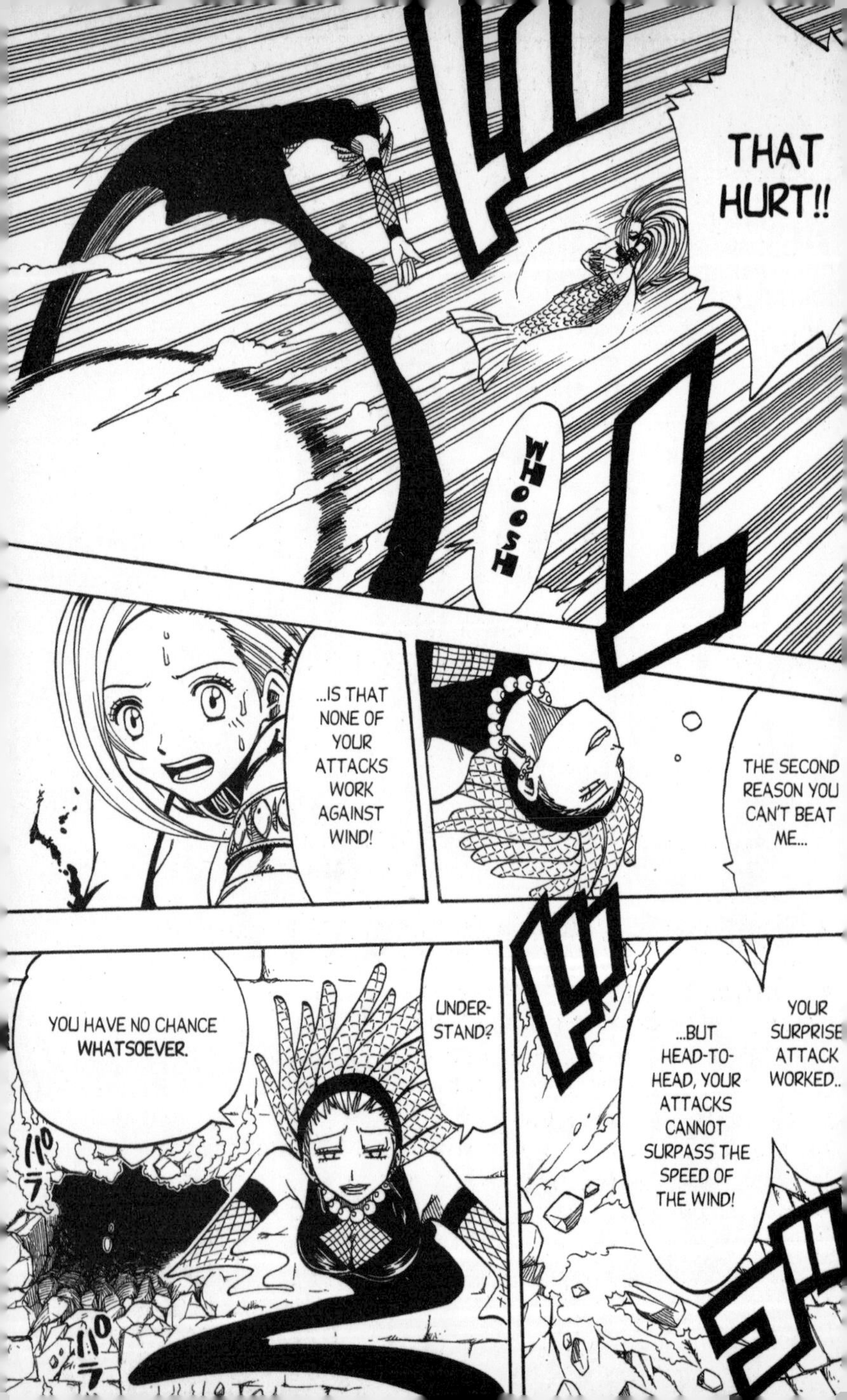
THAT HURT!!
WHOOSH
THE SECOND REASON YOU CAN'T BEAT ME...
...IS THAT NONE OF YOUR ATTACKS WORK AGAINST WIND!
YOUR SURPRISE ATTACK WORKED..
...BUT HEAD-TO-HEAD, YOUR ATTACKS CANNOT SURPASS THE SPEED OF THE WIND!
UNDERSTAND?
YOU HAVE NO CHANCE **WHATSOEVER.**

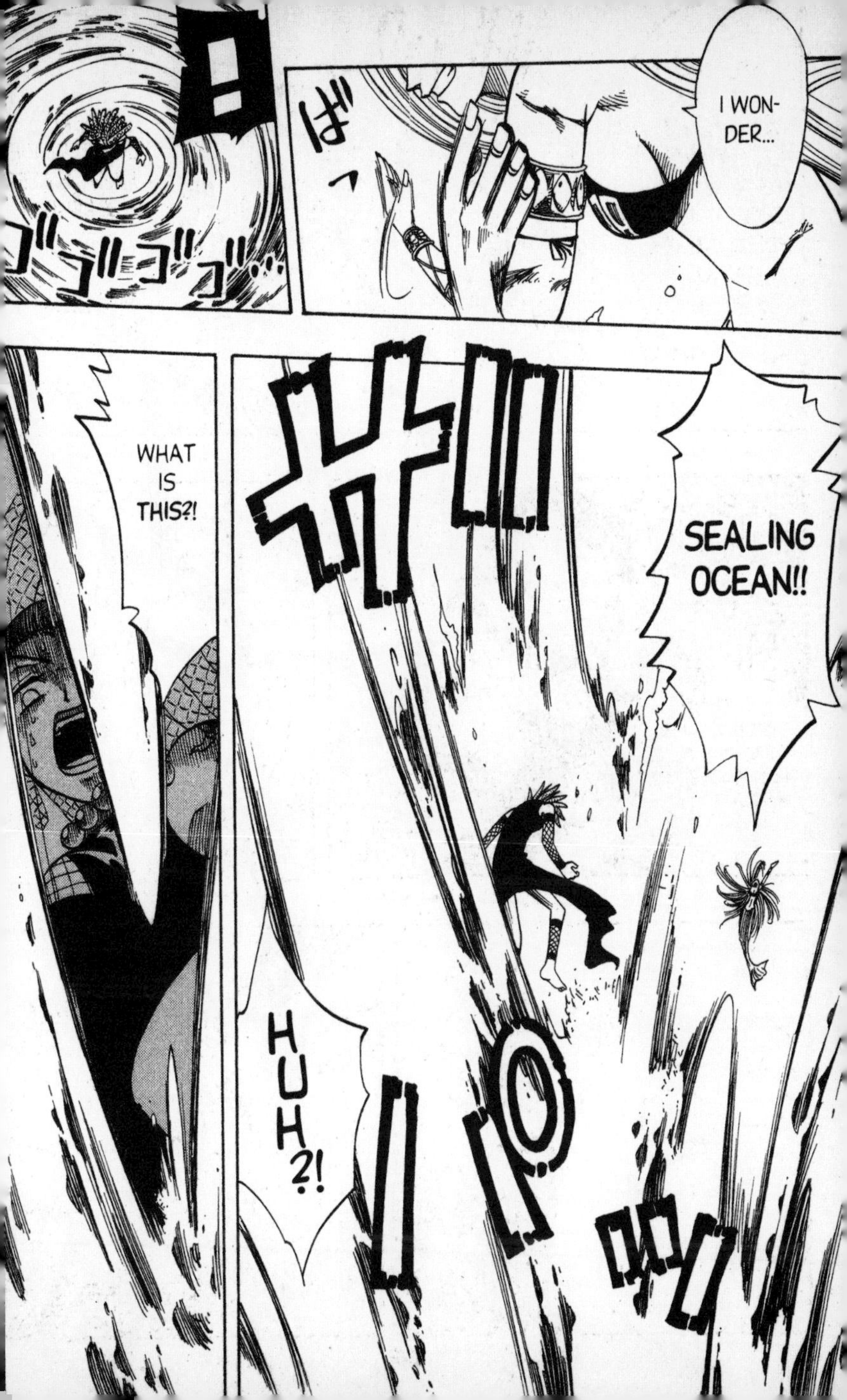

I WONDER...
ばっ
SEALING OCEAN!!
HUH?!
WHAT IS THIS?!

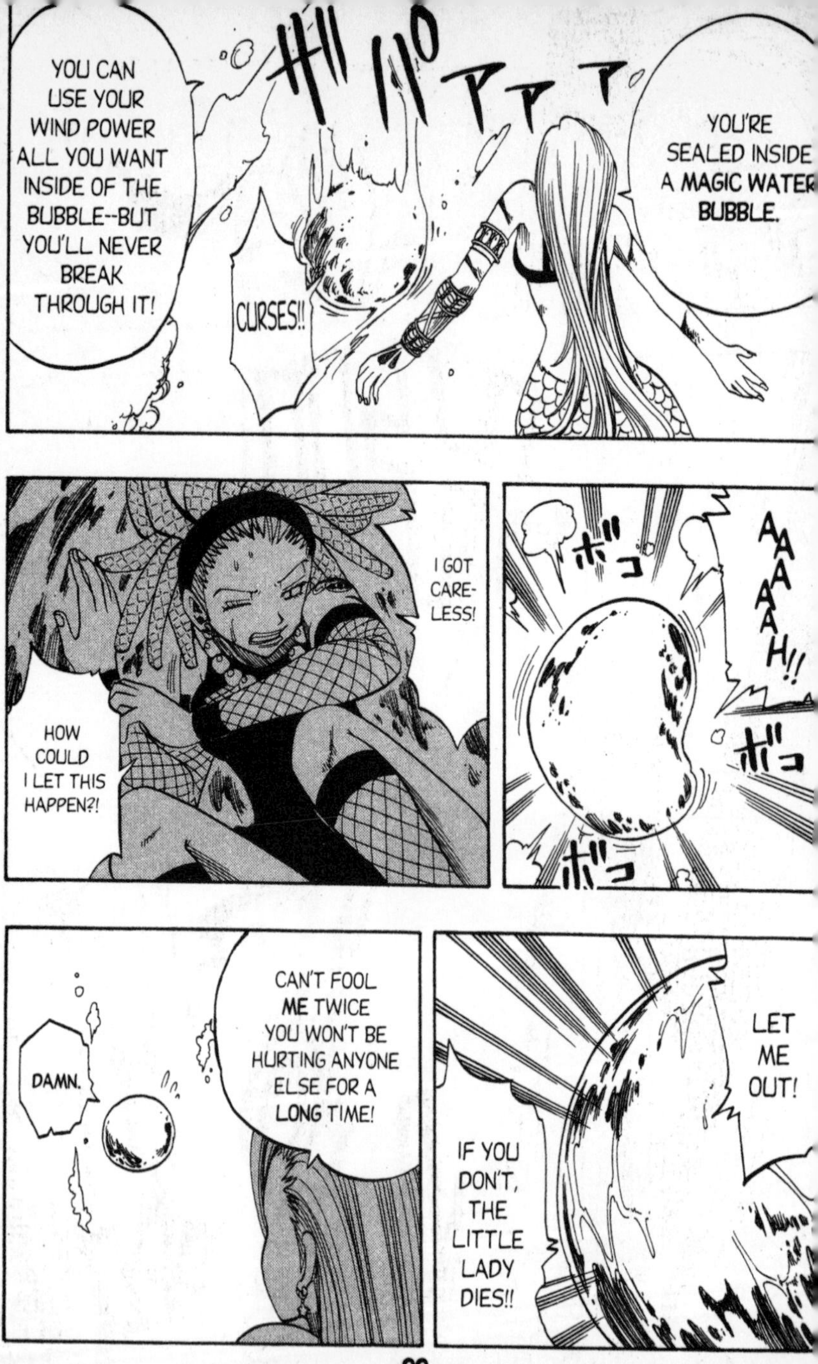

ザパァァァ
YOU'RE SEALED INSIDE A MAGIC WATER BUBBLE.
YOU CAN USE YOUR WIND POWER ALL YOU WANT INSIDE OF THE BUBBLE--BUT YOU'LL NEVER BREAK THROUGH IT!
CURSES!!
ボコ
AAAAAH!!
ボコ
ボコ
I GOT CARE-LESS!
HOW COULD I LET THIS HAPPEN?!
LET ME OUT!
IF YOU DON'T, THE LITTLE LADY DIES!!
CAN'T FOOL ME TWICE YOU WON'T BE HURTING ANYONE ELSE FOR A LONG TIME!
DAMN.

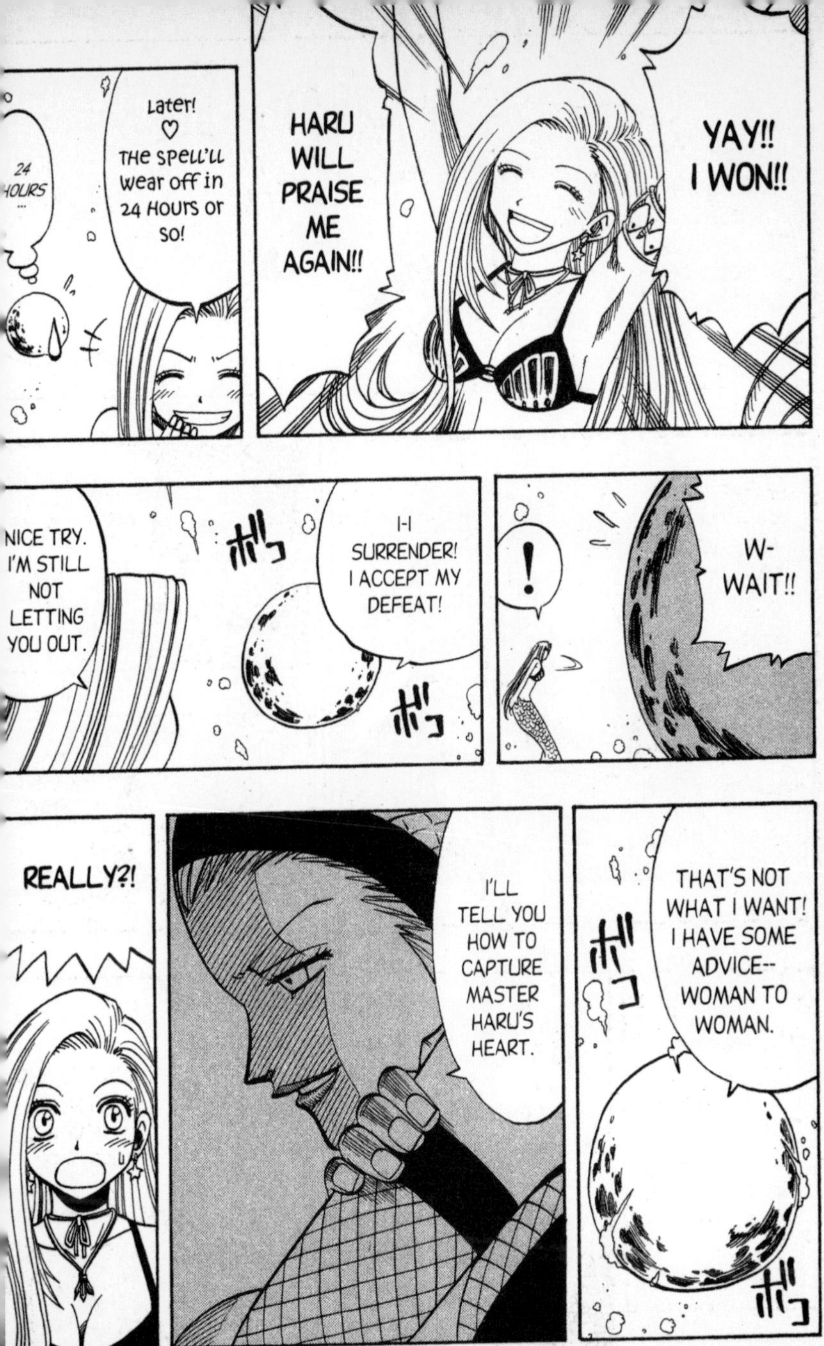
YAY!! I WON!!
HARU WILL PRAISE ME AGAIN!!
Later! ♡ The spell'll wear off in 24 Hours or so!
24 HOURS ...
W- WAIT!!
!
I-I SURRENDER! I ACCEPT MY DEFEAT!
ボコ
ボコ
NICE TRY. I'M STILL NOT LETTING YOU OUT.
THAT'S NOT WHAT I WANT! I HAVE SOME ADVICE-- WOMAN TO WOMAN.
ボコ
ボコ
I'LL TELL YOU HOW TO CAPTURE MASTER HARU'S HEART.
REALLY?!

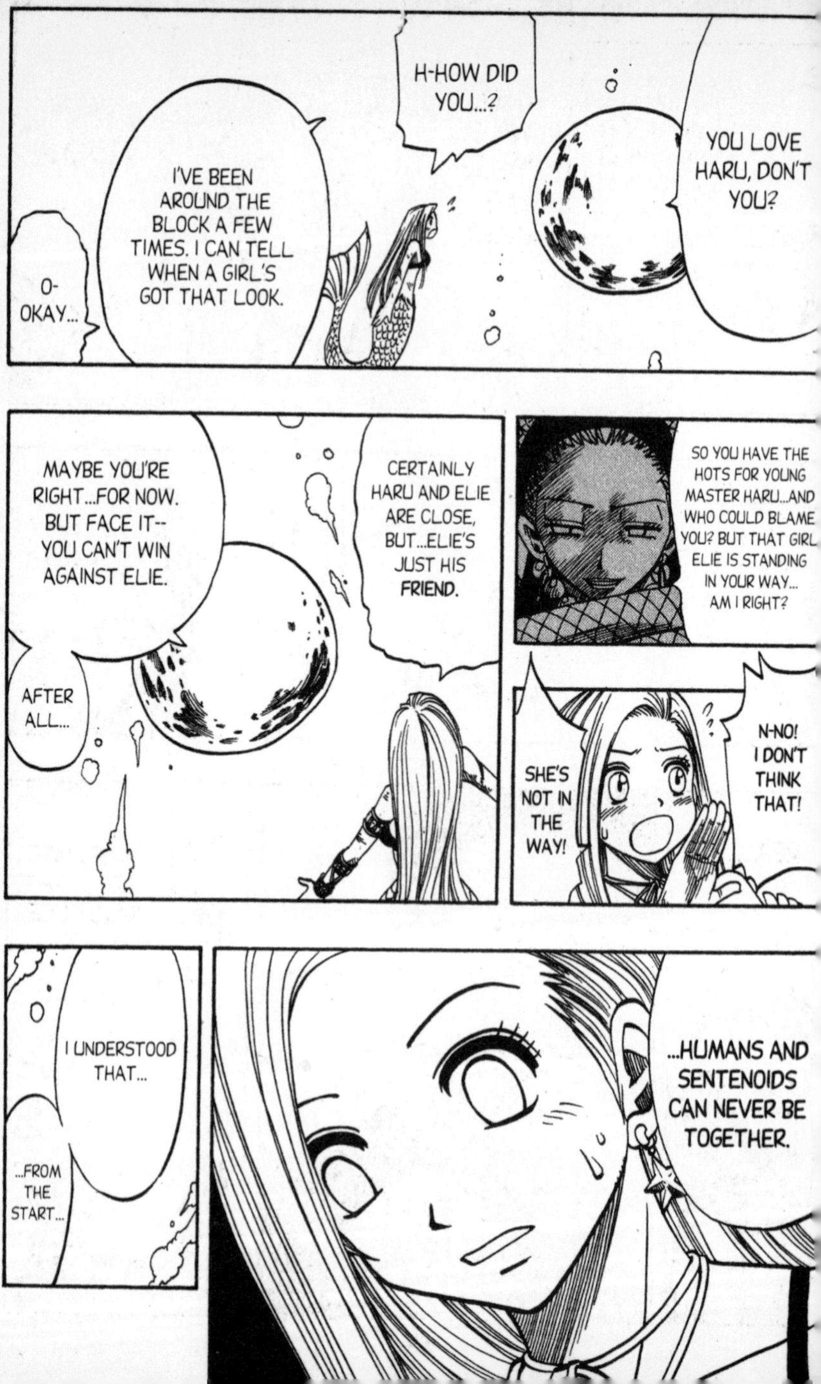
YOU LOVE HARU, DON'T YOU?
H-HOW DID YOU...?
I'VE BEEN AROUND THE BLOCK A FEW TIMES. I CAN TELL WHEN A GIRL'S GOT THAT LOOK.
O-OKAY...
SO YOU HAVE THE HOTS FOR YOUNG MASTER HARU...AND WHO COULD BLAME YOU? BUT THAT GIRL ELIE IS STANDING IN YOUR WAY... AM I RIGHT?
N-NO! I DON'T THINK THAT!
SHE'S NOT IN THE WAY!
CERTAINLY HARU AND ELIE ARE CLOSE, BUT...ELIE'S JUST HIS FRIEND.
MAYBE YOU'RE RIGHT...FOR NOW. BUT FACE IT-- YOU CAN'T WIN AGAINST ELIE.
AFTER ALL...
...HUMANS AND SENTENOIDS CAN NEVER BE TOGETHER.
I UNDERSTOOD THAT...
...FROM THE START...

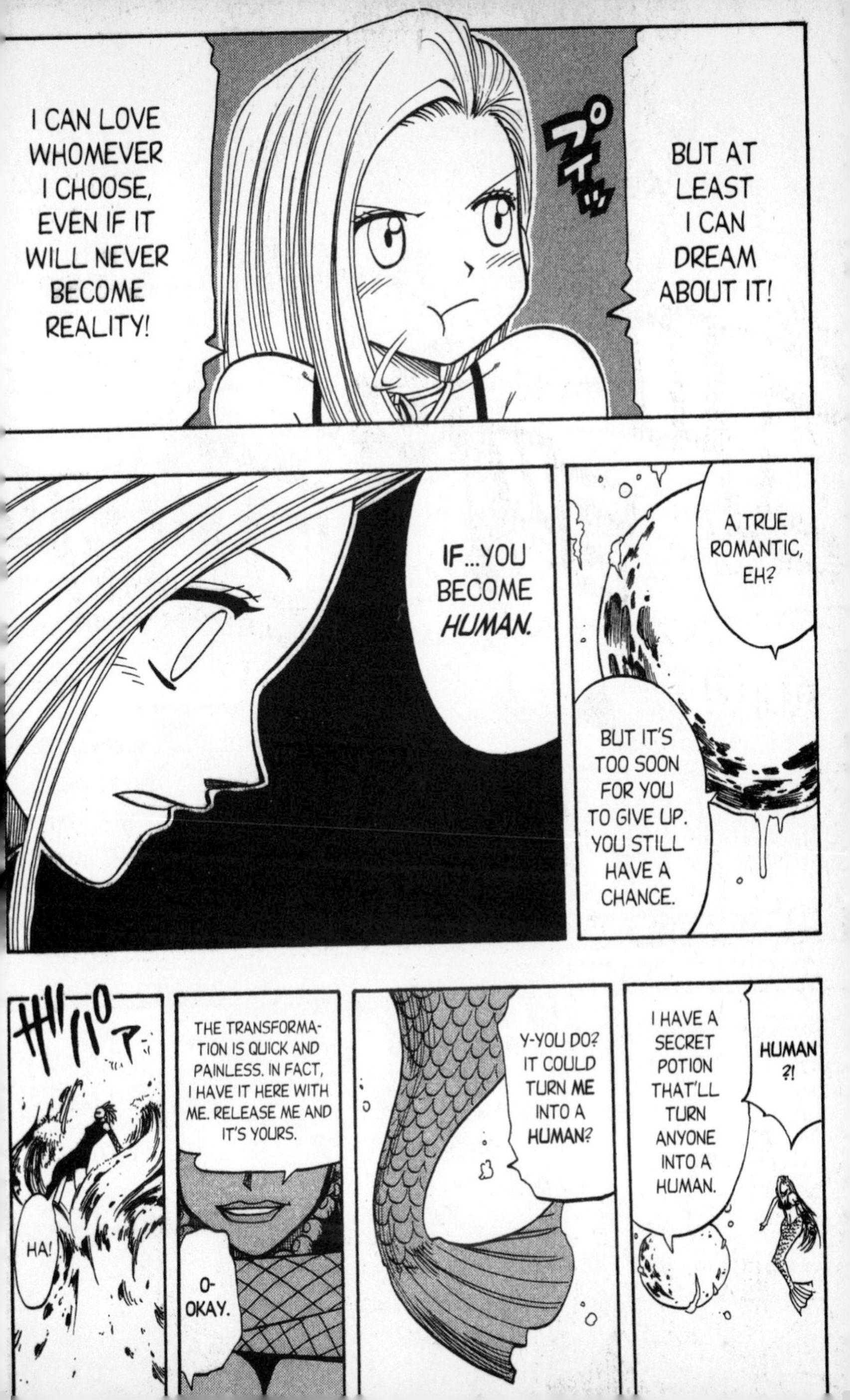
I CAN LOVE WHOMEVER I CHOOSE, EVEN IF IT WILL NEVER BECOME REALITY!
プイッ
BUT AT LEAST I CAN DREAM ABOUT IT!
A TRUE ROMANTIC, EH?
BUT IT'S TOO SOON FOR YOU TO GIVE UP. YOU STILL HAVE A CHANCE.
IF...YOU BECOME *HUMAN.*
HUMAN?!
I HAVE A SECRET POTION THAT'LL TURN ANYONE INTO A HUMAN.
Y-YOU DO? IT COULD TURN **ME** INTO A **HUMAN**?
THE TRANSFORMATION IS QUICK AND PAINLESS. IN FACT, I HAVE IT HERE WITH ME. RELEASE ME AND IT'S YOURS.
O-OKAY.
HA!

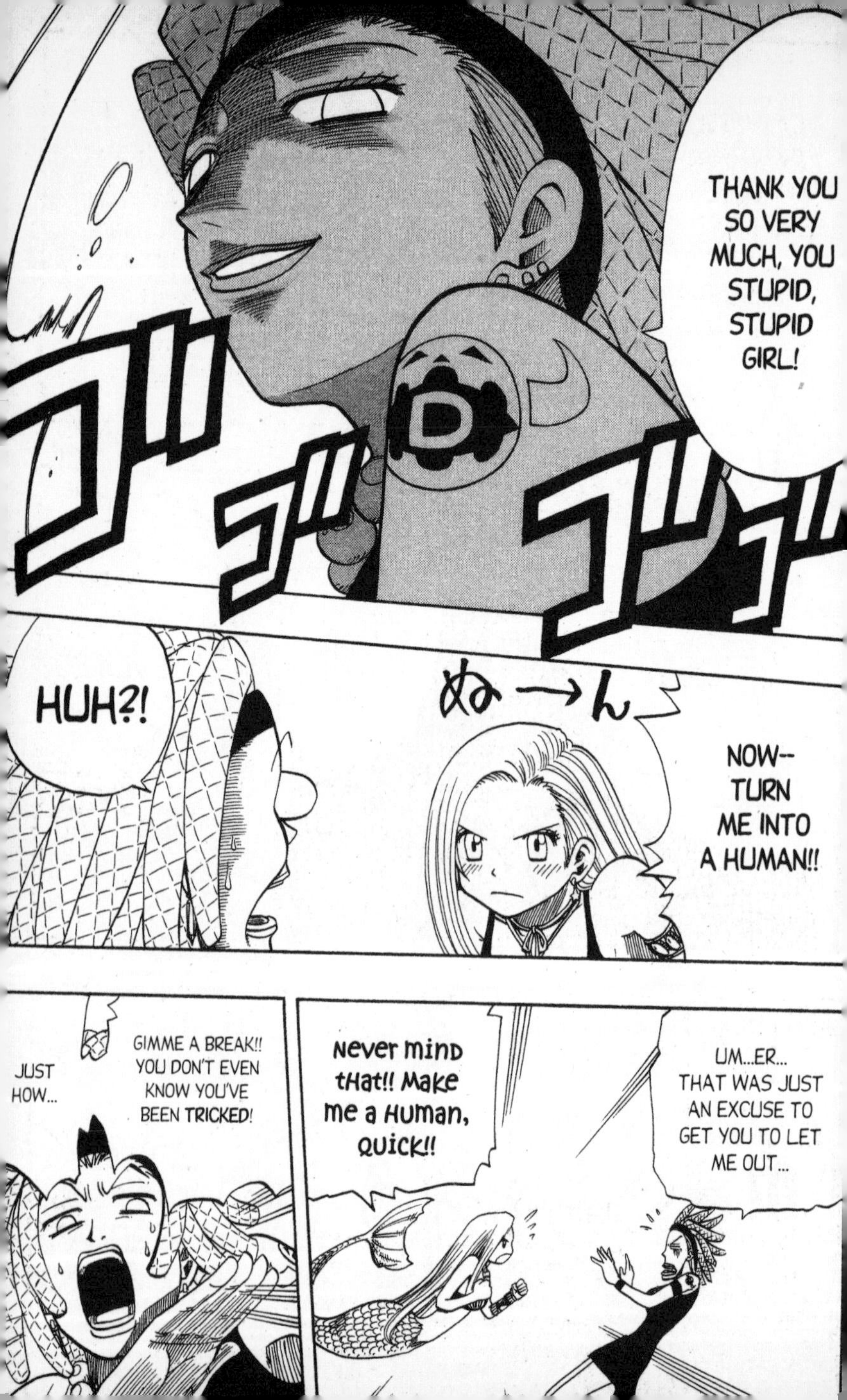
THANK YOU SO VERY MUCH, YOU STUPID, STUPID GIRL!
ゴゴゴゴ
NOW-- TURN ME INTO A HUMAN!!
ぬ→ん
HUH?!
UM...ER... THAT WAS JUST AN EXCUSE TO GET YOU TO LET ME OUT...
Never mind that!! Make me a Human, QUICK!!
GIMME A BREAK!! YOU DON'T EVEN KNOW YOU'VE BEEN TRICKED!
JUST HOW...

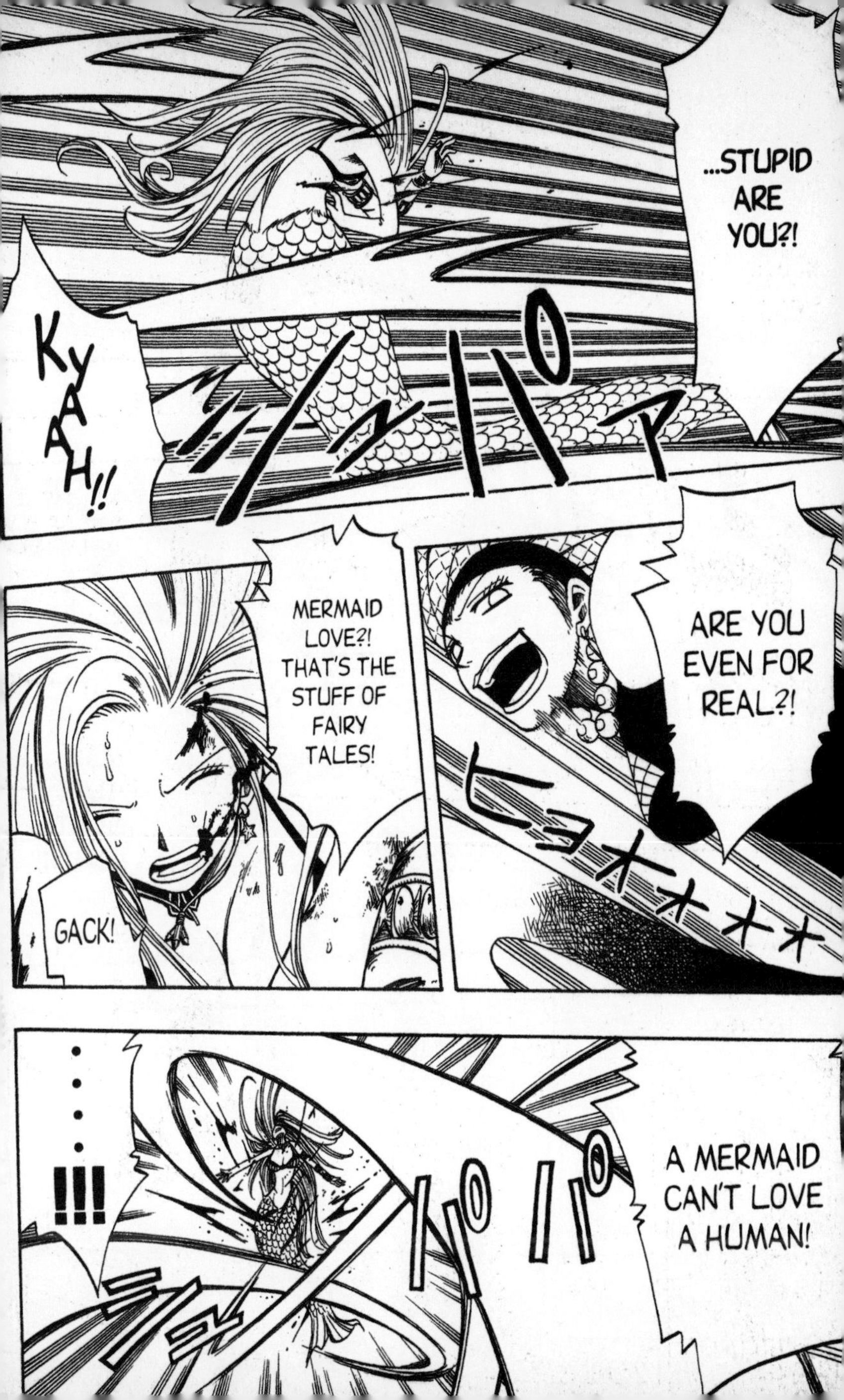
...STUPID ARE YOU?!
KYAAAH!!
ARE YOU EVEN FOR REAL?!
ヒョオオオオオ
MERMAID LOVE?! THAT'S THE STUFF OF FAIRY TALES!
GACK!
A MERMAID CAN'T LOVE A HUMAN!
......!!!

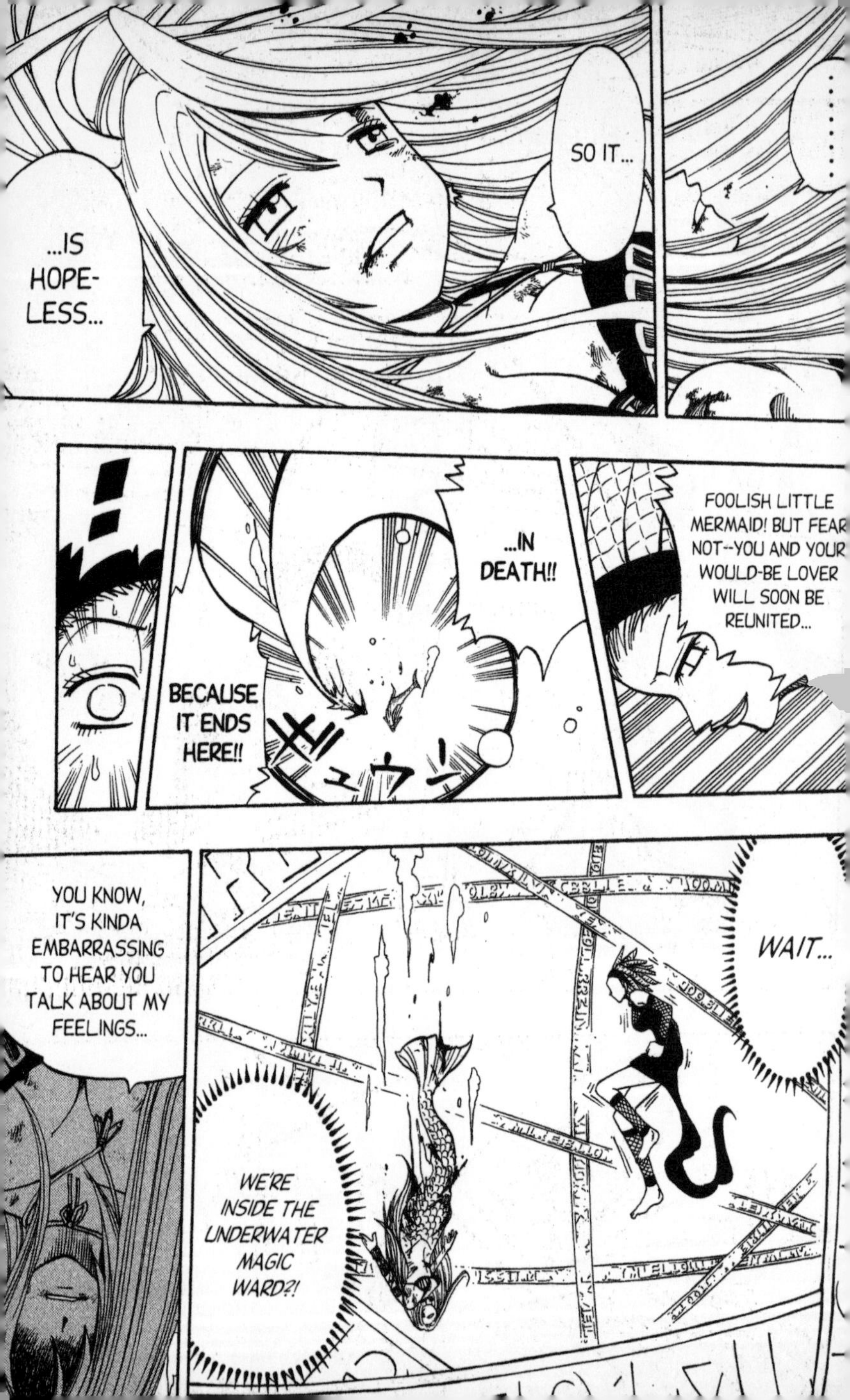
SO IT...
...IS HOPE-LESS...
FOOLISH LITTLE MERMAID! BUT FEAR NOT--YOU AND YOUR WOULD-BE LOVER WILL SOON BE REUNITED...
...IN DEATH!!
BECAUSE IT ENDS HERE!!
!
WAIT...
WE'RE INSIDE THE UNDERWATER MAGIC WARD?!
YOU KNOW, IT'S KINDA EMBARRASSING TO HEAR YOU TALK ABOUT MY FEELINGS...

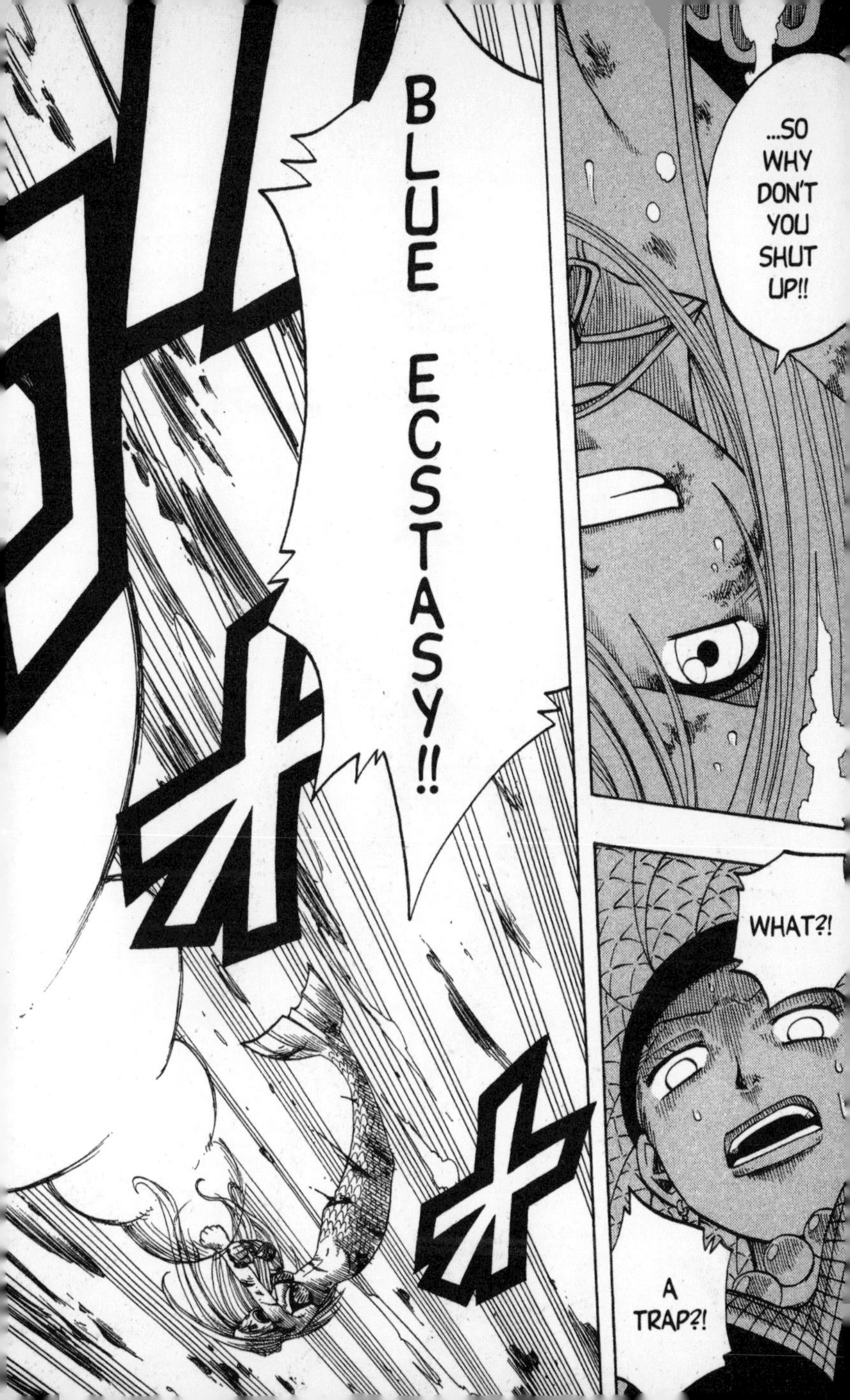
...SO WHY DON'T YOU SHUT UP!!
WHAT?!
A TRAP?!
BLUE ECSTASY!!

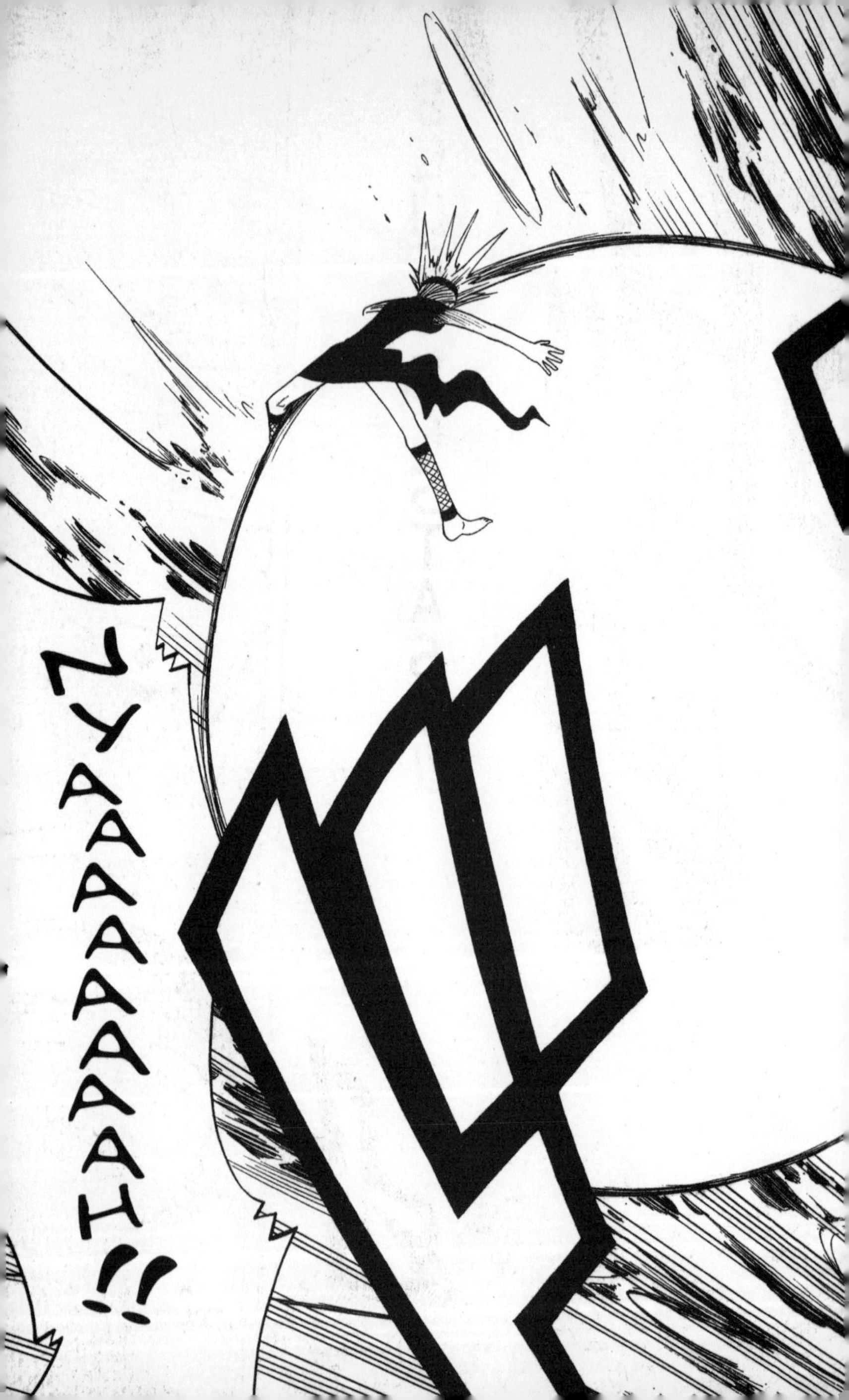
ZYAAAAAAAH!!

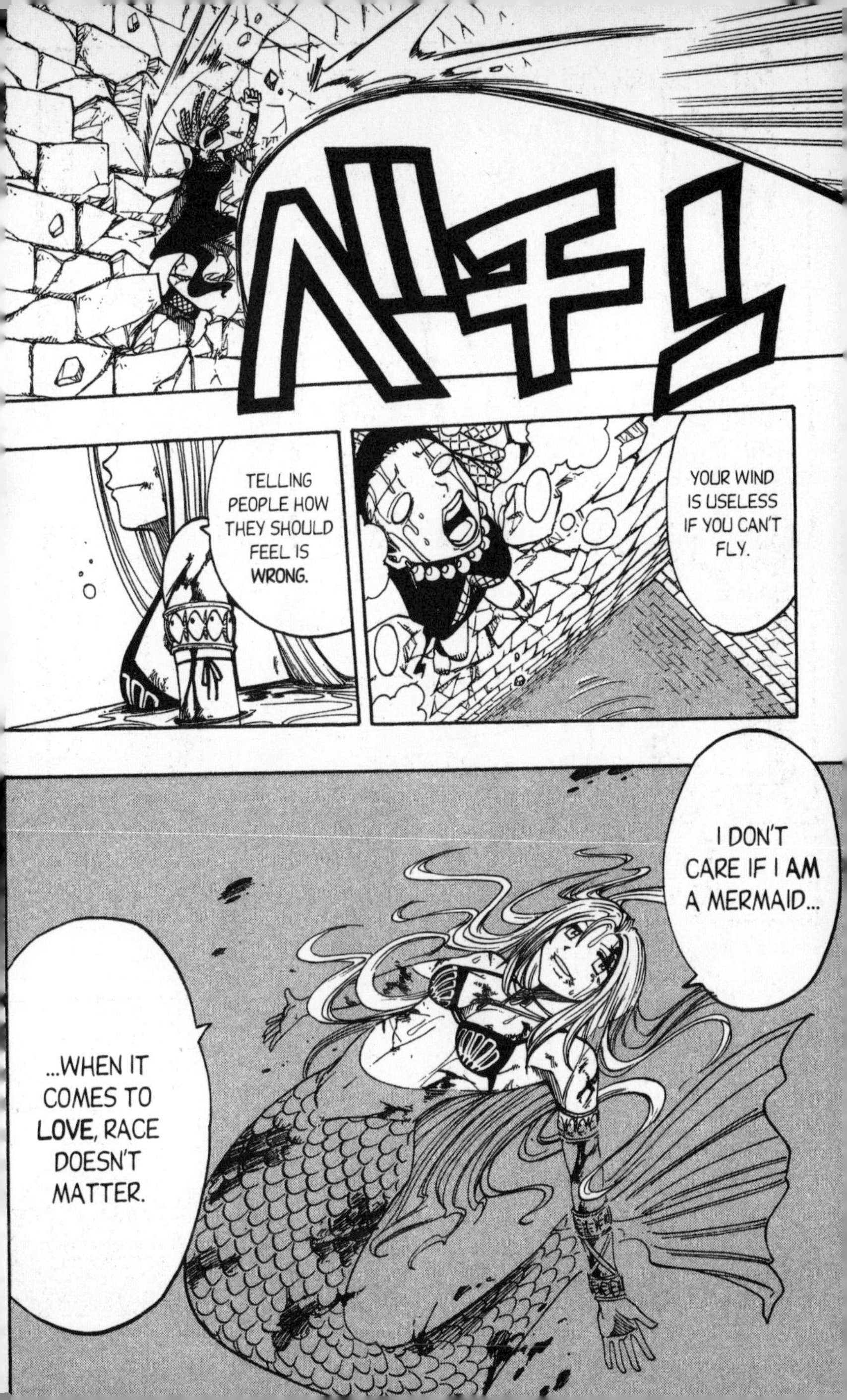
YOUR WIND IS USELESS IF YOU CAN'T FLY.
TELLING PEOPLE HOW THEY SHOULD FEEL IS WRONG.
I DON'T CARE IF I AM A MERMAID...
...WHEN IT COMES TO LOVE, RACE DOESN'T MATTER.

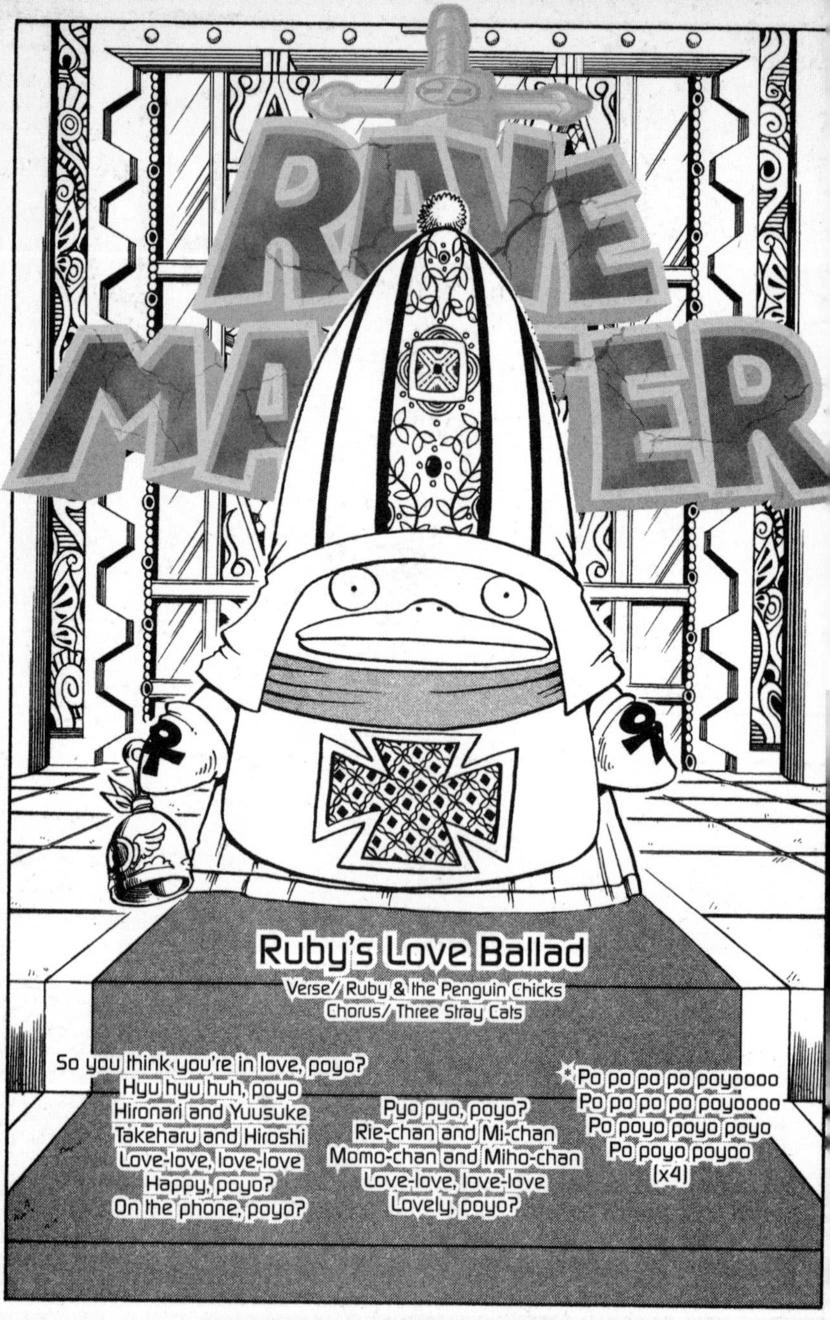
RAVE MASTER
Ruby's Love Ballad
Verse/ Ruby & the Penguin Chicks
Chorus/ Three Stray Cats
So you think you're in love, poyo?
Hyu hyu huh, poyo
Hironari and Yuusuke
Takeharu and Hiroshi
Love-love, love-love
Happy, poyo?
On the phone, poyo?
Pyo pyo, poyo?
Rie-chan and Mi-chan
Momo-chan and Miho-chan
Love-love, love-love
Lovely, poyo?
*Po po po po poyoooo
Po po po po poyoooo
Po poyo poyo poyo
Po poyo poyoo
(x4)

RAVE:120 DARKNESS FALLS

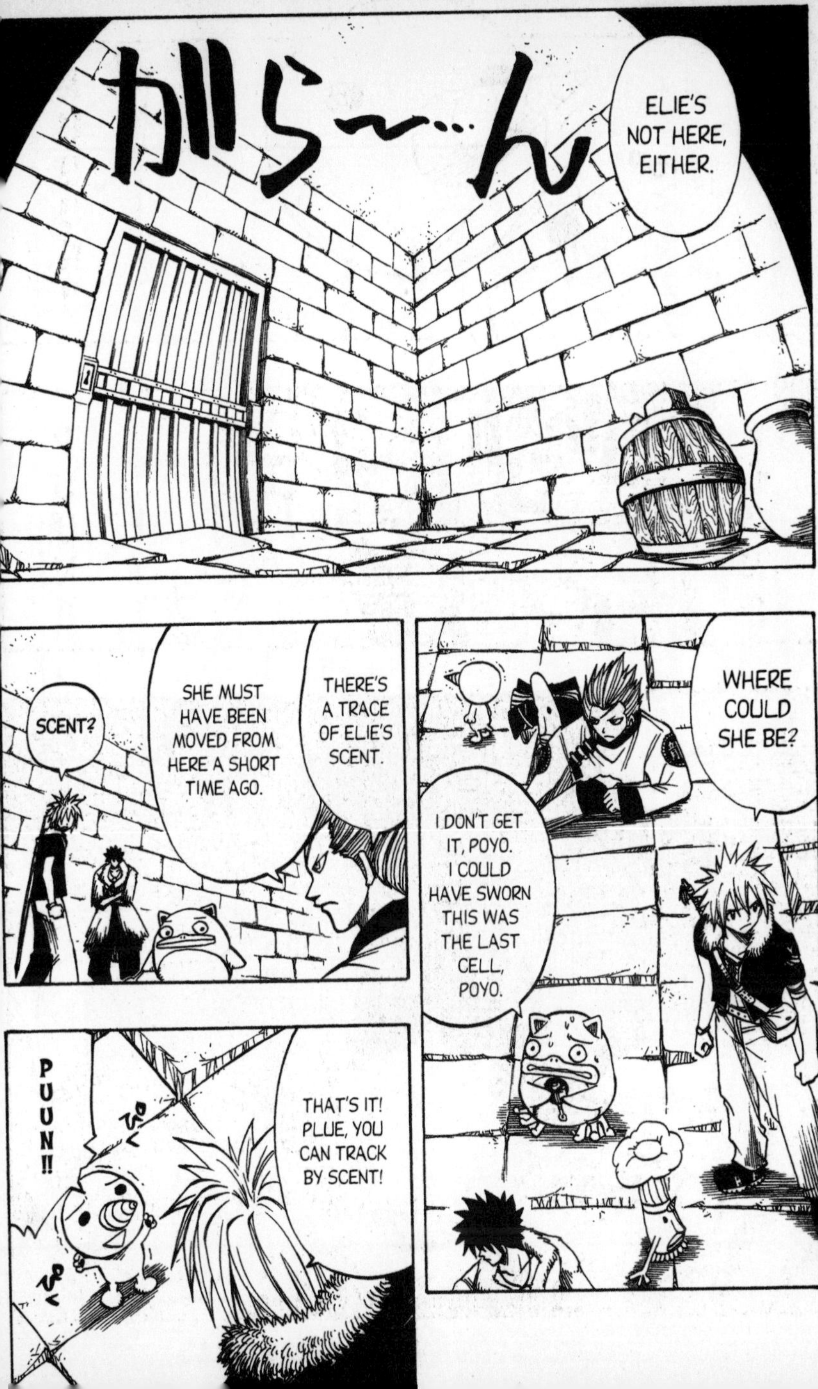
がら～ん
ELIE'S NOT HERE, EITHER.
WHERE COULD SHE BE?
I DON'T GET IT, POYO. I COULD HAVE SWORN THIS WAS THE LAST CELL, POYO.
THERE'S A TRACE OF ELIE'S SCENT.
SHE MUST HAVE BEEN MOVED FROM HERE A SHORT TIME AGO.
SCENT?
THAT'S IT! PLUE, YOU CAN TRACK BY SCENT!
ぴく
PUUN!!
ぴく

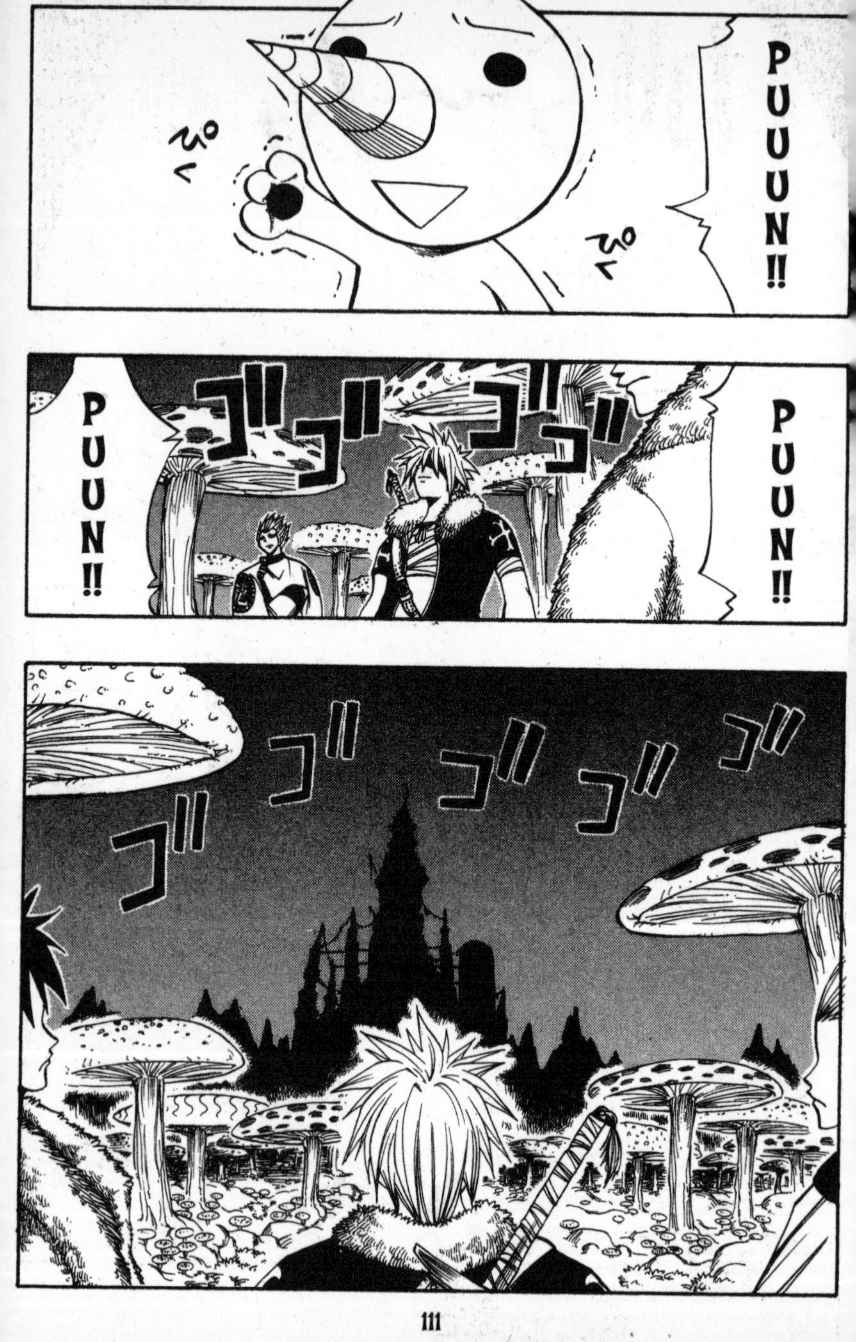
PUUUN!!
PUUN!!
ゴゴゴゴ
PUUN!!
ゴゴゴゴゴ

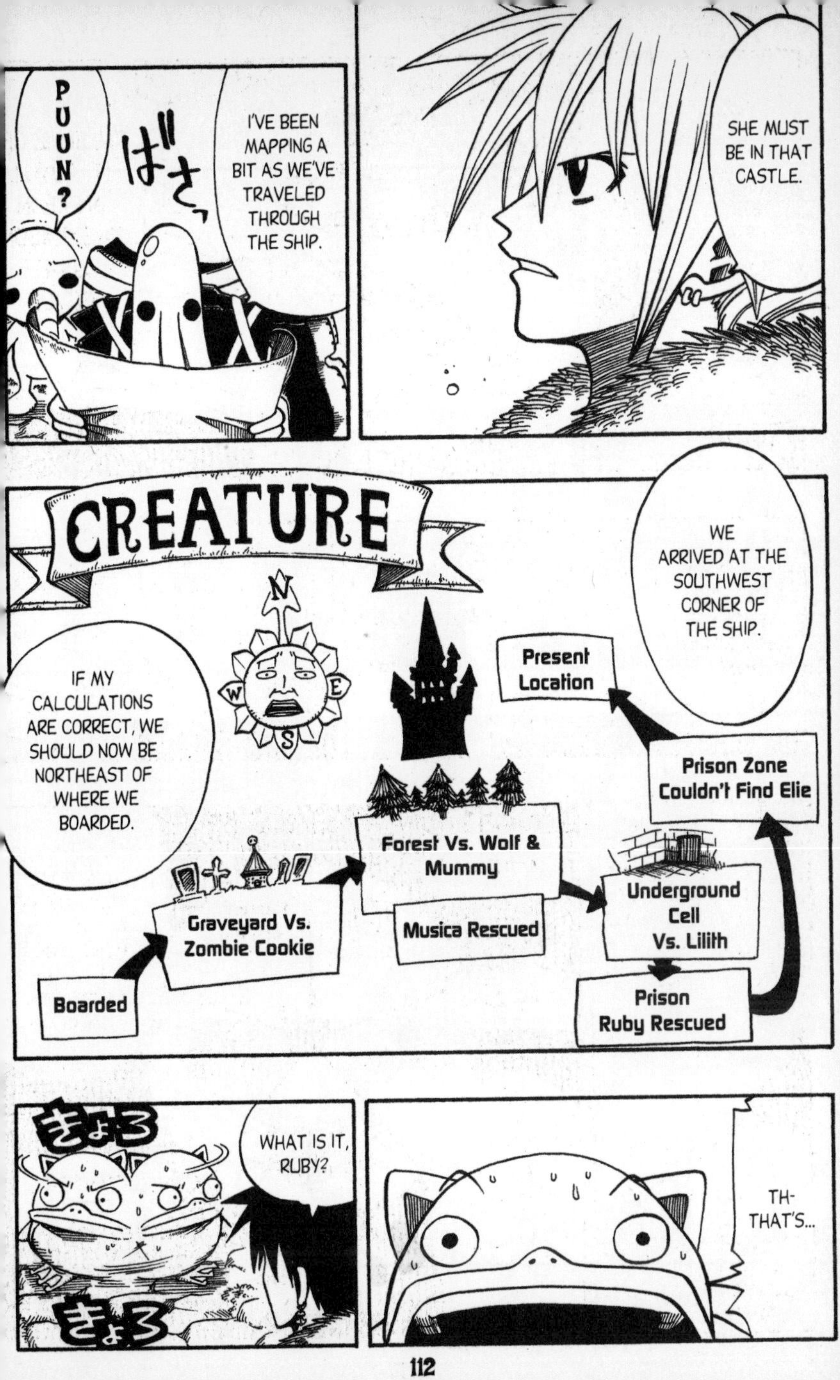
SHE MUST BE IN THAT CASTLE.
I'VE BEEN MAPPING A BIT AS WE'VE TRAVELED THROUGH THE SHIP.
ばさっ
PUUN?
WE ARRIVED AT THE SOUTHWEST CORNER OF THE SHIP.
CREATURE
N
E
W
S
Present Location
Prison Zone Couldn't Find Elie
Forest Vs. Wolf & Mummy
Musica Rescued
Underground Cell Vs. Lilith
Prison Ruby Rescued
Graveyard Vs. Zombie Cookie
Boarded
IF MY CALCULATIONS ARE CORRECT, WE SHOULD NOW BE NORTHEAST OF WHERE WE BOARDED.
TH- THAT'S...
WHAT IS IT, RUBY?
きょろ
きょろ

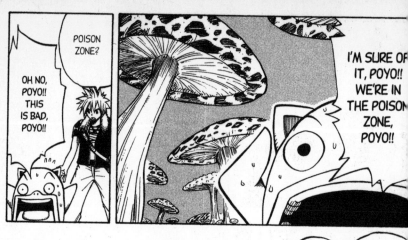

I'M SURE OF IT, POYO!! WE'RE IN THE POISON ZONE, POYO!!
POISON ZONE?
OH NO, POYO!! THIS IS BAD, POYO!!
NOW THAT YOU MENTION IT THERE ARE A LOT OF TOXIC MUSHROOMS HERE.
MR. RUBY, PLEASE CALM DOWN AND EXPLAIN.
SHUDDEr...
DORYU'S SHIP, CREATURE, IS DIVIDED INTO FIVE ZONES, POYO.
ズズズ…
EACH IS RUN BY A DIFFERENT MEMBER OF DORYU'S ARMY, POYO.
COOKIE RAN THE TOMB ZONE, MUMMY AND HIS WOLVES THE WOOD ZONE... LILITH THE TEMPTATION ZONE...
Troll Zone
Present Location
Tomb Zone
Temptation Zone
Wood Zone
THE TROLL ZONE IN THE UPPER-LEFT SECTION IS RUN BY FRANKEN BILLY...
...AND IN THE UPPER-RIGHT CORNER, WHERE WE ARE NOW, IS THE POISON ZONE...
Poison Zone
...WHICH IS CONTROLLED BY THE DORYU GHOST SQUAD'S MIGHTIEST WARRIOR...

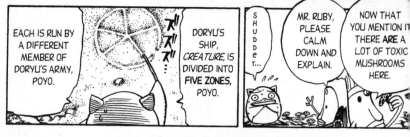

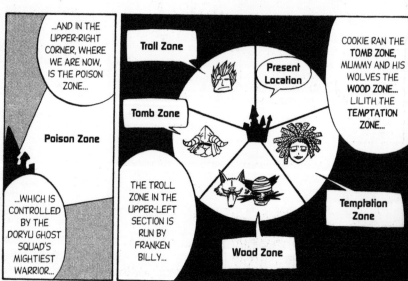

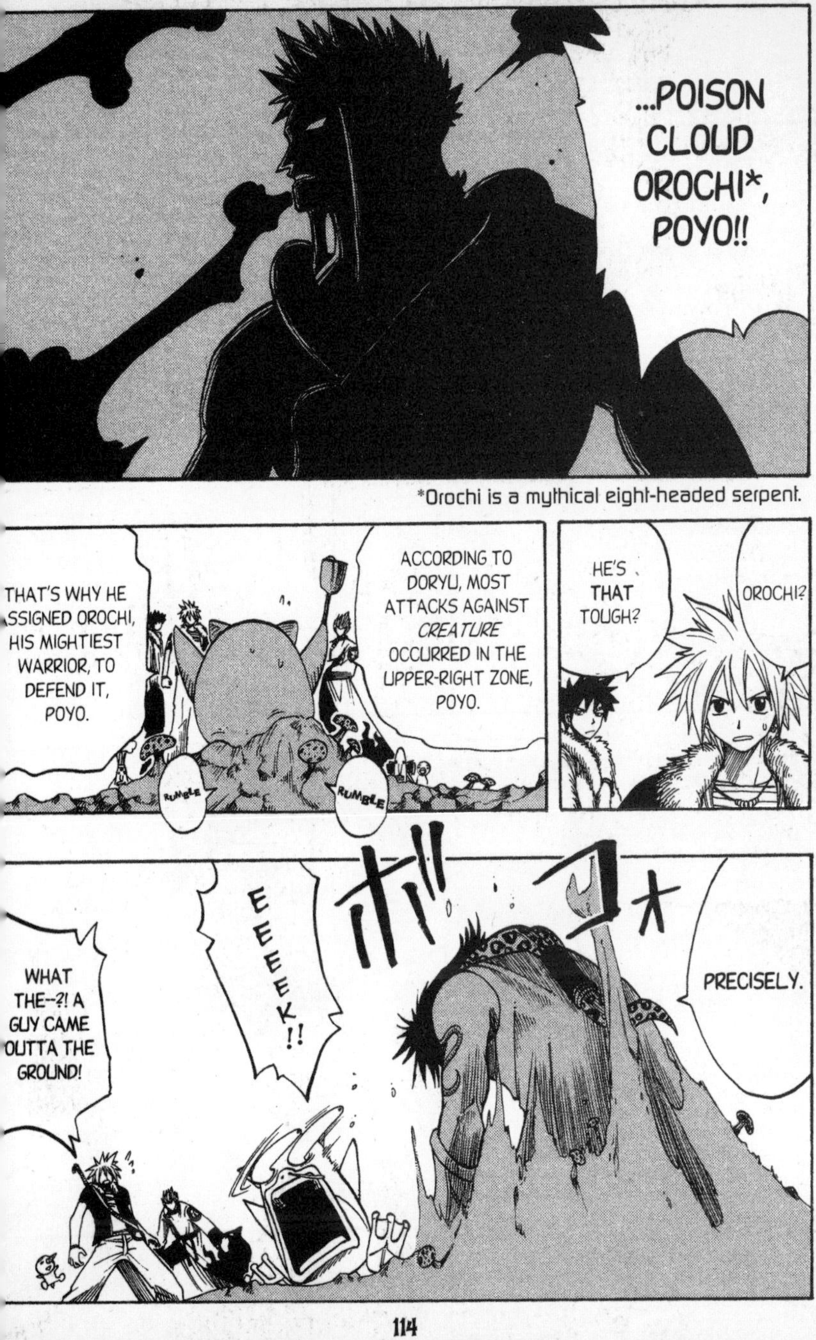

...POISON CLOUD OROCHI*, POYO!!
OROCHI?
HE'S THAT TOUGH?
ACCORDING TO DORYU, MOST ATTACKS AGAINST CREATURE OCCURRED IN THE UPPER-RIGHT ZONE, POYO.
THAT'S WHY HE SSIGNED OROCHI, HIS MIGHTIEST WARRIOR, TO DEFEND IT, POYO.
RUMBLE
RUMBLE
PRECISELY.
EEEEK!!
WHAT THE--?! A GUY CAME OUTTA THE GROUND!

*Orochi is a mythical eight-headed serpent.

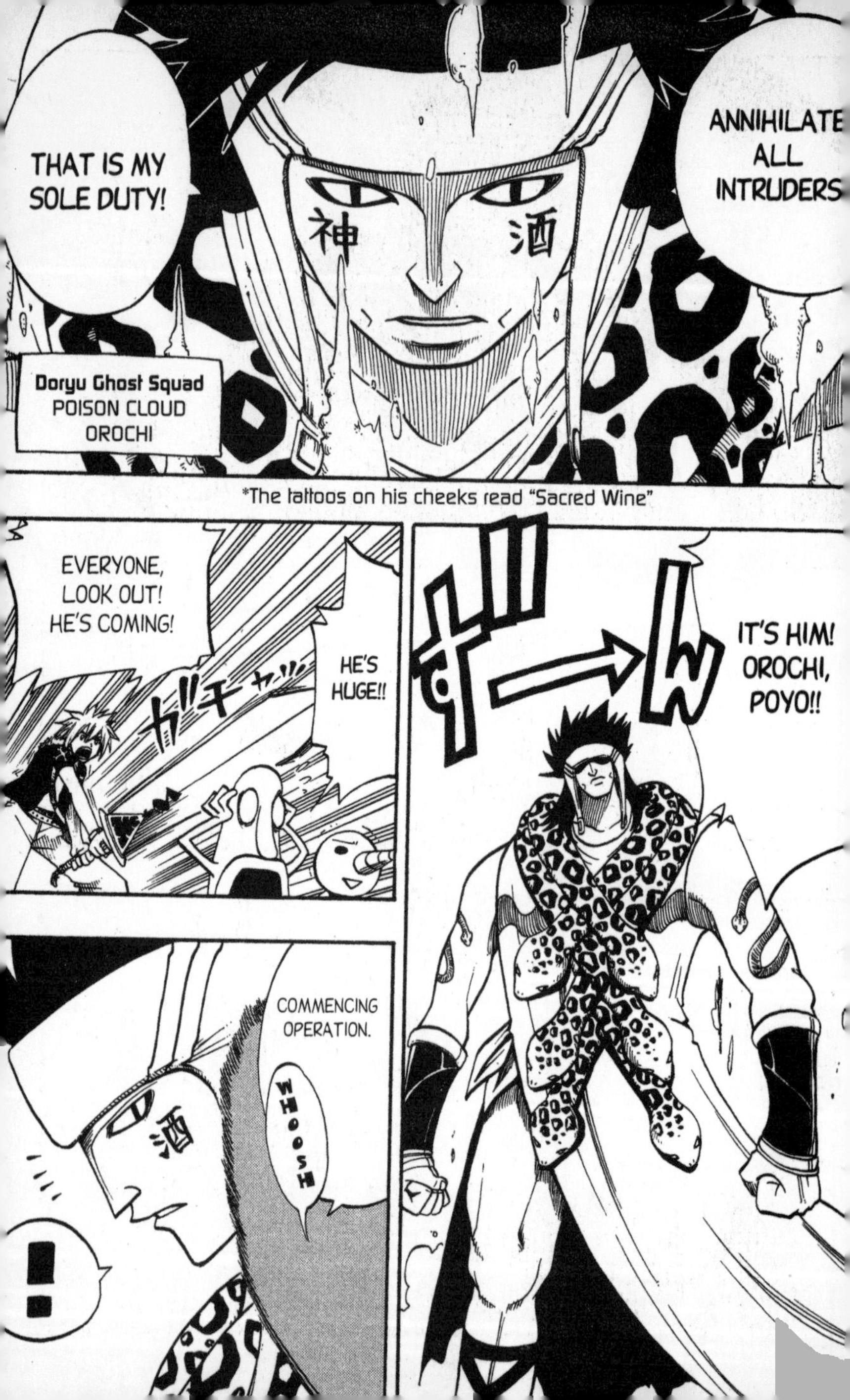
ANNIHILATE ALL INTRUDERS
THAT IS MY SOLE DUTY!
神
酒
Doryu Ghost Squad
POISON CLOUD OROCHI
ずーん
IT'S HIM! OROCHI, POYO!!
EVERYONE, LOOK OUT! HE'S COMING!
HE'S HUGE!!
ガチャ
COMMENCING OPERATION.
WHOOSH
酒
!!
*The tattoos on his cheeks read "Sacred Wine"

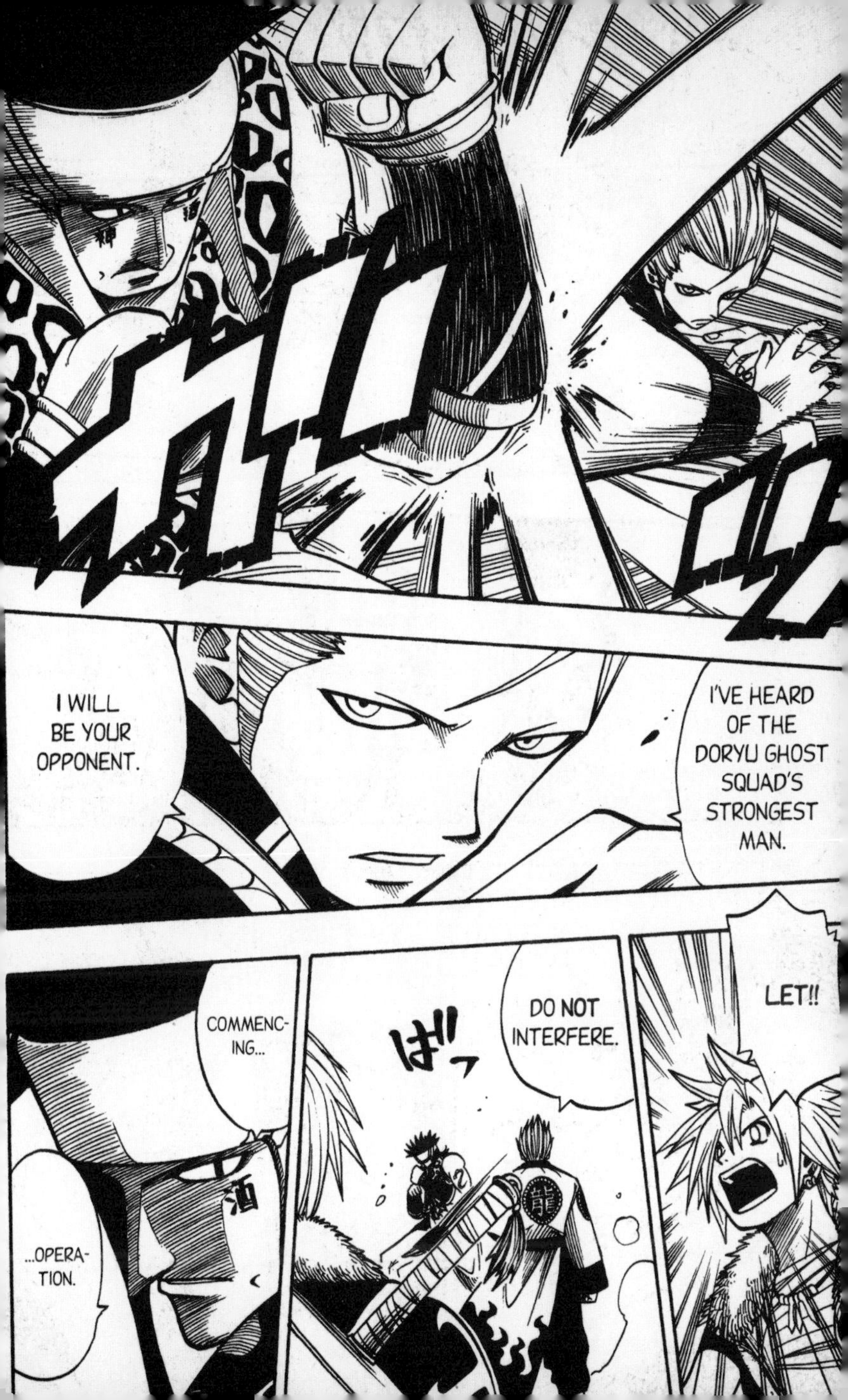
I'VE HEARD OF THE DORYU GHOST SQUAD'S STRONGEST MAN.
I WILL BE YOUR OPPONENT.
LET!!
DO NOT INTERFERE.
ばっ
COMMENC-ING...
...OPERA-TION.

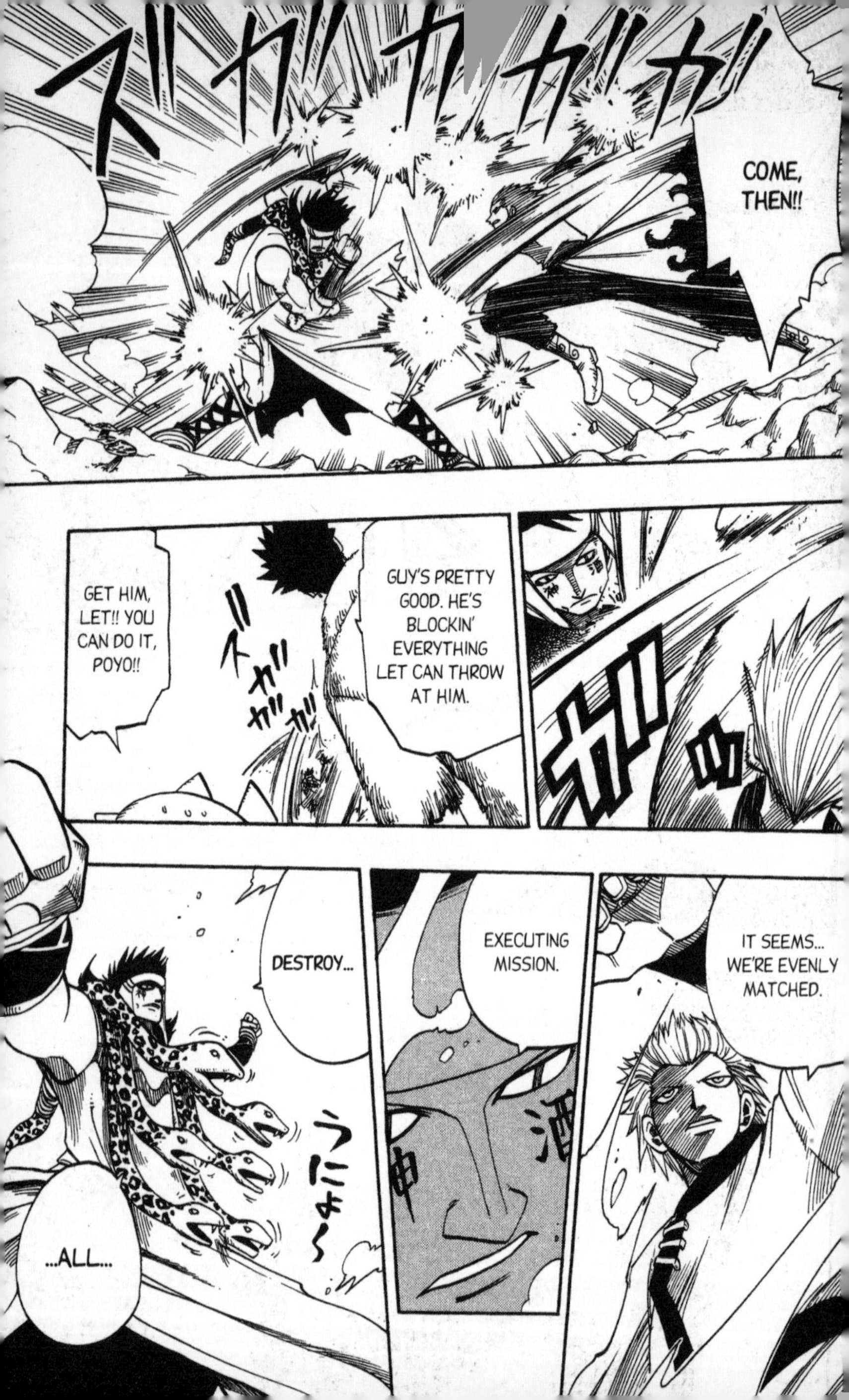
COME, THEN!!
GUY'S PRETTY GOOD. HE'S BLOCKIN' EVERYTHING LET CAN THROW AT HIM.
GET HIM, LET!! YOU CAN DO IT, POYO!!
IT SEEMS... WE'RE EVENLY MATCHED.
EXECUTING MISSION.
DESTROY...
...ALL...
うにょ〜

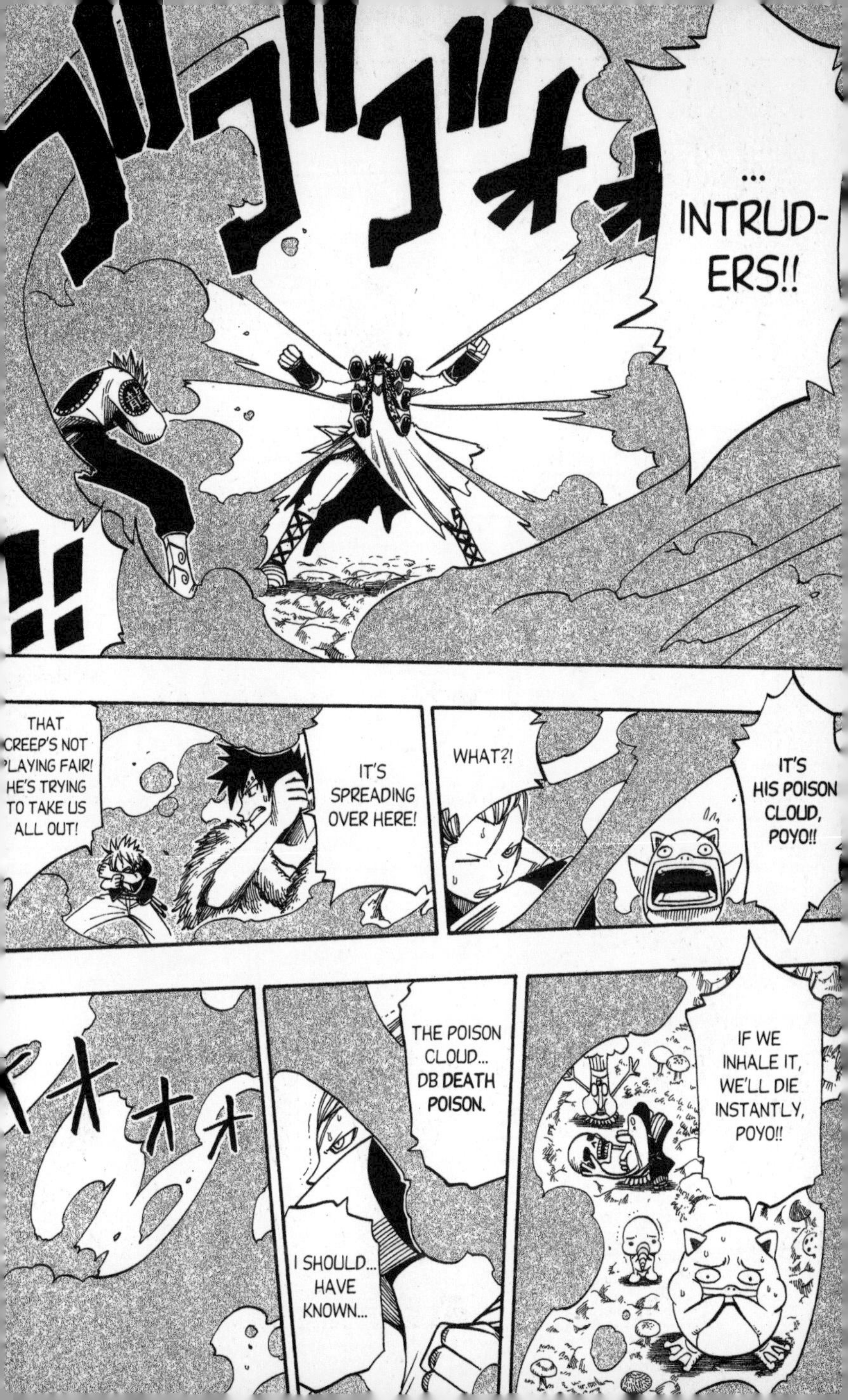

... INTRUDERS!!
!!
IT'S HIS POISON CLOUD, POYO!!
WHAT?!
IT'S SPREADING OVER HERE!
THAT CREEP'S NOT PLAYING FAIR! HE'S TRYING TO TAKE US ALL OUT!
IF WE INHALE IT, WE'LL DIE INSTANTLY, POYO!!
THE POISON CLOUD... DB DEATH POISON.
I SHOULD... HAVE KNOWN...

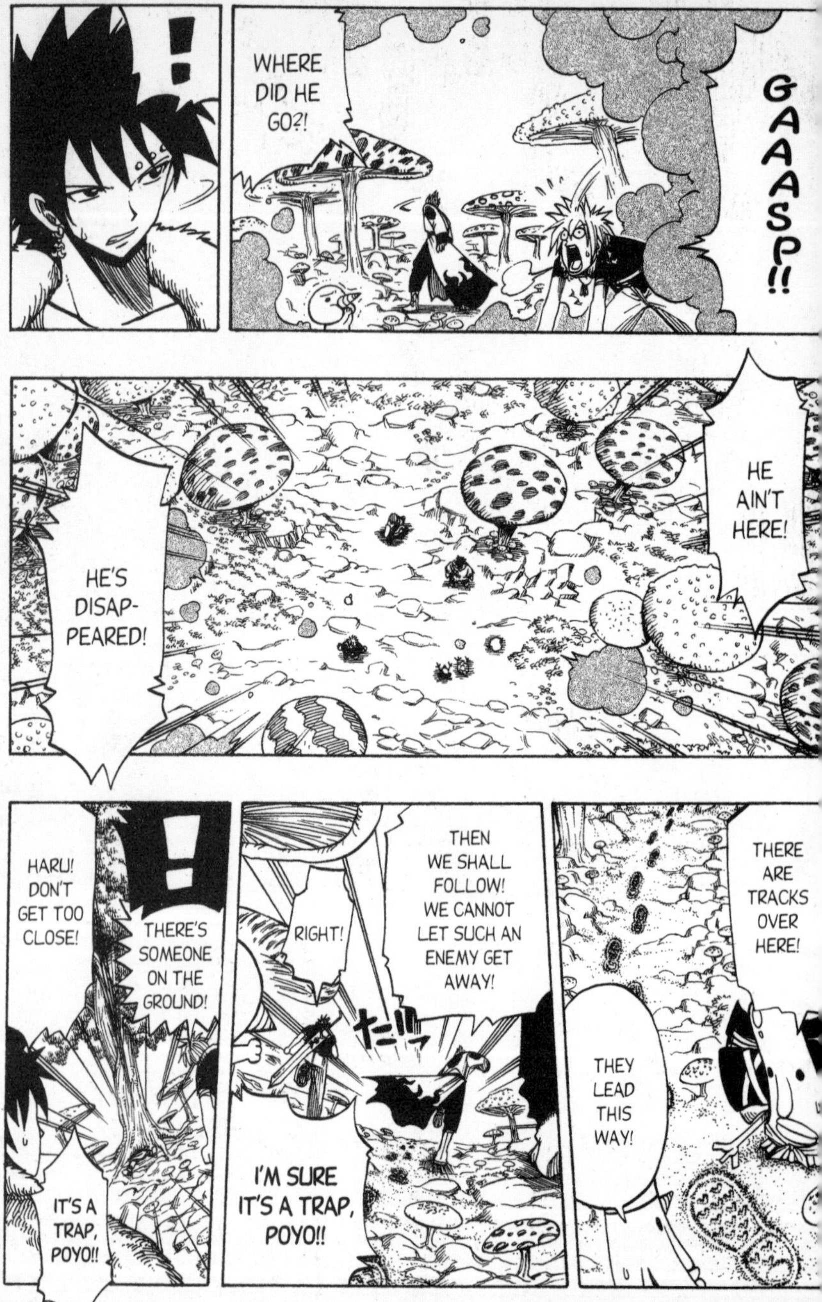
GAAASP!!
WHERE DID HE GO?!
!
HE AIN'T HERE!
HE'S DISAP-PEARED!
THERE ARE TRACKS OVER HERE!
THEY LEAD THIS WAY!
THEN WE SHALL FOLLOW! WE CANNOT LET SUCH AN ENEMY GET AWAY!
RIGHT!
I'M SURE IT'S A TRAP, POYO!!
!
THERE'S SOMEONE ON THE GROUND!
HARU! DON'T GET TOO CLOSE!
IT'S A TRAP, POYO!!

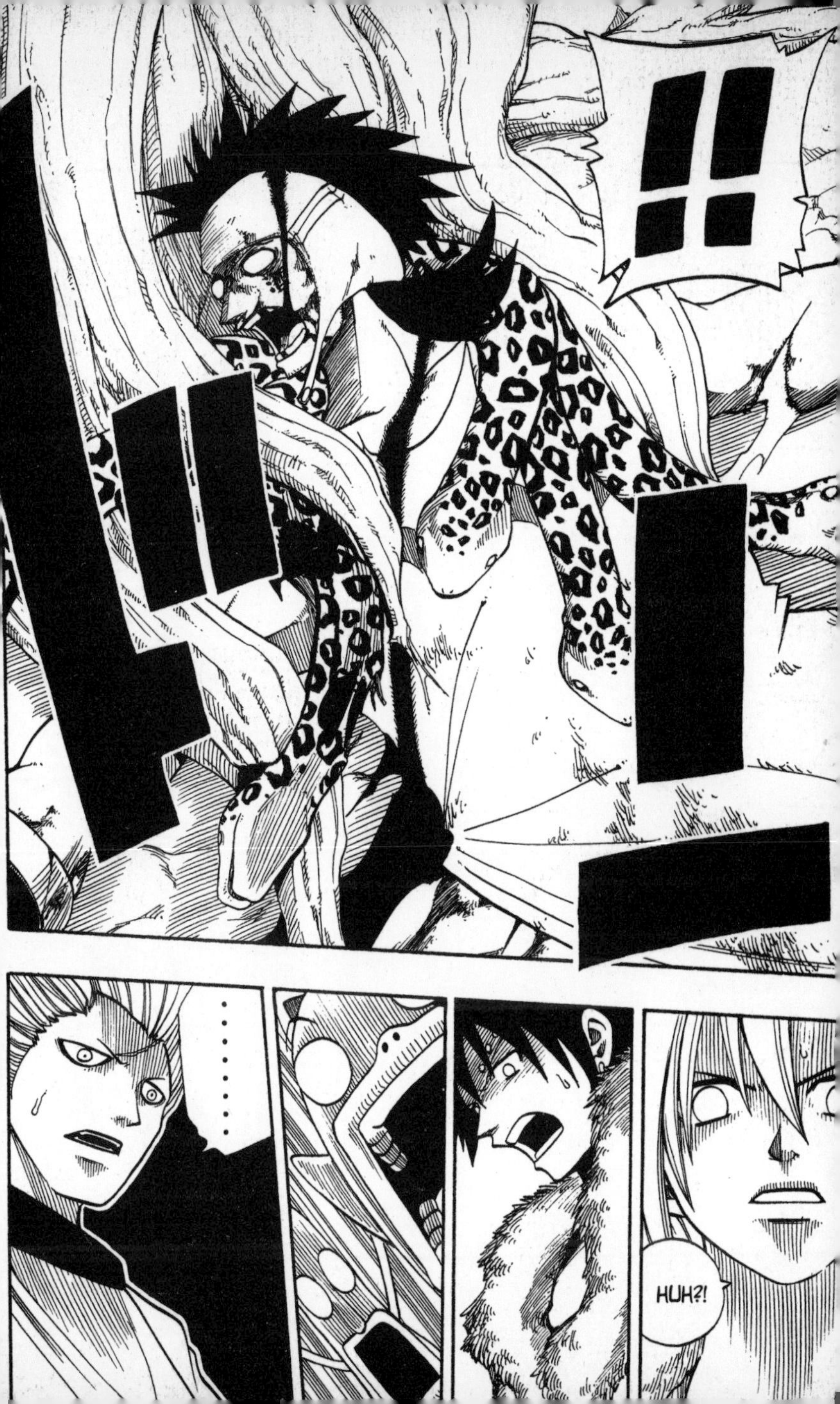
!!
HUH?!
......

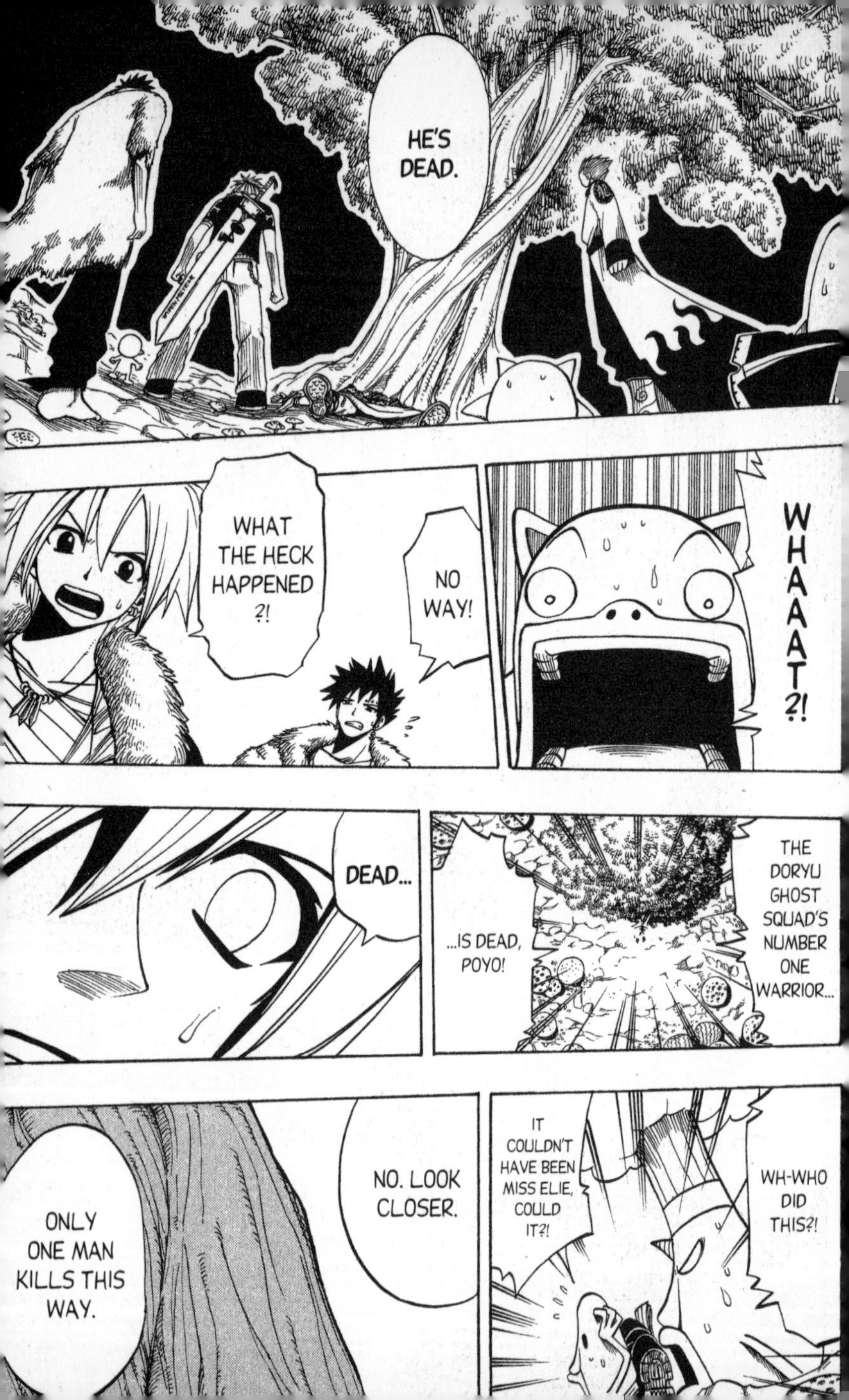
HE'S DEAD.
WHAAAT?!
NO WAY!
WHAT THE HECK HAPPENED?!
THE DORYU GHOST SQUAD'S NUMBER ONE WARRIOR...
...IS DEAD, POYO!
DEAD...
WH-WHO DID THIS?!
IT COULDN'T HAVE BEEN MISS ELIE, COULD IT?!
NO. LOOK CLOSER.
ONLY ONE MAN KILLS THIS WAY.

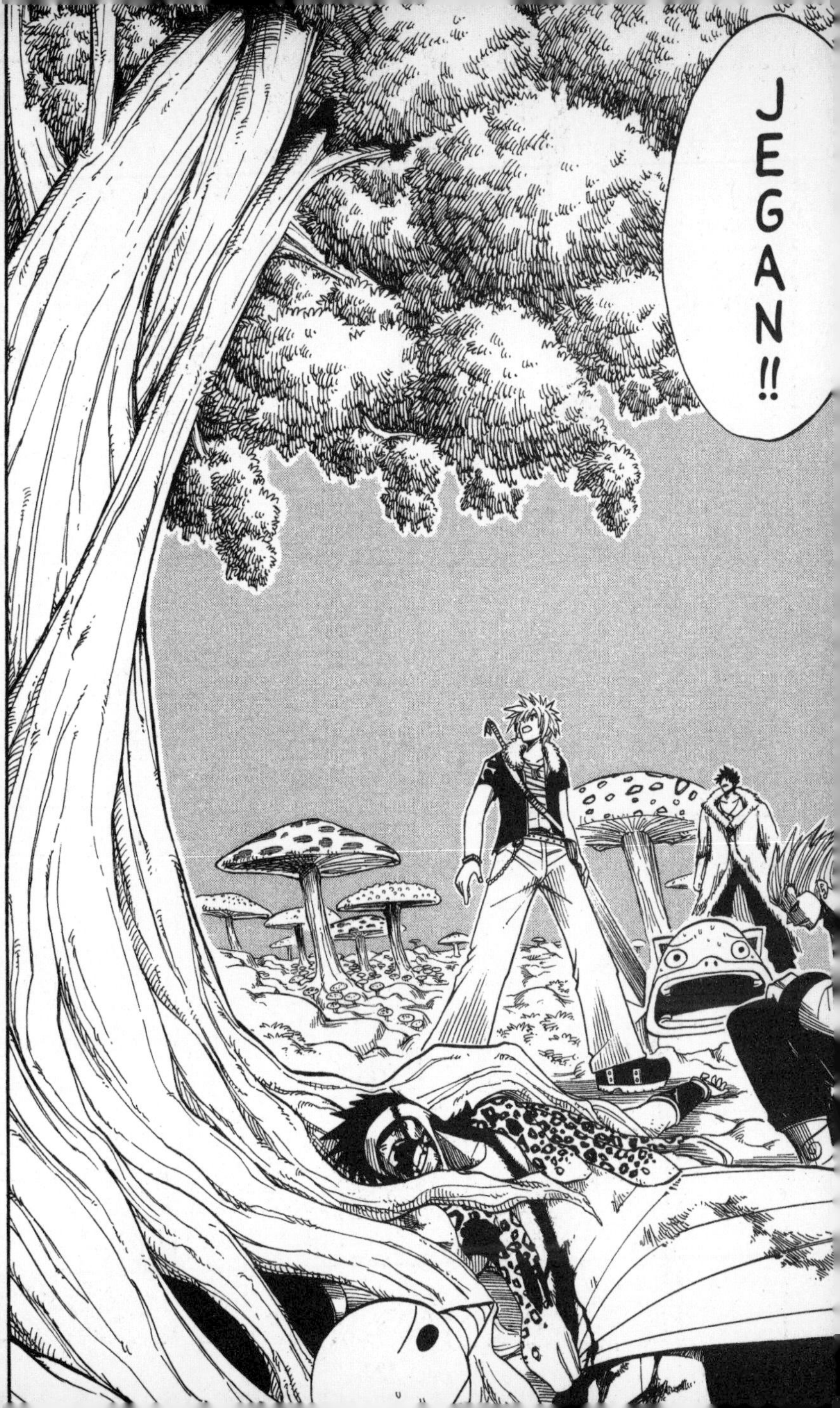
JEGAN!!

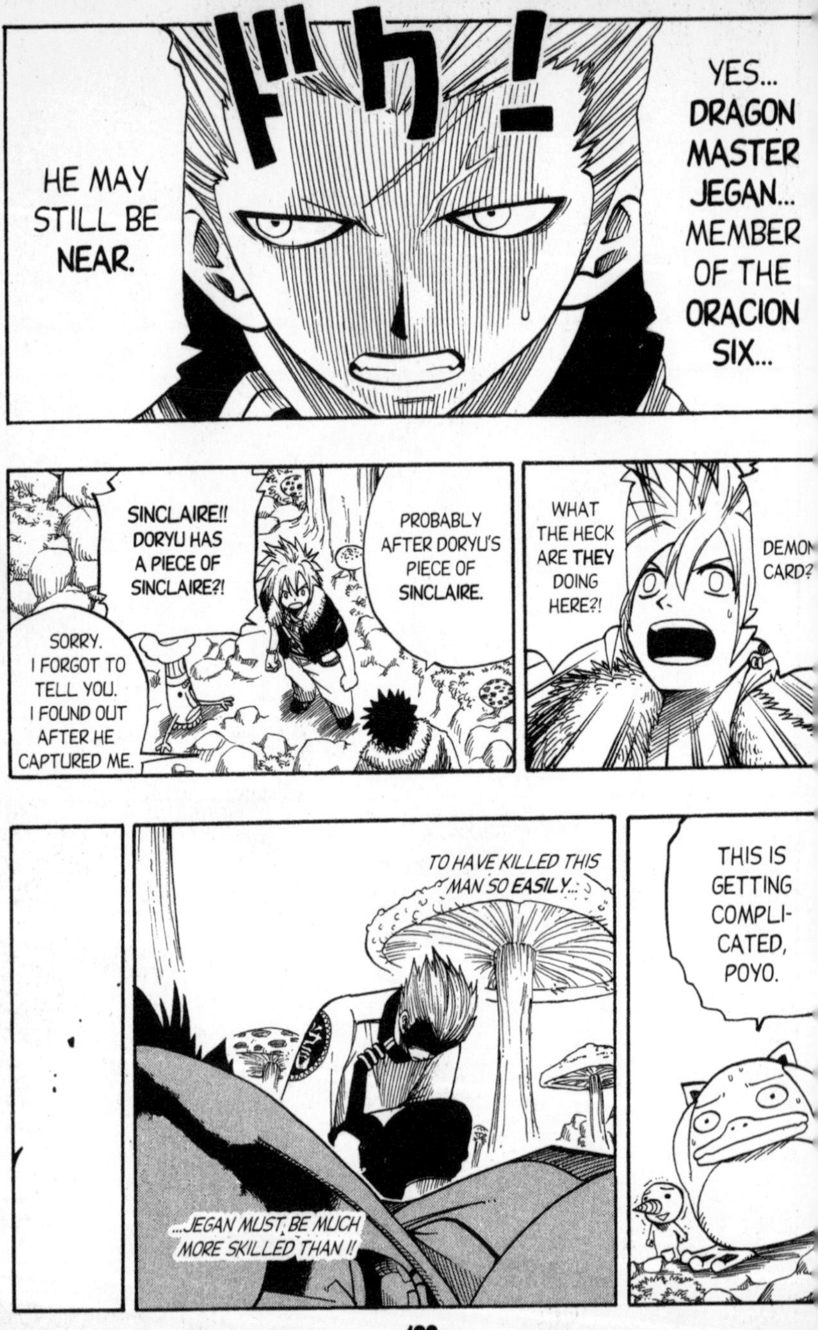
ドク!
YES... DRAGON MASTER JEGAN... MEMBER OF THE ORACION SIX...
HE MAY STILL BE NEAR.
DEMON CARD?
WHAT THE HECK ARE THEY DOING HERE?!
PROBABLY AFTER DORYU'S PIECE OF SINCLAIRE.
SINCLAIRE!! DORYU HAS A PIECE OF SINCLAIRE?!
SORRY. I FORGOT TO TELL YOU. I FOUND OUT AFTER HE CAPTURED ME.
THIS IS GETTING COMPLI-CATED, POYO.
TO HAVE KILLED THIS MAN SO EASILY...
...JEGAN MUST BE MUCH MORE SKILLED THAN I!

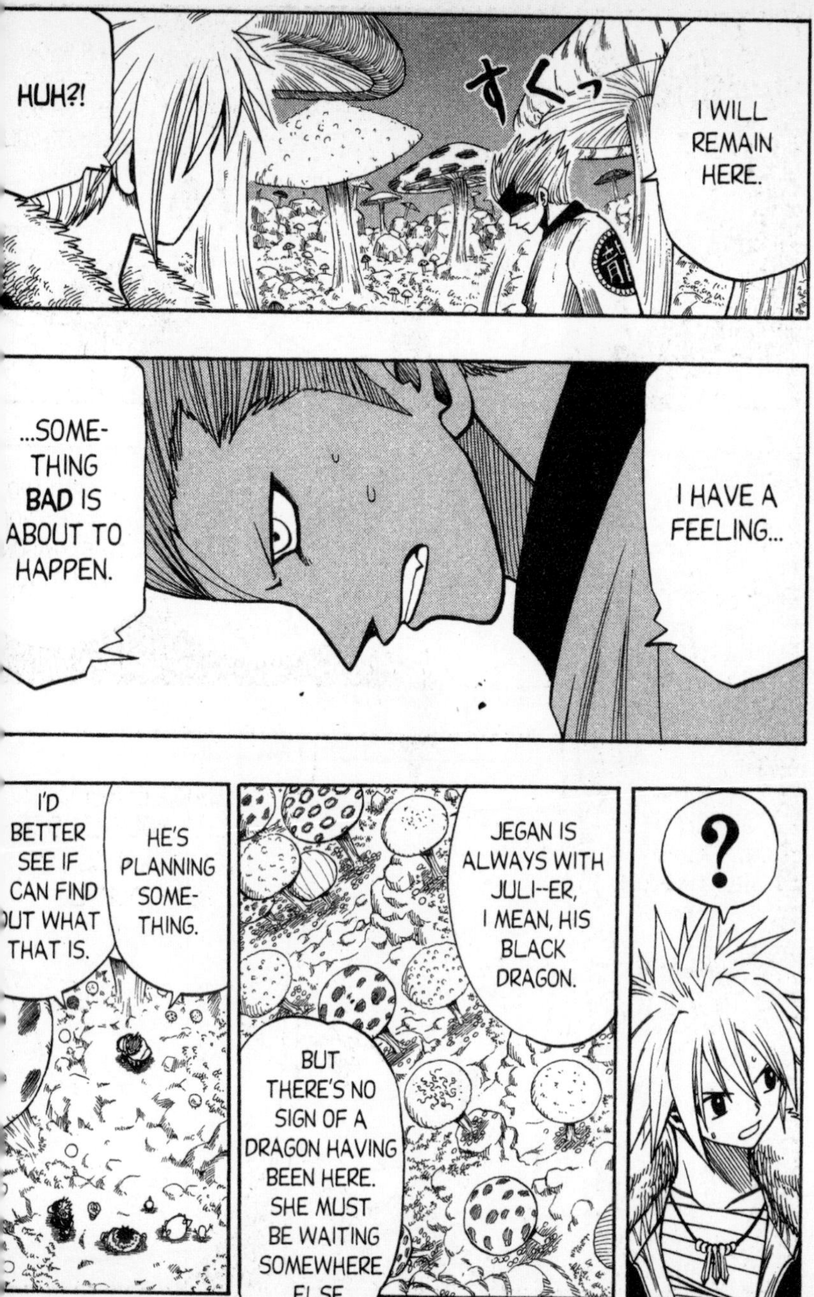
I WILL REMAIN HERE.
すくっ
HUH?!
I HAVE A FEELING...
...SOME-THING BAD IS ABOUT TO HAPPEN.
?
JEGAN IS ALWAYS WITH JULI--ER, I MEAN, HIS BLACK DRAGON.
BUT THERE'S NO SIGN OF A DRAGON HAVING BEEN HERE. SHE MUST BE WAITING SOMEWHERE ELSE.
HE'S PLANNING SOME-THING.
I'D BETTER SEE IF CAN FIND UT WHAT THAT IS.

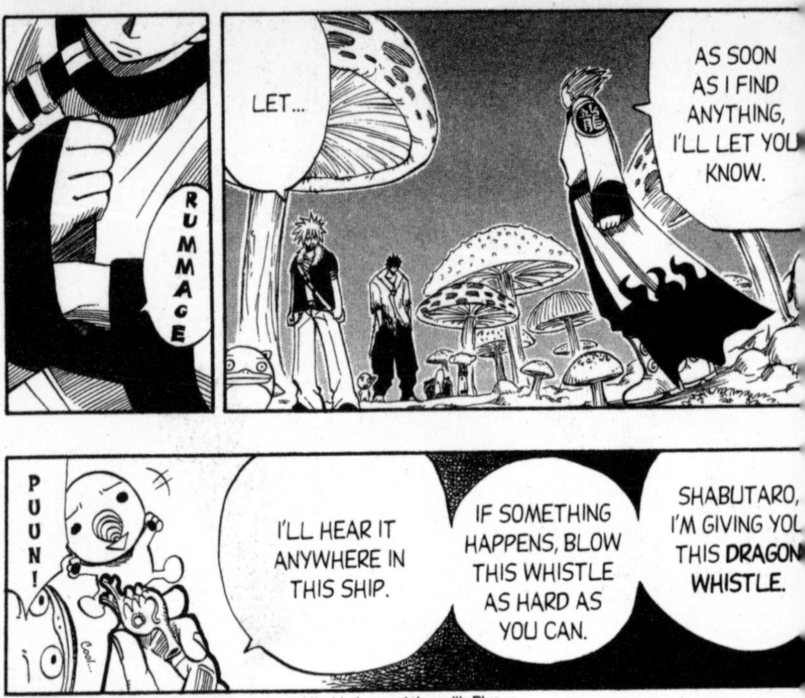
AS SOON AS I FIND ANYTHING, I'LL LET YOU KNOW.
LET...
RUMMAGE
SHABUTARO, I'M GIVING YOU THIS DRAGON WHISTLE.
IF SOMETHING HAPPENS, BLOW THIS WHISTLE AS HARD AS YOU CAN.
I'LL HEAR IT ANYWHERE IN THIS SHIP.
PUUUN!
Cool...

*see vol. 13--Shabutaro is a fabricated word that Let associates with Plue.

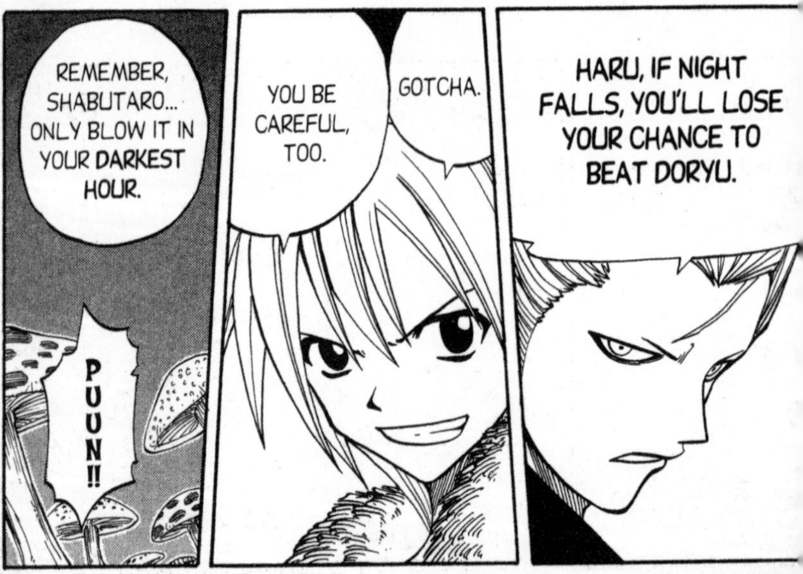
HARU, IF NIGHT FALLS, YOU'LL LOSE YOUR CHANCE TO BEAT DORYU.
GOTCHA.
YOU BE CAREFUL, TOO.
REMEMBER, SHABUTARO... ONLY BLOW IT IN YOUR DARKEST HOUR.
PUUUN!!

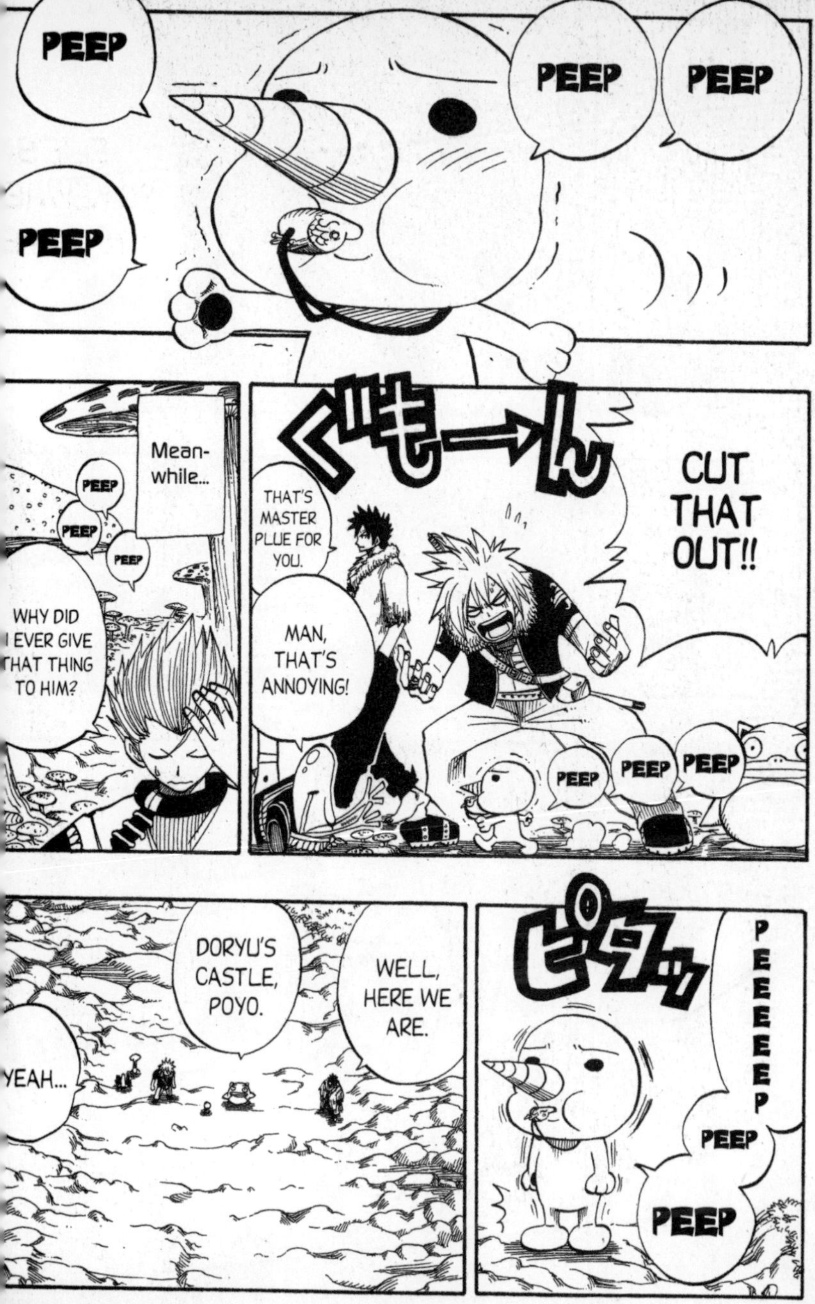
PEEP
PEEP
PEEP
PEEP
ぐもーん
CUT THAT OUT!!
THAT'S MASTER PLUE FOR YOU.
MAN, THAT'S ANNOYING!
PEEP
PEEP
PEEP
Mean-while...
PEEP
PEEP
PEEP
WHY DID I EVER GIVE THAT THING TO HIM?
ピタッ
PEEEEEP
PEEP
PEEP
WELL, HERE WE ARE.
DORYU'S CASTLE, POYO.
YEAH...

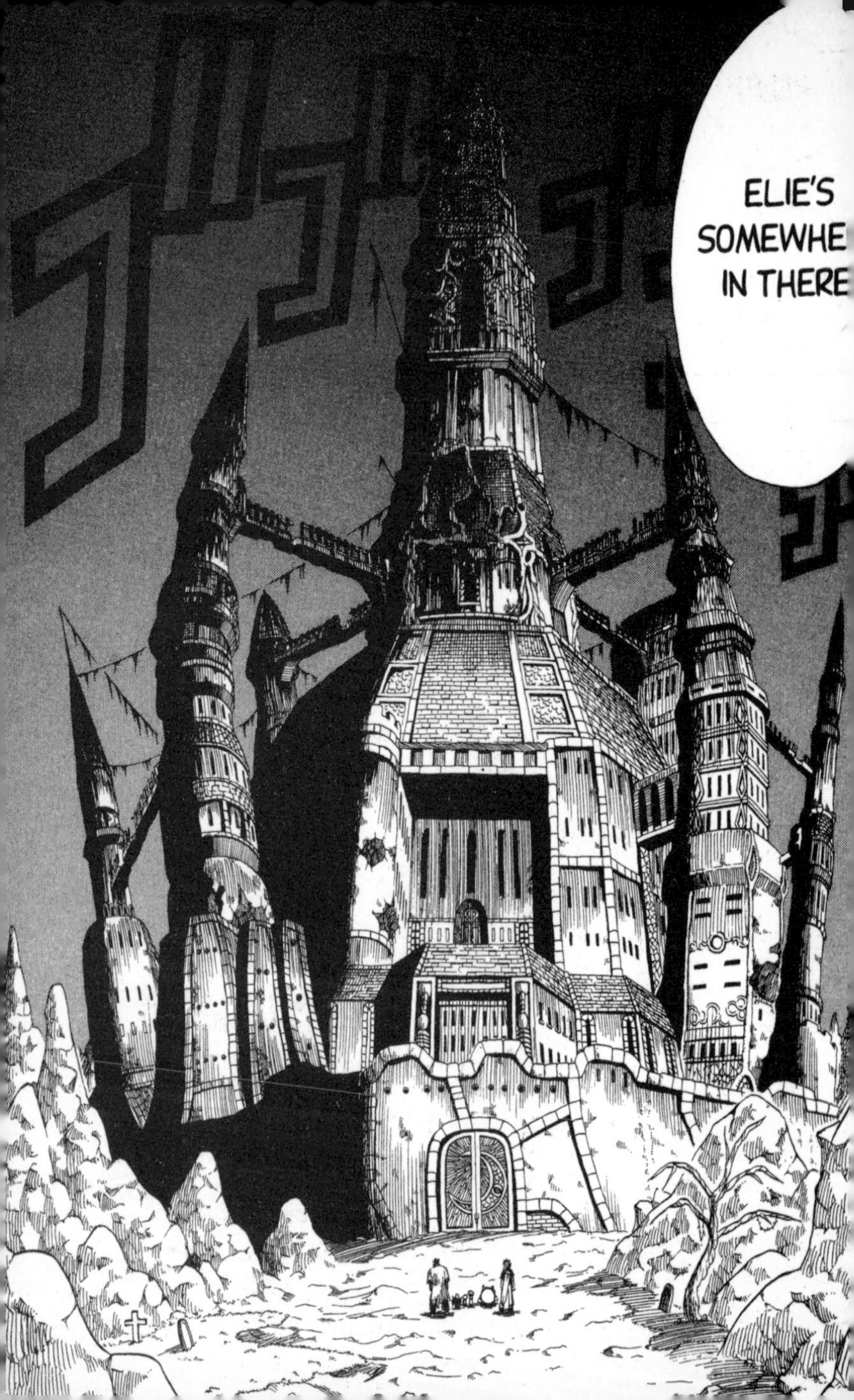
ELIE'S SOMEWHE IN THERE

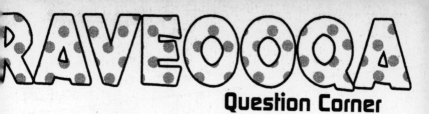

Question Corner

WHAT'S THE ENGLISH ON THE JAPANESE COVER MEAN?

—TABASCO FROM SHIZUOKA PREFECTURE

ENGLISH...? OH! YOU MEAN...

> HARU & FRIENDS
> GO ON A TRIP ROUND THE WORLD
> TO BREAK "DEMON CARD."
> WE CALL HIS WEAPON "RAVE"

YEAH. THAT WAS JUST ME HAVING FUN WITH A LITERAL TRANSLATION. I WONDER WHAT MY ENGLISH-SPEAKING READERS THINK OF IT?

MASHIMA-SENSEI,
YOU WRITE THAT YOU'RE NOT VERY SMART, BUT I THINK YOU ARE.

—COCOA COOKIE FROM HOKKAIDO

REALLY? THANKS (^_^)! BUT IN HIGH SCHOOL, MY SCORES WERE QUITE SOMETHING. EVERYTHING I GOT BACK (EXCEPT FOR MATH) WAS ALL PRETTY WITH RED MARKS. I NEVER GOT BETTER THAN A C IN ENGLISH--OR JAPANESE, EITHER (^^;). ECONOMICS AND SCIENCE WERE LIKE THAT, TOO. THE ONLY SUBJECTS WHERE I DID ALL RIGHT WERE PHYS. ED AND ART, BUT THAT WASN'T GONNA GET ME A JOB. (OR SO I THOUGHT.)

SO, SAD AS IT SOUNDS, I USED MY ILLUSTRIOUS SKILLS TO GET INTO A TRADE SCHOOL, BUT THEY TOLD ME "YOU'LL NEVER GRADUATE WITH GRADES LIKE THAT!" (AND WITH MY TRACK RECORD, THEY HAD EVERY REASON TO THINK THAT). BUT SOMEHOW, I *JUST* MANAGED TO SQUEAK THROUGH AND GET MY DEGREE. SO YOU SEE, I'M REALLY NOT THAT BRIGHT. I'M JUST LUCKY I GOT INTO MANGA BEFORE I ENDED UP A BEAN COUNTER.

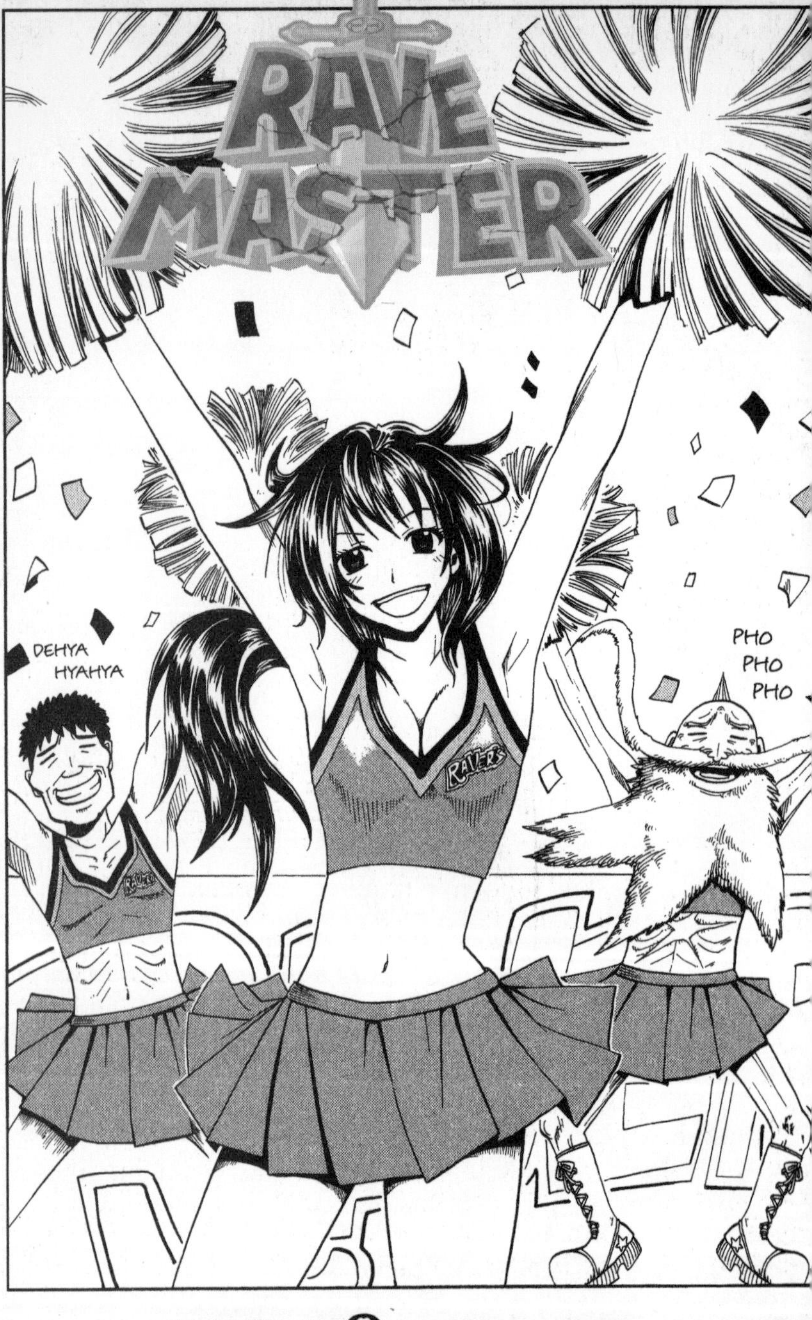
RAVE MASTER™
PHO PHO PHO
DEHYA HYAHYA
RAVERS

RAVE:121 DARKNESS RISING

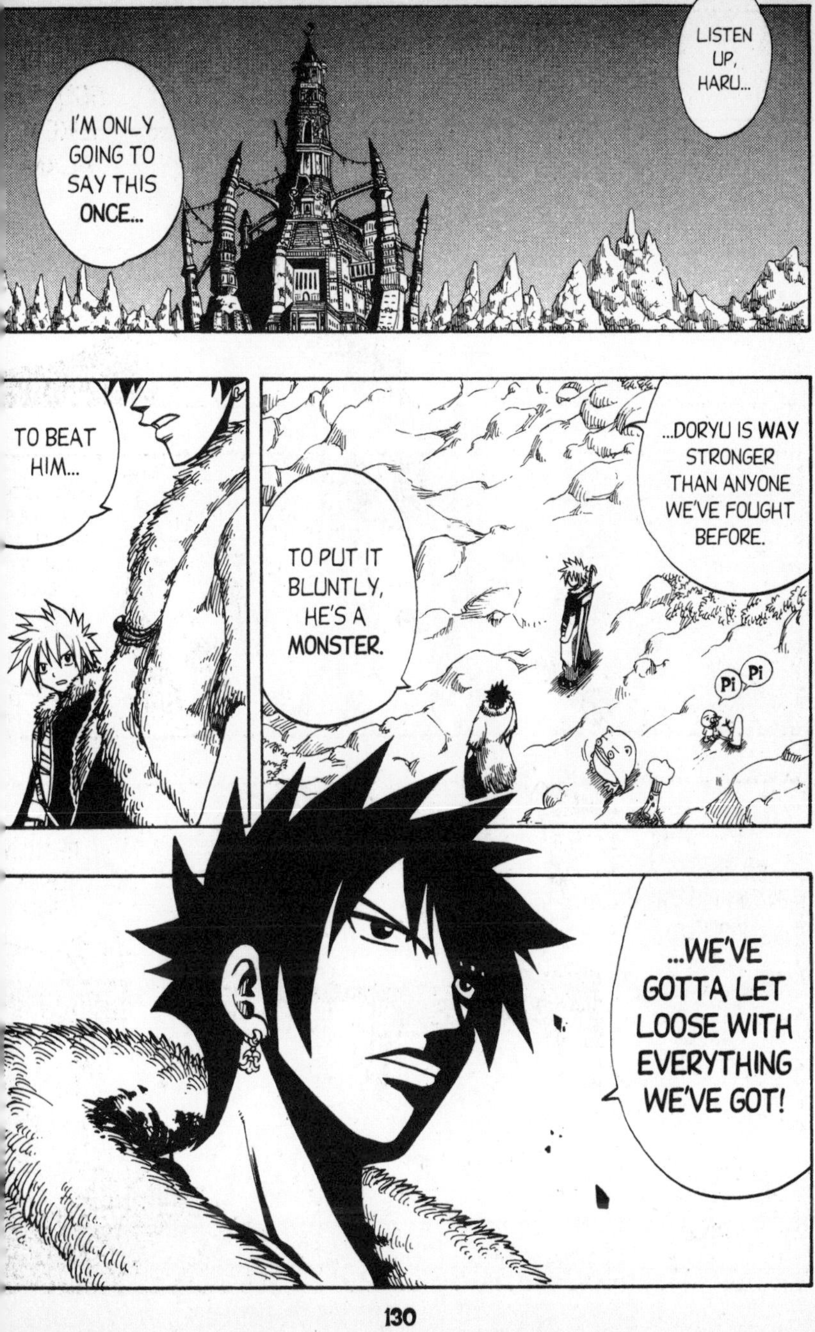
LISTEN UP, HARU...
I'M ONLY GOING TO SAY THIS ONCE...
...DORYU IS WAY STRONGER THAN ANYONE WE'VE FOUGHT BEFORE.
TO PUT IT BLUNTLY, HE'S A MONSTER.
Pi Pi
TO BEAT HIM...
...WE'VE GOTTA LET LOOSE WITH EVERYTHING WE'VE GOT!

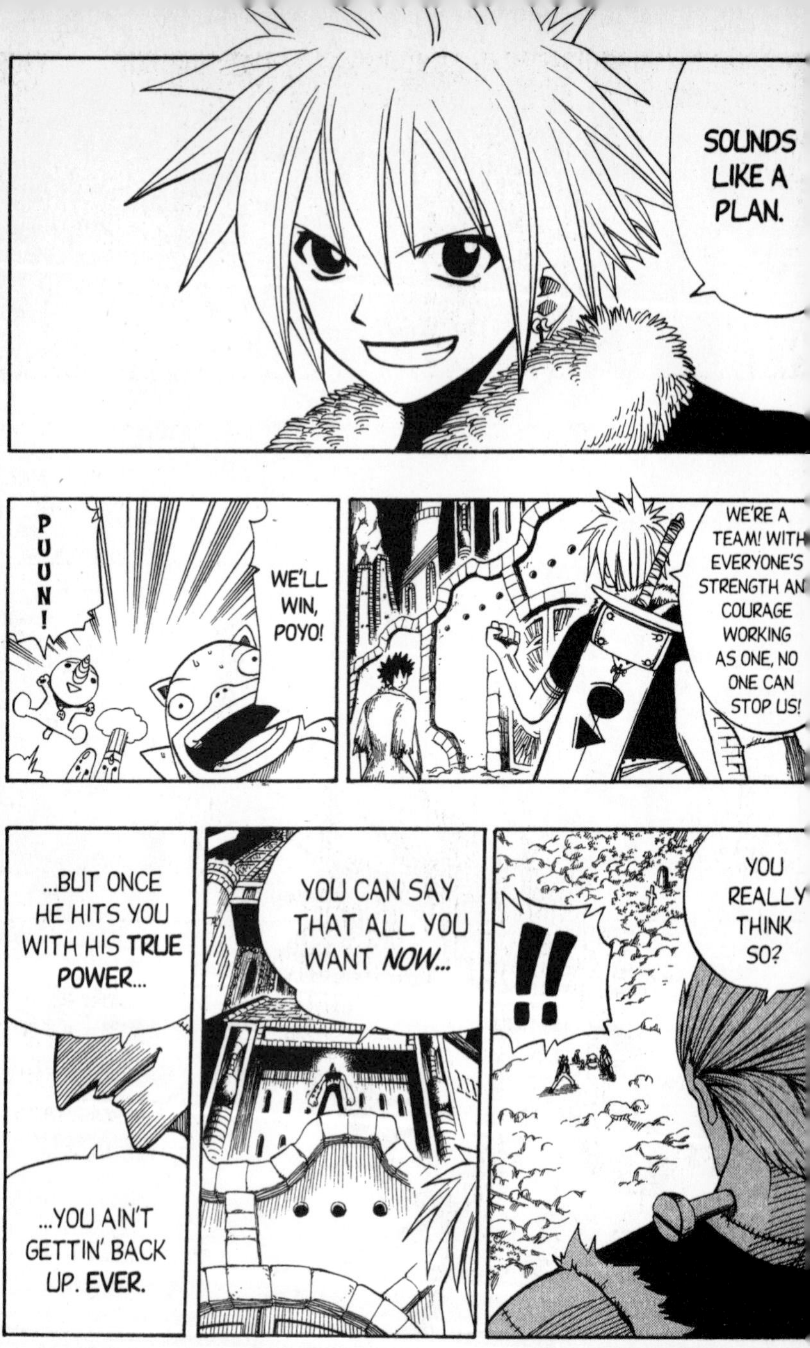
SOUNDS LIKE A PLAN.
WE'RE A TEAM! WITH EVERYONE'S STRENGTH AN COURAGE WORKING AS ONE, NO ONE CAN STOP US!
WE'LL WIN, POYO!
PUUN!
YOU REALLY THINK SO?
!!
YOU CAN SAY THAT ALL YOU WANT *NOW*...
...BUT ONCE HE HITS YOU WITH HIS **TRUE POWER**...
...YOU AIN'T GETTIN' BACK UP. **EVER.**

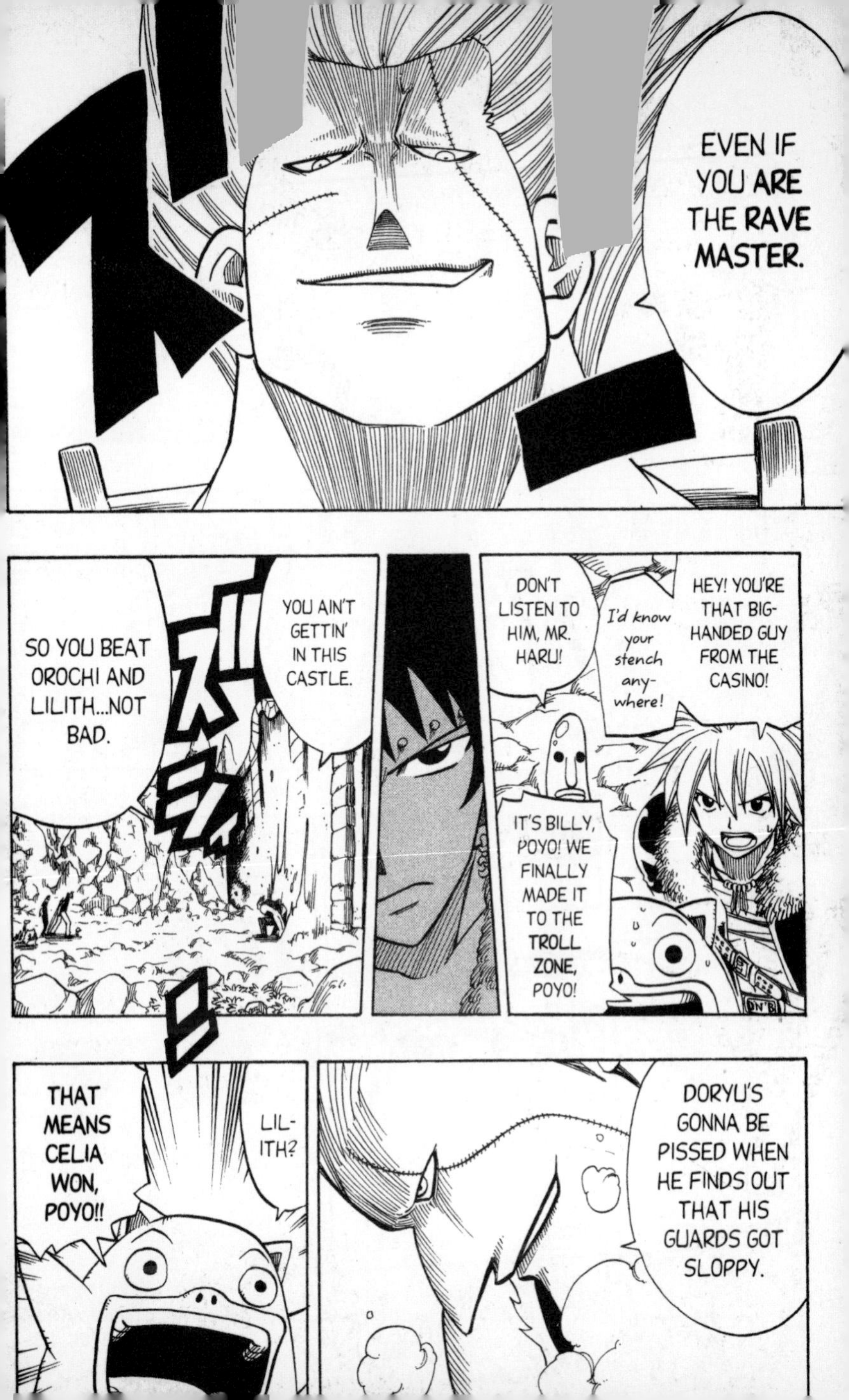
EVEN IF YOU ARE THE RAVE MASTER.
HEY! YOU'RE THAT BIG-HANDED GUY FROM THE CASINO!
I'd know your stench any-where!
DON'T LISTEN TO HIM, MR. HARU!
IT'S BILLY, POYO! WE FINALLY MADE IT TO THE TROLL ZONE, POYO!
YOU AIN'T GETTIN' IN THIS CASTLE.
SO YOU BEAT OROCHI AND LILITH...NOT BAD.
DORYU'S GONNA BE PISSED WHEN HE FINDS OUT THAT HIS GUARDS GOT SLOPPY.
LIL-ITH?
THAT MEANS CELIA WON, POYO!!

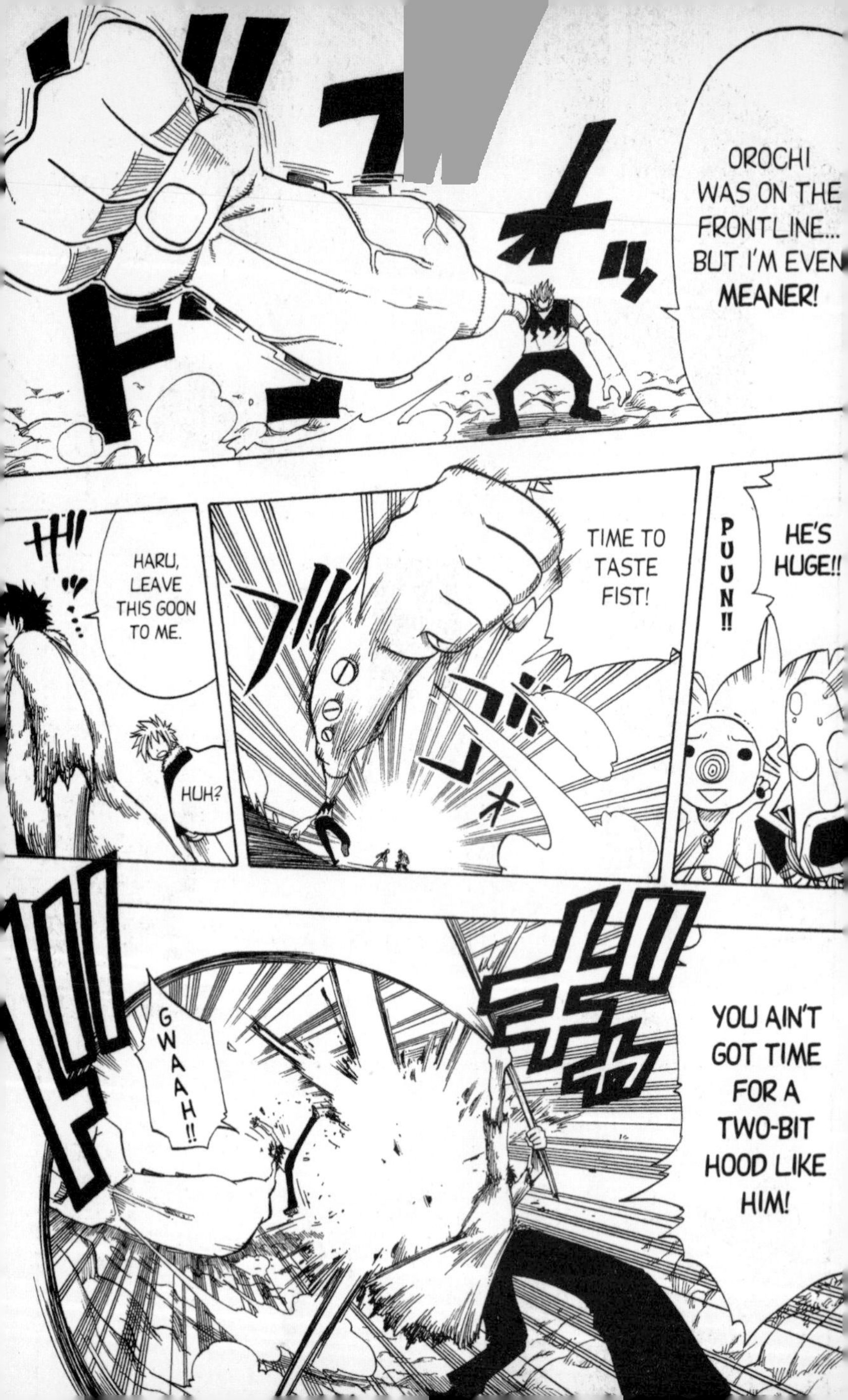
OROCHI WAS ON THE FRONTLINE... BUT I'M EVEN MEANER!
HE'S HUGE!!
PUUN!!
TIME TO TASTE FIST!
HARU, LEAVE THIS GOON TO ME.
HUH?
YOU AIN'T GOT TIME FOR A TWO-BIT HOOD LIKE HIM!
GWAAH!!

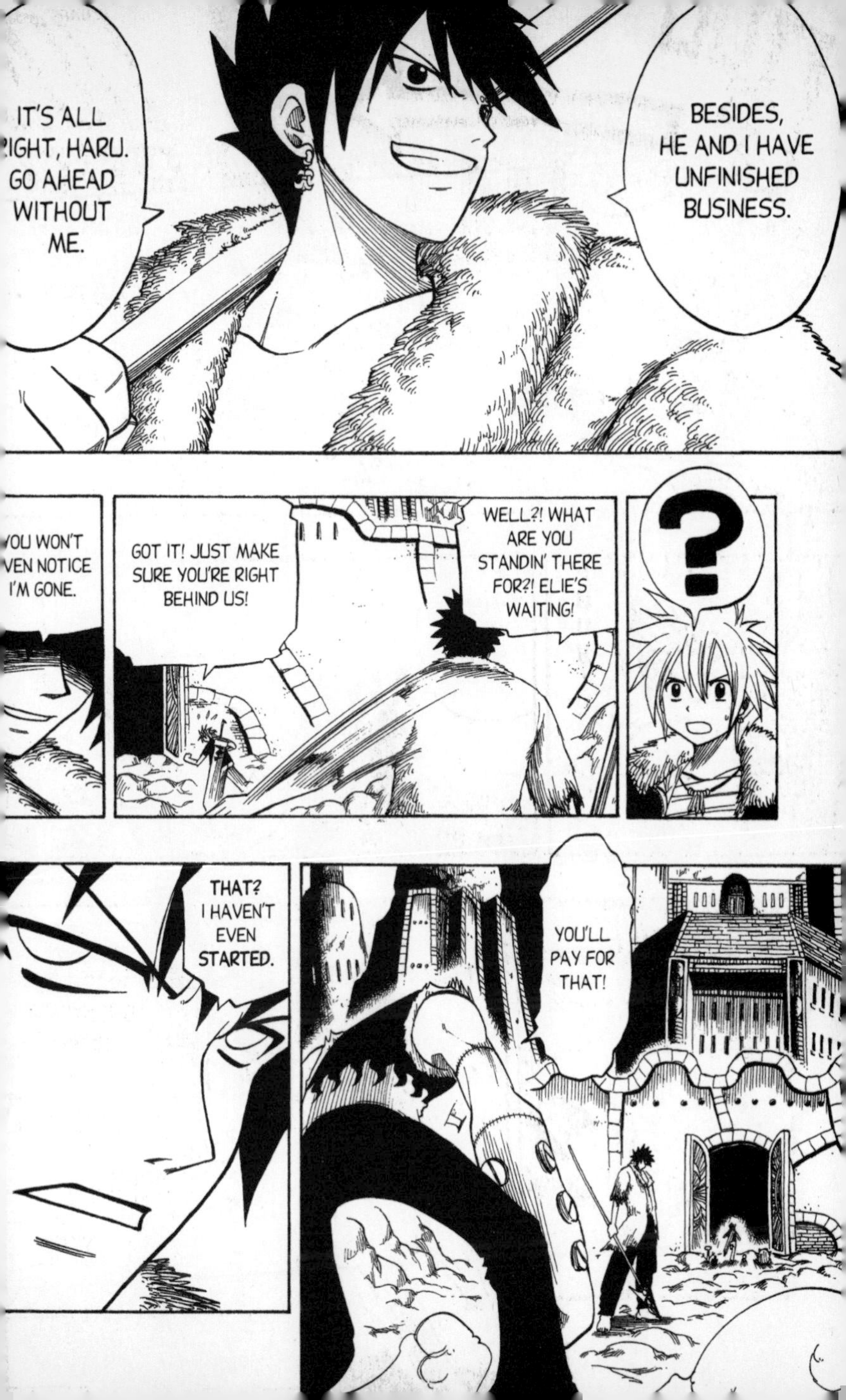
BESIDES, HE AND I HAVE UNFINISHED BUSINESS.
IT'S ALL IGHT, HARU. GO AHEAD WITHOUT ME.
?
WELL?! WHAT ARE YOU STANDIN' THERE FOR?! ELIE'S WAITING!
GOT IT! JUST MAKE SURE YOU'RE RIGHT BEHIND US!
OU WON'T VEN NOTICE I'M GONE.
YOU'LL PAY FOR THAT!
THAT? I HAVEN'T EVEN STARTED.

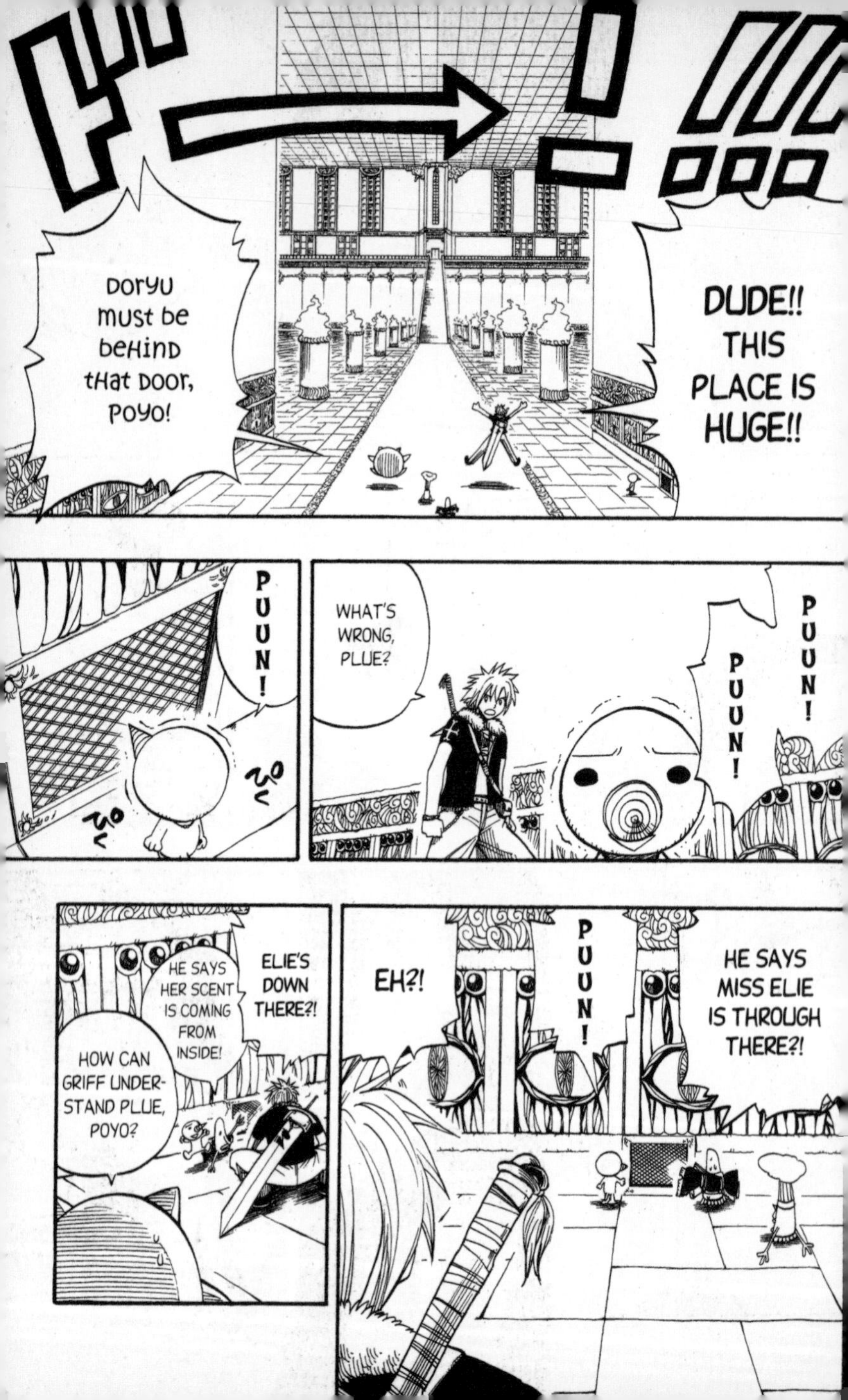
DUDE!! THIS PLACE IS HUGE!!
Doryu must be behind that door, Poyo!
PUUN!
PUUN!
WHAT'S WRONG, PLUE?
PUUN!
HE SAYS MISS ELIE IS THROUGH THERE?!
PUUN!
EH?!
ELIE'S DOWN THERE?!
HE SAYS HER SCENT IS COMING FROM INSIDE!
HOW CAN GRIFF UNDER-STAND PLUE, POYO?

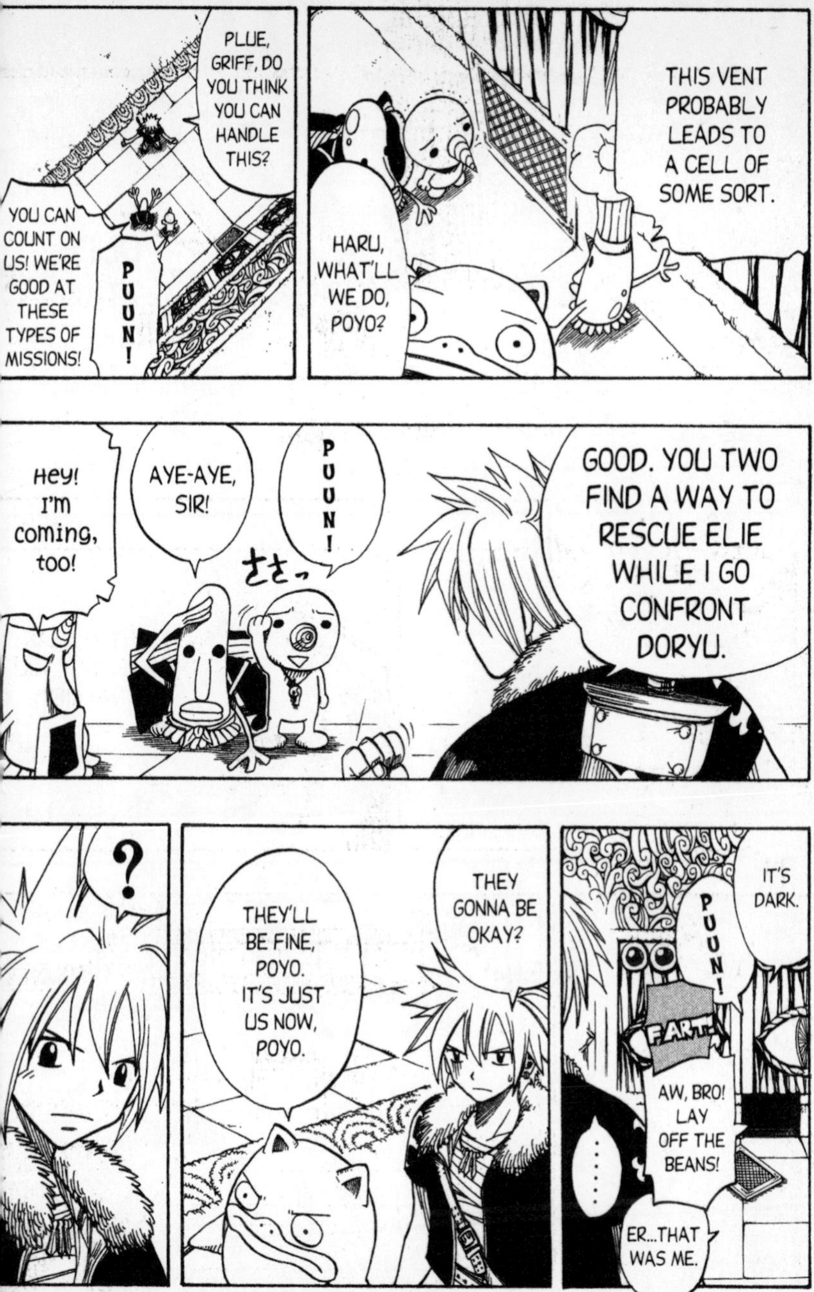
THIS VENT PROBABLY LEADS TO A CELL OF SOME SORT.
HARU, WHAT'LL WE DO, POYO?
PLUE, GRIFF, DO YOU THINK YOU CAN HANDLE THIS?
PUUN!
YOU CAN COUNT ON US! WE'RE GOOD AT THESE TYPES OF MISSIONS!
GOOD. YOU TWO FIND A WAY TO RESCUE ELIE WHILE I GO CONFRONT DORYU.
PUUN!
ささっ
AYE-AYE, SIR!
Hey! I'm coming, too!
IT'S DARK.
PUUN!
FART
AW, BRO! LAY OFF THE BEANS!
.....
ER...THAT WAS ME.
THEY GONNA BE OKAY?
THEY'LL BE FINE, POYO. IT'S JUST US NOW, POYO.
?

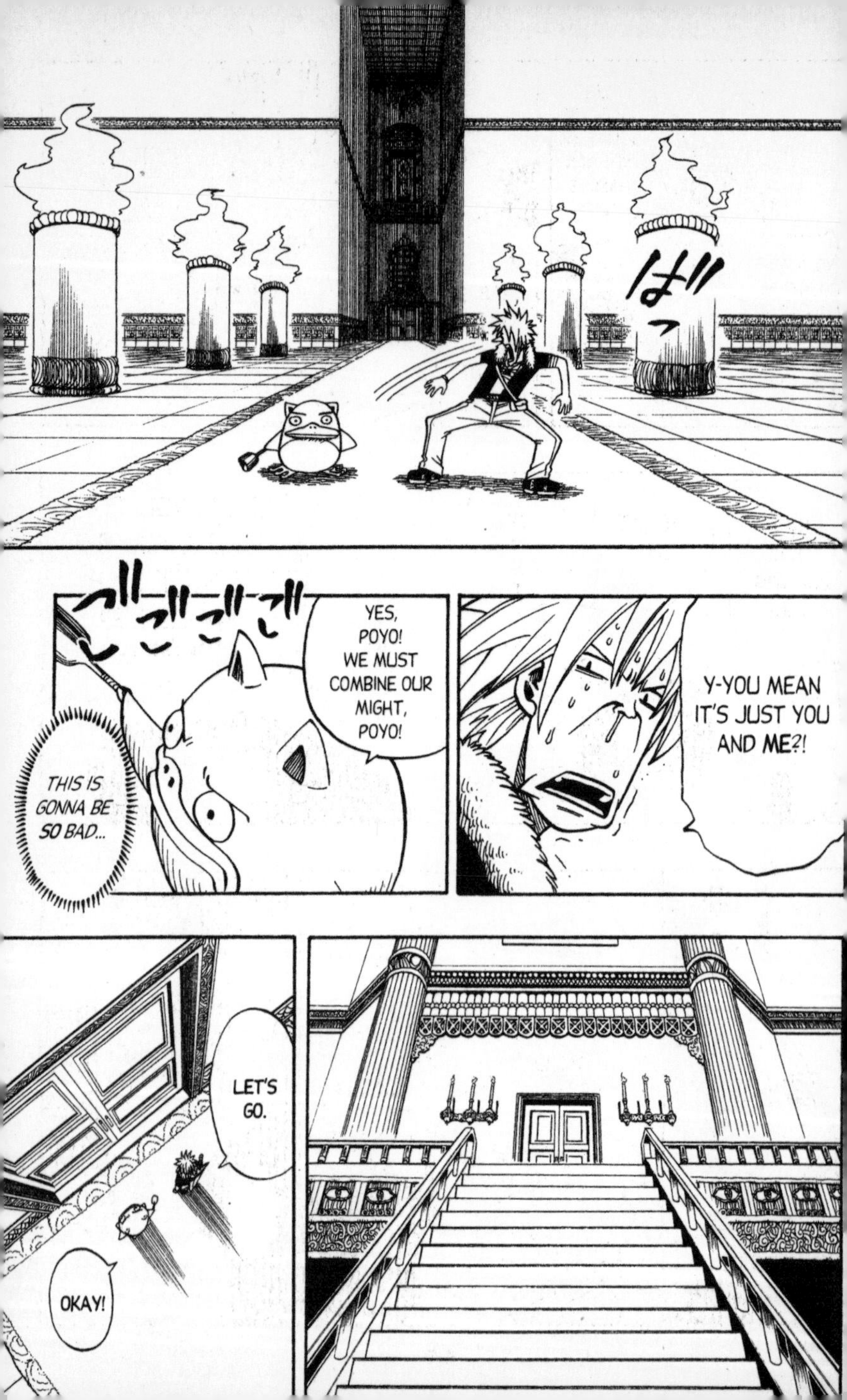
ばっ
Y-YOU MEAN IT'S JUST YOU AND ME?!
YES, POYO! WE MUST COMBINE OUR MIGHT, POYO!
ごごごご
THIS IS GONNA BE SO BAD...
LET'S GO.
OKAY!

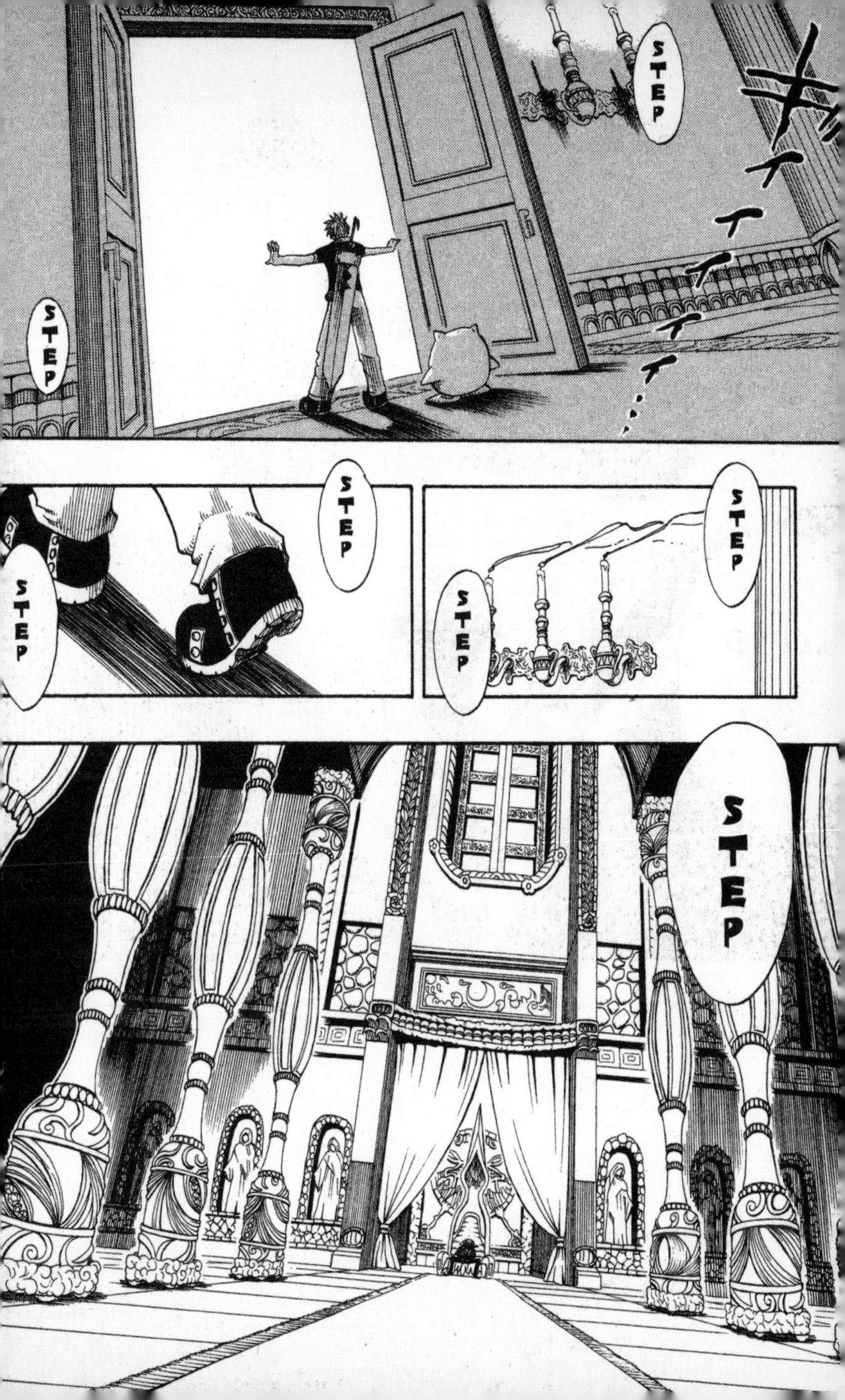
STEP
STEP
STEP
STEP
STEP
STEP
STEP

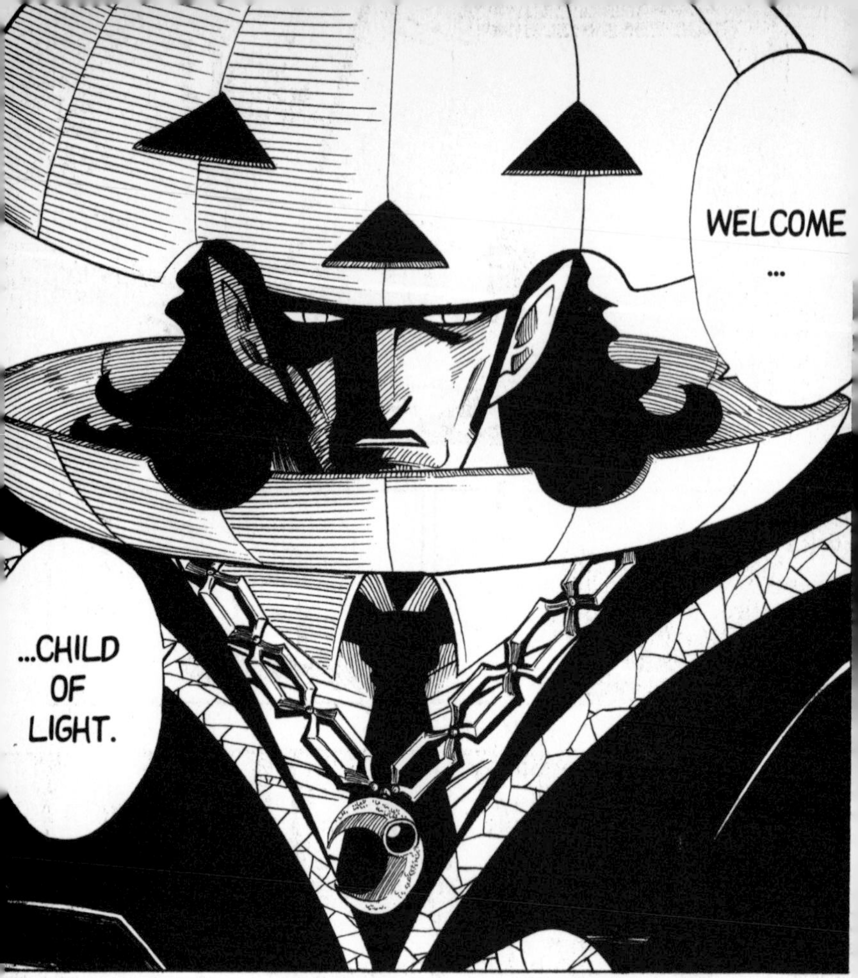
WELCOME ...
...CHILD OF LIGHT.
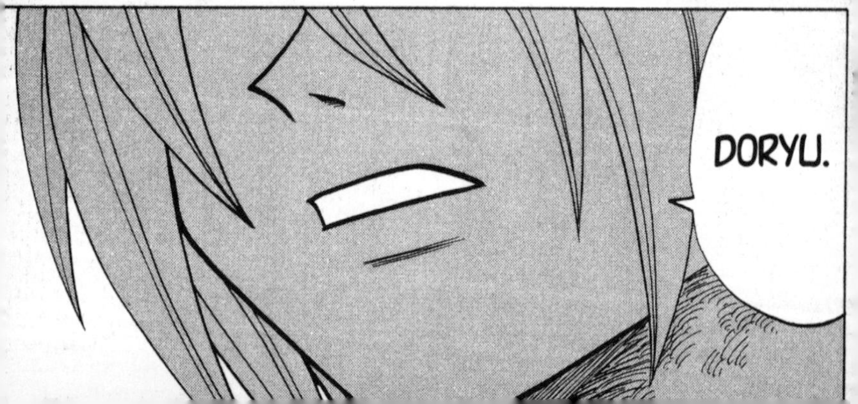
DORYU.

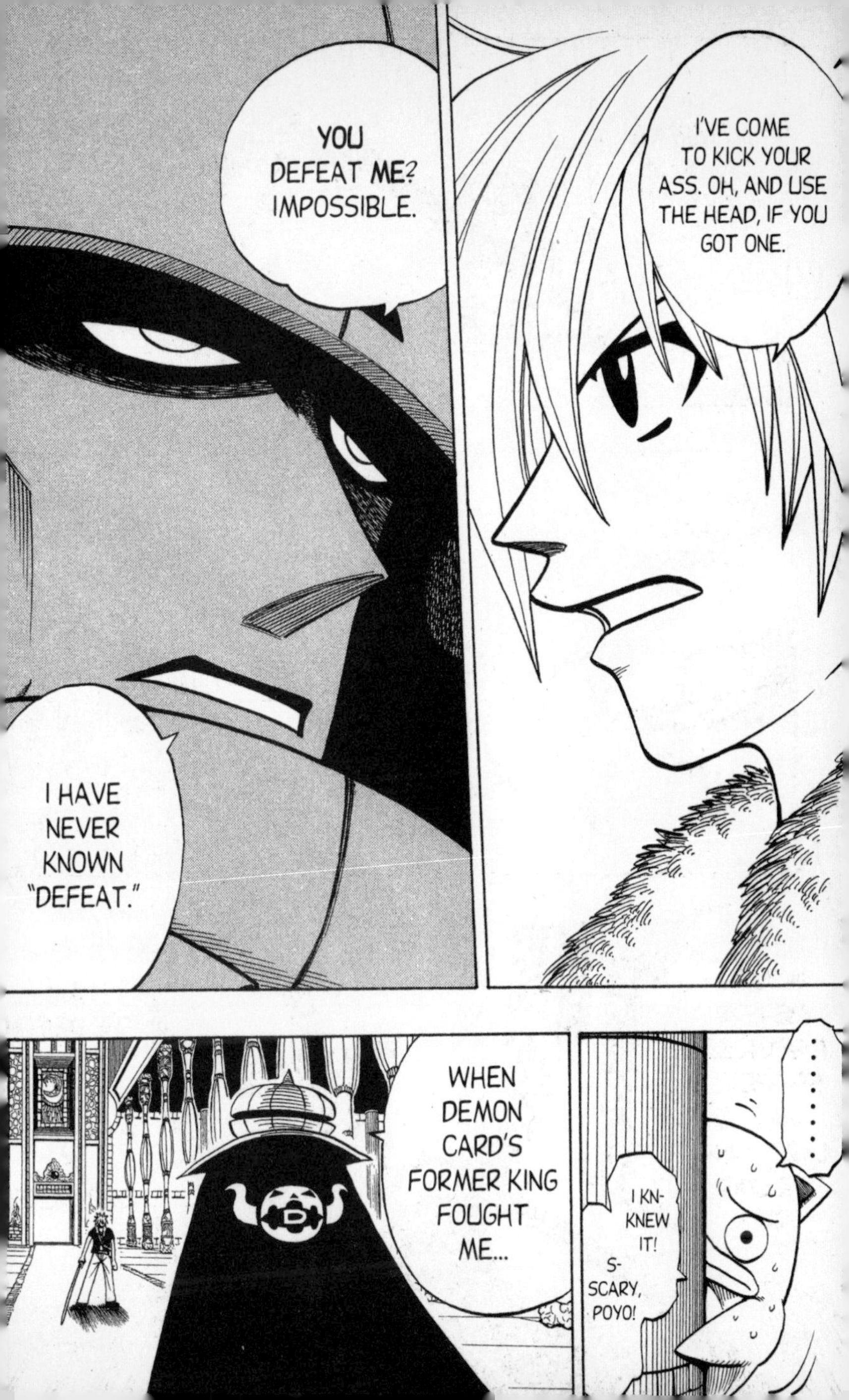
I'VE COME TO KICK YOUR ASS. OH, AND USE THE HEAD, IF YOU GOT ONE.
YOU DEFEAT ME? IMPOSSIBLE.
I HAVE NEVER KNOWN "DEFEAT."
......
I KN-KNEW IT!
S-SCARY, POYO!
WHEN DEMON CARD'S FORMER KING FOUGHT ME...

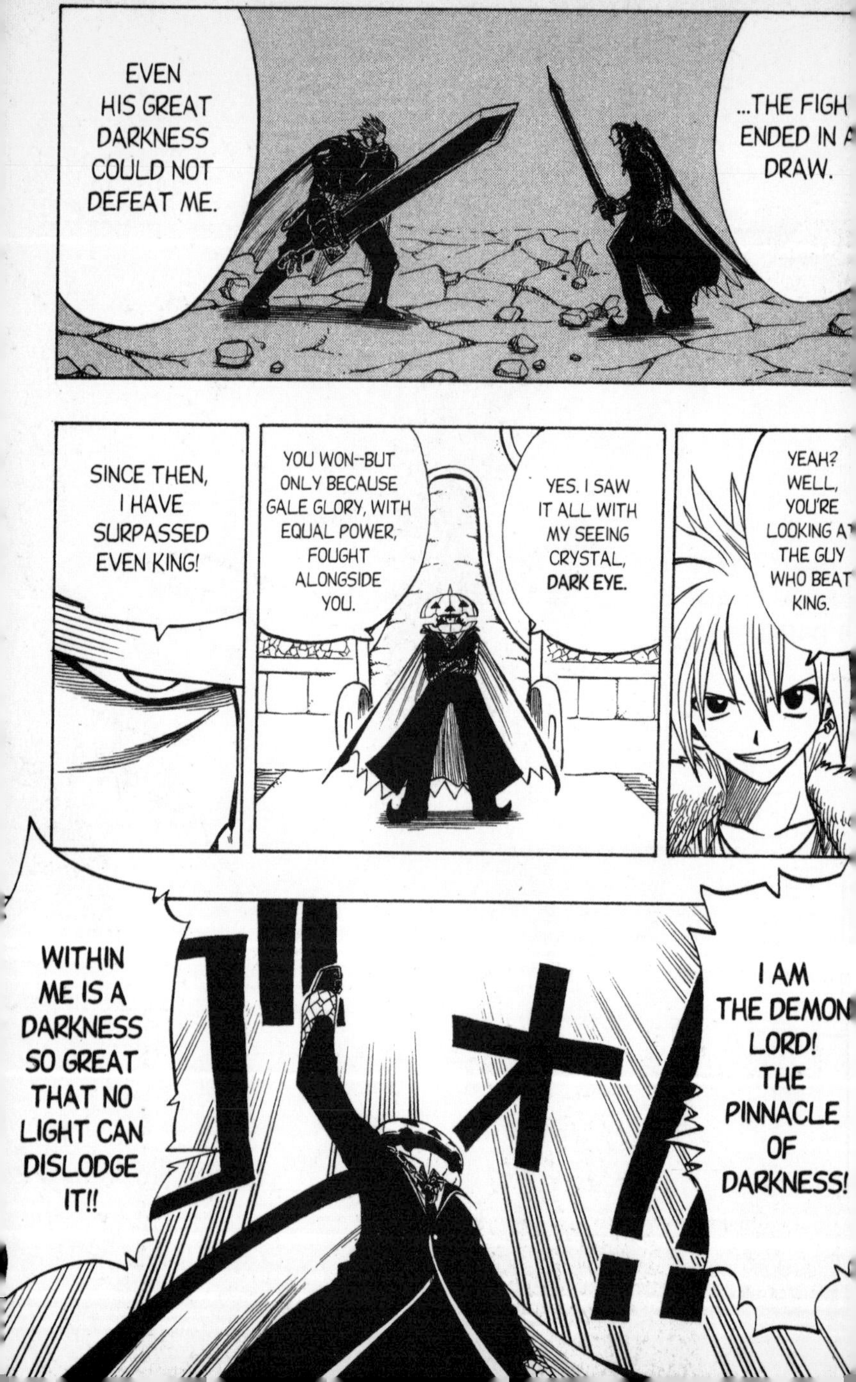

...THE FIGH ENDED IN A DRAW.
EVEN HIS GREAT DARKNESS COULD NOT DEFEAT ME.
YEAH? WELL, YOU'RE LOOKING AT THE GUY WHO BEAT KING.
YES. I SAW IT ALL WITH MY SEEING CRYSTAL, DARK EYE.
YOU WON--BUT ONLY BECAUSE GALE GLORY, WITH EQUAL POWER, FOUGHT ALONGSIDE YOU.
SINCE THEN, I HAVE SURPASSED EVEN KING!
I AM THE DEMON LORD! THE PINNACLE OF DARKNESS!
WITHIN ME IS A DARKNESS SO GREAT THAT NO LIGHT CAN DISLODGE IT!!

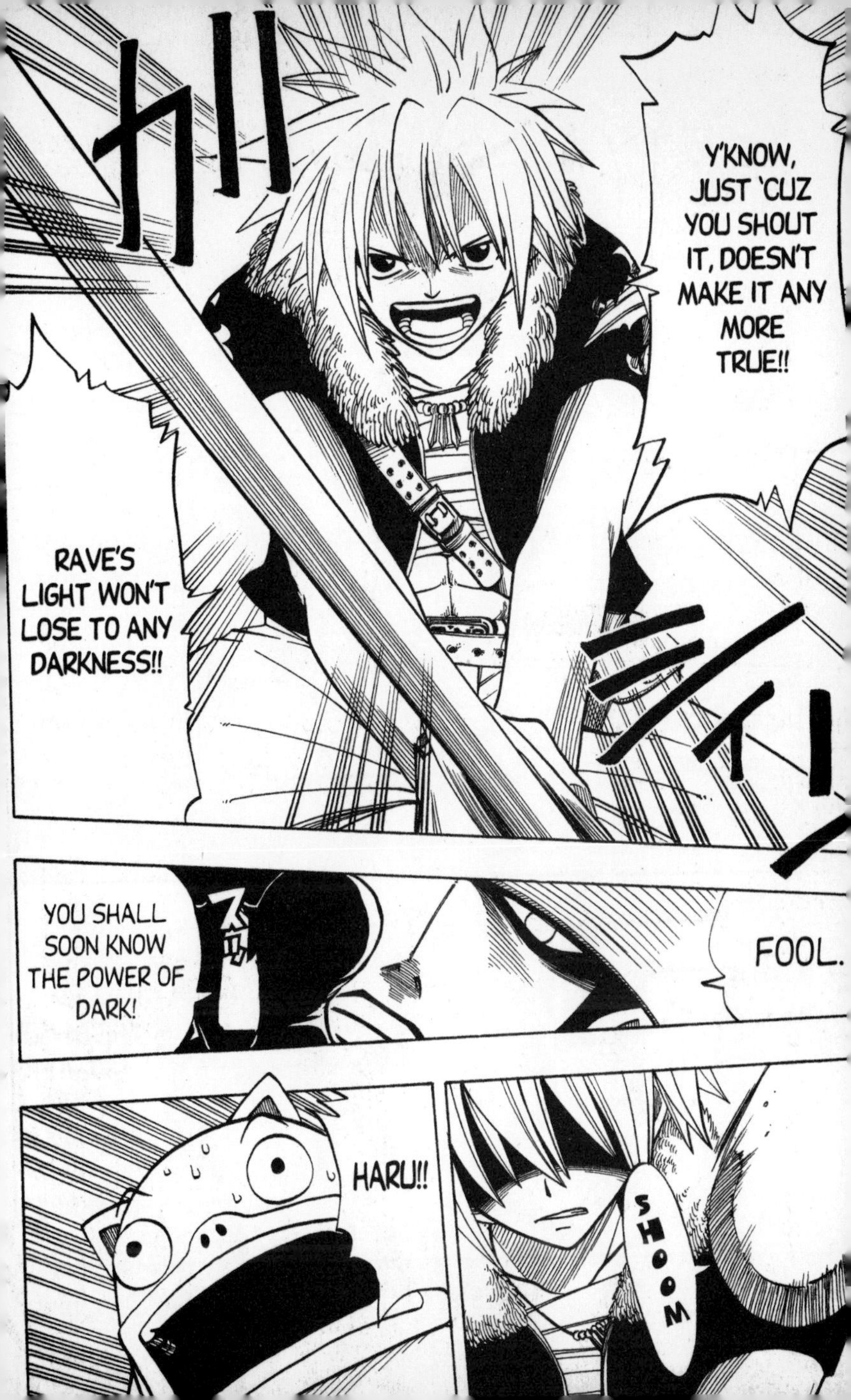

Y'KNOW, JUST 'CUZ YOU SHOUT IT, DOESN'T MAKE IT ANY MORE TRUE!!
RAVE'S LIGHT WON'T LOSE TO ANY DARKNESS!!
FOOL.
YOU SHALL SOON KNOW THE POWER OF DARK!
SHOOM
HARU!!

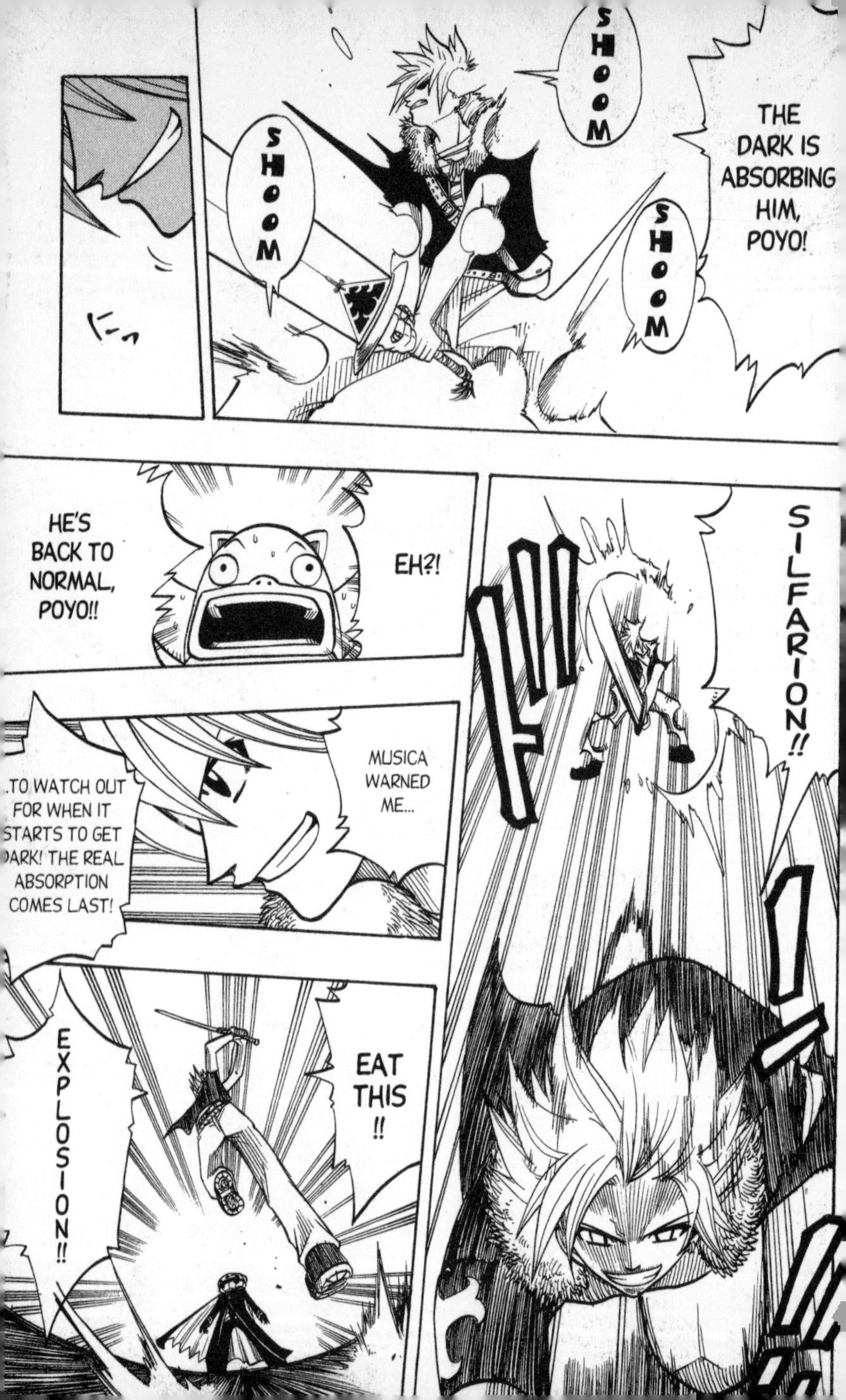
THE DARK IS ABSORBING HIM, POYO!
SHOOM
SHOOM
SHOOM
SILFARION!!
EH?!
HE'S BACK TO NORMAL, POYO!!
MUSICA WARNED ME...
...TO WATCH OUT FOR WHEN IT STARTS TO GET DARK! THE REAL ABSORPTION COMES LAST!
EAT THIS!!
EXPLOSION!!

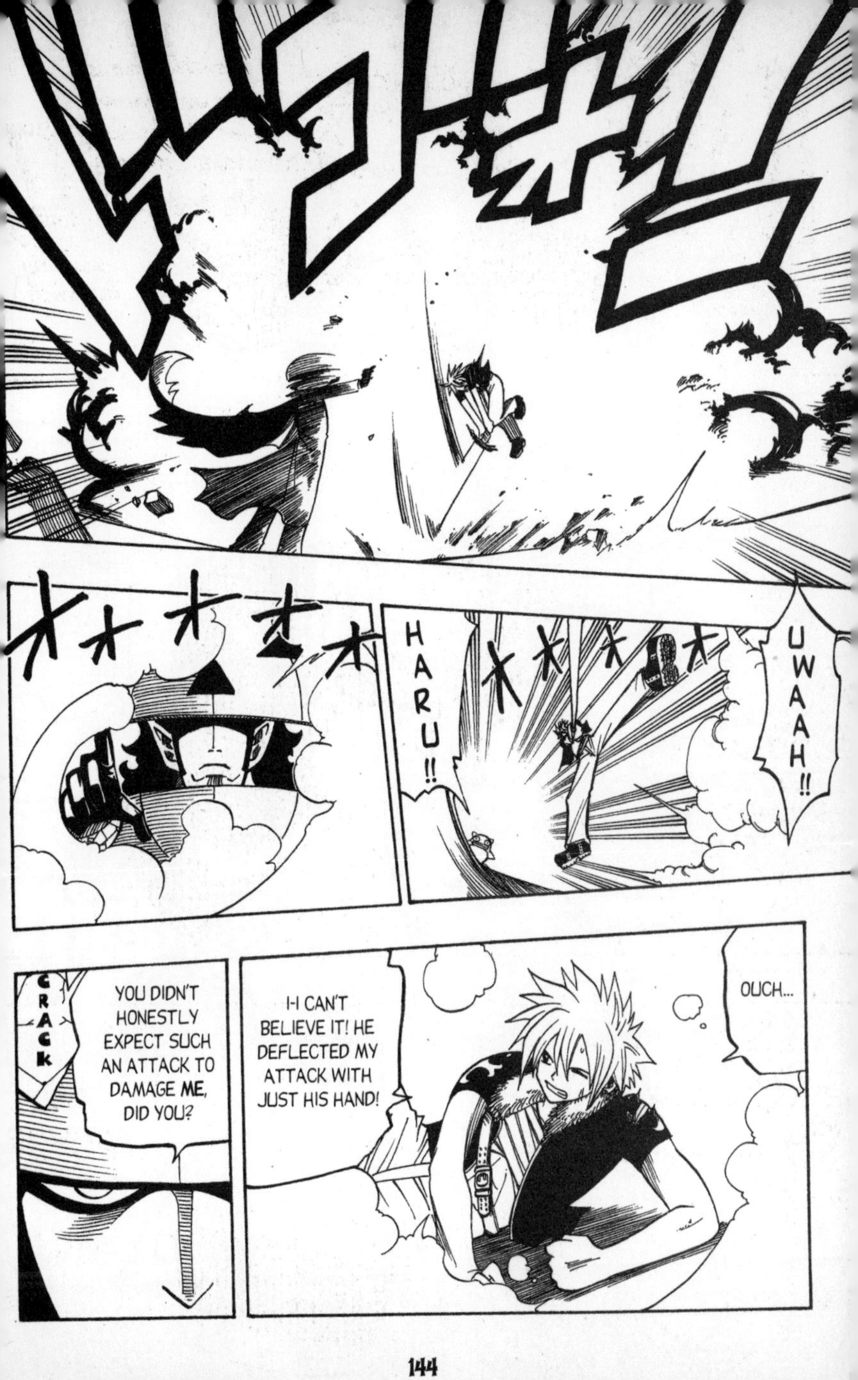
UWAAH!!
HARU!!
OUCH...
I-I CAN'T BELIEVE IT! HE DEFLECTED MY ATTACK WITH JUST HIS HAND!
CRACK
YOU DIDN'T HONESTLY EXPECT SUCH AN ATTACK TO DAMAGE ME, DID YOU?

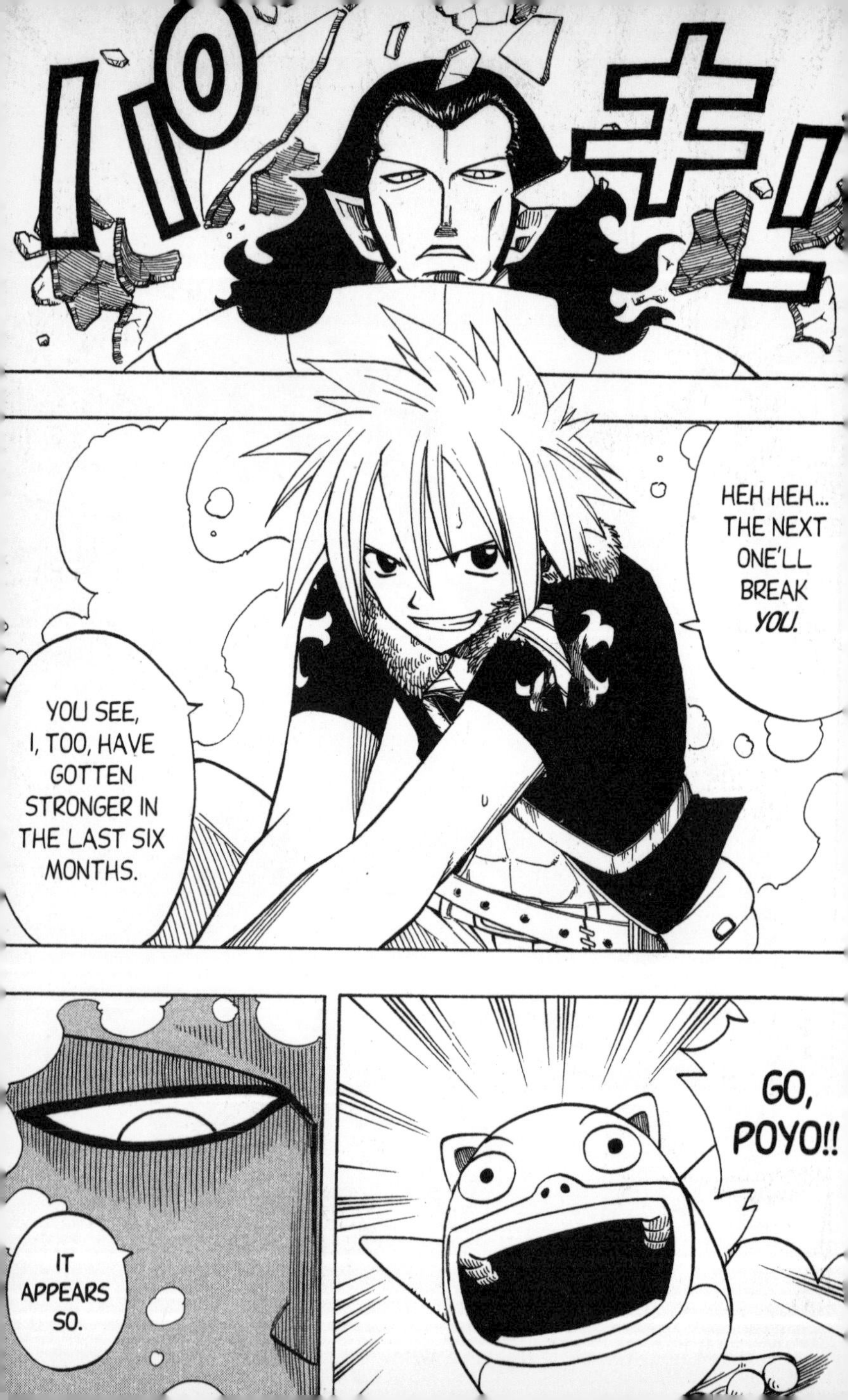
パキ!!
HEH HEH... THE NEXT ONE'LL BREAK *YOU.*
YOU SEE, I, TOO, HAVE GOTTEN STRONGER IN THE LAST SIX MONTHS.
GO, POYO!!
IT APPEARS SO.

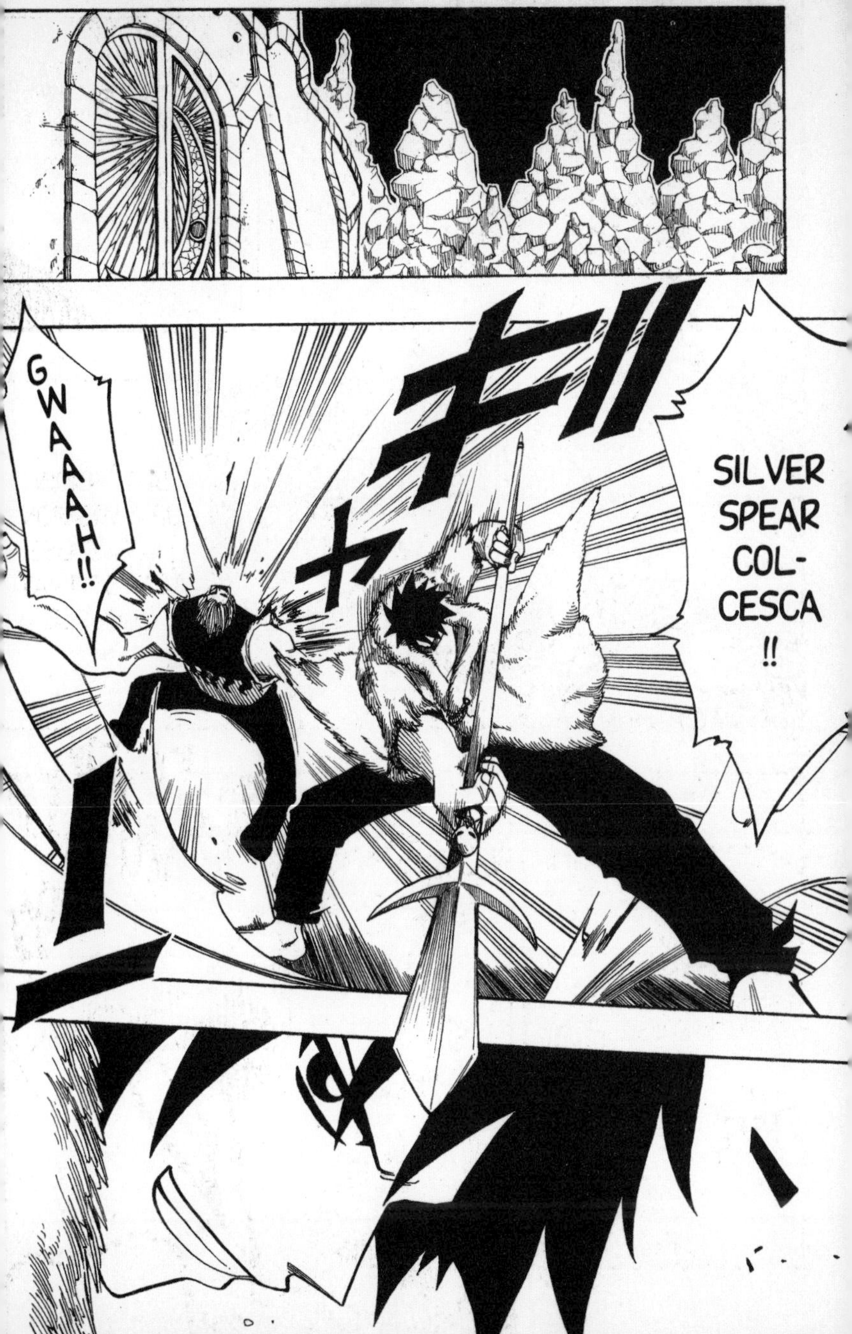
SILVER SPEAR COL-CESCA!!
GWAAAH!!

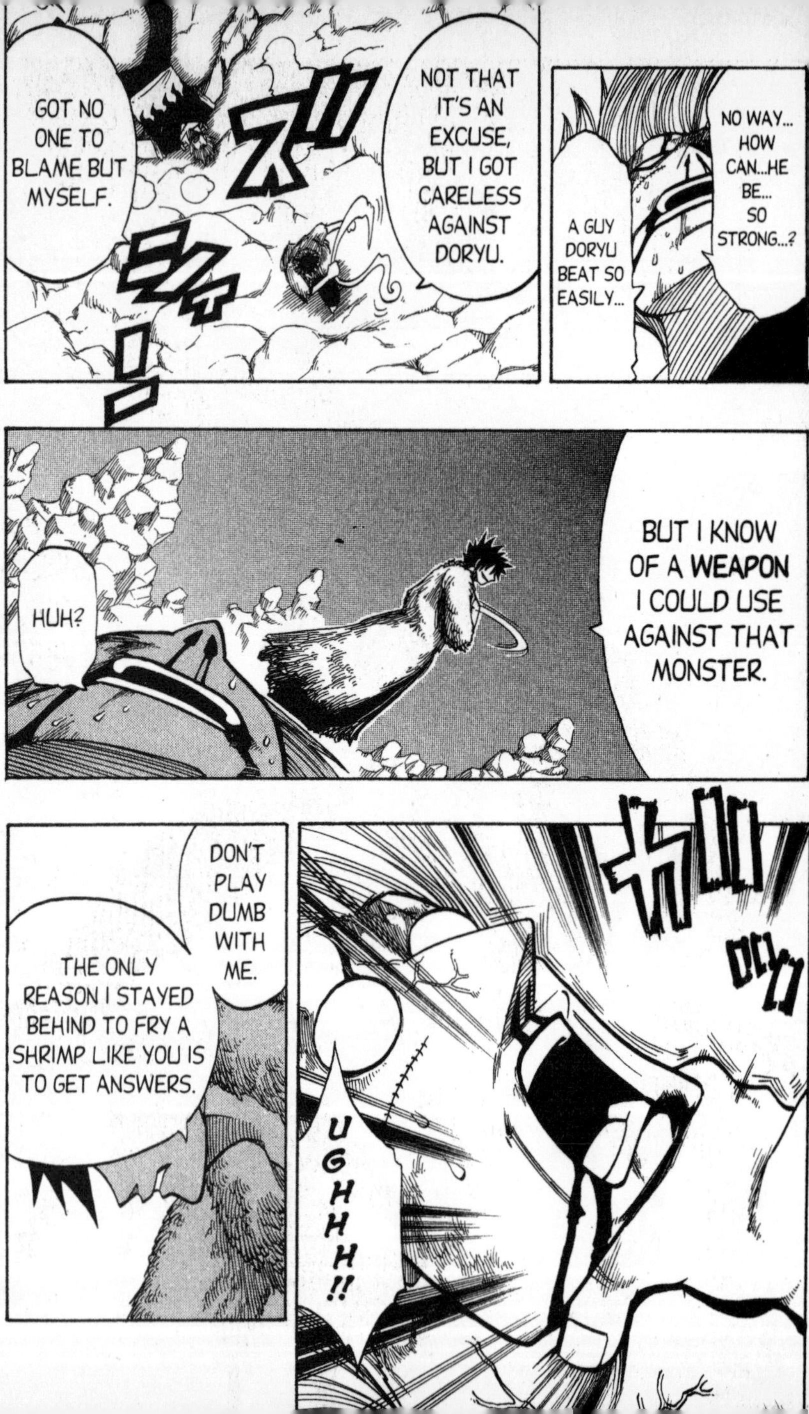
NO WAY... HOW CAN...HE BE... SO STRONG...?
A GUY DORYU BEAT SO EASILY...
NOT THAT IT'S AN EXCUSE, BUT I GOT CARELESS AGAINST DORYU.
GOT NO ONE TO BLAME BUT MYSELF.
BUT I KNOW OF A **WEAPON** I COULD USE AGAINST THAT MONSTER.
HUH?
UGHHH!!
DON'T PLAY DUMB WITH ME.
THE ONLY REASON I STAYED BEHIND TO FRY A SHRIMP LIKE YOU IS TO GET ANSWERS.

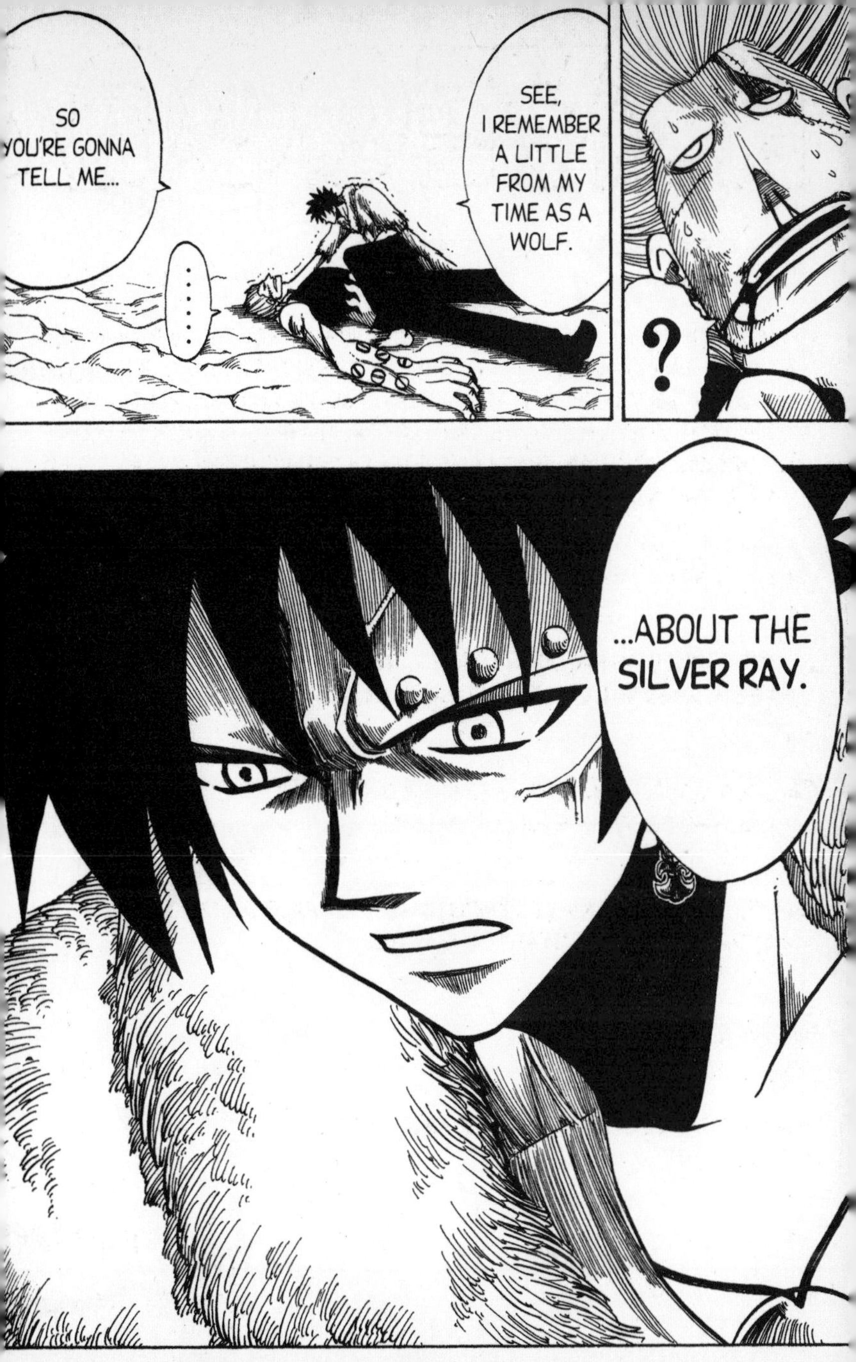
?
SEE, I REMEMBER A LITTLE FROM MY TIME AS A WOLF.
SO YOU'RE GONNA TELL ME...
......
...ABOUT THE SILVER RAY.

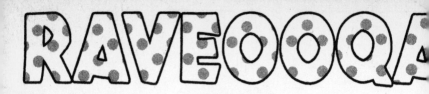

RAVE OOQA

Q. WHAT'S AN ONI-GOB? WHAT'S AN ONI-OGRE?

—HYOGOKEN - LITTLE KUROMACE

A. HUH? WHAT? AH...!! I SEE!! YOU WANT TO KNOW ABOUT "ONI RACE" NAMES. WELL GAWARA, GOB AND YANMA HAVE HORNS ON THEIR HEADS, MAKING THEM ALL "ONI" NO MATTER HOW YOU SLICE IT. THE GOB AND OGRE PARTS ARE DIFFERENT, THOUGH. GOB IS SHORT FOR GOBLIN--WHICH IS A MISCHIEVOUS FAIRY-LIKE CREATURE THAT LIKES TO PLAY PRANKS. OGRES, ON THE OTHER HAND, ARE A LOT BIGGER AND BRUTISH.

Q. SIEG'S AN ELEMENTAL MASTER, RIGHT? WHAT ELEMENT IS HE ALIGNED WITH?

—? - FRIENDS

A. IT'S HARD TO PIN HIM DOWN TO ANY PARTICULAR ELEMENT. BUT, BASICALLY, HE'S ALIGNED WITH "MAGIC" AND HIS ELEMENTAL POWERS STEM FROM THAT.

Q. HAJA'S FACE LOOKS LIKE AN UPSIDE-DOWN FACE, AS WELL AS A KIND-LOOKING ONE. WHAT DOES THIS MEAN, HIRO-KUN?

—MIYAGI-KEN - JABA & OTHERS

A. YES...HE DOES LOOK A LOT KINDER WITH THAT FACE, DOESN'T HE? (^_^) I DON'T THINK IT MEANS ANYTHING AT ALL.

Q. WHAT ARE THE "ENDLESS"?

—MIE-KEN - LEMON & LOTS O' OTHERS

A. THAT'S STILL SECRET. YOU'LL FIND OUT SOON.

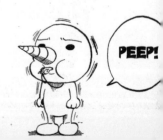

PEEP!

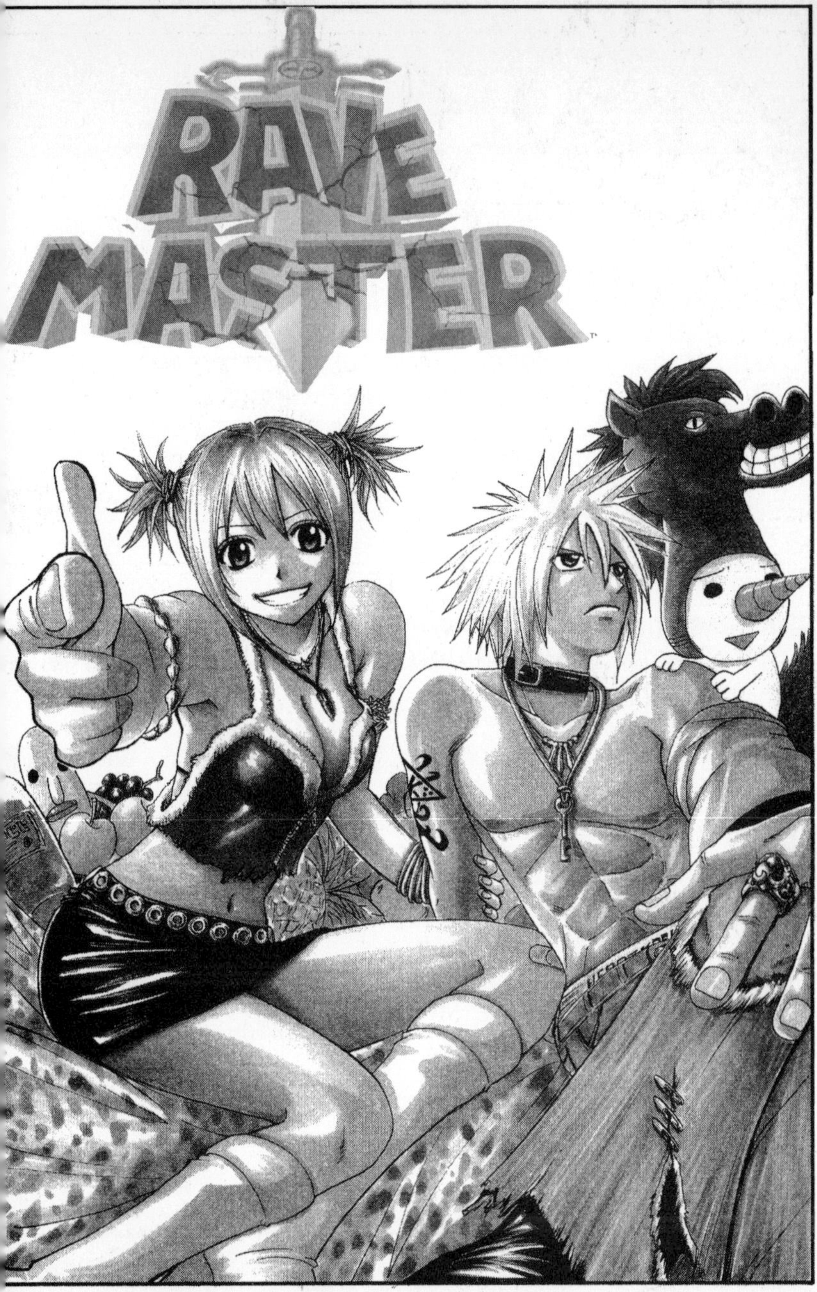
RAVE MASTER

RAVE:122 OUR HOPE, EXTINGUISHED?!

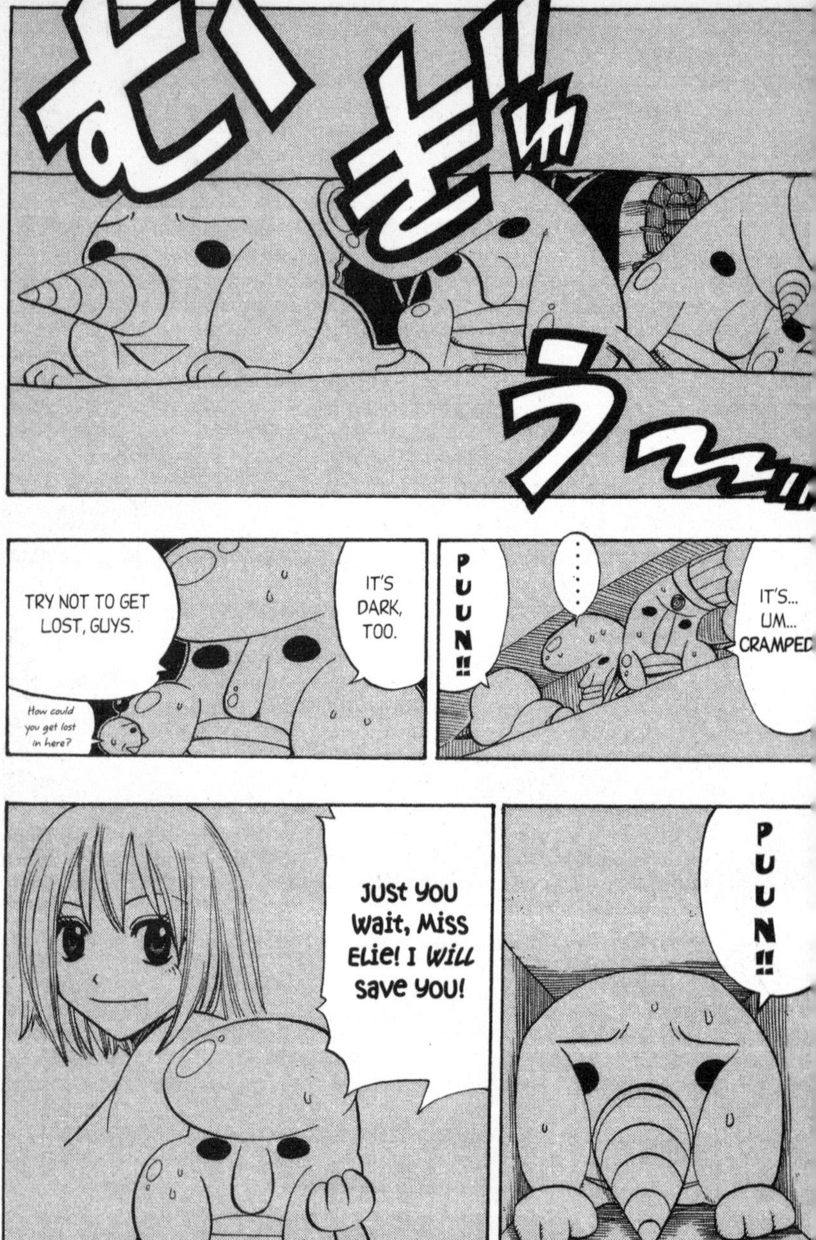
むぎゅう
IT'S... UM... CRAMPED
......
PUUN!!
IT'S DARK, TOO.
TRY NOT TO GET LOST, GUYS.
How could you get lost in here?
PUUN!!
Just you wait, Miss Elie! I *will* save you!

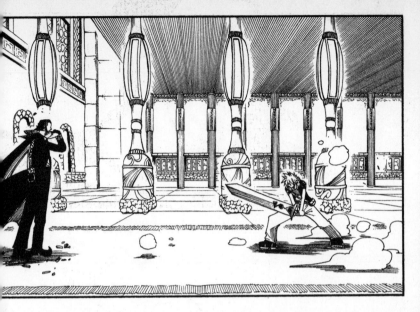

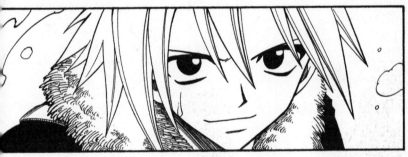

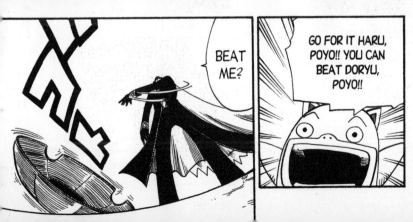

BEAT ME?

GO FOR IT HARU, POYO!! YOU CAN BEAT DORYU, POYO!!

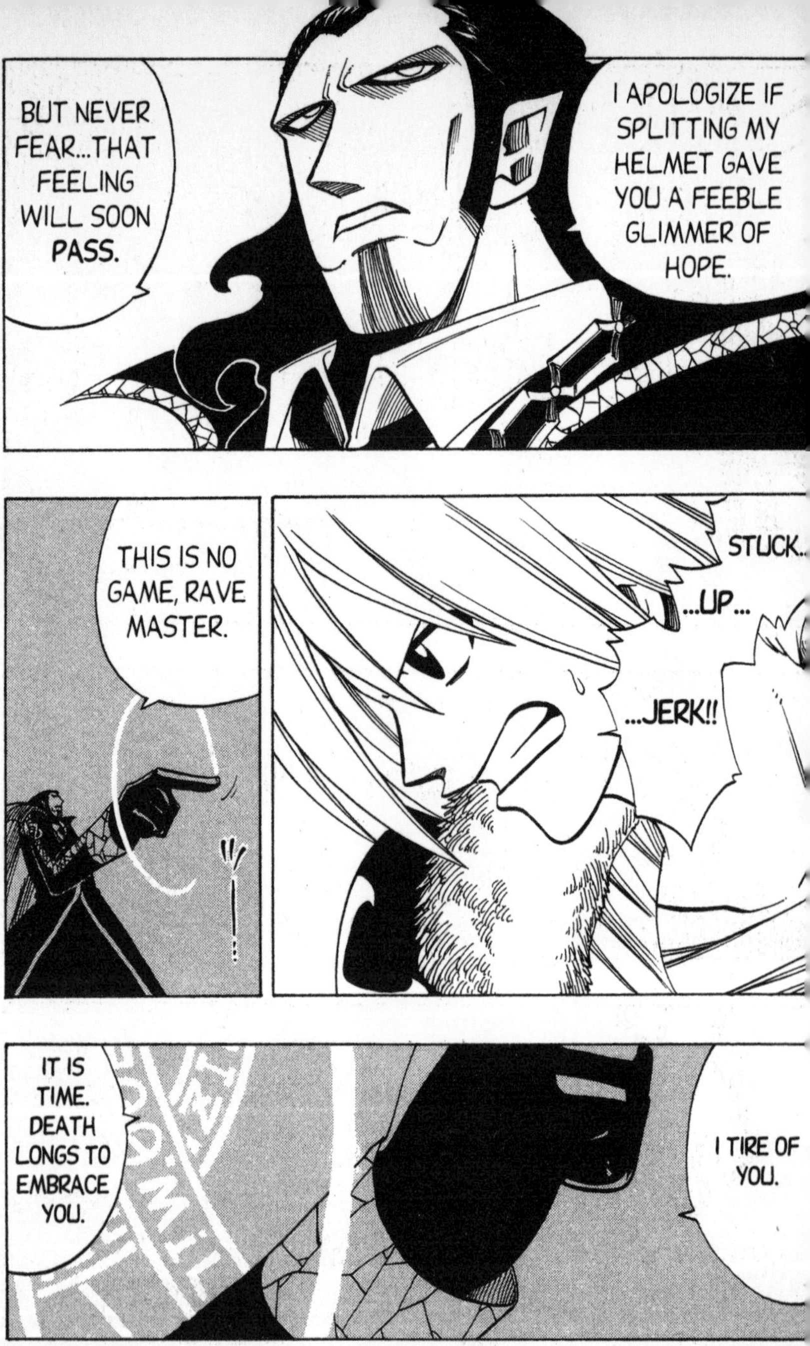
I APOLOGIZE IF SPLITTING MY HELMET GAVE YOU A FEEBLE GLIMMER OF HOPE.
BUT NEVER FEAR...THAT FEELING WILL SOON PASS.
STUCK...
...UP...
...JERK!!
THIS IS NO GAME, RAVE MASTER.
I TIRE OF YOU.
IT IS TIME. DEATH LONGS TO EMBRACE YOU.

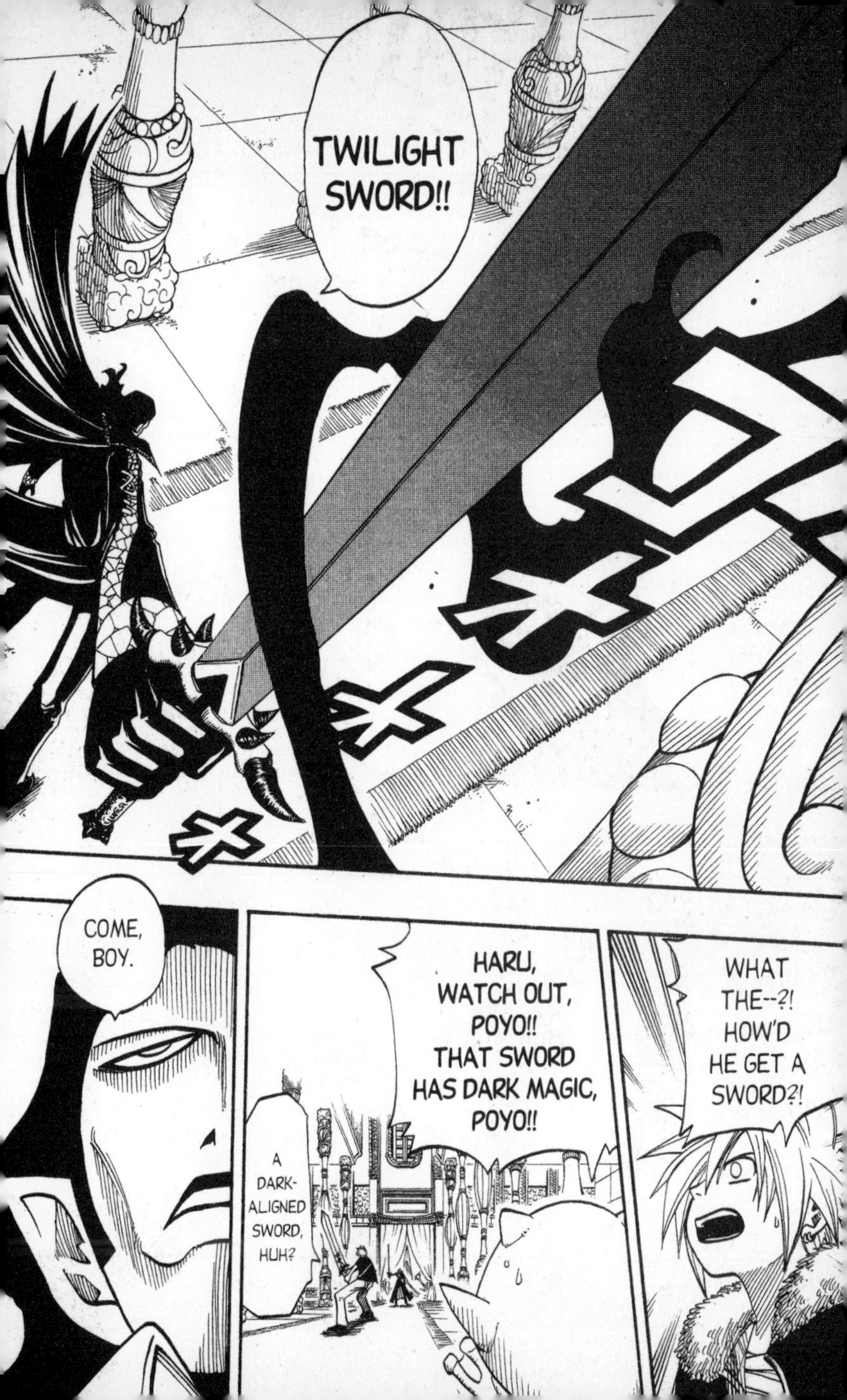
TWILIGHT SWORD!!
WHAT THE--?! HOW'D HE GET A SWORD?!
HARU, WATCH OUT, POYO!! THAT SWORD HAS DARK MAGIC, POYO!!
A DARK-ALIGNED SWORD, HUH?
COME, BOY.

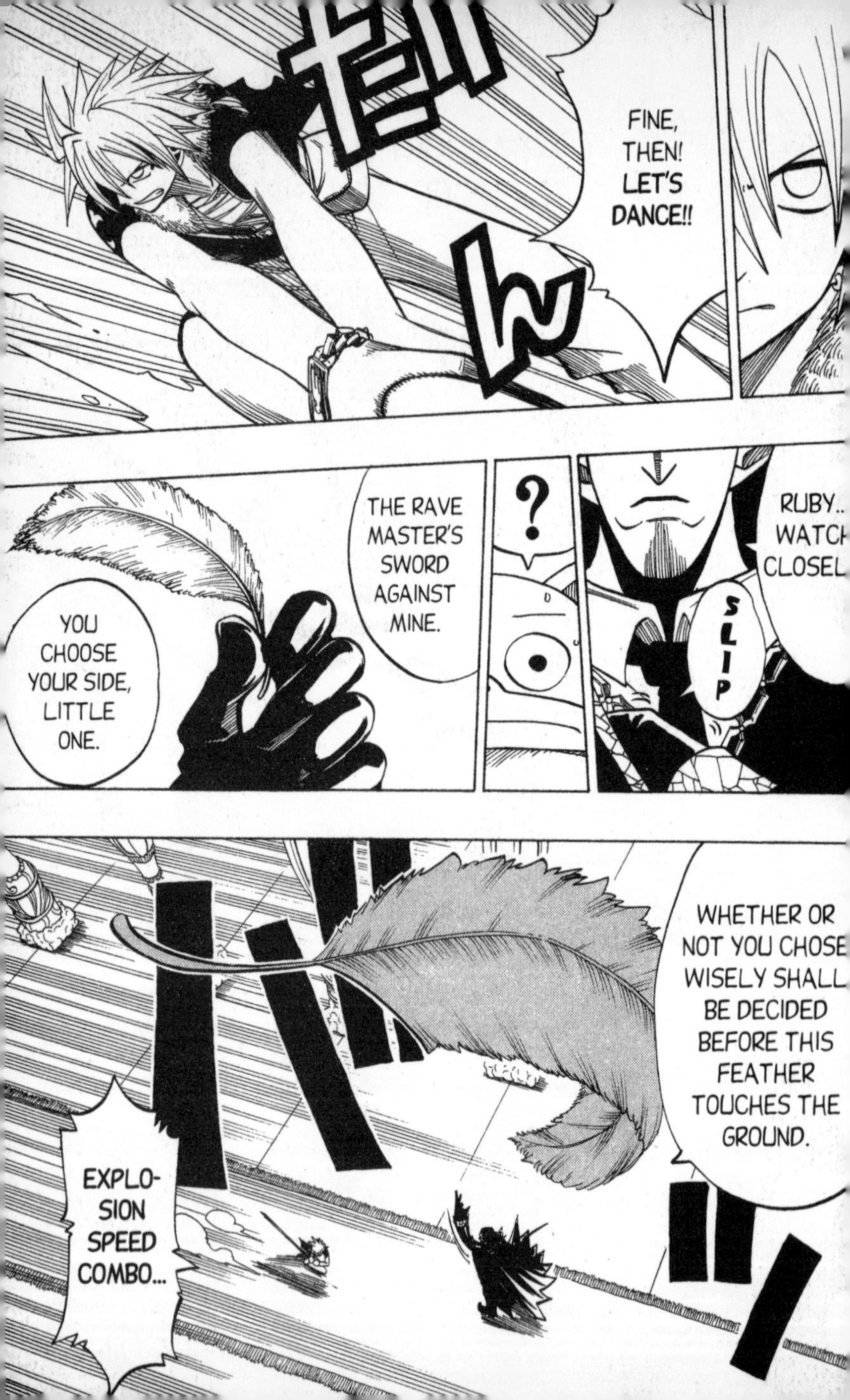
FINE, THEN! LET'S DANCE!!
RUBY... WATCH CLOSEL
SLIP
?
THE RAVE MASTER'S SWORD AGAINST MINE.
YOU CHOOSE YOUR SIDE, LITTLE ONE.
WHETHER OR NOT YOU CHOSE WISELY SHALL BE DECIDED BEFORE THIS FEATHER TOUCHES THE GROUND.
EXPLO-SION SPEED COMBO...

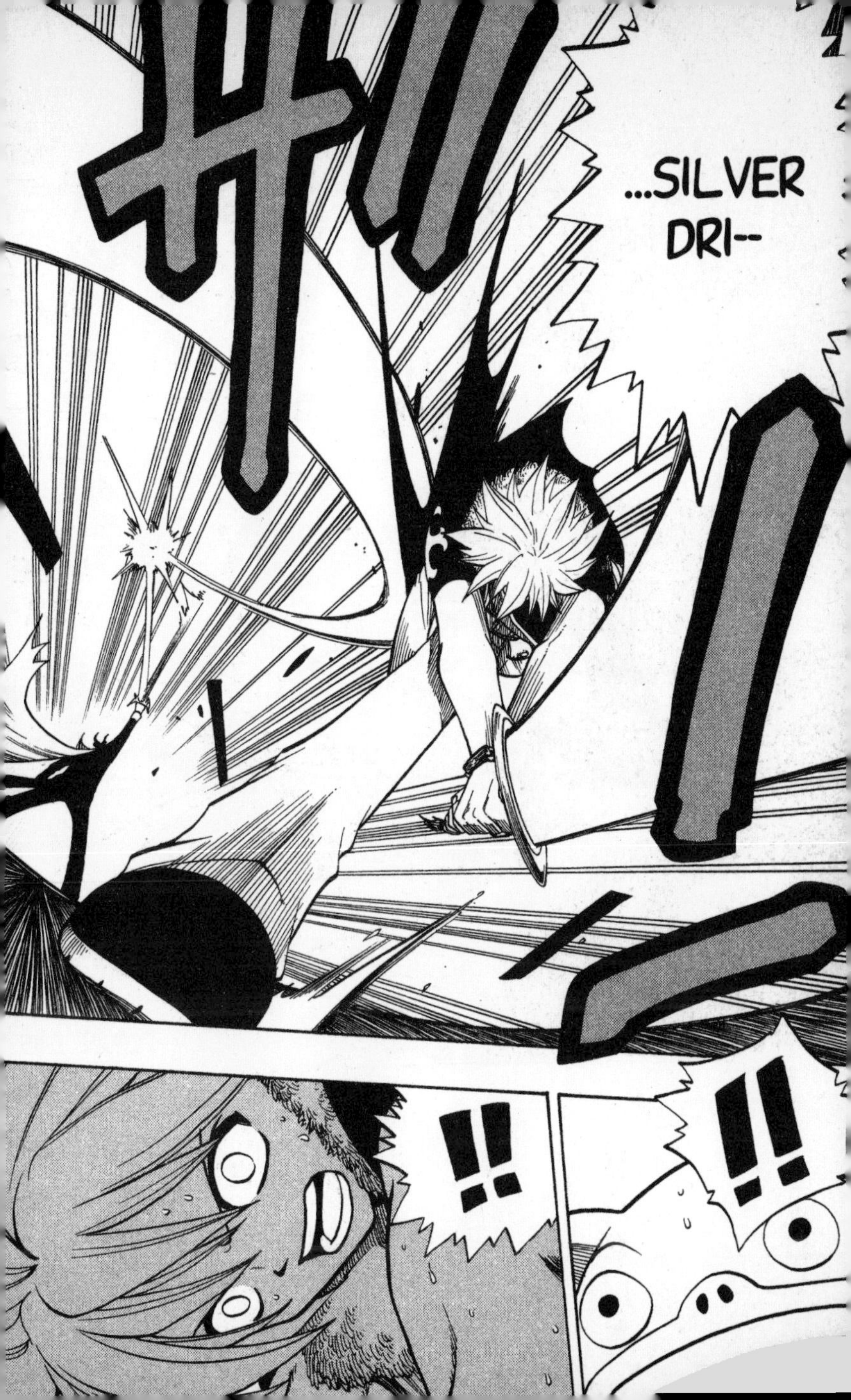
...SILVER DRI--
!!
!!

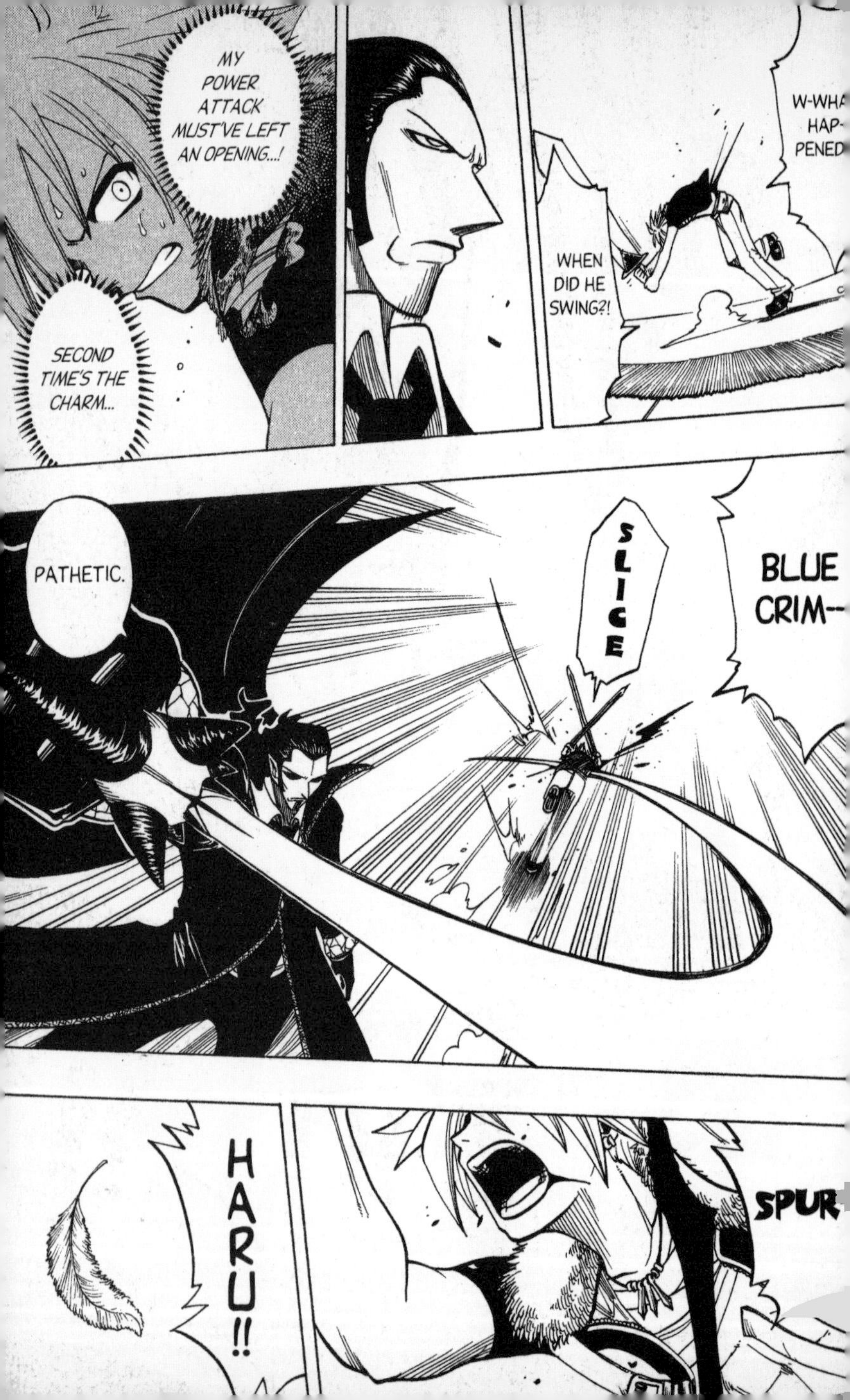
W-WHA HAP-PENED
WHEN DID HE SWING?!
MY POWER ATTACK MUST'VE LEFT AN OPENING...!
SECOND TIME'S THE CHARM...
BLUE CRIM--
SLICE
PATHETIC.
SPUR
HARU!!

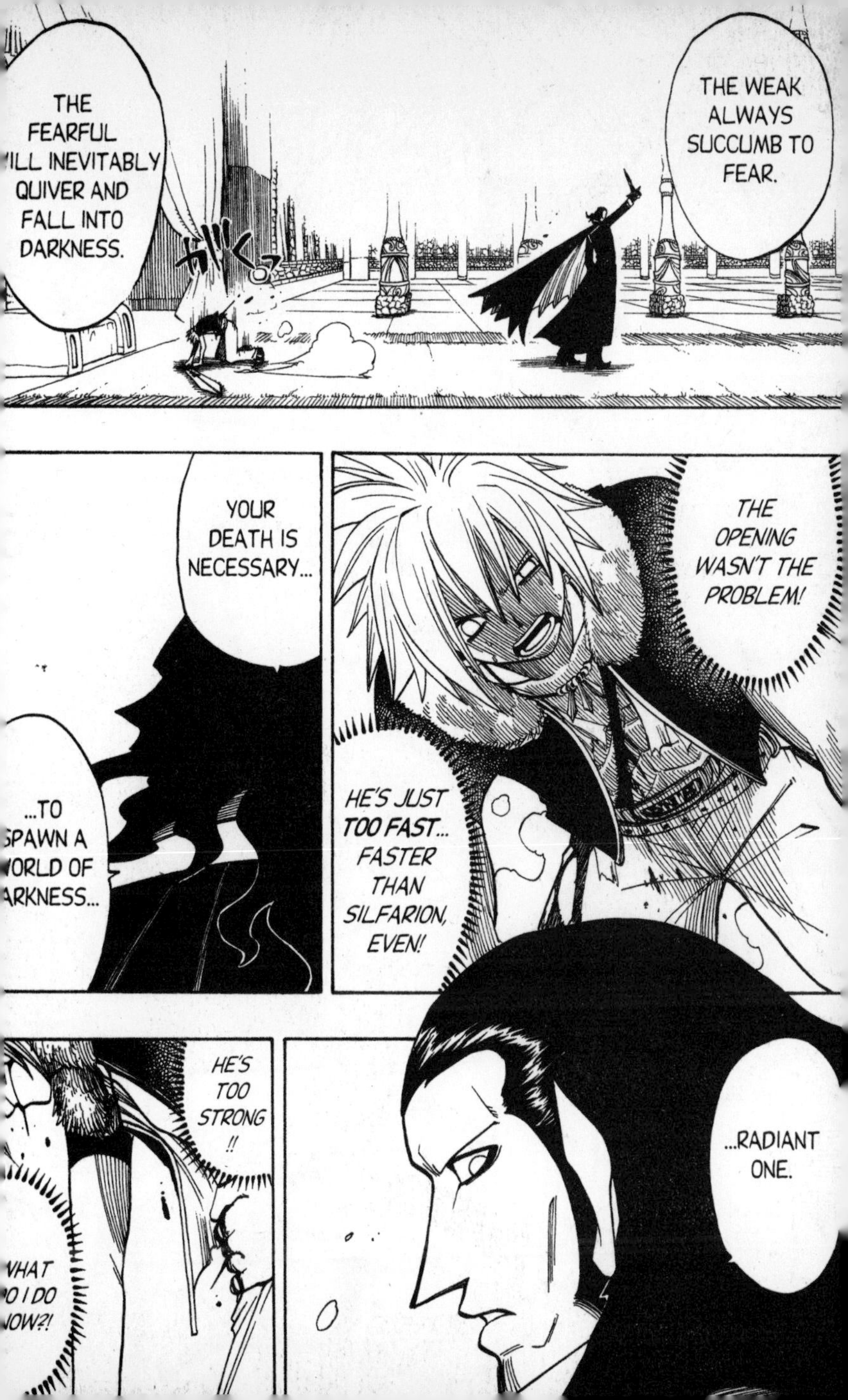
THE WEAK ALWAYS SUCCUMB TO FEAR.
THE FEARFUL ILL INEVITABLY QUIVER AND FALL INTO DARKNESS.
THE OPENING WASN'T THE PROBLEM!
HE'S JUST TOO FAST... FASTER THAN SILFARION, EVEN!
YOUR DEATH IS NECESSARY...
...TO PAWN A ORLD OF ARKNESS...
...RADIANT ONE.
HE'S TOO STRONG !!
HAT O I DO OW?!

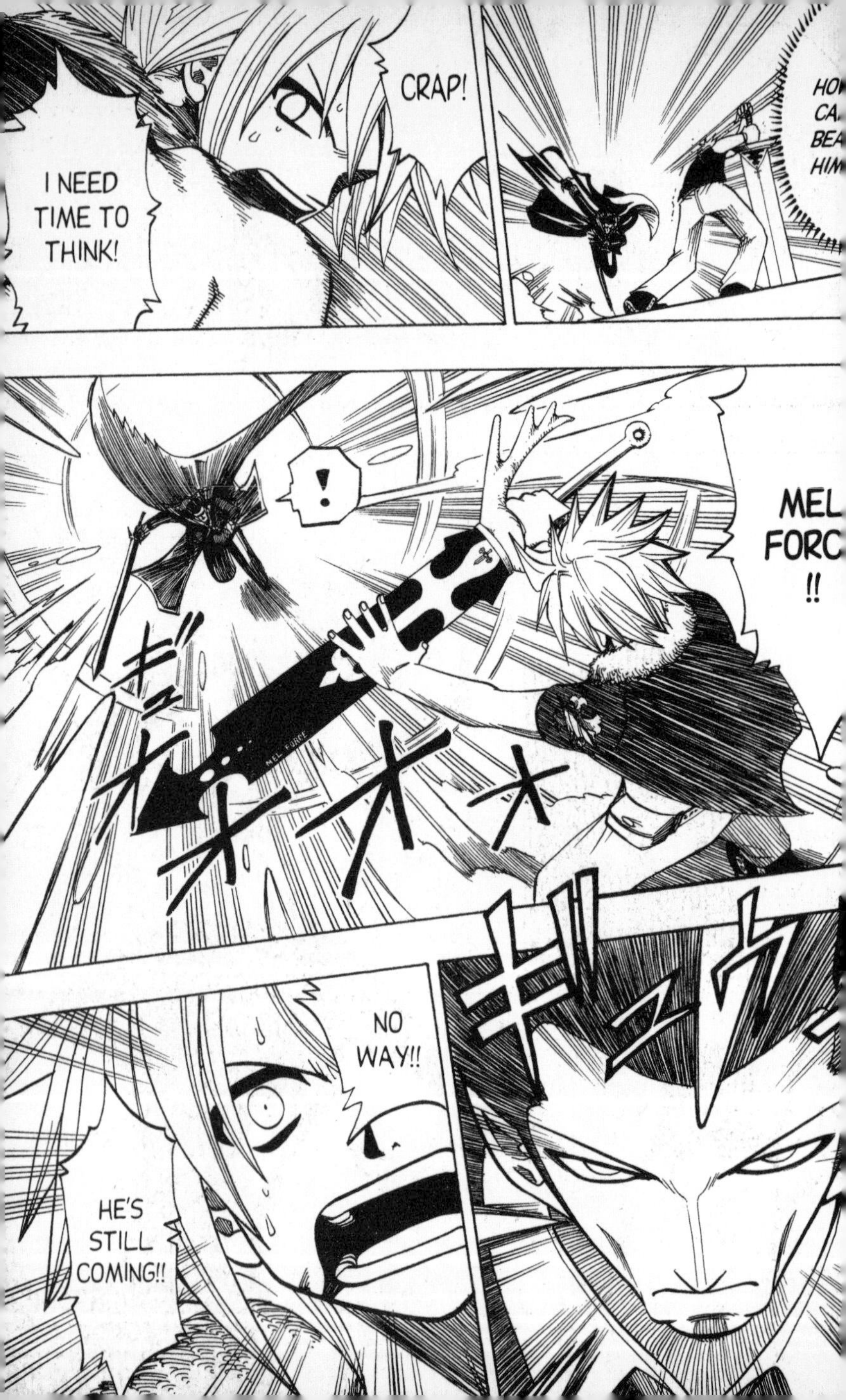
HO CA BEA HIM
CRAP!
I NEED TIME TO THINK!
!
MEL FORC !!
ギュオオオオ
MEL FORCE
ギュウ
NO WAY!!
HE'S STILL COMING!!

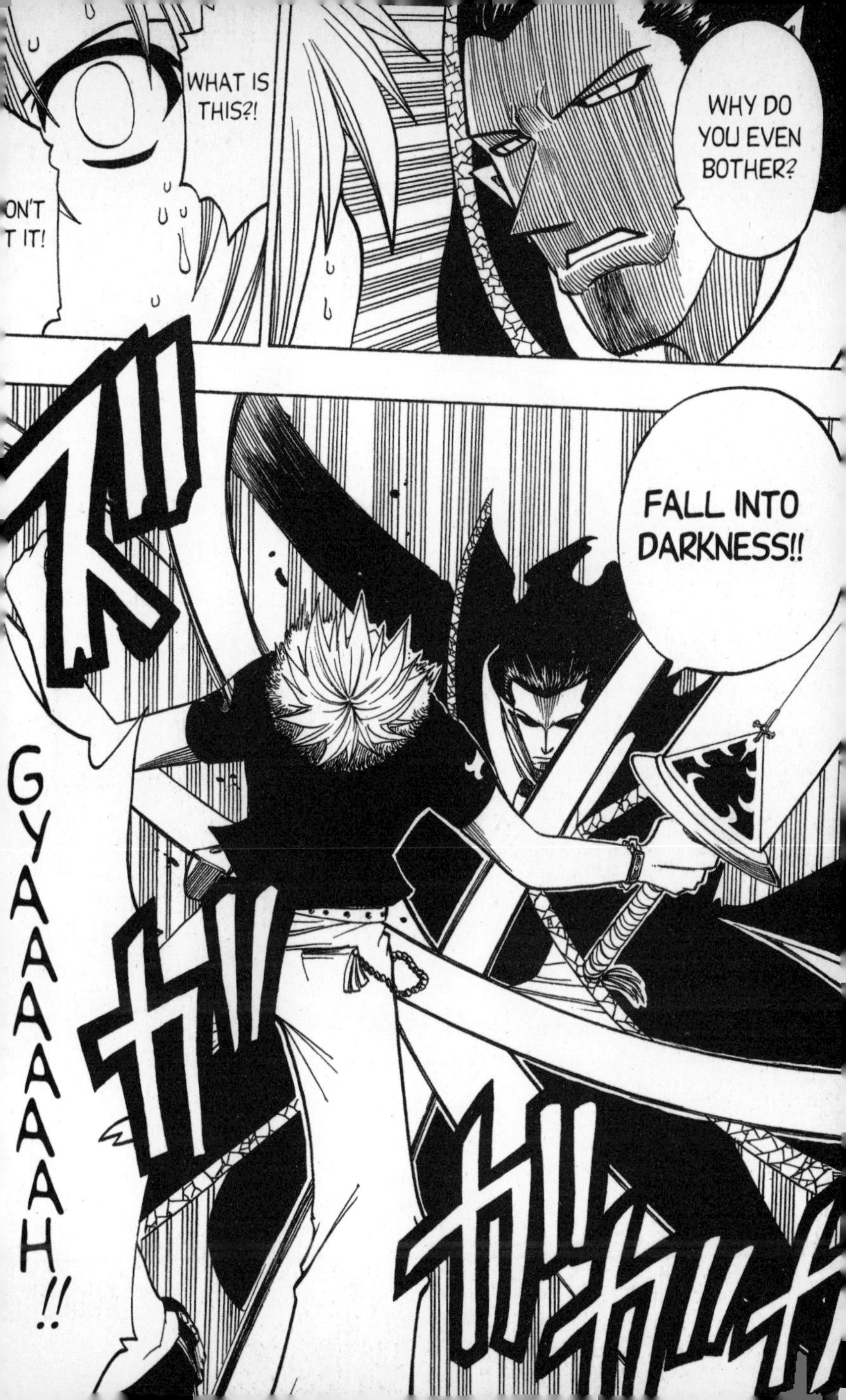
WHY DO YOU EVEN BOTHER?
WHAT IS THIS?!
ON'T
T IT!
FALL INTO DARKNESS!!
GYAAAAAAH!!

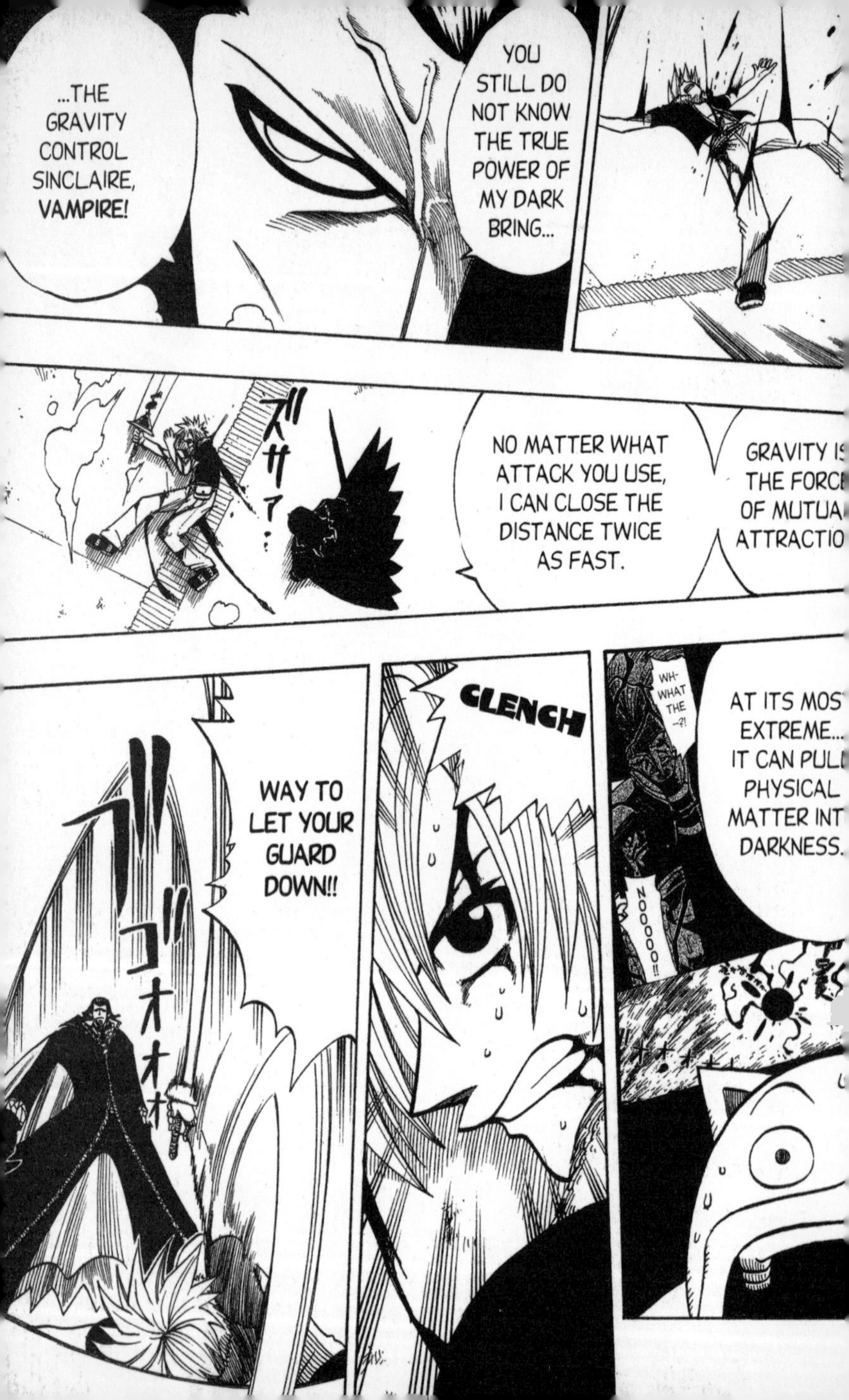
YOU STILL DO NOT KNOW THE TRUE POWER OF MY DARK BRING...
...THE GRAVITY CONTROL SINCLAIRE, VAMPIRE!
GRAVITY IS THE FORC OF MUTUA ATTRACTIO
NO MATTER WHAT ATTACK YOU USE, I CAN CLOSE THE DISTANCE TWICE AS FAST.
ズザァ…
AT ITS MOS EXTREME... IT CAN PULL PHYSICAL MATTER INT DARKNESS.
WH- WHAT THE --?!
NOOOOOO!!
CLENCH
WAY TO LET YOUR GUARD DOWN!!
ゴオオオ

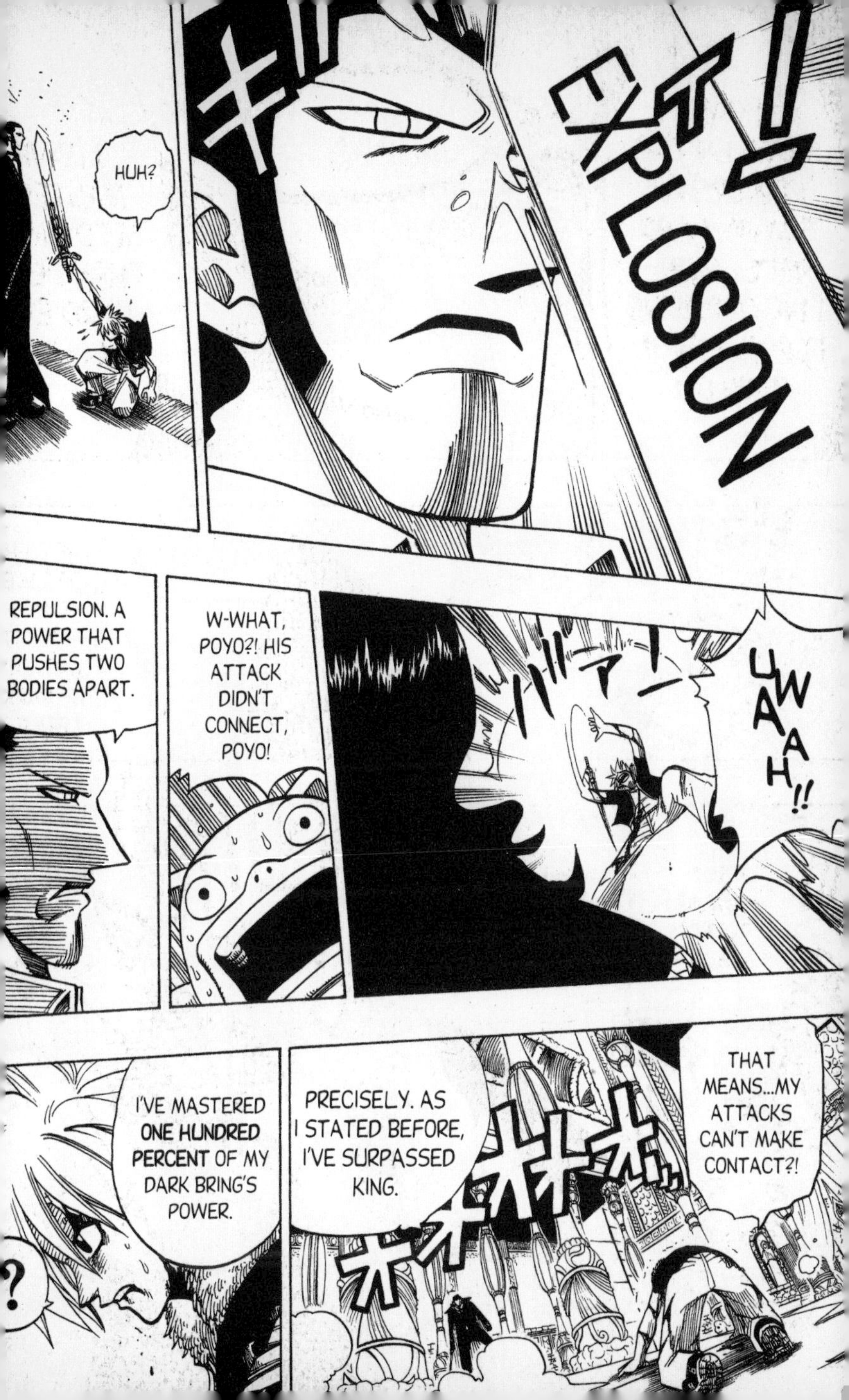
EXPLOSION
HUH?
UWAAH!!
W-WHAT, POYO?! HIS ATTACK DIDN'T CONNECT, POYO!
REPULSION. A POWER THAT PUSHES TWO BODIES APART.
THAT MEANS...MY ATTACKS CAN'T MAKE CONTACT?!
PRECISELY. AS I STATED BEFORE, I'VE SURPASSED KING.
I'VE MASTERED **ONE HUNDRED PERCENT** OF MY DARK BRING'S POWER.
?

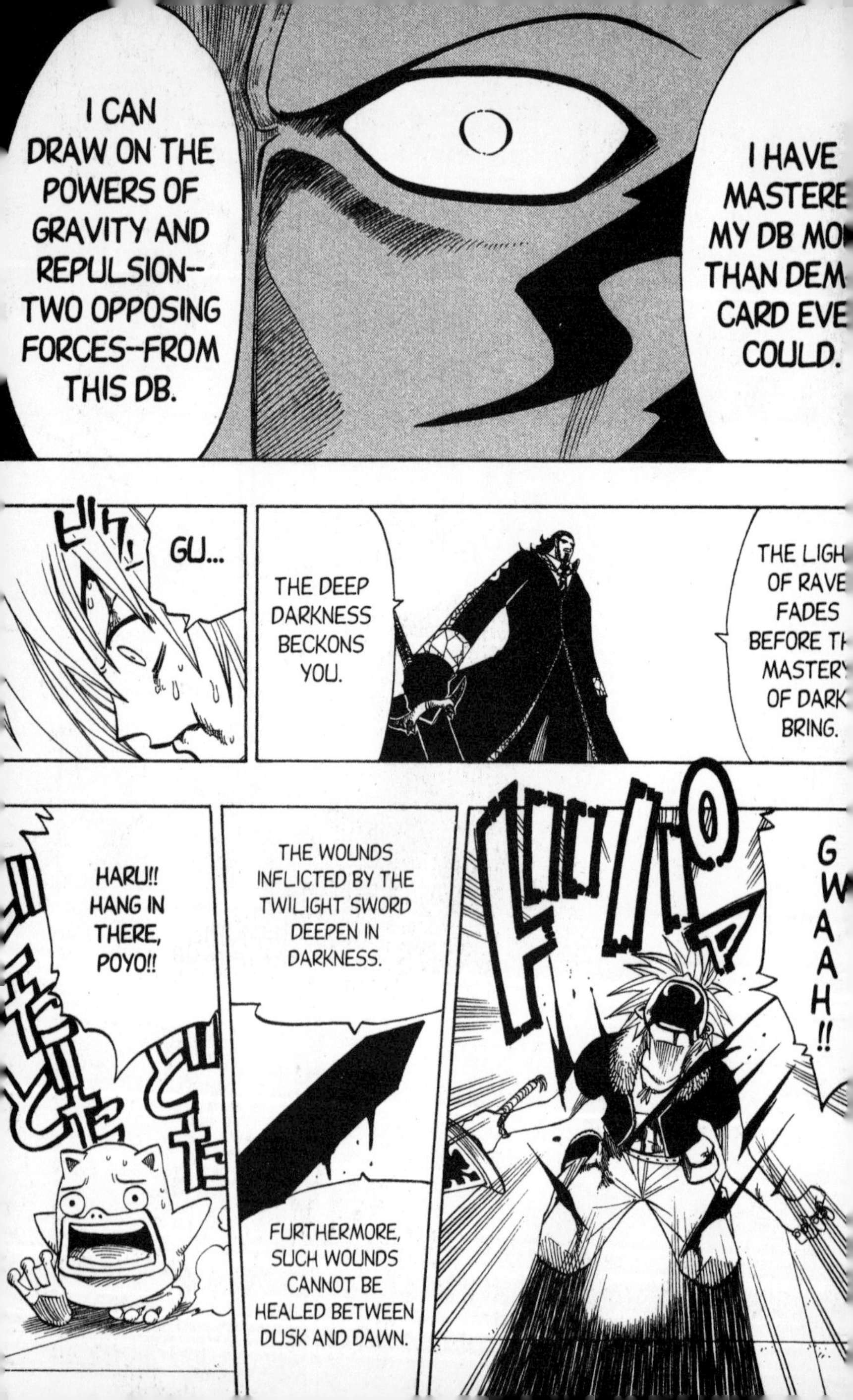

I HAVE MASTERE MY DB MO THAN DEM CARD EVE COULD.
I CAN DRAW ON THE POWERS OF GRAVITY AND REPULSION--TWO OPPOSING FORCES--FROM THIS DB.
THE LIGH OF RAVE FADES BEFORE TH MASTERY OF DARK BRING.
THE DEEP DARKNESS BECKONS YOU.
GU...
GWAAH!!
THE WOUNDS INFLICTED BY THE TWILIGHT SWORD DEEPEN IN DARKNESS.
FURTHERMORE, SUCH WOUNDS CANNOT BE HEALED BETWEEN DUSK AND DAWN.
HARU!! HANG IN THERE, POYO!!

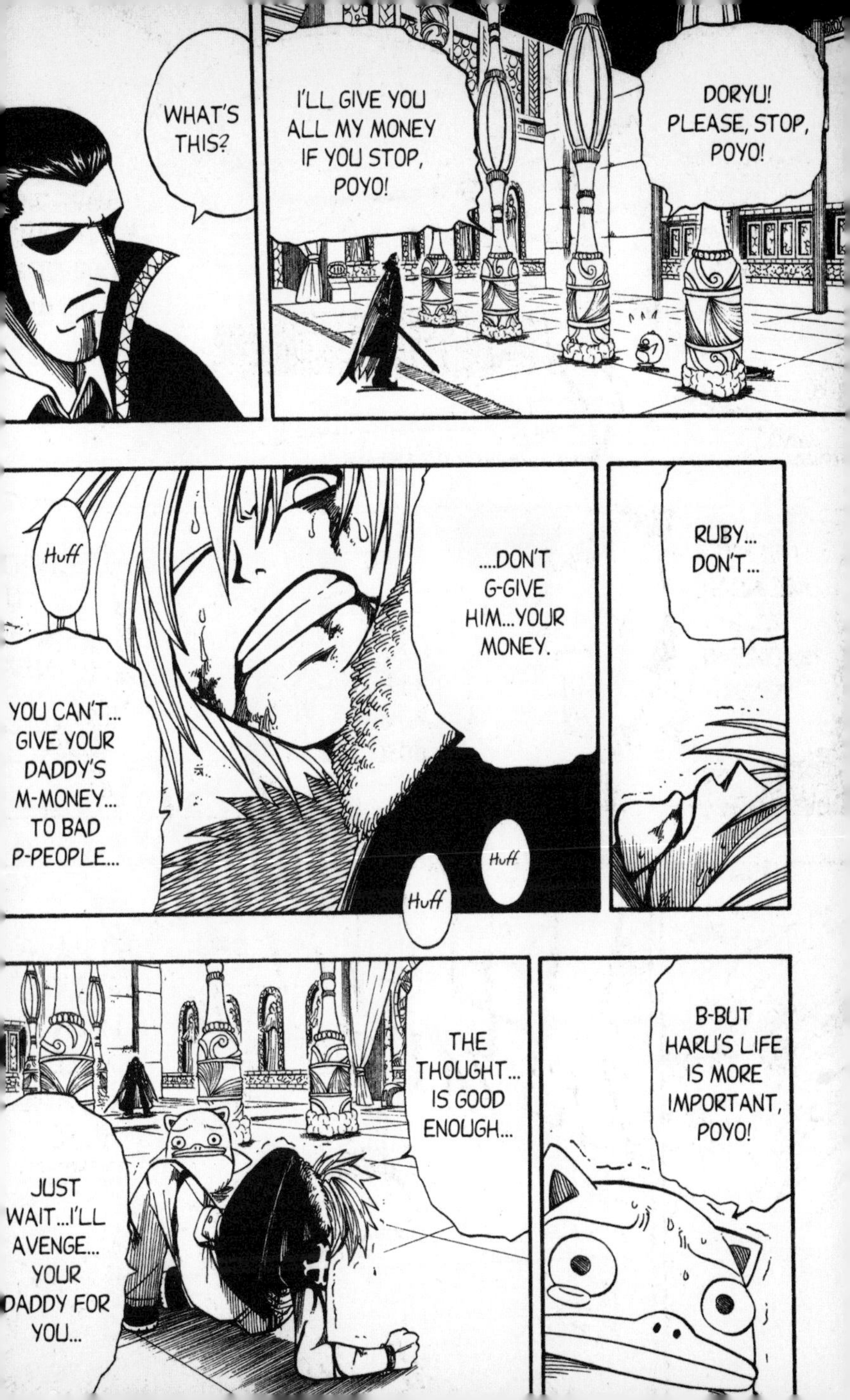
DORYU! PLEASE, STOP, POYO!
I'LL GIVE YOU ALL MY MONEY IF YOU STOP, POYO!
WHAT'S THIS?
RUBY... DON'T...
....DON'T G-GIVE HIM...YOUR MONEY.
Huff
Huff
Huff
YOU CAN'T... GIVE YOUR DADDY'S M-MONEY... TO BAD P-PEOPLE...
B-BUT HARU'S LIFE IS MORE IMPORTANT, POYO!
THE THOUGHT... IS GOOD ENOUGH...
JUST WAIT...I'LL AVENGE... YOUR DADDY FOR YOU...

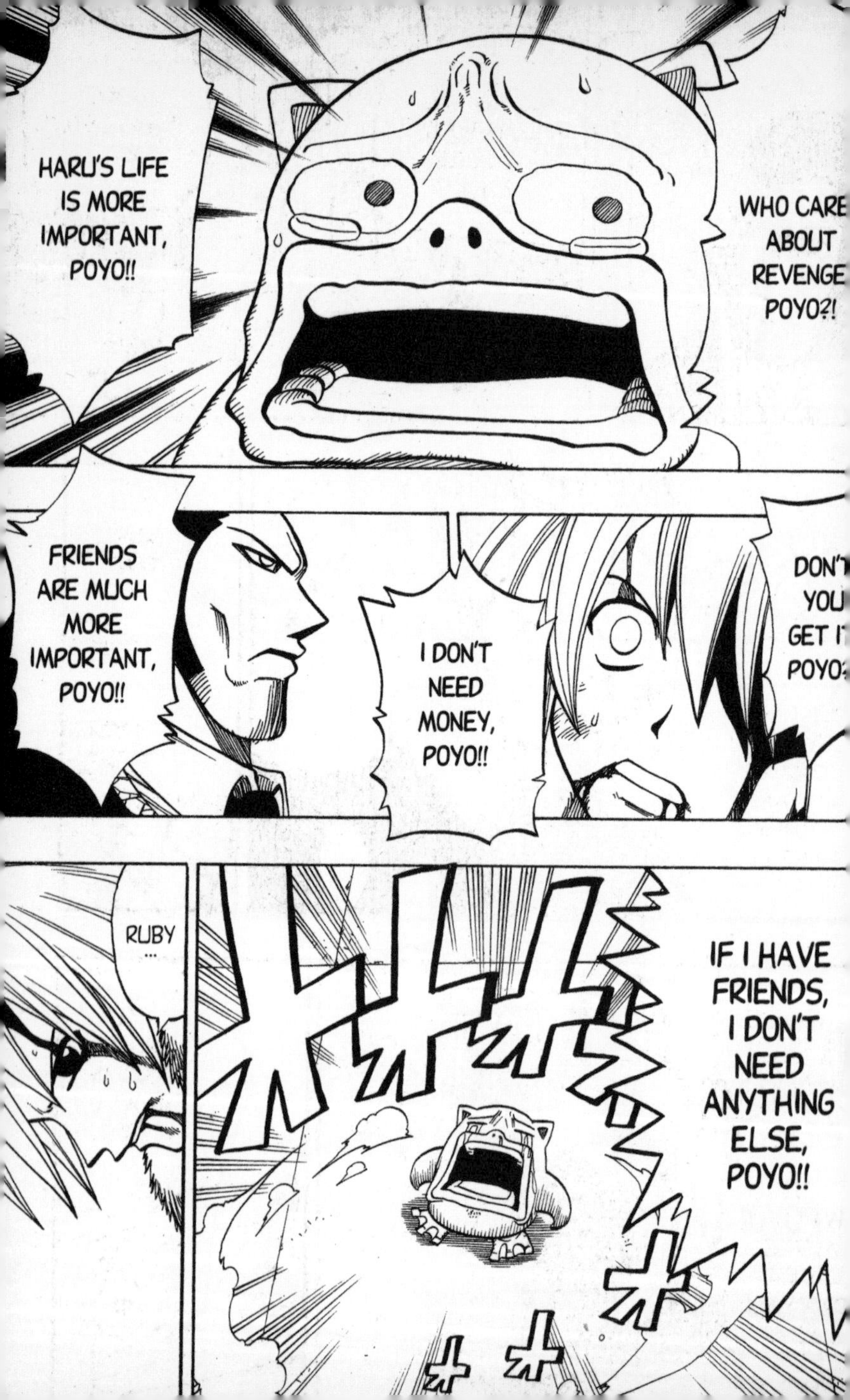
WHO CARE ABOUT REVENGE POYO?!
HARU'S LIFE IS MORE IMPORTANT, POYO!!
DON'T YOU GET IT POYO?
I DON'T NEED MONEY, POYO!!
FRIENDS ARE MUCH MORE IMPORTANT, POYO!!
IF I HAVE FRIENDS, I DON'T NEED ANYTHING ELSE, POYO!!
RUBY ...

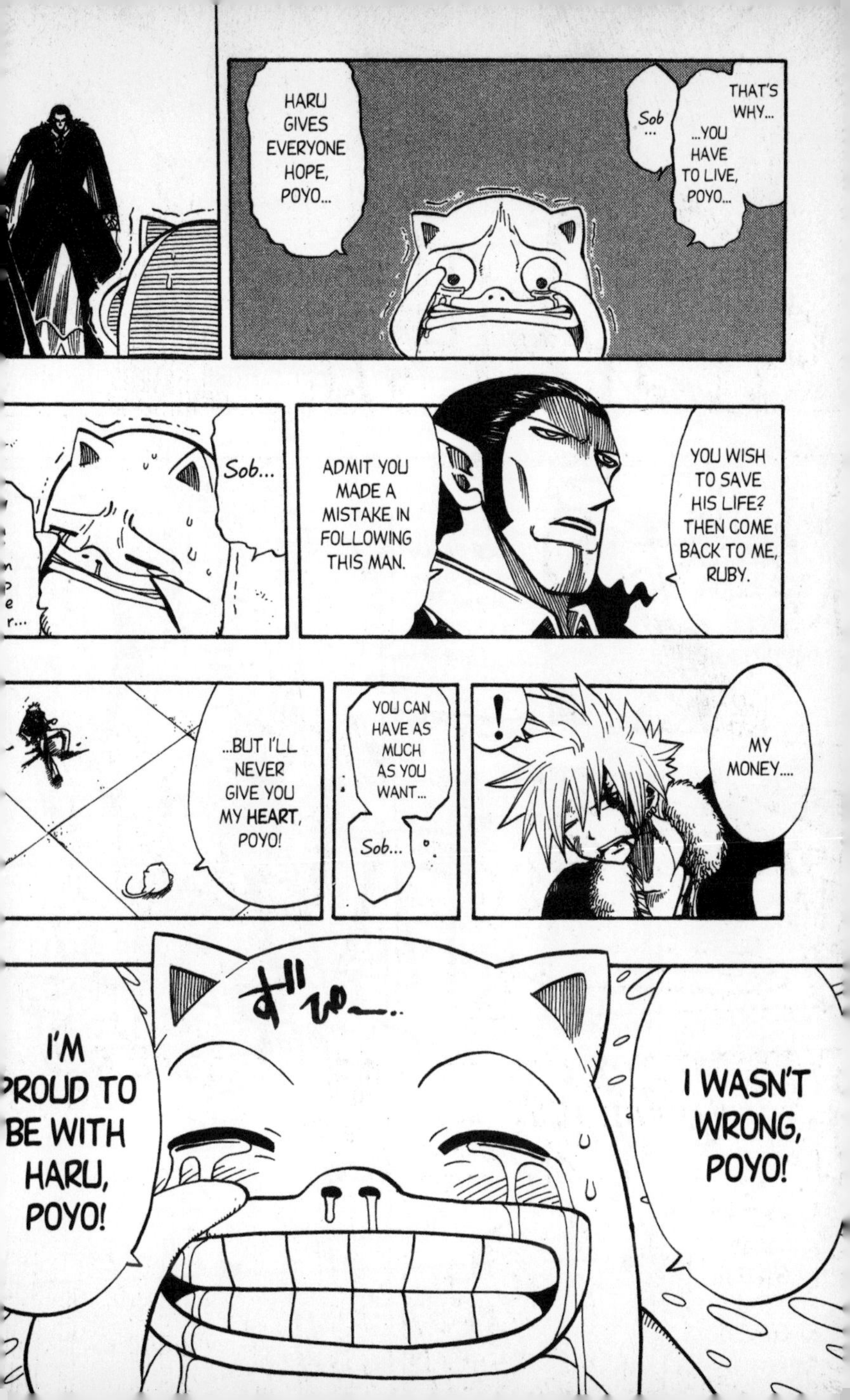
THAT'S WHY... ...YOU HAVE TO LIVE, POYO...
Sob...
HARU GIVES EVERYONE HOPE, POYO...
YOU WISH TO SAVE HIS LIFE? THEN COME BACK TO ME, RUBY.
ADMIT YOU MADE A MISTAKE IN FOLLOWING THIS MAN.
Sob...
!
MY MONEY....
YOU CAN HAVE AS MUCH AS YOU WANT...
Sob...
...BUT I'LL NEVER GIVE YOU MY HEART, POYO!
I WASN'T WRONG, POYO!
ずび〜..
I'M PROUD TO BE WITH HARU, POYO!

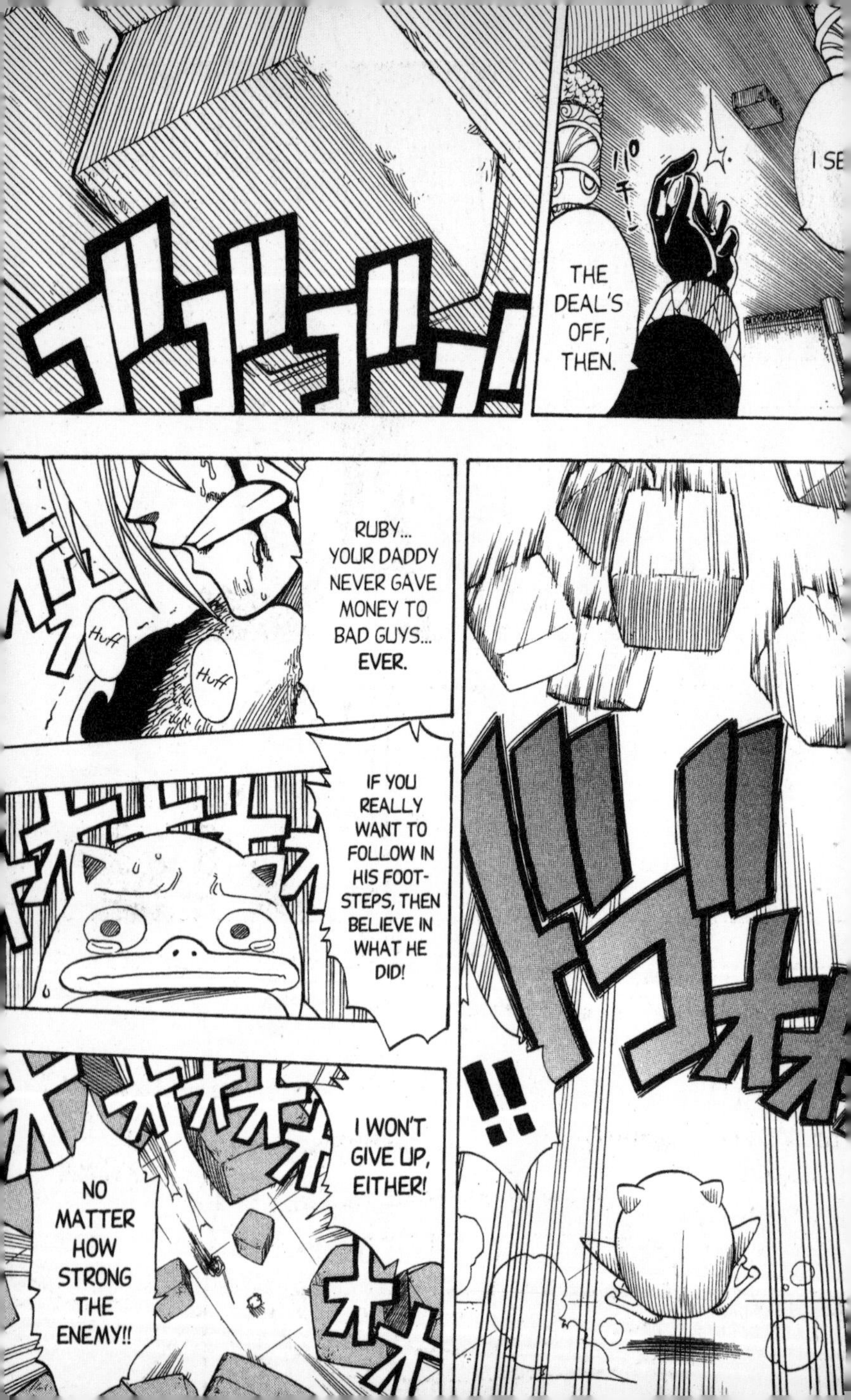

I SE
THE DEAL'S OFF, THEN.
!!
RUBY... YOUR DADDY NEVER GAVE MONEY TO BAD GUYS... EVER.
Huff
Huff
IF YOU REALLY WANT TO FOLLOW IN HIS FOOT-STEPS, THEN BELIEVE IN WHAT HE DID!
I WON'T GIVE UP, EITHER!
NO MATTER HOW STRONG THE ENEMY!!

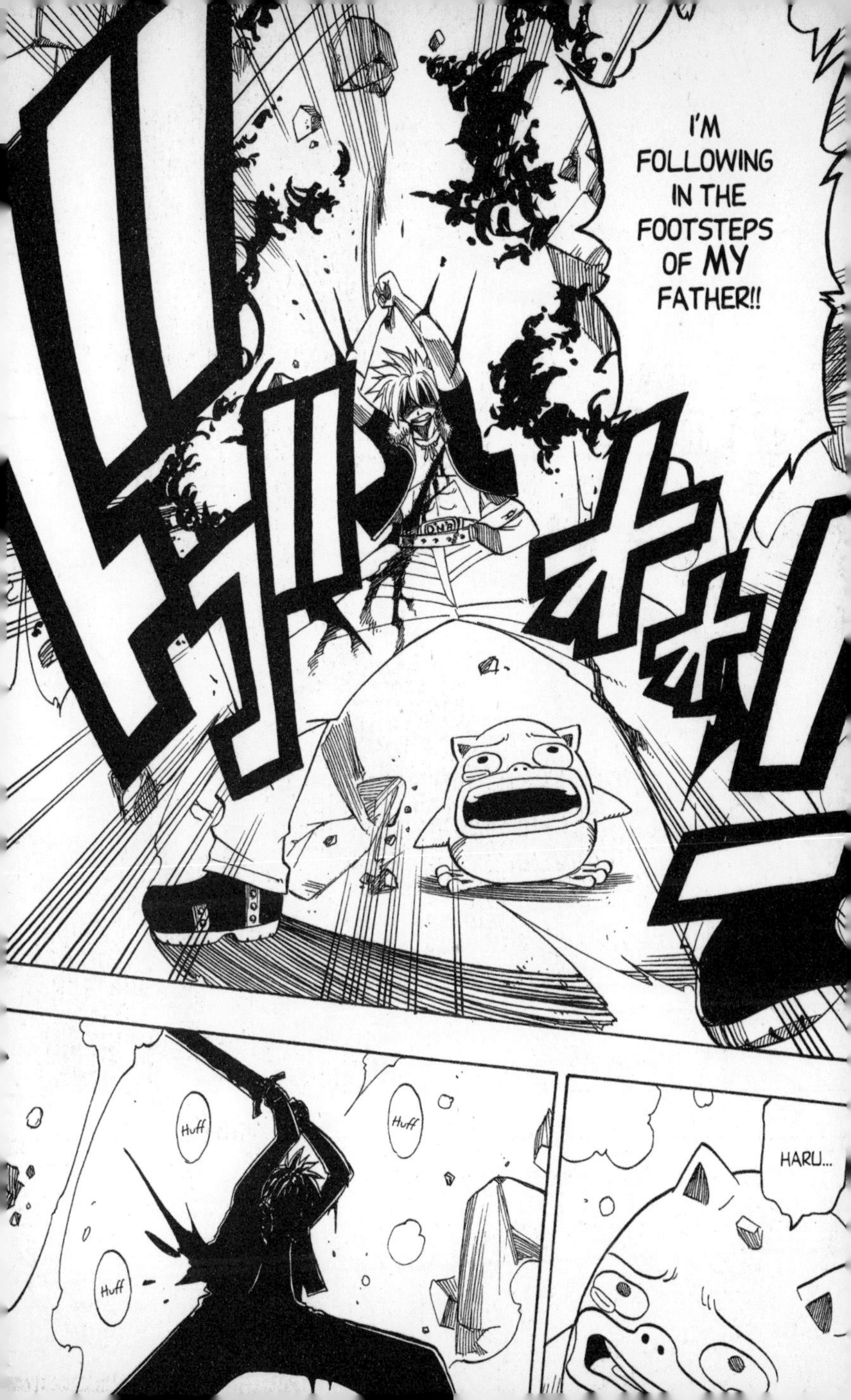
I'M FOLLOWING IN THE FOOTSTEPS OF MY FATHER!!
HARU...
Huff
Huff
Huff

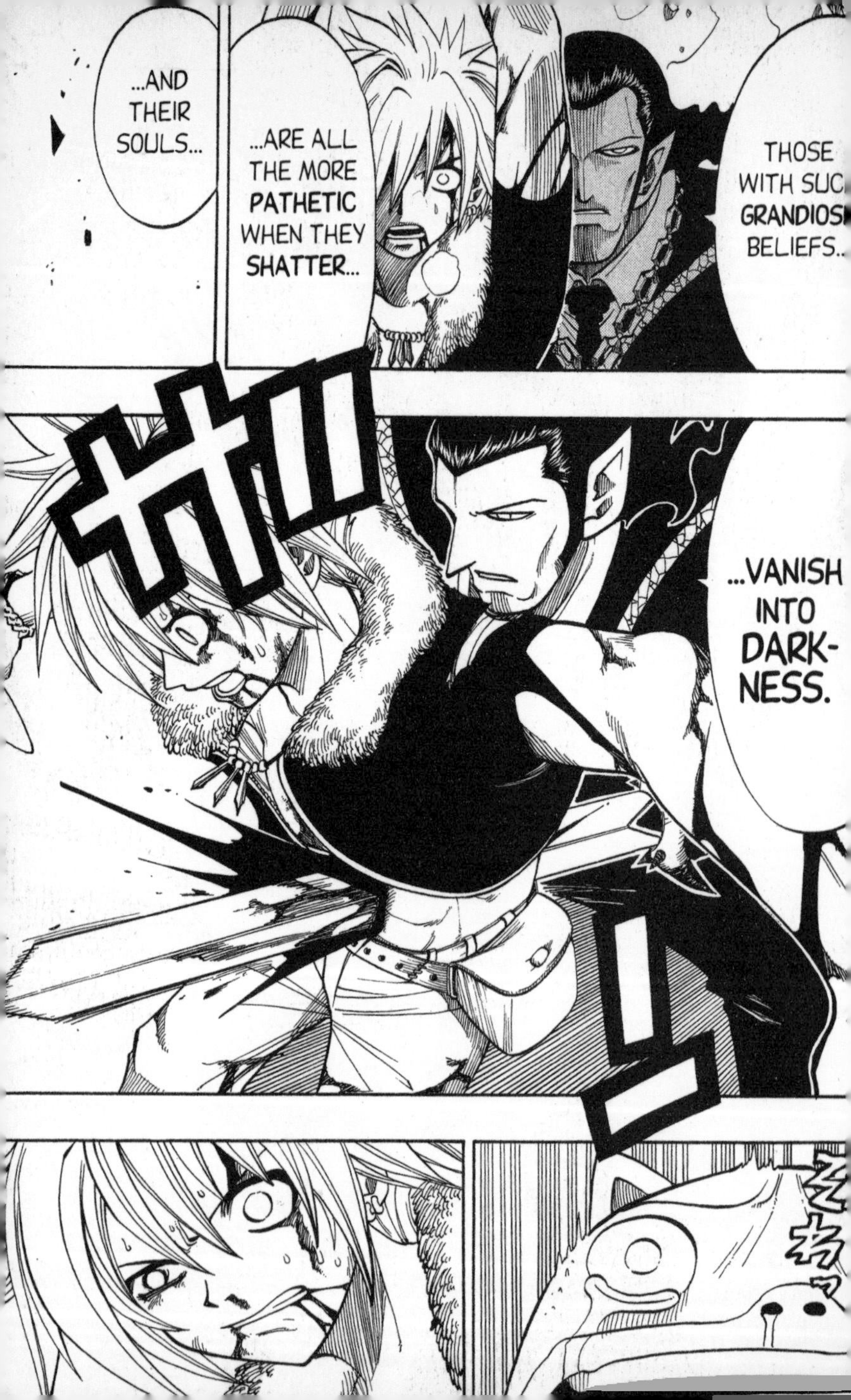
THOSE WITH SUC GRANDIOS BELIEFS..
...ARE ALL THE MORE PATHETIC WHEN THEY SHATTER...
...AND THEIR SOULS...
...VANISH INTO DARK-NESS.

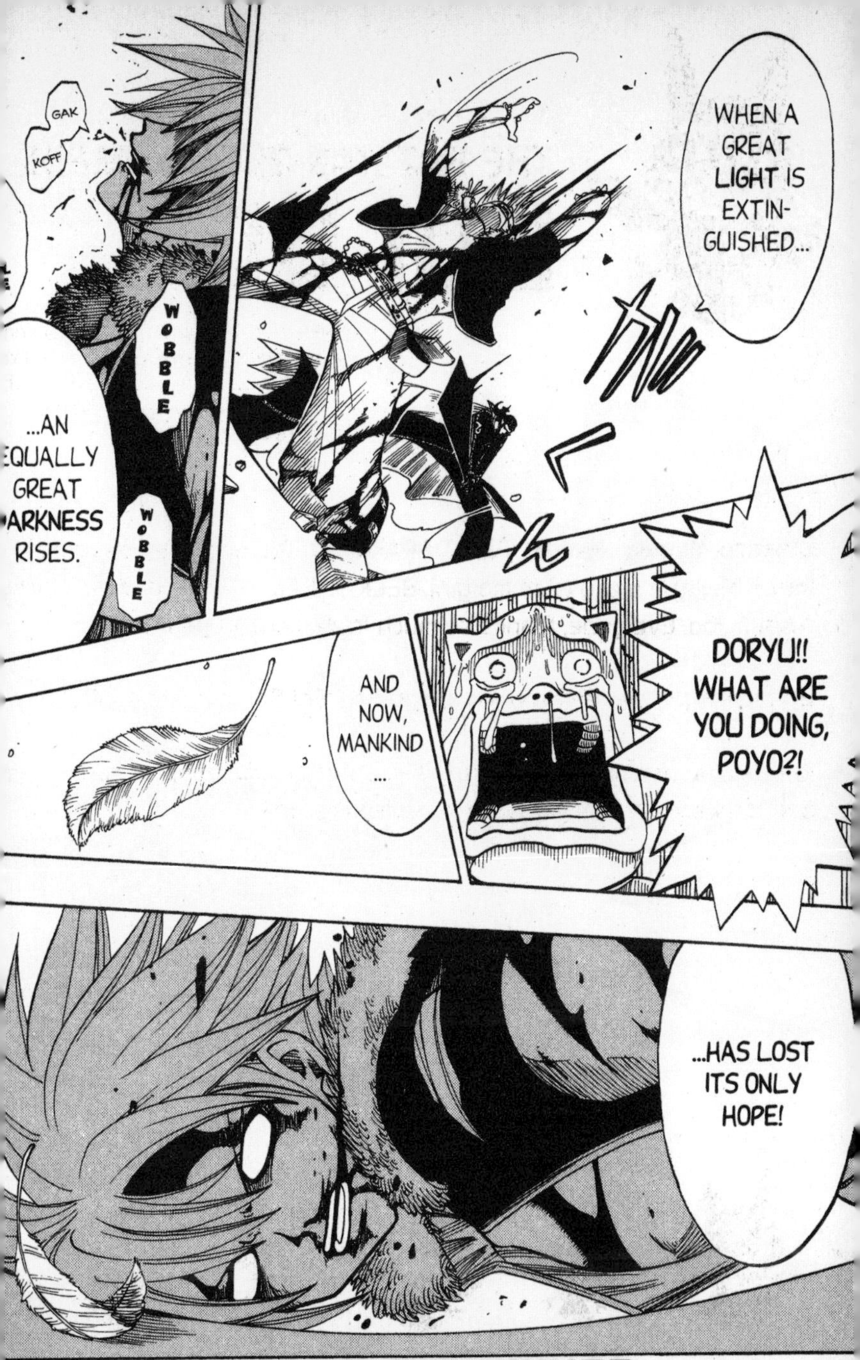
WHEN A GREAT LIGHT IS EXTIN-GUISHED...
GAK
KOFF
WOBBLE
...AN EQUALLY GREAT ARKNESS RISES.
WOBBLE
DORYU!! WHAT ARE YOU DOING, POYO?!
AND NOW, MANKIND ...
...HAS LOST ITS ONLY HOPE!

TO BE CONTINUED

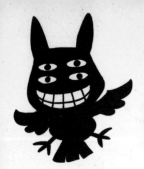

The votes have been tallied!

THE BAT HAS BEEN NAMED!!

BOI BOI

Well, I didn't think I'd get one thousand plus votes for a small fry character like this. Really, I'm surprised. Boi Boi, huh? It definitely has a ring to it--so the name's final!!

Other candidates were JIO, PISKO, BRAKKI, etc. The most popular name was KIKI (by a pretty wide margin). BECKY, BEAL, and lots of other wacky names, too. Everyone, thanks so much for sending in your votes!!

By the way, it'll be a little while longer until Boi Boi appears again.

Well, this worked out pretty nicely. There're more little guys where he came from, so keep checking in--and keep having fun!!

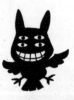

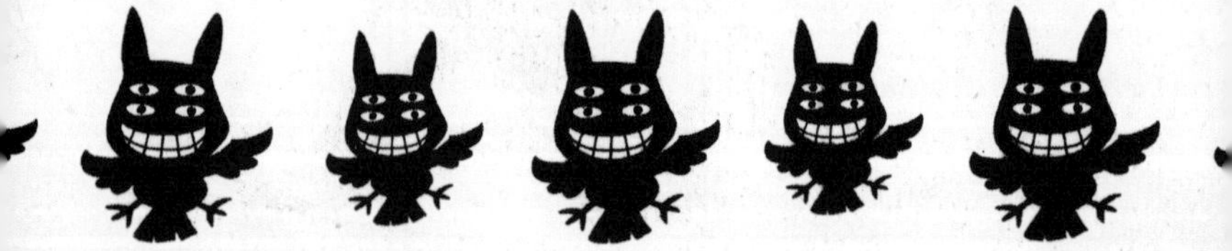

#14 - Love Is Good

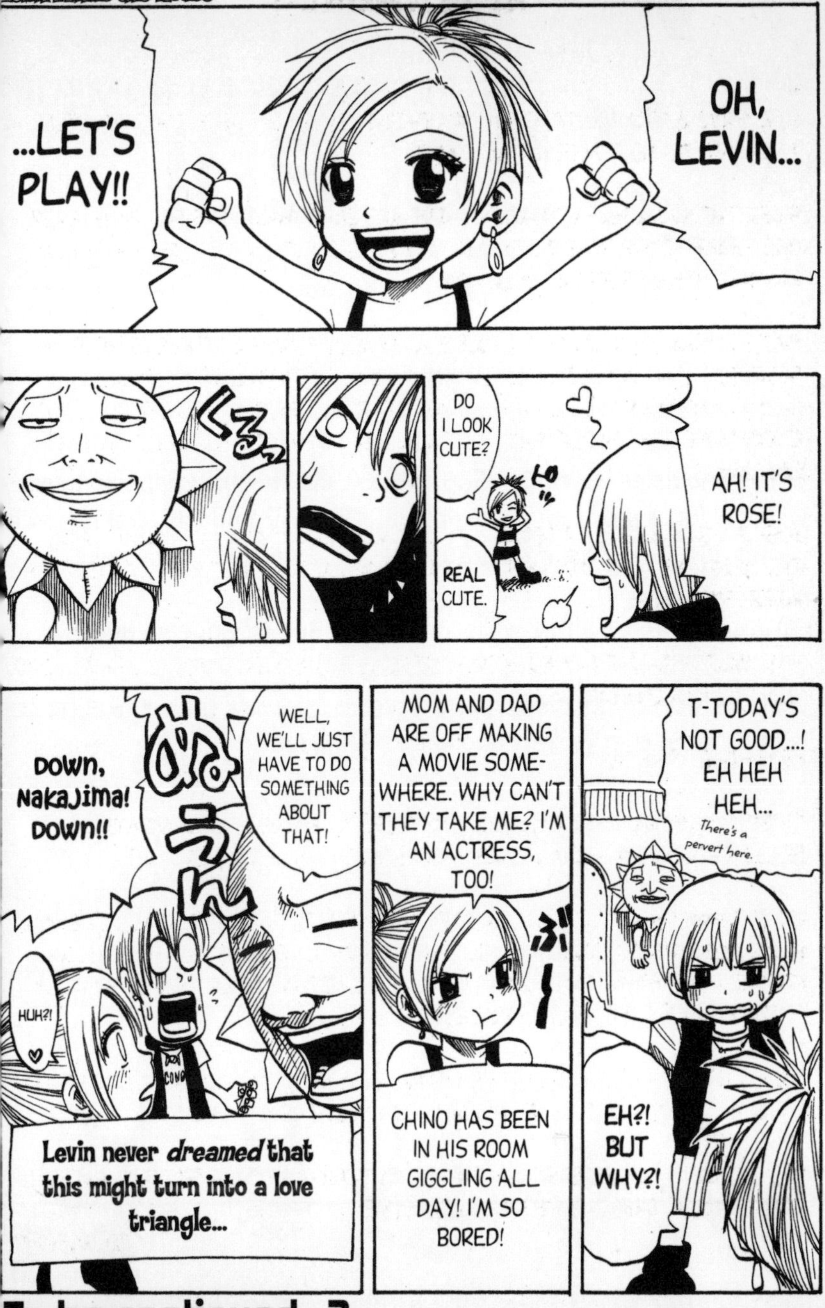
OH, LEVIN...
...LET'S PLAY!!
AH! IT'S ROSE!
DO I LOOK CUTE?
REAL CUTE.
くるっ
T-TODAY'S NOT GOOD...! EH HEH HEH...
There's a pervert here.
EH?! BUT WHY?!
MOM AND DAD ARE OFF MAKING A MOVIE SOMEWHERE. WHY CAN'T THEY TAKE ME? I'M AN ACTRESS, TOO!
ぶ
CHINO HAS BEEN IN HIS ROOM GIGGLING ALL DAY! I'M SO BORED!
WELL, WE'LL JUST HAVE TO DO SOMETHING ABOUT THAT!
ぬうん
DOWN, NAKAJIMA! DOWN!!
HUH?!
Levin never *dreamed* that this might turn into a love triangle...

To be continued...?

"AFTERWORDS"

HI, EVERYONE! DID YOU TAKE THE TRASH OUT? MASHIMA, HERE. THIS TIME I'LL TALK ABOUT THE FUN, FUN **RAVE** STAFF!

FIRST THE MANAGER--ACTUALLY THERE ARE **EIGHT** MANAGERS FOR RAVE. EVERYONE'S FREE TO GIVE THEIR OPINION. I MAY BE THE AUTHOR, BUT IT'S A BIG HELP HAVING LOTS OF SUPPORT EVERY DAY.

MATSUKI-SAN (NICK: M KISHI) IS QUITE A MIRACLE-WORKER. HE KEEPS ME FROM BEING TOO LONG-WINDED WHEN I WRITE HERE (^_^). IF YOU WANT TO KNOW EVERYTHING THEN YOU'LL HAVE TO WAIT FOR THE "**RAVE** 0" GUIDE BOOK. I'LL COVER EVERYTHING ELSE IN DUE TIME. (LIKE THE REAL STORY BEHIND RUBY'S WAY OF SPEAKING.)

YOSHIDA-SAN: A REAL VETERAN. HE'S THE NICE MAN WHO KEEPS AN EYE ON ALL THE NEW KIDS (LIKE ME!) HE'S ALSO A SERIOUS ACTOR. JUST SIMPLY A REALLY INTERESTING GUY!

YOSHIMOTO-SAN (NICK: PUYO): FOR SOME REASON MATSUKI-SAN CALLS HIM "PUYO." HE'S OUR MAN ON WHEELS.

NEXT--THE ASSISTANTS!

CHIEF NAKAMURA (A.K.A. NAKAMURA OF SASUGA): EXTREMELY DEDICATED AND REALLY GOOD AT HIS JOB. WEARS SHORTS, EVEN IN THE WINTER.

CHAP CHINKERS: A CLASSIC HORROR FILM BUFF. FIRST IN LINE FOR ALL THE NEW BLOCKBUSTERS, TOO. AROUND THE TIME THIS VOLUME CAME OUT HE QUIT TO PURSUE HIS OWN WRITING. THINKS DIFFERENTLY FROM OTHER PEOPLE--REALLY QUITE A CHARACTER. THANKS FOR EVERYTHING!

MANGA ROCK (^_^): THAT'S HIS PEN NAME. LOVES ROCK & GUITAR, JUST LIKE I DO. SAYS AND DOES A LOT OF INEXPLICABLE THINGS. A REAL PRANKSTER.

WELL, THAT'S THE **RAVE** STAFF. I'M PRETTY BORING, SO IT'S GREAT TO HAVE ALL THESE FUN, INTERESTING PEOPLE AROUND ME!

- HIRO MASHIMA

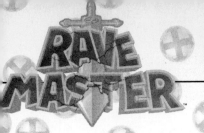

RAVE MASTER Fan Art

HEY, ASPIRING MANGA ARTISTS! WANT TO SEE YOUR PICTURES IN PRINT? WELL, IF YOU THINK YOU CAN DRAW A COOL-LOOKING HARU, A SEXY ELIE OR A FUNNY PLUE, SEND 'EM THIS WAY! WE'LL PICK ONE LUCKY WINNER FROM EACH ROUND AND SEND THEM A SPECIAL PRIZE! WHAT DO HAVE TO LOSE? NOTHING!

HOW TO SUBMIT:

1) SEND YOUR WORK VIA REGULAR MAIL (NOT E-MAIL) TO:

RAVE MASTER FAN ART
C/O TOKYOPOP
5900 WILSHIRE BLVD.
SUITE 2000
LOS ANGELES, CA 90036

2) ALL WORK SUBMITTED SHOULD BE IN BLACK-AND-WHITE AND NO LARGER THAN 8.5" X 11". (AND TRY NOT TO FOLD IT TOO MANY TIMES!)

3) ANYTHING YOU SEND WILL NOT BE RETURNED. IF YOU WANT TO KEEP YOUR ORIGINAL, IT'S FINE TO SEND US A COPY.

4) PLEASE INCLUDE YOUR FULL NAME, AGE, CITY AND STATE FOR US TO PRINT WITH YOUR WORK. IF YOU'D RATHER WE USE A PEN NAME, PLEASE INCLUDE THAT TOO.

5) IMPORTANT: IF YOU'RE UNDER THE AGE OF 18, YOU MUST HAVE YOUR PARENT'S PERMISSION IN ORDER FOR US TO PRINT YOUR WORK. ANY SUBMISSIONS WITHOUT A SIGNED NOTE OF PARENTAL CONSENT CANNOT BE USED.

6) FOR FULL DETAILS, PLEASE CHECK OUT HTTP://WWW.TOKYOPOP.COM/ABOUTUS/FANART.PHP

DRAW US! PUUN!

RAVE
EISEN METEOR

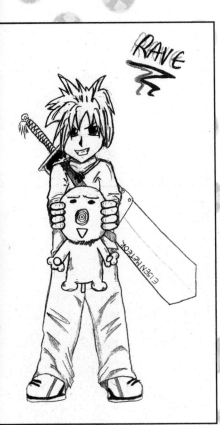

HARU COMES BEARING...THE RAVE BEARER? HARU GIVES THE GIFT OF PLUE, COURTESY OF ANNIE. GREAT JOB!

ANNIE R.
AGE 10
BOULDER, CO

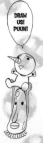

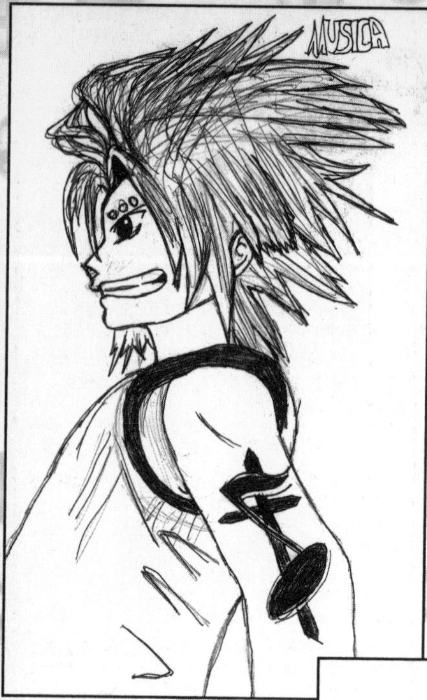
MUSICA

CONFIDENT AND PROUD (JUST THE WAY WE LIKE HIM), MUSICA LOOKS READY TO SHOW OFF HIS SILVER. THANKS FOR THE COOL PICTURE, FAYTH!

FAYTH S.
WEST BLOCTON, AL

SARA, YOU'VE BROUGHT A TEAR TO ALL OF OUR EYES WITH THIS BEAUTIFUL RECREATION OF AN EMOTIONAL MOMENT FROM VOLUME 6. NICE WORK!

SARA K.
AGE 17
HUNTINGTON BEACH, CA

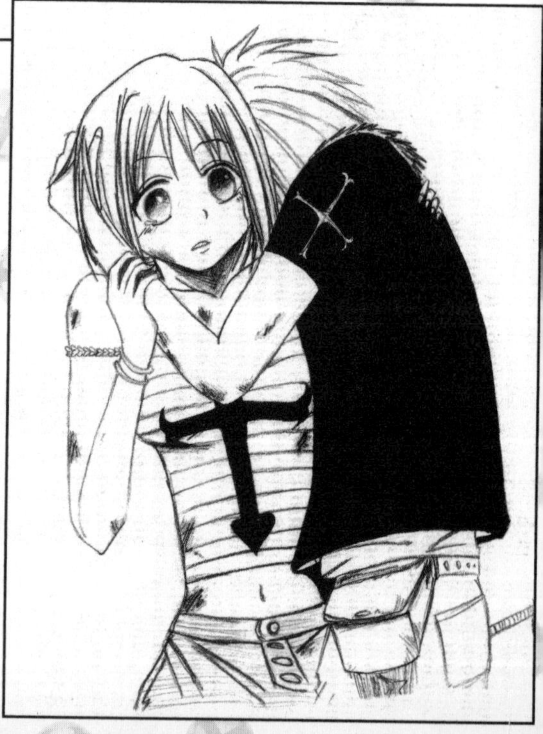

UH-OH...IT LOOKS LIKE SOMEONE'S BURIED PLUE'S LOLLIPOP AND LEFT HIM WITH A STALK OF CELERY. NOW WHO WOULD DO SOMETHING LIKE THAT? DEMON CARD, OF COURSE! VERY NICE, COLIN!

COLIN F.
SAN FRANCISCO, CA

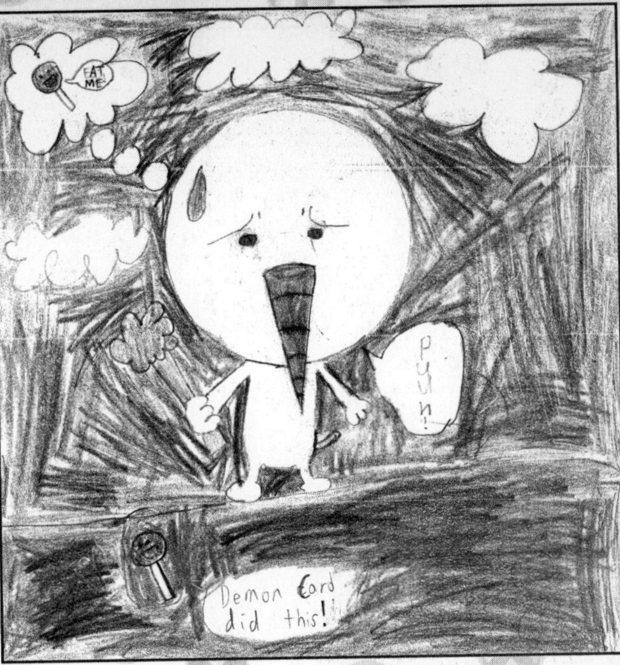
EAT ME!
Pyun!
Demon Card did this!

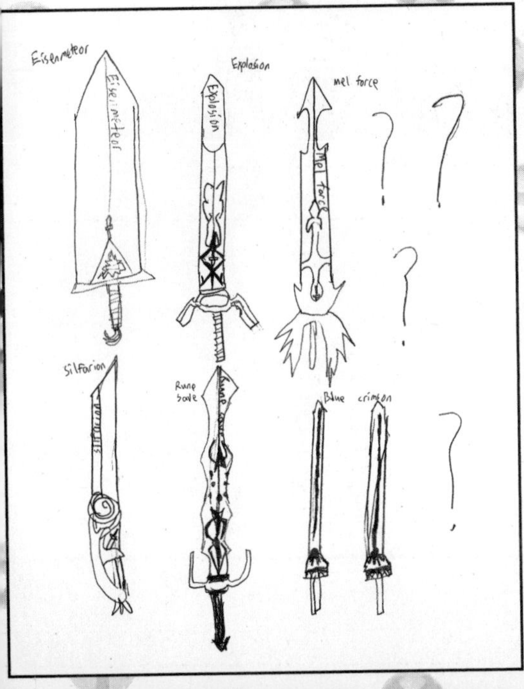
Eisenmeteor
Explosion
mel force
Silfarion
Rune save
Blue
crimson

A GOOD SWORDSMAN NEEDS A GOOD SWORD, AND THERE'S NO BETTER BLADE THAN THE TEN POWERS. BENJAMIN'S AWESOME ART SHOWCASES A FEW OF THE SWORD'S MORE POWERFUL FORMS.!

BENJAMIN C.
AGE 11
HUMBOLDT, IA

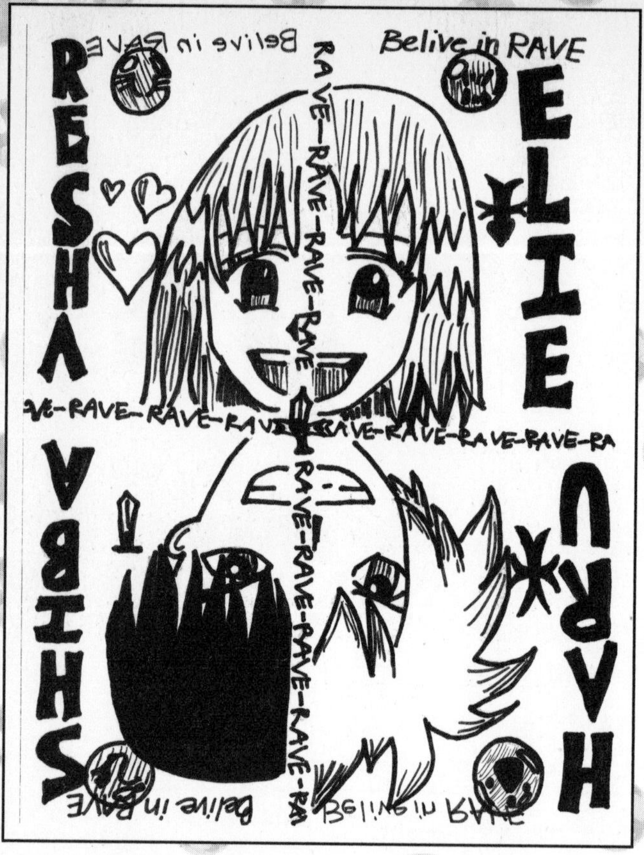
Belive in RAVE
RESHA
ELIE
SHIBA
HARU
RAVE-RAVE-RAVE-RAVE

TWO GENERATIONS OF HEROES ARE BROUGHT TOGETHER IN THIS IMAGINATIVE ILLUSTRATION. KELLY REMINDS US TO "BELIEVE IN RAVE" BY GIVING US A LOOK AT OTHER PEOPLE THE STONES HAVE INSPIRED.

KELLY B.
AGE 11
FLOWER MOUND, TX

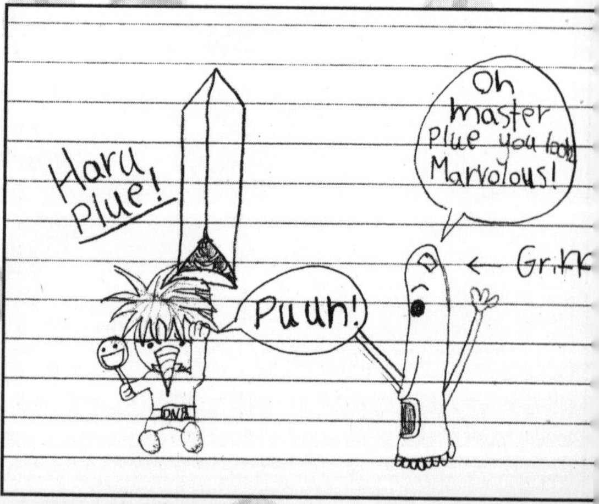
Haru plue!
Oh master Plue you look Marvolous!
Puuh!

WHEN THE RAVE MASTER'S AWAY, THE RAVE BEARER WILL PLAY...**WITH THE TEN POWERS!** THAT'S SOME REALLY FUNNY STUFF, GRANT!!

GRANT B.
AGE 11
NOVI, MI

WITH A SWORD *THAT* MASSIVE STRAPPED TO MY BACK, I'D BE FEELING LIKE I COULD TAKE ON THE WORLD. GOOD FOR US THAT HARU'S ONLY INTERESTED IN TAKING ON DEMON CARD. SWEET PICTURE, RYAN!

RYAN K.
AGE 13
WEST ISLIP, NY

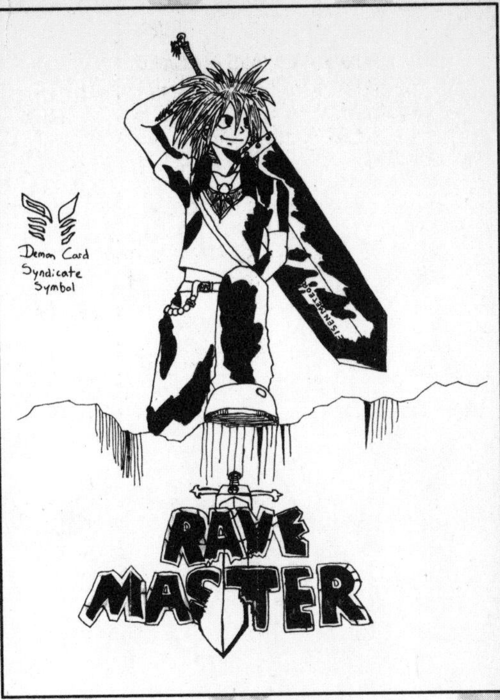
Demon Card
Syndicate
Symbol
RAVE
MASTER

THIS FUN DRAWING OF OUR HEROES PERFECTLY CAPTURES THE PERSONALITY OF THE GROUP, FROM MUSICA'S ATTITUDE, TO GRIFF'S ADMIRATION OF PLUE, TO ELIE'S HOPEFULNESS. THANKS FOR READING, ALEXIS!!

ALEXIS S.
AGE 11
ALTA LOMA, CA

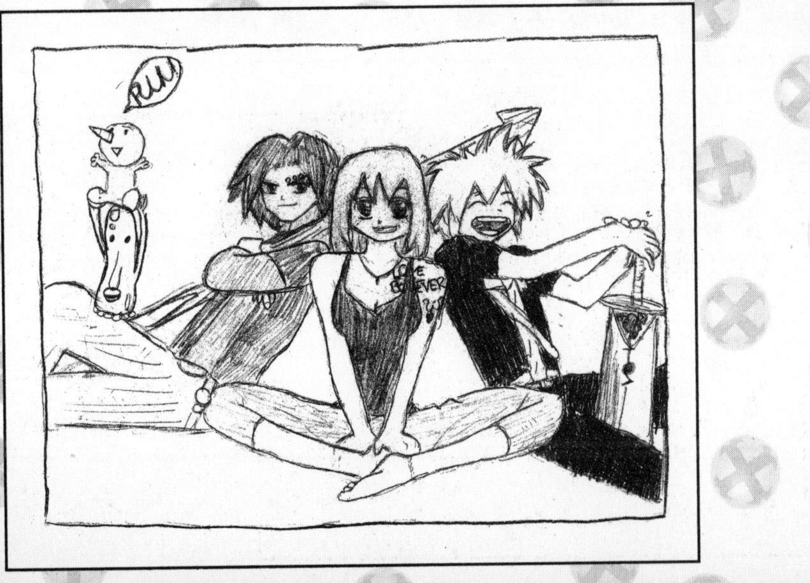

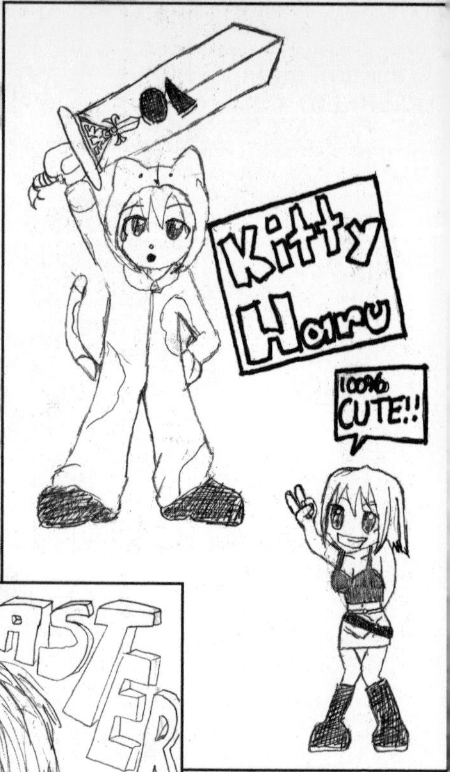
Kitty Haru
100% CUTE!!

FUNNY, I ALWAYS ASSUMED HARU WAS A DOG PERSON. BUT AFTER SEEING HIM AS A KITTY, I'M INCLINED TO AGREE WITH ELIE. CUTE DRAWING, JULIE!

JULIE W.
AGE 13
CYPRESS, CA

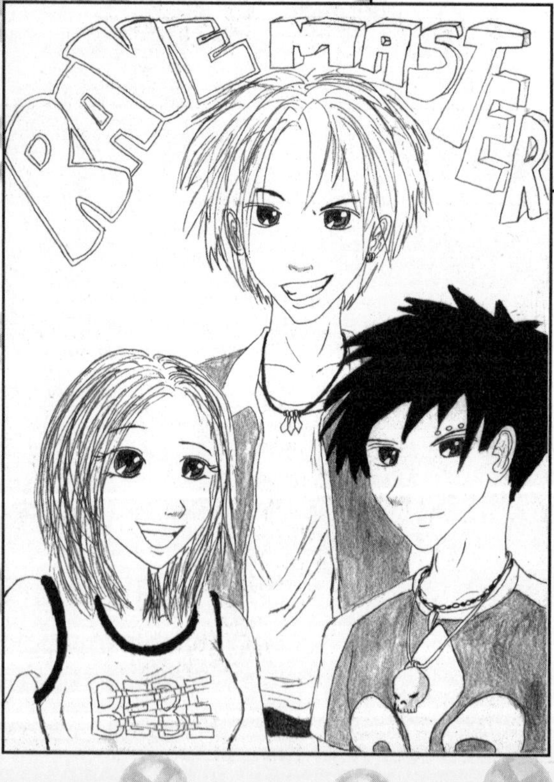
RAVE MASTER
BEBE

ELIZABETH HAS DRAWN HARU, ELIE AND MUSICA SO STYLISHLY THAT YOU CAN ALMOST IMAGINE THEM HANGING AT THE LOCAL MALL (THUMBING THROUGH THE PAGES OF RAVE MASTER, OF COURSE).

ELIZABETH S.
AGE 15
CHAPEL HILL, NC

Rave Master ART SPECIAL 5

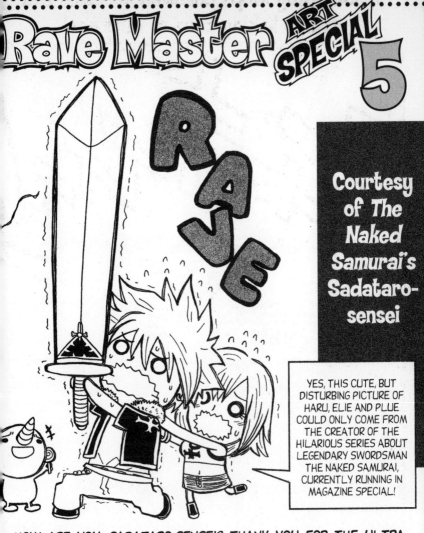

RAVE

Courtesy of *The Naked Samurai's* Sadataro-sensei

YES, THIS CUTE, BUT DISTURBING PICTURE OF HARU, ELIE AND PLUE COULD ONLY COME FROM THE CREATOR OF THE HILARIOUS SERIES ABOUT LEGENDARY SWORDSMAN THE NAKED SAMURAI, CURRENTLY RUNNING IN MAGAZINE SPECIAL!

HOW ARE YOU, SADATARO-SENSEI? THANK YOU FOR THE ULTRA CUTE PICTURE! I KNOW YOU'RE BUSY BUT LET'S HANG OUT SOME TIME. (LAUGHS) I KNOW WE'RE ABOUT THE SAME AGE (YOU'RE SLIGHTLY YOUNGER) AND WE'RE BUDDIES, BUT YOU SHOULD KNOW THAT I HAVE A LOT OF RESPECT AND ADMIRATION FOR YOU AND YOUR WORK. LET'S KEEP WORKING HARD! I'LL TREAT YOU TO SOME STEAKS NEXT TIME.

Whoa! Ruby stops counting his coins and starts taking care of business!

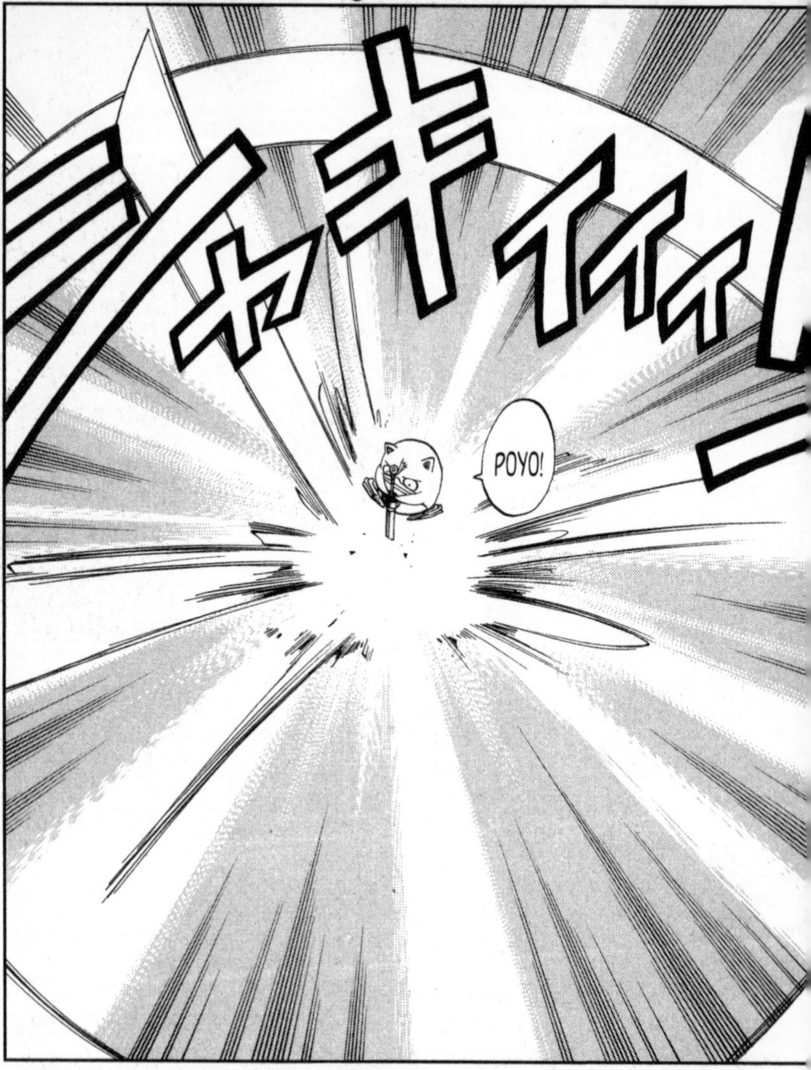

POYO!

With Haru in serious trouble, the daunting task of rescuing Elie falls on...Ruby? Well, not quite, but the spotlight falls on other characters in our next volume of Rave Master!

Rave Master Volume 16
Available August 2005

TOKYOPOP SHOP

WWW.TOKYOPOP.COM/SHOP

HOT NEWS!
Check out the
TOKYOPOP SHOP!
The world's best
collection of manga in
English is now available
online in one place!

ARCANA

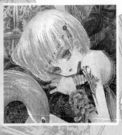

TOKYO MEW MEW A LA MODE

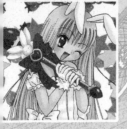

MBQ and other
hot titles are
available at
the store that
never closes!

MBQ

- LOOK FOR SPECIAL OFFERS
- PRE-ORDER UPCOMING RELEASES!
- COMPLETE YOUR COLLECTIONS

SPOTLIGHT TOKYOPOP MANGA SUPPLEMENT

BECK: MONGOLIAN CHOP SQUAD

OT OLDER TEEN AGE 16+

ROCK IN MANGA!

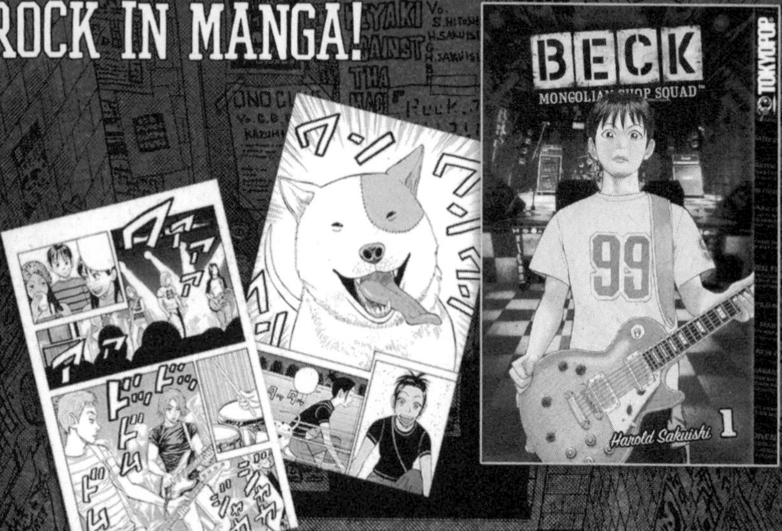

BECK
MONGOLIAN CHOP SQUAD
TOKYOPOP
99
Harold Sakuishi 1

Yukio Tanaka is one boring guy with no hobbies, a weak taste in music and only a small vestige of a personality. But his life is forever changed when he meets Ryusuke Minami, an unpredictable rocker with a cool dog named Beck. Recently returned to Japan from America, Ryusuke inspires Yukio to get into music, and the two begin a journey through the world of rock 'n' roll dreams! With cameos of music's greatest stars—from John Lennon to David Bowie—and homages to supergroups such as Led Zeppelin and Nirvana, anyone who's anyone can make an appearance in *Beck*...even Beck himself! With action, music and gobs of comedy, *Beck* puts the rock in manga!

HAROLD SAKUISHI'S HIGHLY ADDICTIVE MANGA SERIES THAT SPAWNED A HIT ANIME HAS FINALLY REACHED THE STATES!

FOR MORE INFORMATION VISIT: WWW.TOKYOPOP.COM

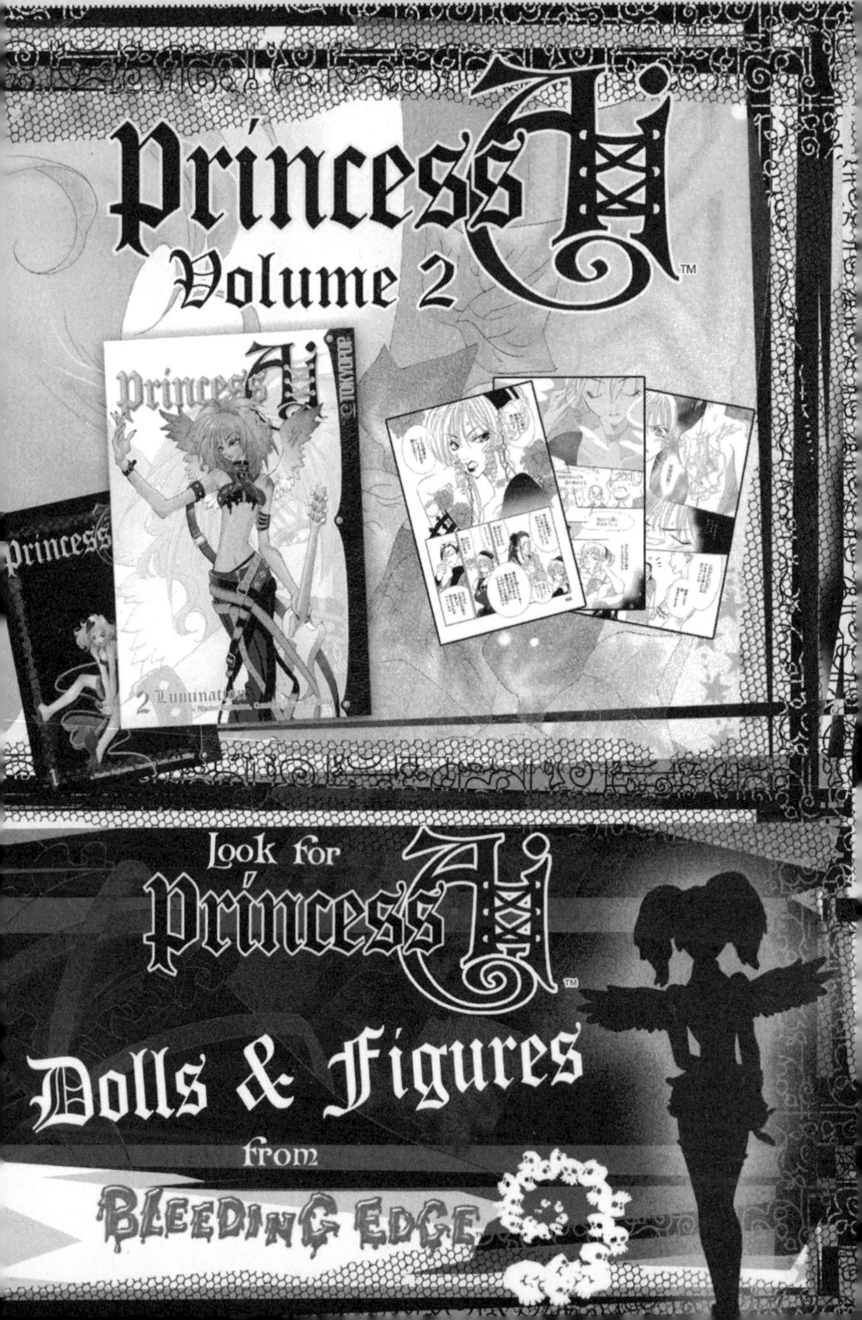
Princess Ai™
Volume 2
Look for Princess Ai™
Dolls & Figures
from
BLEEDING EDGE

A Diva Torn from Chaos
A Savior Doomed to Love

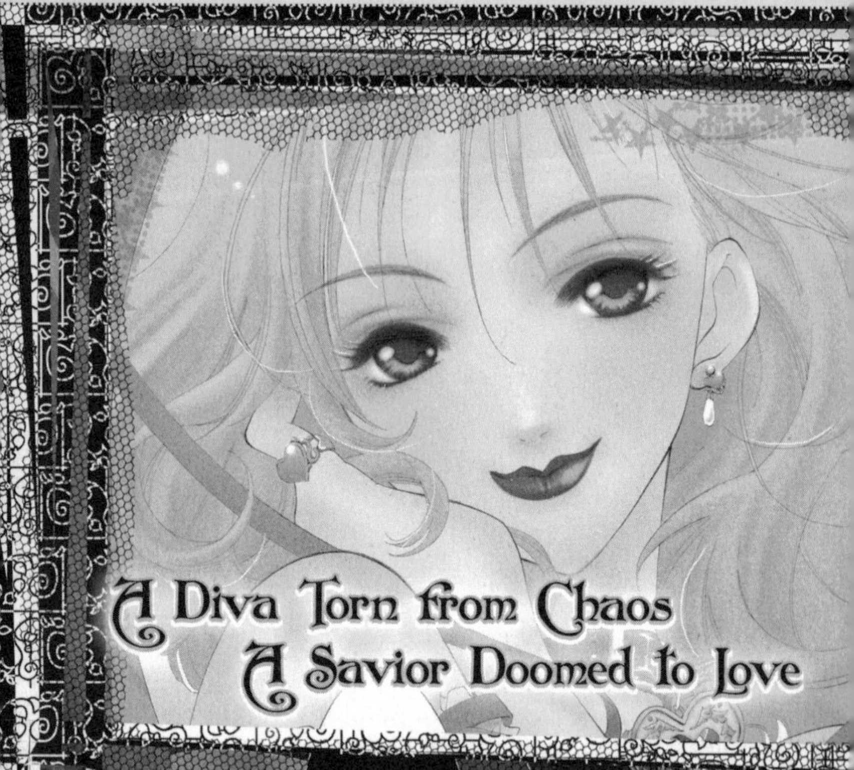

Volume 2
Lumination

Ai continues to search for her place in our world on the streets of Tokyo. Using her talent to support herself, Ai signs a contract with a top record label and begins her rise to stardom. But fame is unpredictable—as her talent blooms, all eyes are on Ai. When scandal surfaces, will she burn out in the spotlight of celebrity?

T
TEEN
AGE 13+

Preview the manga at:
www.TOKYOPOP.com/princessai

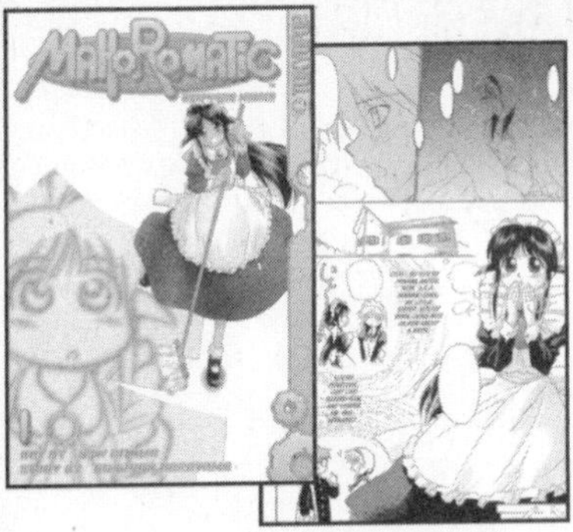
MAHOROMATIC

BY BUNJURO NAKAYAMA AND BOW DITAMA

MAHOROMATIC: AUTOMATIC MAIDEN

Mahoro is a sweet, cute, female battle android who decides to go from mopping up alien invaders to mopping up after Suguru Misato, a teenaged orphan boy... and hilarity most definitely ensues. This series has great art and a slick story that easily switches from truly funny to downright heartwarming...but always with a large shadow looming over it. You see, only Mahoro knows that her days are quite literally numbered, and the end of each chapter lets you know exactly how much—or how little—time she has left!

~Rob Tokar, Sr. Editor

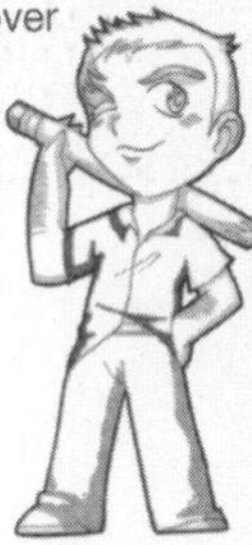

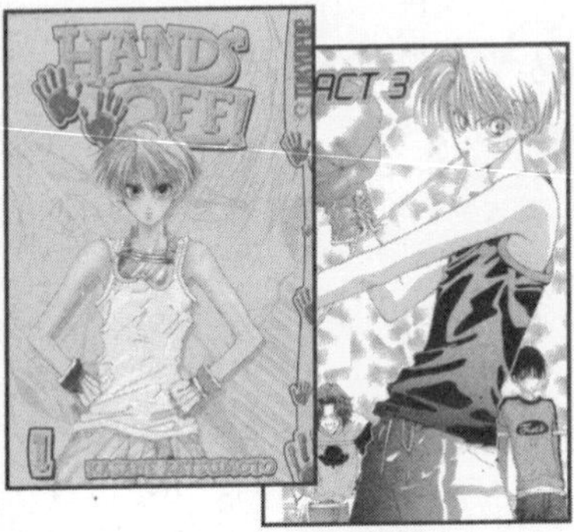
HANDS OFF!
ACT 3

BY KASANE KATSUMOTO

HANDS OFF!

Cute boys with ESP who share a special bond... If you think this is familiar (e.g. *Legal Drug*), well, you're wrong. *Hands Off!* totally stands alone as a unique and thoroughly enjoyable series. Kotarou and Tatsuki's (platonic!) relationship is complex, fascinating and heart-wrenching. Throw in Yuuto, the playboy who can read auras, and you've got a fantastic setup for drama and comedy, with incredible themes of friendship running throughout. Don't be put off by Kotarou's danger-magnet status, either. The episodic stuff gradually changes, and the full arc of the characters' development is well worth waiting for.

~Lillian Diaz-Przybyl, Jr. Editor

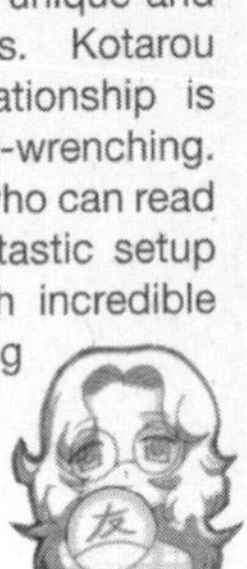

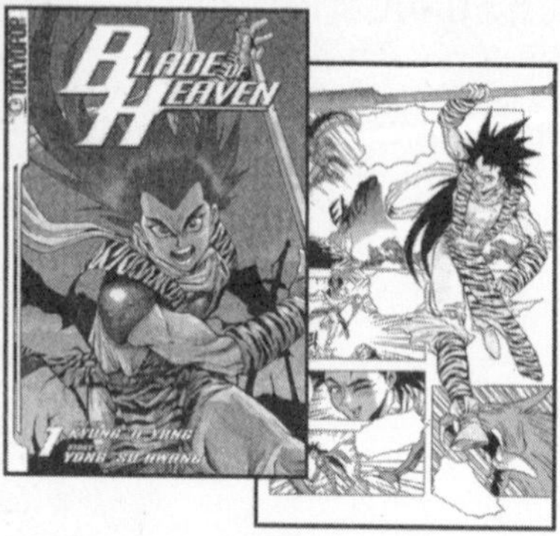
Blade of Heaven
TOKYOPOP

BY YONG-SU HWANG
AND KYUNG-IL YANG

BLADE OF HEAVEN

Wildly popular in its homeland of Korea, *Blade of Heaven* enjoys the rare distinction of not only being a hit in its own country, but in Japan and several other countries, as well. On the surface, Yong-Su Hwang and Kyung-Il Yang's fantasy-adventure may look like yet another "Heaven vs. Demons" sword opera, but the story of the mischievous Soma, a pawn caught in a struggle of mythic proportions, is filled with so much humor, pathos, imagination—and yes, action, that it's easy to see why *Blade of Heaven* has been so popular worldwide.

~Bryce P. Coleman, Editor

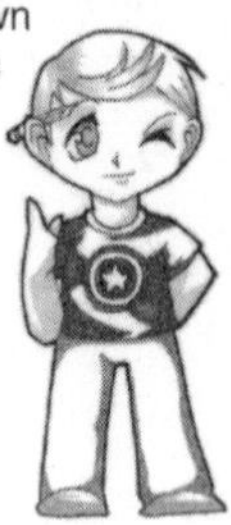

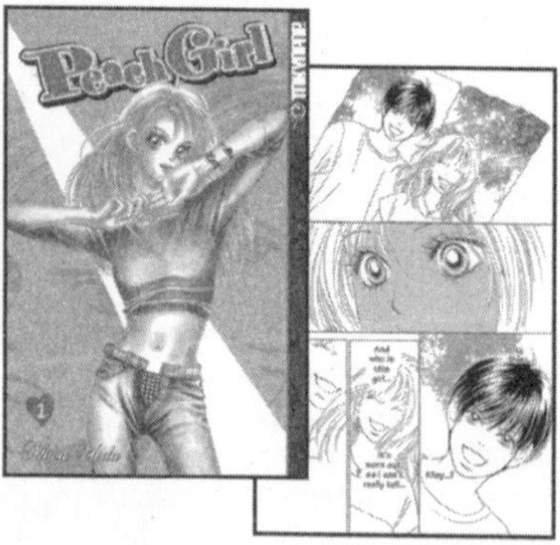
Peach Girl
TOKYOPOP

BY MIWA UEDA

PEACH GIRL

Am I the only person who thinks that *Peach Girl* is just like *The O.C.*? Just imagine Ryan as Toji, Seth as Kiley, Marissa as Momo and Summer as Sae. (The similarities are almost spooky!) Plus, Seth is way into comics and manga—and I'm sure he'd love *Peach Girl*. It has everything that my favorite TV show has and then some—drama, intrigue, romance and lots of will-they-or-won't-they suspense. I love it! *Peach Girl* rules, seriously. If you haven't read it, do so. Now.

~Julie Taylor, Sr. Editor

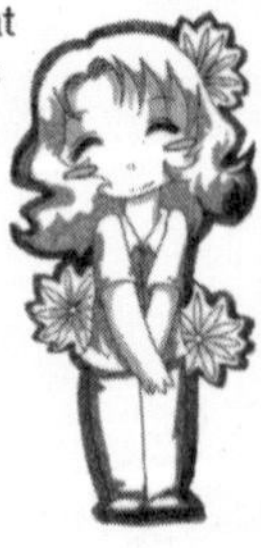

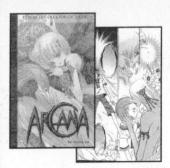

ARCANA
BY SO-YOUNG LEE

Inez is a young orphan girl with the ability to communicate with living creatures of all kinds. She is the chosen one, and a great destiny awaits her! Inez must bring back the guardian dragon to protect her country's fragile peace from the onslaught of a destructive demon race.

From the creator of TOKYOPOP's *Model* comes an epic fantasy quest filled with wizards, dragons, deception and adventure beyond your wildest imagination.

T TEEN AGE 13+

© SO-YOUNG LEE, DAIWON C.I. Inc.

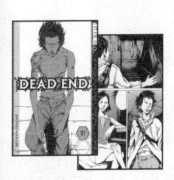

DEAD END
BY SHOHEI MANABE

When Shirou's memory is suddenly erased and his friends are brutally murdered, he is forced to piece together clues to solve a shocking and spectacular puzzle. As we follow Shirou's journey, paranoia assumes an air of calm rationality and the line between tormenter and prey is often blurred.

OT OLDER TEEN AGE 16+

© Shohei Manabe

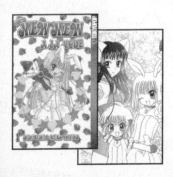

TOKYO MEW MEW A LA MODE
BY MIA IKUMI AND REIKO TOSHIDA

The cats are back, and a new Mew emerges— the first Mew Mew with *two* sets of animal genes. Half cat, half rabbit, Berry joins the Mew Mew team just in time: a new gang is about to appear, and its leader loves wild game like rabbit—well done and served for dinner!

The highly anticipated sequel to *Tokyo Mew Mew* (*Mew Mew Power* as seen on TV)!

Y YOUTH AGE 10+

© Mia Ikumi and Kodansha

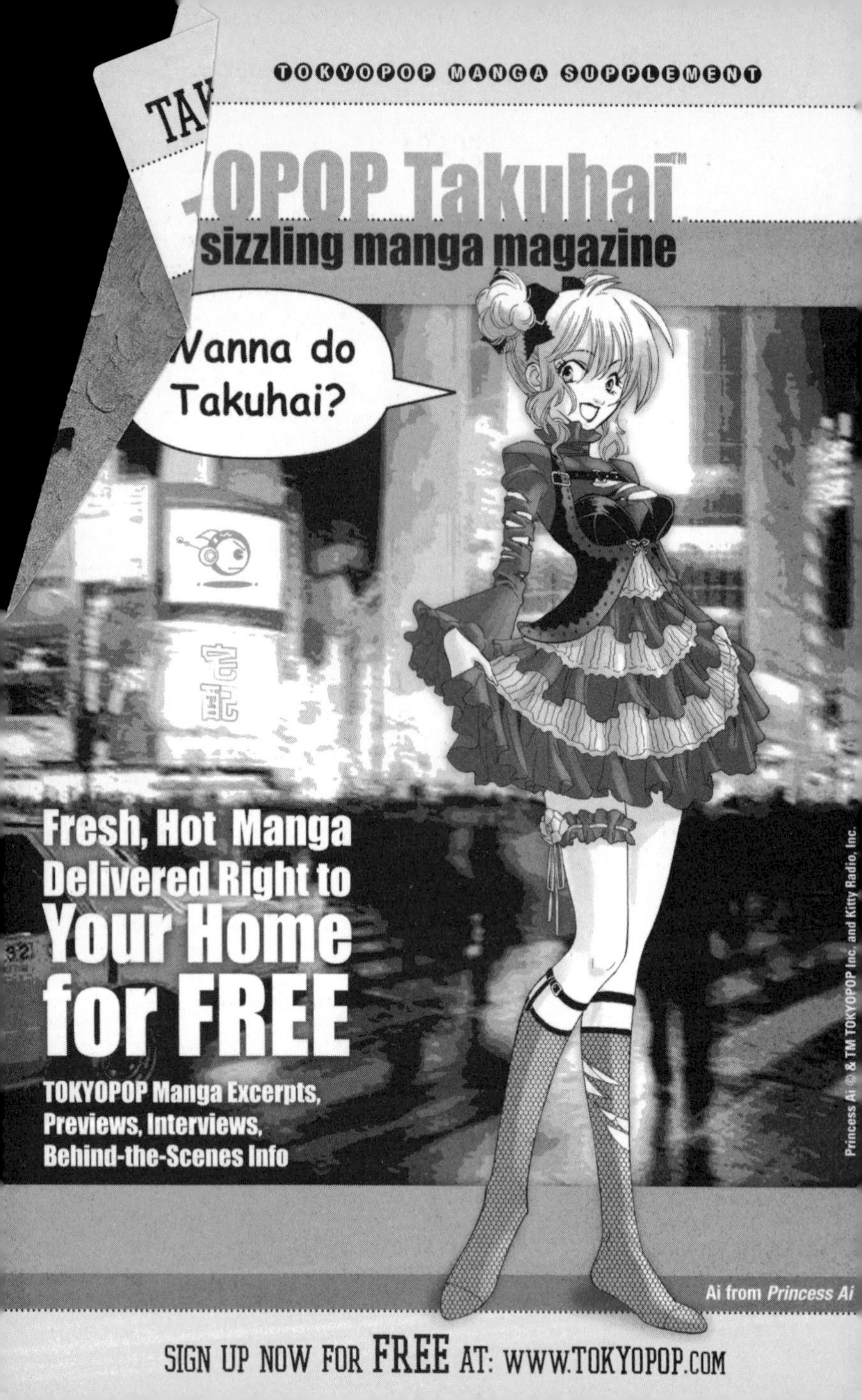
TOKYOPOP MANGA SUPPLEMENT
TAK
-OPOP Takuhai™
sizzling manga magazine
Wanna do Takuhai?
Fresh, Hot Manga Delivered Right to Your Home for FREE
TOKYOPOP Manga Excerpts, Previews, Interviews, Behind-the-Scenes Info
Princess Ai © & TM TOKYOPOP Inc. and Kitty Radio, Inc.
Ai from *Princess Ai*
SIGN UP NOW FOR FREE AT: WWW.TOKYOPOP.COM

SPOTLIGHT TOKYOPOP MANGA SUPPLEMENT

BLAZIN' BARRELS

Sting may look harmless and naïve, but he's really an excellent fighter and a wannabe bounty hunter in the futuristic Wild West. When he comes across a notice that advertises a reward for the criminal outfit named Gold Romany, he decides that capturing the all-girl gang of bad guys is his ticket to fame and fortune!

MIN-SEO PARK HAS CREATED ONE WILD TUMBLEWEED TALE FILLED WITH ADVENTURE GALORE AND PLENTY OF SHOTGUN ACTION!

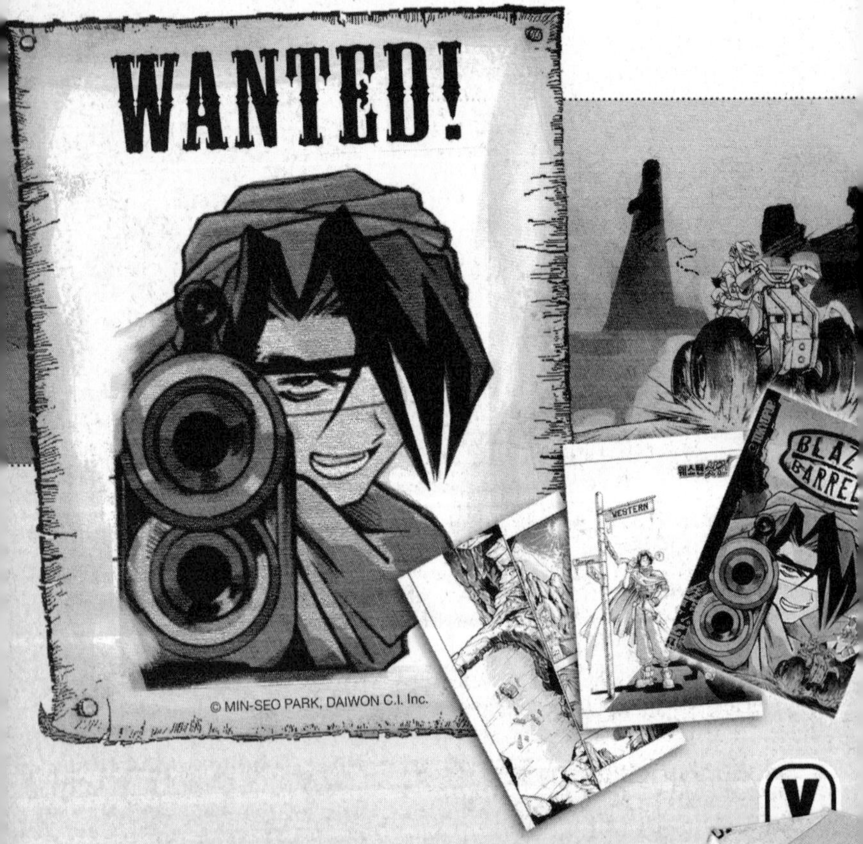
WANTED!
WESTERN
© MIN-SEO PARK, DAIWON C.I. Inc.

FOR MORE INFORMATION VISIT: WWW.TOKYOPOP.C

STOP!

This is the back of the book. You wouldn't want to spoil a great ending!

This book is printed "manga-style," in the authentic Japanese right-to-left format. Since none of the artwork has been flipped or altered, readers get to experience the story just as the creator intended. You've been asking for it, so TOKYOPOP® delivered: authentic, hot-off-the-press, and far more fun!

DIRECTIONS

1
2
3
4
5
6
7
8
9
10

If this is your first time reading manga-style, here's a quick guide to help you understand how it works.

It's easy... just start in the top right panel and follow the numbers. Have fun, and look for more 100% authentic manga from TOKYOPOP®!

100% AUTHENTIC MANGA
品質第一公式商品

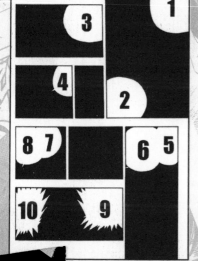

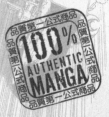